CURRENT RESEARCH IN ETHNOMUSICOLOGY

Edited by
Jennifer C. Post
Middlebury College

A ROUTLEDGE SERIES

CURRENT RESEARCH IN ETHNOMUSICOLOGY
JENNIFER C. POST, *General Editor*

THE GYPSY CARAVAN
From Real Roma to Imaginary Gypsies in Western Music and Film

David Malvinni

ROUTLEDGE
New York & London

Published in 2004 by
Routledge
711 Third Avenue,
New York, NY 10017

Published in Great Britain by
Routledge
2 Park Square, Milton Park,
Abingdon, Oxfordshire OX14 4RN

First issued in paperback 2014
Routledge is an imprint of the Taylor and Francis Group, an informa business

Transferred to Digital Printing 2005

Copyright©2004 by Taylor & Francis Books, Inc.

Library of Congress Cataloging-in-Publication Data

Malvinni, David
    The gypsy caravan : from real Roma to imaginary gypsies in Western music and film / David Malvinni
    p. cm. -- (Current research in ethnomusicology ; v. 11)
    Includes bibliographical references (p.   ) and index.
    Discography
    ISBN 978-0-415-96999-4 (hbk)
    ISBN 978-0-415-86145-8 (pbk)
    1. Romanies--Music--History and criticism. 2. Music--History and criticism. I. Title. II. Series
ML3545.M24 2004
781.6'816291497--dc22
                                                                2003021587

Contents

List of Musical Examples

MUSICAL EXAMPLES

Preface

Whether in the clichés of the Hungarian restaurant with its cloying violinist, scenes from Bizet's *Carmen*, or Hollywood's *Golden Earrings* with Marlene Dietrich, the connection made between Gypsies and music seems almost like a reflex. Yet when we try to figure out in either a musical, social, or historical sense how to frame this discussion, we find ourselves stranded between fact and fiction.

The phenomenon known as "Gypsy music" has been viewed both as a treasure (Liszt) and a contaminant (Bartók). Despite recent work on the subject its power, nature, and historicity remain unclear. My thesis is that Gypsy music, as understood by Liszt and others in the nineteenth century, is not simply a musical style, nor another exoticism (the German-centric view), but a consciousness of the communicative essence of music; differently put, it is the power of musical performance to convey a "passionate" impression on the listener. Yet because Gypsy music appears stuck between reality and the imaginary — what Gypsies or "Roma" might play versus creative appropriations by composers — I propose the mystique of "Gypsiness" to theorize it. Gypsiness articulates the collection of ideas about the Gypsies or "Roma," whose musical expression reduces to the mock equation, $I+V=E$: the player experiences and impresses upon the audience immediate, spontaneous emotions (E) through the rhapsodic perception of improvisation (I) combined with an evocative, erotic, and fantastic virtuosity (V).

The confusion over the identity of Gypsies was present from the start, in many instances with the Roma's encouragement. Originally from North India, Roma groups entered Western Europe roughly 600 years ago; to protect themselves from persecution they promoted the idea that they were pilgrims from "Little Egypt." The extent to which they mixed with indigenous nomadic groups along the route to and in Europe is not known, and perhaps impossible to determine. In Europe, Christianity seems to have been adopted quite early by many Roma. Music was among the professions cultivated by the nomadic Roma, and brought them early fame in the West. Because the Roma refused to assimilate, keeping their rituals and lifestyle basically intact, outsider status has remained with them, leaving profound marks on their culture.

Gypsy music became a Western subject of reflection during the last half of the nineteenth century, at a time when nationalism, exoticism, and Romanticism combined to exert a re-evaluative influence on the way music was conceived. Franz Liszt was the first to consider Gypsy music as a European topic of discourse in his book *The Gypsy in Music*. For Liszt, Gypsy music represented the holy grail of what Western composers had sought for centuries: the achievement of a pure musicality, combined with a depth of emotion (the natural expression of the Gypsies' misfortune). When the Gypsy fiddler improvised on a tune, according to Liszt, he was able to produce a kind of music that synthesized the rational and the irrational, technical competence and depth of feeling. Furthermore, that Central European composers had contact with Gypsy musicians makes for a different kind of exoticism than that of *Scheherazade* or *The Mikado*: unlike portrayals of the Orient as an "exoticism-from-outside," Gypsy music was experienced as an "exoticism-from-inside."

Rebelling against this exotic Romanticism, many have sought to combat the stereotype of the Gypsy virtuoso. In the twentieth century there have been violent reactions to Gypsy music, especially in the case of Hungarian scholarship; Bartók devoted much energy to distinguishing urban or popular Gypsy song (which for Bartók was really Hungarian in origin) from "peasant" or village Hungarian musics, while essentially bypassing the role of Roma instrumental musicians in this ideally contained Hungarian village.

In spite of this, Gypsiness with its Romantic, extravagant, and exaggerated imagery appears to be impervious to empirical revelations. And this locates precisely the excitement of a study of Gypsiness in music: to determine how an irrational construction can somehow prove more persuasive than scientific discourse. In short, audiences connect directly and immediately to Gypsiness in music; it is this communicative ability that helps to explain compositional interest in appropriating models and gestures of Gypsiness, even in the case of a resisting Bartók.

Romantic ideas about Gypsiness remain stunningly present in the marketing of music as Gypsy. In order to package something as Gypsy music, producers rely on the age-old stereotypes of Gypsiness. Commercialism draws its basic image of the Gypsy from the one formalized by Liszt. And if there exists a desire for cultural escape in European society, musical Gypsiness certainly fulfills such a need.

Any book purporting to deal with Gypsy music cannot neglect the politics of studying Roma. Indeed, my attempt to reevaluate Gypsiness is possible only through the recent surfacing of political issues in the last decades. For example, Tony Gatlif's film *Latcho drom* (*Safe Journey*, 1993) not only summarizes the current diasporic understanding of Gypsy music — Gypsy as world music — but makes a strong political statement about the continuing oppression of Roma communities. It has also brought to wider public attention the devastation of the Holocaust on the Roma — one of *Latcho*'s scenes a Gypsy survivor is shown outside of Auschwitz singing about life in the concentration camp. As Holocaust victims the Gypsies have also been the subject of recent studies (it is estimated that 600,000 perished under the Nazis).

Indeed, it has become increasingly clear that any treatment of "Gypsiness," of "Gypsy music," of "Roma music," must respond in some way to the political climate encompassing Roma marginalization. In other words, it is no longer possible to think about Gypsy music without considering the Roma-rights movement. A Roma intellectual could charge this book as yet another attempt by the *Gadje* (non-Gypsy) to rip off the Gypsies, to build a career from Gypsy music, at a time when urgent political action is needed. This adds a level of complication to the study, in that a political position is inscribed, automatically, into any treatment of Gypsy music.

Thus I will discuss music's appropriation by the Roma-rights movement. The movement is actively creating a Romani self-awareness, one that is trying to unite the diverse communities of Roma. Music plays an important role both in solidifying identity, as in the adoption of the Romani anthem, "Jelem, Jelem," ("I went, I went"), and more broadly in symbolizing the Gypsy contribution to world culture — jazz guitarist Django Reinhardt has emerged as a leading poster image of Roma culture. However, a problem remains in this process of creating a transnational identity: despite the plea for representation in local and national governments, much of the Roma community remains separatist and distrustful of outsiders, actively shrouding itself in mystery. Exemplifying this musically, Roma musicians will sometimes revert to being eerily complicit in embodying Gypsiness, a stereotype that politically speaking should be rejected.

Because this book attempts to engage with Gypsiness on a deconstructive level, it became increasingly necessary for me to cite the continental heritage, from Kant to Derrida. This may serve to annoy some musicologists. Yet the philosophical context not only serves as serious and rigorous underpinning for the unfolding of the topic, but is intended as a deepening and in some cases radicalizing of the tendency for deconstructive counterpoint in recent musicology. (As the pendulum of the discipline appears to have swung decisively against the New Musicology, my move may appear to some as risky and untimely.)

Finally, my book will propose that the contemporary "imagined community" of the Roma relies on Gypsiness in music as a marker of identity. Insofar as Gypsiness resists reason, so too does national discourse. The symbolic power of Gypsiness is its ability to reach across various genres, from nineteenth- and twentieth-century art-music to folk and folkloristic styles, and now global (world) pop and, increasingly, fusion genres. Bringing these together under one roof is not as difficult as even ten years ago — one major factor which makes such a wide-ranging study possible is the Internet. Yet the sheer variety of information available makes studying Gypsiness complicated, in that each of these categories has its own specific disciplinary context and understanding, however, it also situates Gypsiness as a compelling arena for testing the limits of interdisciplinarity in music studies.

Acknowledgments

First and foremost I thank Michael Beckerman. The initial call to study Gypsy music and the Roma grew out of his doctoral seminar in nineteenth-century music with the title "Gypsy Music," winter 1997 at the University of California, Santa Barbara. As advisor, mentor, and friend, Mike has been a major source of intellectual and emotional support throughout the writing of this book. He has always inspired me to think beyond what I believed possible.

The committee members, Scott Marcus and Pieter van den Toorn, provided expert guidance and trenchant criticism on this manuscript and my progress. Studying Middle Eastern music under Scott helped me in understanding Gypsy music as a phenomenon of world music. Diagnosed in 2001 with A.L.S., Robert N. Freeman deserves special mention as an honorary member of the committee. "Dr. Bob" (as he liked to be called) also played a significant role in my development as a musicologist. Carol Silverman focused my topic early on, and her pioneering work on the Roma and their music has made a deep impression on me.

My wife, Valerie Malvinni, has been everything to me while writing. She has given me great feedback on many of the ideas about Gypsiness in string playing. When I came up with the strange notion that I wanted to play violin like my Gypsy friends, she patiently gave her time to help me learn how to play. For that gift I will always remain grateful.

My parents, Joseph and Maryanne Malvinni, sister Denise, and family have always been there when I needed them, and without them this book would not have happened.

Two who unselfishly gave their expertise in Russian and Romanian matters, respectively, must be acknowledged: Ildar Khannanov and Marin Marian-Bălaşa. Ildar's knowledge of Russian-Gypsy music is vast, and he sat with me on countless Saturday afternoons teaching me the subtleties of this world. Marin hosted me while in Bucharest, and helped get me to Clejani.

My first contact with a discourse on Roma was through the e-mail list group, "Romnet," moderated by Ian F. Hancock; I thank Professor Hancock for allowing me onto to the list. All of those who participated in Romnet had a decisive influence on my formative thinking on Roma issues.

In the course of preparing a manuscript as wide-ranging as this one is, there have been numerous people I have met here and in my travels who have influenced my formulations, in some cases profoundly. To all of these, and others whom I may have not have mentioned, I express my sincere thanks and gratitude: David E. Schneider, Judit Frigyesi, László Kelemen, Rudko Kawczynski, Marko Knudsen, Asmet Elesovski, the participants of the "Good Practice Projects" Conference (Hamburg, 2001), William Rosar, Speranta Radulescu, Margaret Beissinger, Phil de Fremery, Michel Winter, Stéphane Karo, Jonathan Bellman, Lynn Hooker, Tom Merino, Ken McNaughton, Rana Halprin, Michael Stewart, Jasmine Dellal, Alejandro Planchart, William F. Prizer, Tim Cooley, Miriam Whaples, Jacques Derrida, Ivan Fischer, Sonia Tamar Seeman, Kalman Balogh, the musicians of *Gypsy Caravan*, and Ökrös Ensemble.

I also thank the Roma of the Strada Lautarilor in Clejani, who welcomed me into their community. Catherine "Tara" Manole was my translator there, and to her I owe a special debt of gratitude. Though I have met, studied, and played with many Roma musicians during the last five years, there are two virtuosos from Clejani whose dedication to the violin and friendship stand out for me: Caliu, of Taraf de Haïdouks, and his son, Robert. More than anyone, they have taught me what Gypsy music is.

Chapter One

The Relative Neglect of Gypsy Music: Nationalism, Interest, and Advocacy in Musicology

We pose the question: How is the spiritual shape of Europe to be characterized? Thus we refer to Europe not as it is understood geographically, as on a
map, as if thereby the group of people who live together in this territory would
define European humanity. In the spiritual sense the English Dominions, the
United States, etc., clearly belong to Europe, whereas the Eskimos or Indians
presented at curiosities at fairs, or the Gypsies, who constantly wander about
Europe, do not.

Edmund Husserl, *The Crisis of the European Sciences,* 273

Gypsy musicians and performers have been legendary in Europe for centuries. With
a nod here or there, still, the musicological community has never fully recognized the
Gypsies' influence on and interrelation with artistic traditions. But what is surprising
is that Gypsy music continues to suffer this lack of engaged investigation by the developing matrix of ethnomusicology and New Musicology.[1] Despite some recent
smaller studies on the topic, the basic parameters for discourse remain those set up by
Liszt in the mid-nineteenth century. For reasons we shall explore further on, if scholarship is hindered by an inability or unwillingness to think outside of traditional
boundaries, the same cannot be said of the concert hall, where Gypsy music remains
almost a programmatic requirement for every major orchestra or opera house. Here
imaginative attempts have been staged to promote Gypsy music in its progression
from a "folk" or popular music to an appropriated style in art music.[2] Nor film for
that matter, as we shall see.

Although Gypsy music both as appropriator and as appropriated has begun to be recognized, this book's goal is to expand and to widen considerably the range of what is understood by the phenomenon.

For, there has also been a dramatic shift in studying and writing about Gypsies as both a cultural and an ethnic group. Symbolic of this paradigm shift is the linguistic turn away from the word "Gypsy," eschewed for the term "Rom" (plural "Roma"). This latter word can mean "man" or "person" in the Gypsy language, which itself is called "Romani." The first worldwide indication of this linguistic rethinking of identity began with the movement for what has become "Roma rights." The movement began in the mid-1960s, and its effect on shaping Roma identity has been profound. Indeed, many Roma as well as Roma scholars now consider it offensive to use the term "Gypsy" (see Chapter Eleven).

To a certain extent musicologists have acknowledged the paradigm shift in Roma studies, while neither wishing to explore the full implications of this shift, nor even to question the work in Roma studies, carried out by a politically aware group whom we will dub "Romanologists." At the broadest level, the historical factors behind this musicological neglect are nationalism and advocacy. In short, there is no clear *stake*, national or otherwise, involved in the promotion of Gypsy music as a musicological topic of discourse. And this is somewhat paradoxical when we realize that the phenomenon of Gypsy music now reaches the widest audience of its history, through the marketing channels of classical-music promotion, the world-music industry, and film producers.

Hence this book's thesis is that the category of Gypsy music represents one of the great populist aesthetic intrusions into European nineteenth- and twentieth-century art music, while conceptually remaining a blurry, hidden, and marginalized topic. The historical and political reasons for this marginalization run deep, and cross disciplinary lines. Further, the mirage of investigating Gypsy music is that unlike some other ethnically marginalized musics, the identity of Gypsies is not so clearly known. Indeed for some, like the philosopher Husserl said, the Gypsies do not figure into the "spiritual shape of Europe"!

However, as an initial framework to understand why statements like this have occurred, we begin by analyzing nationalism, which has in fact been problematized in musicology for at least the last two decades. It is only by seeing that many of the narrative stories of Western music have implicit and sometimes massive nationalist implications that we can begin to appreciate why Gypsy music has escaped the purview of sustained musicological discourse.

NATIONALISM

The study of nationalism is now a hotly pursued area in musicology.[3] In a latest article for *The New Grove Dictionary of Music and Musicians*, second edition, Richard

Taruskin criticizes, ironically, the nationalist basis for Willi Apel's formulation of nationalism for an edition of his *Harvard Dictionary of Music* in the late 1960s, where national schools are viewed negatively as a "reaction to the supremacy of German music." Taruskin writes:

> Musical nationalism is hence cast willy-nilly as a degenerate tendency that represents [Taruskin here is quoting Apel] "a contradiction of what was previously considered one of the chief prerogatives of music, i.e., its universal or international character, which meant that the works of the great masters appealed equally to any audience." And consequently, "by about 1930 the nationalist movement had lost its impact nearly everywhere in the world." One of the principal achievements of recent musical scholarship [read: New Musicology] has been to discredit this definition and all its corollaries, themselves the product of nationalist agenda.[4]

Though we agree with Taruskin's verdict, still, we might ask: what writing is *not* the product of "nationalist agenda?" Who escapes the tendency to protect a national heritage?[5]

In any case, the disinterest in writing about Gypsy music is inscribed within the larger context of nationalism and national schools. If national schools like the Hungarian or the Czech are marginalized,[6] still, at the very least they have their defenders and adherents. By contrast there are no national adherents to defend or to advocate Gypsy music *as* Gypsy. And beginning in the twentieth century other national schools, especially the Hungarian, sought to downgrade the importance of Gypsy music (analogically, the same way German-music adherents like Adorno downgraded so-called folkloristic music of the Eastern European schools).

However, this negative marking by nationalism, unequivocal in denying Gypsies their place within Europe, simultaneously drives a fascination toward finding, and after Derrida, losing, the culture and music of the Gypsies.[7] In Heidegger's terms, the Event (*Ereignis*) institutes the space for meditating on Gypsy music, which again, can only be accessed through what constructs and deconstructs it, national discourses.[8] In other words, the discourse on Gypsy music is always already within the national dimension. At the same time, we have to be attentive to what Derrida has called the "obliterating" effects of the proper, where the attempt to sign at the same time is responsible for destroying an identity, through the logic of expropriation. For this book this translates into the idea that all operations of creating identity are suspect. Take the following example, the signing of the legal document. With the death of the one who signs, the signature becomes the property of other entities — the state, the family, the legal system itself — through the process of expropriation beyond the mastery and control of any of these entities, including the one who signs.

For music historiography, ideas of the proper are articulated in the debates over so-called program music and nationalism. Indeed, the idea of a national school itself contradicts the notion that music *as* music, so-called "absolute music," has any meaning outside of concrete ethnic, social, and historical interests.[9] In writing the history of composition, one may decide who and what belongs to national school based on geography: a birthplace is usually enough to establish whether a composer is Polish, Hungarian, or Czech. As in Chopin, Liszt, and Dvořák, respectfully; the first two émigrés who paradoxically wrote nearly all of their significant works on foreign soil, Dvořák writing important works while he was residing in the United States. Of course this is a simplification of the structure of national identity, but the point is, the attachment of a proper and ethnic noun to these proper names seems undeniably tied to a notion of music that affirms while denying national identity.[10] Yet no one denies that a national school becomes complicated when writing history — are Dvořák's "American" works American, or are they Czech? Or, on the contrary, one might maintain that nationality is only a secondary factor, not a question that matters *vis-à-vis* the substance of "music itself."

Unlike phenomena within national schools, Gypsy music in its generality deals with more than any single nation — it is the essence of a *transnational* musical phenomenon. And Roma do not have any aspirations for a homeland, for a historic/utopian resting place; call it "Romestan" for lack of a better word. Thus the investigation of Gypsy music is burdened already with the relationship of Gypsies to their host countries. Do the Gypsies simply function as performer/entertainers in a client-service economic exchange? And do they have their "own" music (both in terms of identity and more concretely, as intellectual property in the marketplace), apart from these transactions? Furthermore, is there anything that unites and gathers Gypsy music *as* Gypsy, as a film like *Latcho drom* seems to suggest? Or what happens when we investigate these various musics together — Hungarian-Gypsy, Spanish-Gitano, French-Manouche, or German-Sinti — as *Latcho* in fact does?[11]

Thus one major area for exploring the idea of Gypsy music is the very notion that there is a set of identifying characteristics that distinguish Gypsy music from any other, no matter what the host country might be. If we accept the statement that aspects of Gypsy music could be found in nearly every national music of the European tradition (this is what is at stake in studying appropriation), are we essentializing or reducing Gypsy music to a set of identifying traits that are fictional? On the one hand, a nationalist would consider Gypsy music embodying the "Gypsy" as a parasite tradition, one that does not add anything to the musical repository of the nation; whereas on the other, those interested in Gypsy music *per se* might argue that it adds everything. These complications are nowhere more urgent than in the case of Central/Eastern Europe and Russia, where today the majority of the world's Roma live. In fact, it is in large part because of this that this book's focus covers this geographic terrain.

INTEREST AND ADVOCACY: DECONSTRUCTING NATIONALISM

Scholars in the countries of the former Soviet bloc might harbor no small resentment, however, toward those from the West pursuing the study of Gypsy music in their respective traditions.[12] In addition to bias against the Gypsies, these scholars feel suspicious that the Western interest in Gypsy music might have more to do with the fact that Gypsy music paints a romantic image that is readily and easily marketable. Indeed, many of the CDs and other productions that have come out in the last decade seem to bear this out.

Although this might be true to some extent, the topic of interest as it intersects with national questions is more complicated than a simple postulating of capitalist endeavor. In a philosophical sense, what would be an interest, for example, that is purely devoted to music *as* music, beyond any strategy of marketing? Why are we interested? Why study, investigate, analyze music — what motivates such projects? Can there be interest in music that is disinterested, a claim some music theorists might make for their analytical investigations? This surely recalls Kant's famous and paradoxically dictum in his aesthetics, that in principle, the liking or the disliking in the beautiful should be disinterested.[13]

In any case, to conjure up the discourse practice of Marxism, do we not detect an interest, a class one, a *national* one, perhaps a personal one, behind every discourse on music?[14] Can musicologists be compared with advocates in the legal sense, or political lobbyists when aesthetically evaluating music?

To continue with the legal analogy: perhaps the goal of musicology has been really to build an airtight case for a given musical style, piece, or culture, one that goes beyond the available evidence to establish the argument for aesthetic validity beyond any reasonable doubt. In terms of advocacy, if we detect an interest, even in what sets itself up as the purest, most theoretical, and abstract discourse of the "great" Germanic work, this interest increases exponentially when dealing with so-called national schools. Here, the advocate must construct a massive case from a small number of historical facts. This idea of a limit to the facts, of circumscribing, should not be overlooked, because a national school must be predicated on the tangible, on something that is definable; whereas in the "universal" stream of music (German music), the music is simply powerful, sublime, beautiful, beyond interest; one does not necessarily need to define or to limit the aesthetic experience. In the twentieth-century distillation of national schools, usually only one or two great composer per generation can be admitted, so that the lines of filiations can be drawn. Namely, the father passes as a model for the son, as in "couples" Smetana and Dvořák, Glinka and Musorgsky, and Rimsky-Korsakov and Stravinsky. Though models like these are used to show influences within a national school, it might also apply to the German lines of transmission, as in the couples Haydn and Mozart (a double relation, where Mozart serves as both son and later father, Haydn learning from him), Beethoven and Mendelssohn (with the ghosts of Handel and Bach haunting them both), Schumann and Brahms, and in the twentieth century, Schoenberg and his sons, the "brothers" Berg and Webern. It is impossible to deny the huge patriarchal implications of these fatherly and fraternal relations. Yet what separates the national couples from the German ones is that the national composers are measured against their respective peer in the Austro-Germanic world.

THE VIENNESE DISRUPTION[15]

Yet even in the case of the German music, the idea of its purity is always already disrupted by the land to the South, especially the Imperial city of Vienna. "South" here denotes both direction and place matters, as a particular historical determination, qualified through privations — less intellect, less seriousness, less work, less interest; lazy, perhaps even trivial.[16] In quick and schematic terms: Austria is marked by impurity, as a site of crossing and intransigence, where Romans settled and Italians (Fux being the notable exception to this Southern influx) served emperors as court composers through Joseph II; a place the Ottoman forces tried to capture, where Hungarian refugees would find security during these Muslim invasions; where Gypsies were to settle since at least the early eighteenth century. Mozart and Haydn, two composers steeped in what we will propose as "Austrianness," perhaps knew the music of both the Turks and the Gypsy verbunkos bands quite well.[17]

But before looking at Gypsies, to return to the larger historical problematic that situates the context for Gypsy and other so-called "peripheral" (see Taruskin) musical narratives, how can we think German music (the hegemonic music in the Western art-music tradition) without this Austrian disruption, a disruption that not only complicates what we think of as German, but also seems to define German music itself? Vienna: site of what has come to be globally marketed as Classic music in its most essential form, witnessed by a three-century march of composers, from Haydn to Mozart to Beethoven to Schubert to (skipping a generation) to Bruckner to Brahms to Mahler to Schoenberg to Webern to Berg. What begs to be situated: how does this Southern atmosphere change the course of German music? That German music was always already (or, from the start) contaminated by Southern influence is shown by Vivaldi and Corelli's influence on J. S. Bach, the greatest representative of the so-called Lutheran, Northern, and Saxon Baroque. Here we should never forget this Lutheran moment, the Reformation as a Northern reaction against Southern laziness, corruption, and Catholicism. The cultural and intellectual repercussions from of the Reformation are also at the essence of the origin of the discourse of German music — especially in the latter's moral, rational, and Christian specificity.

As is well known, because musicology was codified and systematized as a scientific endeavor in the late nineteenth century by German scholars, as *Musikwissenschaft*, its early heroes from Bach to Handel to Mozart tended to be German-speaking composers. Now, so the standard narrative goes, these composers became the inspiration for art-music movements in smaller, less powerful, and nascent states. However, and here is where the plot thickens, just as composers of the late nineteenth century were trying to reproduce the axiomatic of German music, they at the same time became mesmerized by the hypnotic force of awakening national sentiment. Nationalism as a movement requires at least two things: 1) an ethnic group, an ethnicity that is linguistically unified through the mother tongue; and 2) that the ethnic/tribal group occupies and inhabits a quasi-defined geographical location, a place that is either a sovereign state or on its way to becoming one. This latter aspect is a claim; as a prepared dwelling, the nation with a claim to statehood inaugurates a kind of thinking that is tied to the history of the oath, contract, and promise (sovereign nations exist through a complex legal phenomenon of the right of the national border, a right that is conferred through the promise inherent in the legal contract). This factor has been emphasized in studies of nationalism: without it, without the aspiration to sovereignty, nationalism stands powerless.[18] Sovereignty: the right to make war, to decide on the exception,[19] to produce treaties and pacts, and an aspect usually overlooked, to produce the decision that is the basis for art. Composers responded to nationalism (again, this is the traditional narrative) by creating a music that was national, grounded in the nation and the people, in the production of a national essence. Yet, we can add, the "national" composer seeks sovereignty outside of music itself (music itself as the territory claimed and occupied by universal or "German" music). In particular, the national composer did this by turning to the national essence, which sovereignty sanctions as national property: in musical terms, folk music, the unwritten music of the people.

Indeed, it is from this standpoint, from folk and oral music, that it first becomes possible to think about Gypsy music. Gypsy music is usually unwritten, and when appropriated by composers, this unwritten aspect survives in the notion of a "Gypsy performance style," one heavily laden with emotion. Though Gypsy music is entangled with the interest in folk music, what distinguishes the two is precisely the performance style. In Bartók's terms, folk music is performed "naturally" without emotion, without virtuosity, and without any flourish, while Gypsy music includes all of these traits by definition. Yet if to think about Gypsy music entails a tentative reformulation of what folk music is, we are also led to what motivates the opening of this difference, namely, the national interest. To reconstitute this essential difference, of national interest versus Gypsy music, is a contradictory and perhaps endless task, especially as new political and national configurations continue to re-align our understanding of who a Gypsy or Roma is.

Thus although the topic of advocacy in musicology remains somewhat a *terra incognita*, requiring a discourse unto itself, still, the relevance for Gypsy music is quite clear: that without some advocacy, the residue of nineteenth-century Gypsy music in art music will remain hidden, forever banished to the realm of what Carl Dahlhaus has called "trivial music."[20] Risk is involved in any advocacy to some extent, though less so in the case of an already canonized composer or aesthetic movement; for us, the risk of advocacy is that Gypsy music will turn out to be a vague generality, a superimposed category, or an exoticism among exoticisms. Specifying what is individual, interesting, and singular about Gypsy music thus becomes the goal of advocacy, while simultaneously, this advocacy of Gypsy music must consider its relationship to the hegemonic German-centered vision of music, a construct whose unity we will have to challenge endlessly.

THE QUESTION: WHAT IS GYPSY MUSIC?

What is Gypsy music? What is Gypsy as a predicate? This announcing would mark the beginning of a discourse on Gypsy music, of a way out of the neglect, yet at the same time, introduces a linguistic violence. As we have already indicated, political and Romani-rights advocates (again, the question of advocacy) vigorously denounce the word "Gypsy."[21] Their argument presupposes the primacy of linguistic phenomenon over conceptuality. Restated, the assumption is that the material signifier dictates the concept. Thus a concept of Gypsy already prejudices, because the word itself recalls racist semantics, as in the resonance with "to gyp," with its vicious connotations of dishonesty, lying, falsehood, thievery, and untruth. For Roma-rights advocates, the investigation that starts from the question "What is Gypsy music" may be already biased and biasing, it judges without knowing its prejudgment.[22]

Yet against this, as an eruptive event within music history, we can still try to pose a series of questions beginning with question, "what is Gypsy music?" Not as a statement against the worldwide process for political rights of an oppressed ethnicity, but rather as a question of music history. For example, how had composers experienced, understood, interpreted, and finally appropriated Gypsy music? Was Gypsy music just another exotic music language among others? Or was it more powerful, since composers had direct access to Gypsy performers (whereas Japanese, Indian, or Native performance might be harder to come by)? How do we engage with a music that exists as written and yet seems more essential in its unwritten, performative form? To seek a possible path to answering to these and other questions, and as part of our own advocacy for Gypsy music, we shall first follow a strategy that privileges the discourse on Gypsy music in order to build the case for the importance of this music. We start by setting up a basic dialectic, one between Franz Liszt and Béla Bartók.

LISZT'S *THE GYPSY IN MUSIC*

The discourse of Gypsy music proper begins with Liszt's book *The Gypsy in Music*.[23] It could also be the inaugural moment of the reception history of Gypsy music: that is, Liszt's effort to come to terms with what he hypothesized was a new force poised to enter the Western art-music tradition, as executed in his *Hungarian Rhapsodies*. Here we will list some motifs found in Liszt's "book" on the Gypsy, while reserving another kind of analysis of Liszt for Chapter Five: 1) animality, nature, and children; 2) contrast with the Jew; 3) avoidance of work; 4) cruelty and suffering from persecution and wandering; 5) virtuosity in a masculine, virile form; 5) the "racial affinity" between Magyar and Gypsy[24]; 6) the origins of Hungarian music; 7) rhapsody as the Bohemian/Gypsy epic; and 8) Bihary and Czermak. Each of these motifs demands careful treatment, especially as each continues to mark an area of relevance for the contemporary situation and context for Gypsy music.

Still, as an indication of Lisztean sentiment, we will cite a long passage that contains the ideas that instigated the debate about the origins of Gypsy music that continues to this day:

> We do not disguise from ourselves that the theory of Hungarian *national* songs being purely of Bohemian [Gypsy] origin is much more hazardous than that of the Zingani [Gypsies] being the *authors* of their own dance music. It is one instantly encountering difficulties scarcely to be attacked or even turned aside; being in flagrant contradiction with the ideas generally received in our country [France] on this subject. Certainly we must admit that it does not rest upon any document, and is based upon deductions which some may regard as vague. But these deductions are nevertheless of such strength as to range us upon the side of those who hold even the most *ancient national* songs of Hungary — those therefore upon which modern art has not the faintest claim have been originally borrowed [*abgelauscht*] from the Bohemians; deliberately borrowed by those who fitted them Hungarian words...Before all, let it be observed that the melodies now called *national* were not composed by the nation, but by *individuals*. Their popularity is determined and maintained by the resemblance between the inspiration from which they sprang and the *national feeling*; and it is this union which has imprinted upon them a *national character*.[25]

This is a passage about authorship (and we will hold off on discussing the question of authorship of this book) and musical property that raises the issue of how a melody comes to belong to a nation. The melodies in question are the ones found in Hungary, which Liszt thinks are really Gypsy in origin. The Hungarians borrowed these melodies, fitting them out with Hungarian words. Furthermore, showing that he remains above all a composer, in Liszt's view the author of a melody is always an individual or single person. The nation appropriates the song of the individual if the song fits the "national character," the atmosphere and "feeling" of the nation.

But Liszt confesses his own nervousness at the boldness of his thesis concerning the Bohemian origins of Hungarian music: "certainly we must admit that it does not rest upon any document, and is based upon deductions which some may regard as vague." Namely, there is no proof for his view, and his reservation is that his argumentation remains obscure. What bothers Liszt is that there is no external data — nor can there be, by definition — that connects what he *believes* to be true, through a kind of knowledge that only a musician can have access to.

Yet what is really at stake in Liszt's view? Why the interest in Gypsy music? The answer is to be found, perhaps, not merely in Hungarian or Gypsy musics, rather in the genesis of Liszt's own music. That is, Liszt as an individual — the cosmopolitan, wandering virtuoso and aspiring composer — likely wanted to find a way to justify aesthetically and conceptually the validity of his own music. His description of Gypsy music reads like an analysis of his own brilliant music, especially his conception of music as rhapsody. And his relationship to Hungary, his place of birth, was complicated by the failure of the 1848 revolution for Hungarian independence. Liszt is related to Hungary in an analogous fashion to the way that, in his opinion, might be compared to the way that the Gypsy is related to Hungary: belonging without belonging, outside while inside, and responsible for Hungarian national music while not being Hungarian. For Liszt, the Hungarians' national character and sentiment feels a special affinity and fascination for Gypsy music, which it in turn makes its own, fits out with Hungarian words; by a similar process, the Hungarian will find his own nationally essence, musically, in the *Rhapsodies*.

GYPSY MUSIC AND THE MOCK EQUATION OF GYPSINESS (I+V=E)

As a way of thinking about Gypsy music, and also to avoid essentializing it, we propose the concept of Gypsiness, which denotes a conceptual way of engaging with Gypsy music as a performative and communicative phenomenon. I first began to work with the idea in Michael Beckerman's doctoral seminar on Gypsy music.[26]

The basic idea is this: in order to conceptualize the topic immediately, we represent Gypsiness by an equation: I+V=E. "I" means improvisation, an activity which implies freedom and the ability to choose the formal design based on the moment. "V" indicates virtuosity, a realm that unites physical prowess and mental precision; with virtuosity, any technical obstacle can be overcome. But hardly noticed about virtuosity is that it cannot be copied — in its pure concept, the virtuoso is the one whose knowledge is utterly unique and singular. The virtuoso adds his or her life to the music, as it were. Added together, I and V create E, emotion (expression), a condition of feeling the music inwardly. Audiences might perceive the inwardness of music performance as the product of a passionate engagement with the emotional turmoil and joy of life — that the artist has first-hand experience of the emotional content. The concept of an audience is itself a convenient abbreviation employed by musicologists to provide the necessary background for the reception of music in a given era. Yet it also compounds some difficult contextual problems — in addition to the non-universality/unity of any audience, what do we really know about the structures of belief, especially those below or on the brink of consciousness, of an "audience," especially a historically situated one? And the idea of an "equation" for Gypsiness has its risks, too, especially in a philosophically oriented discourse, grounded in the Humanities — it might be perceived as pseudo-scientific, put forth in bad faith. But for me, the idea of Gypsiness as an equation, I+V=E, comes down to a meditation on how the performer tries to charge the raw listening atmosphere with added energy. In this sense it is less about the audience, but is the search for the way to impress something on the listener, to grab the listener's attention toward the music. Negatively, the act of impression can be interpreted as manipulation; in the best sense, impression is the coming-together in ecstatic union. Thus, if the passive listener remains unmoved, unaffected by the performance under Gypsiness, at any moment the performer has the right, so to speak, to demand the full attention of the listener — and this, we are arguing, is usually accomplished through a combination of I and V. I and V are not arbitrary signs, but historically are the musical conventions for generating sonic excitement, here and now.

The originality of the idea of Gypsiness is startling, especially when we consider some of its implications. What has traditionally been experienced as the "mystique" of Gypsy music, its specific and definite, yet equivocal power, is captured by the movement of Gypsiness. For, the equation denotes the purest expression of what we can call the communicative essence of music, the relationship to the tympanum (the inner ear). If the discourse on Gypsy music is about anything, it comes down to the search for the significance of this relationship. Indeed, the question of Gypsy music might turn on the question of the meaning of music itself — namely, what is the ultimate purpose of music-making?

BARTÓK'S CRITIQUE OF LISZT

Bartók opposed Liszt's assimilation of Gypsy-Hungarian music, especially its priority granted to the Gypsy, attempting to reverse Liszt's thesis. Bartók's argument is a two-part one, based on his ethnomusicological excursions to the Transylvanian countryside: 1) the real, authentic Hungarian music is peasant music, and not the urban music of the Budapest cafés or the aristocrat's Gypsy bands that Liszt thought; and 2) the music played by Gypsies — what Bartók will call popular art songs — does not belong to the Gypsies, but is rather music composed by Hungarian noblemen (a group that Bartók was hostile toward). Again, as in the case of Liszt, Bartók's writings stand in need of careful and close scrutiny, here we will only give some indications of the criteria for a music to be authentically of the people, which for Bartók means peasant in origin and spirit: a) the music is anonymous; b) the music originates as "the outcome of changes wrought by a natural force whose operation is unconscious in men not influenced by urban culture"; c) the peasants or group must inhabit a given geographical region over a relatively long period of time; d) the tune must be sung by a majority; e) aesthetically, the folk tune exhibits "an expressive power devoid of all sentimentality," a "conciseness of form," and a "simple" quality.

Though Bartók's criteria are aimed at peasant music, they are simultaneously a critique of Gypsy music. For Bartók, Gypsy music does not stand up to any of these criteria. Still, we may ask, what is Bartók's motivation for his interest in peasant music, and why is he so interested? Though we can perhaps discover profound biographical reasons as to why Bartók wants to unearth what he considers real and authentic Hungarian music (especially his relationships to his parents), the relevant point for us here is that Bartók's own Modernistic art music cannot be understood apart from these ethnomusicological studies.[27] Bartók's aesthetic evaluation that peasant music is a treasure, on the same level as the highest art music (Beethoven), and that it possesses an "an expressive power devoid of all sentimentality" is a characteristic and generous description of his own music. And again, nationalistic discourse is implicated in Bartók's de-valuation of Gypsy music: Hungarian music is pure, authentic, and simple, whereas Gypsies are cheap performers of the worst kind of Hungarian popular music.[28]

THE CURRENT STATE OF RESEARCH ON GYPSY MUSIC

If Gypsy music has been unfairly neglected by musicology (and perhaps ethnomusicology and anthropology), the causes seem to coalesce around nationalistic debates, especially in the case of Hungary, the site that we will be privileging in the discourse of Gypsy music. In both the pro (Liszt) and the contra (Bartók) positions, aesthetic and personal (compositional) biases seem hopelessly entangled in the viewpoints put forward.

To get a broader perspective on the Hungarian debate, it might at this point be worth to look at the current state of research concerning Gypsies as a people. Who are the Gypsies, as understood by contemporary scholarship?

Angus Fraser's book *The Gypsies*, itself part of a series titled "The Peoples of Europe," is the best general book to date on Gypsies as a people.[29] Fraser quotes the linguist Alexandre Paspati when he writes that "*la véritable histoire de la race Tchingianée est dans l'étude de leur idiome*" ("the true history of the Gypsy race is in the study of their language").[30] The language of the Gypsies, called Romani, is used as the basis for nearly every claim made on the historical origins of the Roma. What seems most likely is that the Roma originated in Northern India, leaving there around the tenth century, traveling through Persia, Armenia, and finally Turkey and Greece before entering European-Balkan territory probably by the thirteenth century. Linguists know this from careful study of Romani, a language related to Sanskrit, peeling away the historical layers (loan words) in archeological fashion. Beyond this, there survives little documentation to prove anything: "how far that [the language] can be equated with the origin and evolution of Romani-speakers is a more speculative matter, and the equivalence cannot be taken for granted."[31] Matters of speculation include: why the Roma left India, which nomadic tribes actually makeup the Roma, and if and how the present-day Roma in Europe including Turkey (a population estimated at twelve million) are related to groups remaining in countries south of Turkey such as Syria. Though scholarship continues to offer hypotheses to answer these questions, the reasoning is not based on surviving documents, but again, on archeological-style claims, such as the similarity of rituals and pollution laws between European and Indian groups, and the survival of vocabularies.[32] Yet through artistic means, especially films (we will analyze in considerable detail *Latcho drom* in Chapter Ten), connections are proposed that cannot be supported through surviving documents.

Because the Roma originate outside of Europe, the most recent approach to studying Roma is to consider their music as a world music.[33] This is done by ethnomusicologists and anthropologists who argue that the best way to understand music is locally, through a cultural context with somewhat definite geographic boundaries. This receives a formulation through the notion of a music culture, which can be studied in either "etic" (internal) or "emic" (external) fashion. Whether and how such a distinction is possible, the goal of fieldwork consists in constructing an etic understanding, and one that honors the dignity of the subject who is under the microscope.

In the model developed under recent fieldwork, one analyzes Roma music according to national divisions. However, in the process the signifier "Roma" becomes split and fragmented, with a violent cutting that never quite separates it from a transnational sense of "Gypsy." Roma in different countries and even within the same countries are defined as locally grounded communities, yet somehow related. Thus although localness might remain the ideal, still, the reality of transnational, large-scale constructs still manages to reassert its dominion over these smaller communities. Ethnomusicologists might successfully delimit various Gypsy spheres — flamenco, musique manouche, Sinti or hot jazz, various Balkan wedding and funeral traditional musics, and most recently rock and popular Roma bands.[34] Yet our argument, here, is that studies and recordings of these musics occur always already happen within a large-scale, worldwide marketing of Roma music, a market of Gypsiness that is aimed largely at non-Roma. In any case, in terms of the question of advocacy, it seems clear that the ethnomusicological approach can lead to an advocacy and privileging of Roma music, as a phenomenon worthy of study.

Now, for Western music historiography, the status of Gypsy music is not nearly so vast and "worldwide." To date there have been two strategies proposed, mostly focusing on the nineteenth century, and with much overlap. The first is found in Jonathan Bellman's excellent book *The Style Hongrois in the Music of Western Europe*,[35] which represents a cogent introduction to the way in which Gypsy music (as the *style hongrois*, note that Gypsy music is already entangled with Hungarian in his presentation) is quoted and "spoken" by Western composers, including Weber, Schubert, Liszt, and Brahms. Bellman proposes that with Brahms, the *style hongrois* reaches its historical apogee: "it is somewhat ironic that Brahms, who did not have a personal agenda with his use of this music [the *style hongrois*], would bring it to its further development."[36] After Brahms, Bellman feels it is all "decline and disappearance." Bellman seems interested not in Gypsy music per se, but rather in trying to understand how the dialect of the *style hongrois* figures in the music of the aforementioned composers.

The ethnomusicologist Max Peter Baumann wrote an article that neatly tries to summarize how Roma music is "reflected" (a word that is in the title of the article) in Western art music and opera. Baumann goes beyond Bellman in trying to accommodate and to enlarge the concept of Gypsy music in Western music. Baumann's agenda is more centered on the Roma than Bellman's, and his political bias is stated at the conclusion:

> In these closing years of the twentieth century the question of Gypsy music arises in a completely new connection in view of the interpretation constructions that have become shaky on the one hand and the "transformed" reality of Roma and Sinti on the other in the context of the civil rights movement and minority research.[37]

What Baumann refers to here is the Romani-rights movement, a movement generating power through the interconnection of Roma in various countries, especially through the existence of online and Web-based (e-mail) activities.

A second strategy in understanding Gypsy music is that of Bálint Sárosi, a Hungarian ethnomusicologist who has continued the work laid down by Bartók and Kodály. Sárosi has written the only book that bears the general title *Gypsy Music*.[38] However, after an initial attempt at a general survey, the book's focus reverts to a consideration of the Liszt-Bartók polemic, again, Hungarian versus Gypsy music, and the issue of musical-intellectual property. Sárosi writes in the tradition of Bartók-Kodály: "they [the Gypsies] do not play or sing Gypsy music but always *the music of the area concerned*."[39] Sárosi's thesis is that Gypsies appropriate the music of the host country. Differently put, we could say that the Gypsies performers play the music of the host country, as paid entertainers.

CONCLUSION: THE ADVOCACY OF GYPSY MUSIC

This chapter has tried to situate the reception of the neglect of Gypsy music in terms of its historic, aesthetic, and scholarly determination *vis-à-vis* nationalism and its discontents. As such, we have proposed that Gypsy music's neglect is relative. In other words, there does exist a tradition of a discourse of Gypsy music beginning in the nineteenth century with Liszt; and Liszt's positive evaluation has its legacy in the contemporary worldwide marketing of Gypsy CDs and films. The negative rebuttal to Liszt has occurred primarily in Hungarian circles, themselves perhaps resentful of German chauvinism against Hungarian music.

In terms of national schools, a treatment of Gypsy music allows us to pose questions about the writing of music history. Proponents of a given national school, including the German, must argue a case for the importance and significance of a given musical tradition. Historiographically, nationalism infects and contaminates every discussion of music — one thinks of early German scholarship of Bach and Handel. Furthermore, because there is no Romestan, if Gypsy "nationalism" continues to grow, it is free from the demand for sovereignty, unattached to any agenda trying to buttress the glory of the state. Thus Gypsy music could turn out to be one of the only types of music to exist in the West without any kind of state or national advocacy.

The international Roma-rights movement (led by Ian F. Hancock among others) of the last couple of decades has tried to promote an understanding of the Roma that would reconstitute the Gypsy contribution to culture and the arts.[40] However, this type of advocacy has relied heavily on the historiography of European scholars. Furthermore, the difficulty of building a case for the significance of Gypsy music lies in the disparateness of the historical material. In a certain sense, the significance of the *style hongrois* could only be perceived after the fall of Communism when Gypsy bands from behind the Iron Curtain came to worldwide attention.

Although the interpretation of Gypsy music is based on works and a popular style (the Budapest café style, or the *style hongrois*) that are well known in music history, still, the unfolding of this phenomenon remains static in interpretative studies. That is, advocates have not articulated the need for urgency in thinking about Gypsy music. But the urgency presents itself through the Roma-rights movement. Racism against Roma thrives in the countries where the majority of Roma live. Some writers have even begun to ring the alarm of a possible pre-genocidal situation in countries where ethnic cleansing is not unimaginable. Police actions, civil unrest, and civil war (though the distinctions between all three seem blurry) caused by economic and legal breakdowns in Eastern Europe and the former Soviet states are producing an atmosphere that is at the very least hostile and dangerous to numerous Roma. And yet in the West, we are able to attend concert events and festivals featuring Gypsy musicians with full awareness of the human-rights violations against the Roma community. The marketing of this music by concert promoters has begun to consider the political and economic plight of the Gypsies, but perhaps only in the name of how the suffering and persecution of Gypsies has deepened their capacity for emotional performance.

Thus the connection between music and politics revolves around the idea of music-making in the face of suffering, persecution, and cruelty. Even Liszt was aware of what he called the "cruel" treatment of Gypsies by outsiders. And yet, how can we make sense of this connection between art and reality? Does their music depend on political understanding? Is the music of the Gypsy fiddler conditioned by the suffering (a concept that is perhaps impossible to define), and if so, how?

Chapter Two

Alms, Virgins, and *Feuerzeichen*: Literature's Place in Configuring Gypsiness

The Gypsies have no writing, peculiar to them, in which to express their language. Writing, or reading, is, in general, a very uncommon accomplishment with any of them; nor must either of these attainments be at all expected among the wandering sort.... Music is the only science in which the Gypsies participate, in any considerable degree: they likewise compose, but it is after the manner of the Eastern people, extempore.

H. M. G. Grellman, *Dissertation on the Gypsies*, 87-88

Gypsies are the human types of this vanishing, direct love of nature, of this mute sense of rural romance, and of *al fresco* life, and he who does not recognize it in them, despite their rags and dishonesty, need not pretend to appreciate anything more in Callot's etchings than the skillful management of the needle and the acids. Truly they are but rags themselves; the last rags of the old romance which connected man with nature.

Charles Leland, *The Gypsies*, 13

One of our tasks is to try to demarcate "Gypsiness" in the ceaselessly shifting boundaries of representation, musical or otherwise. To prepare for instantiations of Gypsiness in music, however, we shall start with Gypsies as they are represented in literature. The relevance of this topic to my broader argument about Gypsiness in music can be summarized thus: 1) literature demonstrates in an intentional, denotative way European opinions about Gypsies; 2) literature shows the wide dissemination of the signifier "Gypsy" across European culture; and 3) as signifiers, "Gypsy" and "music" function in ways that approximate one another.

Developing this last point, both "Gypsy" and "music" can refer to mysterious, dreamlike realities that escape Enlightenment rationality. Each conjures up images and ideas that seem graspable via literary conventions, and yet through their illusory epistemological status paradoxically remain outside of the convention that intends to mark their uniqueness. For, with the signifiers "Gypsies" and "music" we enter the dimensions of nature, magic, and their combination in the supernatural — at essence, the psychological territory of the dream — inescapably linked with the charged atmosphere of desire and raw emotion. For nineteenth-century commentators, the hallucination of the dream imparted the force of Gypsy music performance, and sealed its closeness to nature.

If it is through the writing of Europeans that historical knowledge of Gypsy culture and music survives, literature bears witness to how "Gypsy" and "music" became an almost automatic association in popular culture.[1] In the presence of vanishing oral history, literature gives a precious glimpse of the historical representation of Gypsies. Furthermore, in terms of our subject matter — understanding the historical reality of as well as misrepresentations of Gypsy music — the signifier "Gypsy" appears to have been a marketable cultural phenomenon from the time of their entrance into Europe.

The circulation of "Gypsy" in the textual economy occurred as a subgenre of European colonial writing. The passages quoted in the chapter heading come from the nineteenth century, a time when the English upper-class invented the field of "Gypsy lorism." Though they intended their remarks as scientific, today their remarks seem relevant only in a literary context.

Before focusing on the reception of Gypsies in literature, we will give a short historical introduction to the close relationship of literature and music.

ON LITERATURE AND MUSIC

In his *Poetics* Aristotle was one of the first to consider the relationship of music and literature. As is well known, the philosopher defined art, including music (*mousikē*), as imitation (*mimesis*) of life. Further, Aristotle wrote that there is no poetry without music, and that poetic compositions use a combination of "rhythm, music, and meter."[2] Thus in Aristotle, both music and poetry imitate life, and are so closely tied that there is no word, strictly speaking, for poetry without music.

With Dante, Petrarch, and Chaucer (among others) the literary arts became a catalyst for fixing and codifying the representation of a national language. Along with this national integration the ancient bonds with music began to loosen. And yet, the closeness of the two arts persisted. In particular, literary forms continued to evoke the power of music, both by describing contexts for music, and by quoting lyrics of songs. Still, despite detailed accounts of music making (Castiglione's *Courtier*, as one classical example), it often remains difficult to assess the truth of linguistic descriptions of music. Namely, how do we know if we can trust what a writer says about music? And more broadly, when a writer refers to music, is it as real sound in time, or instead as symbolic content, or a mixture of the two? Broader still, what does literature (the same holds for the iconographic arts) tell us about music history?

Considered from the side of music, the central role of poetic forms in vocal music is obvious. However, in the case of so-called absolute or "pure" instrumental music, we find ourselves on shakier ground. The analogy of music and language has a long tradition, harkening back to at least the Baroque aestheticians who formalized a rhetorical theory to explain how music can be denotative.

If we say that music is *like* a language, what is the semantic status of this "like?" Do we invent the denotative quality of music? Addressing this in his philosophy of music, Adorno's initial comparison of music and language is deceptive. Adorno argues that though music "says" something, it creates no semiotics that is transferable, that is, the content of what music says cannot be detached from the actual music.[3] In this way, music distances itself from language — music operates, in other words, at a non-intentional level, and attaches itself to a specific context (usually a work). Once this environment (again, a work) is abandoned, isolated musical gestures, passages, or events take on new and radically different meanings. Without delving into the complicated aesthetic debates of twentieth-century theory after Adorno, suffice as it may that music is no longer as readily comparable with language as it once was thought in previous periods.

THE CRITICAL RECEPTION OF GYPSIES IN LITERATURE

Along with the complications of the triadic relationship music-language-literature, there is an increasingly strong tendency to disassociate Gypsies from their fictional images. In her multi-disciplinary bibliography on Gypsies, Diane Tong includes a chapter called "Portrayal of Gypsies." She states her thesis in the following way:

> When Gypsies are portrayed in the arts, they and their culture are often sacrificed to the needs of the artists portraying them — with the hostility and/or romanticism — as the quintessential Other. Interpreters of images of Gypsies have different and often contradictory explanations of the same works, but once again Gypsies themselves are almost always absent from the debate.[4]

Tong implies that artistic portrayals of Gypsies say more about the artists. Further, she argues that critics of these writers repeat the mistakes of these writers by avoiding Gypsies "themselves," by which she apparently means "real" Gypsies. Finally, for Tong, these "fantasies" impede the "Romani struggle for equal rights."

Despite what Tong says, the best overall and available resource dealing with Gypsies in literature is by a non-Gypsy. Frank Timothy Dougherty's 1980 dissertation in

Comparative Literature is titled *The Gypsies in Western Literature*. His study looks at the representation of the Romany people in Western literature. Because nothing like his study actually exists, why was this dissertation never published? Many reasons are possible: 1) non-interest mingled with varying degrees of prejudice by literary scholars; 2) Roma or activist resentment for interest in the topic of literary representation of Gypsies;[5] 3) it simply was not good enough; 4) he never tried to publish it or he tried the wrong presses.

In any case, for Dougherty, the literary heritage begins with Cervantes, and reaches maturity in the Romantic period. He provides an excellent commentary and bibliography on the major writers and key genres (including the picaresque or rogue genre). He writes:

> It is one of the rewards of this study that the most salient names in the history of the Gypsies in literature rank among the most salient names in the history of world literature.

He continues:

> Shortly after Scott, and across the English Channel, Esmeralda, Carmen, and their ilk became the Romantic rage, and their creators originated the idealized perception of Gypsies still in evidence today.[6]

Dougherty argues that one of the general themes in this literary heritage is the "individual's search for identity and self-fulfillment," a broad enough statement to apply to perhaps all literature, in fact. We could add that with the Gypsies, Europeans had what they considered an exotic ethnicity living in close proximity; there was no need to travel to seek out human or cultural difference. However, Dougherty also asserts that the main difficulty of interpretation becomes one of delimitation — choosing which authors and works to analyze.

As an instance of musicological forays into literary criticism, Bellman's book on the *style hongrois* (cited in Chapter One) contains a chapter called "Stereotypes: The Gypsies in Literature and Popular Culture." Bellman's reason for including this chapter is that "the extramusical associations [stereotypes drawn from literature] made it [the *style hongrois*] even more effective for a composer to use."[7] These literary associations were both "positive" and "negative." For Bellman, one of the "guiding principles" of the literary representation of Gypsies was the "exaggeration of the most relevant part of the stereotype";[8] Gypsies do not appear for what they are in themselves, but rather, to exemplify whatever it is the author needs, be it freedom, theft, sex, baby stealing, or simply romantic atmosphere. Bellman writes in a somewhat misleading way that:

> For the late twentieth century, of course, the relevance of this *thoroughly fictional*
> Gypsy is quite diminished. Today's surviving Gypsy stereotype, the residue from
> Romantic literature and Viennese operettas, is relatively benign.[9]

This statement makes three misguided assumptions: 1) the idea that Gypsy stereotypes are "thoroughly fictional." That is, there is no truth to fiction, fiction shows the
working of the imagination and has no basis in reality; 2) that the fictional Gypsy is
no longer present in today's world; and 3) that the fictional Gypsy does not tell us
anything of importance.

These ideas can be challenged. In order for the fictional accounts to be so consistent, it seems impossible to maintain that they are thoroughly the work of imagination. Surely, the accounts of baby stealing, lawlessness, and cannibalism have no
basis in reality; but the other tropes in the stereotype — fortune-telling, horse-trading, music, dancing, and begging — are based on some shared, communal notions of
a "real" European experience of Roma culture, though perhaps seen entirely from the
outside. And the stereotypes, as we shall see in Chapter Eleven, are anything but presently "benign," and remain massively present in the worldwide spectacle and *digita-
lization* of Gypsy music.

FARSA DAS CIGANAS (1521)

Gil Vicente (1470?-1536?) was a Portuguese dramatist and poet whose surviving pieces for the stage number over forty. Some of these are in Spanish, some in Portuguese,
and curiously, many involve a mixing of these two languages (twenty-five of his works
include Castilian). As a humanist writer, his early pieces follow in the tradition of
Juan del Encina. He was attached to the courts of Manuel I and John III, for whom
he wrote his many *autos* and *farsas* ("*auto*" is a one-act play, commonly with a religious
theme). Like Encina, Vicente was also an accomplished musician who wrote songs
(including two "*ensaladas*," a genre that involves a mixing of musical and textual elements, literally "salads") for his numerous plays.[10] Vicente's music for the songs, if
there was any, has either not survived, or awaits discovery. Perhaps some of the music
would have been improvised.

Farsa das Ciganas may well be the first literary work to have Gypsies as the main
characters, and certainly the first in Spanish to do so.[11] As such it deserves our attention. This *farsa* was performed in the presence of King John III at Évora during the
first year of this monarch's reign (1521-57). This King would later issue ineffectual
edicts banning Gypsies from his dominion.

The language of the play is written in the precursor for modern Spanish, referred
to as "Old Spanish." However, in order to evoke the flavor of the Gypsy dialect of
Granada in Seville, Vicente adds a "z" to the endings of many of the words. In

English, this sounds like "th," and is supposed to sound like a lisp, without the psychosexual connotations thereof.

The characters are eight Gypsies, four females named Martina, Cassandra, Lucrécia, and Giralda, and four males named Liberto, Cláudio, Carmélio, and Auricio. The first dialogue contains Christian references, to the cross and the Virgin Mary, though perhaps with some irony. The women appear to advertise their Christianity to increase/enhance their change of getting alms (*limuzna*) from the ladies. The men then interrupt, and exaggerate the attributes of various horses (*rocin, caballoz, potro, burricos*) they have for trade. Auricio even wants to trade his female burro for a greyhound (*galgo*). Martina becomes irritated and interrupts this business; she would rather that they sing (*cantemos*). The song (*cantiga*) *"En la cocina estaba el asno"* compares an ass to a potential groom:

> *En la cocina el asno*
> *Bailando*
> *Y dijéronme, don asno,*
> *Que vos traen casamiento*
> *Y os daban en axuar*
> *Una manta y un paramiento*
> *Hilando.*

> In the kitchen the ass [was]
> Dancing
> But they told me, Sir ass,
> May they bring you marriage
> And give you as a dowry
> A blanket and a spun vestment.

The Gypsies sing and dance to this comic song. The "ass" both parodies the men's horse dealings, and pokes fun at the groom — the ass whose dowry is, appropriately for an ass, a blanket and spun vestment.

Numerous plays during the Renaissance contain songs. Sometimes these songs can be used to add atmosphere to the drama, and are not necessary, strictly speaking, to the plot. Yet here, in a play about Gypsies, the song is central to the effectiveness of the play. The play lacks a goal-oriented storyline — it is after all a farce — and would be severely lacking in content without the song. In the courtly performance, the song was probably the centerpiece of the play, fore-shadowing the fortune telling (which often concerns the prospects of marriage) with which the play concludes. (In other plays, Vicente commonly opens and closes with a song.)

In the last section, the Gypsy girls try to impress the ladies with the various kinds of magic (*hechizo*) that they know. For example, through magic one can know the thoughts (*pensamientoz*) of others, or change the will (*voluntad*) of a man, and most importantly, know when one can chase down (*cazar*) a husband (*marido*). Palm reading is evident: "Show your hand," (*Mustra la mano*), for certainly the lines tell good things (*buena dicha*, literally the good-saying; also *buena ventura*, good fortune). The rest of the play tells of future great and honorable marriages (including one to the *Alcazar de Zal*), again, based on the predictions of fortune telling. The play abruptly ends with Lucrécia admonishing the audience that "never did people so honorable/ Give such so little reward ("*No vi gente tan honrada/Dar tan poco galardon*"). This is to tell the ladies that they need to give more to the Gypsies/actors.[12] It also indicates that the Gypsies expect a greater recompense for their services.

Only 100 years after the Gypsies first entered Italy (1417), *"Farsa das Ciganas"* offers a vivid picture of activities for which Gypsies are already (in-)famous by this time: begging, horse-trading, singing and dancing, magic, and palm-reading. Significantly, none of these activities produces any product, but are based, rather, on a performative condition. And the moral of Vincente's *"Farsa"* seems to say that if you offer nothing to the Gypsy, you will receive nothing in return.

"LA GITANILLA" (1613)

Miguel de Cervantes Saavedra began work on his twelve *Exemplary Novels* (*Novellas Ejemplares*) contemporaneously with his *Don Quixote I* (1605). For music historians, "La Gitanilla" is the most important of the novellas (short stories), having served as the basis for the libretto of Carl Maria von Weber's opera *Preciosa*. Bellman has analyzed this story as "particularly accommodating to a race-conscious sensibility."[13] Of course, he means German writers, including Achim von Arnim and Pius Alexander Wolff.[14] Weber's *Preciosa* uses Wolff's German translation of the Cervantes. Bellman concludes that despite the association of thieving and easy virtue, however, Cervantes's Gypsies "still get passably gentle treatment."[15] As we shall see, Cervantes's treatment is anything but "passably gentle."

The opening of the story (also quoted in Bellman, but not as the opening) sets forth a tight image of Gypsies as thieves (*ladrones*):

> It would seem that gypsies, men [*gitanos*] and women [*gitanas*] alike, came into the world for the sole purpose of thieving [*para ser ladrones*]: they are born of thieving parents [*nacen de padres ladrones*], study to be thieves, and end up polished and perfect thieves, in whom the impulse to steal [*la gana de hurtar*] and stealing [*hurtar*] are one and the same thing, extinguished only by death [*la muerta*].[16]

The first sentence of the novella is emphatic: Cervantes employs the word "*ladrones*" four times, like a mantra. Again, as the opening to the narrative, this statement conditions the rest of the work. It informs the understanding of Gypsies, especially in contrast to the Christian references unleashed toward the end.

Now, sexual difference erases itself before the violent activity of thieving: both men and women, "*gitanos*" and "*gitanas*" alike, are thieves. Furthermore, Cervantes leaves unresolved the nature-versus-nurture controversy — Gypsies are born of thieving parents, but they must study to be thieves. And it does not seem to matter, in any case; for Gypsies steal ("*hurtar*") until they are taken ("*quitan*," translated in the quotation as "extinguished") by death: not merely a natural death, but probably the punishment of death for stealing (the death penalty frequently emerges in Gypsy literature).

Death leads to the metaphor of darkness. Weather conditions — the burning of the sun and the harshness of the wind — have no impact on the heroine, Preciosa:

> Neither sun nor wind, nor all the inclemencies of the heavens [*las inclemencias del cielo*], to which Gypsies are exposed more than others, could darken [*deslustrar*] her face or tan her hands; and, what is even stranger, for all her rough upbringing, she seemed to have been born with finer qualities [*de mayores prendas*] than a Gypsy girl, for she was most courteous and well-spoken [*bien razonada*].[17]

Preciosa's skin refuses to become dark like the Gypsies' skin; in comparison with Gypsy girls, she possesses "finer qualities." Mentioned is her ability to speak well. The word "*razonda*" is derived from the Latin for reason, "*ratio*." Implied is that Gypsies do not possess reason. Another finer quality seems to be a white skin color — the exposure to the elements of nature could not darken her face. "*De[s]lustrar*" also has the senses of tarnishing, disgracing, or soiling, as in staining one's honor or reputation. Thus the play on the image of light is spectacular in this passage: light (sun and heavens) must be resisted in order to maintain lightness of skin. Furthermore, this whiteness of skin is not only a finer quality, but manifests what is inside the subject, the ability to possess reason. In these aspects, Preciosa, as a Gypsy, remains exceptional.

Again, and also at the beginning of his story and before the plot begins, Cervantes exposes Preciosa's musical abilities:

> Salió Preciosa rica de villancicos, de coplas, seguidillas y zarabandas y de otros versos, especialmente de romances, que los cantaba con especial donaire.[18]

> Preciosa turned out to have a rich [knowledge] of villancicos, coplas [verses], seguidillas, zarabandas, and other types of verse, especially romances [ballads], which she sang with special grace (my translation).

The genres of the songs named are popular. Scholars who have scrutinized Cervantes's references to music are not in agreement about exactly what he has mind; but it seems that Cervantes could mean a kind of music found in the cancieneros.[19] In his book on music in Cervantes, Adolfo Salazar plausibly states that the songs sung by Preciosa were monodies (*"monódicos"*), accompanied only by her tambourine (*sonajas*) and dancing.[20]

The mention of these genres places the story within the context of the early history of flamenco. The "seguidilla" is one of the most ancient forms of this repertoire, in that its verse forms recall the possibly Arabo-Andalusian *muwashshah*.[21] Note that Cervantes does not include a seguidilla in this story (Salazar quotes one from the story *"Rinconete and Cortadillo,"* but he seems to have altered Cervantes's longer line breaks.

If we turn to the narrative, the plot of "Gypsy Maid" is based on the premise and myth of Gypsy baby-stealing. The stunning Preciosa (the name itself means "beautiful") was stolen from her rich and noble parents by an old Gypsy who assumed the role of grandmother. Toward the end of the story, the supposed grandmother confesses to the rightful parents that it was she who took Preciosa, whose real name is Doña Constanza de Azevedo.

The old Gypsy asks for forgiveness for her great sin (*"el perdón de un gran pecado mío"*), showing that Cervantes's Gypsies were Christian. Indeed, the old Gypsy's plea echoes Preciosa's own cry for mercy, as she begs the Corredigor (governor) for pardon for her betrothed Andrés Caballero. Like Preciosa, Andrés is not a Gypsy, but a nobleman from Madrid whose real name is Don Juanico. To test the strength of his love, Preciosa demands of him that he become a Gypsy for approximately two years time; if he passes all of the tests, then she will marry him. Andrés is about to receive the death sentence by hanging for the murder of a soldier who thought Andrés a dishonorable thief. Preciosa's clemency speech to the Corredigor employs the Latin word for mercy, *"misericordia,"* and is the climax of the story:

> ¡Señor, misericordia, misericordia! ¡Si mi esposo muere, yo soy muerto! ¡Él no tiene culpa [...][22]

> Sir, mercy, mercy! If my husband dies, I am dead! He is not guilty [my translation]

Again, the appeal to *"misericordia"* reinforces a Christian orientation of forgiveness of sins. Though brought up a Gypsy, the fictional Preciosa seems on familiar terms with a European tradition of pleading for pardon.

And this huge overture to Christian themes raises some significant problems, at the borderline of fiction and history: why did Gypsies, allegedly fiercely resistant to assimilation, appropriate Western forms of religion so quickly? The typical answer (Fraser et al.) runs that they did so to avoid further persecution; however satisfying this answer may be, it does not address the larger problematic of how to believe in not believing. To be sure, if one assumes that Gypsies practice the local religious beliefs for purely pragmatic reasons, than one must remain cynical about what Gypsies actually believe. Thus what we can call the "persecution card" does not seem to address a deeper undercurrent of Christianity which European Gypsy culture has acquired. What Cervantes's Gypsies show is that from the European perspective, Gypsies accepted the essential tenets of Christianity.

MOLL FLANDERS (1722) AND *TOM JONES* (1749)

Gypsies appear in the early English novel of the first half of the eighteenth century. These novels frequently center on the life and times of some controversial personage. In both *Moll Flanders* and *Tom Jones*, the Christian theme of redemption figures prominently in the rehabilitation of the title characters, both of whom are orphans.[23]

Daniel Defoe's novel on the famous London prostitute is told in first-person narrative. Moll's first recollection is vague, but it contains a reference to Gypsies:

> The first account that I [Moll Flanders] can recollect, or could ever learn ofmyself, was that I had wandered among a crew of those people they call *Gypsies*, or Egyptians; but I believe it was but a very little while that I had been among them, for I had not had my skin discoloured or blackened, as they do very young to all the children they carry about with them; nor can I tell how I came among them, or how I got from them.

> It was at Colchester, in Essex, that those people left me; and I have a notion in my head that I left them there (that is, that I hid myself and would not go any farther with them), but I am not able to be particular in that account; only this I remember, that being taken up by some of the parish officers of Colchester, I gave an account that I came into the town with the Gypsies, but that I would not go any farther with them, and that so they had left me, but whither they were gone that I knew not, nor could they expect it of me; for though they send round the country to inquire after them, it seems they could not be found.[24]

Left unanswered is the question of how this early childhood experience informs Moll's life. Assumed is that it contributes to Moll's early turn to promiscuity. Again, the issue of darkness emerges as central in marking difference: the Gypsies, being dark themselves, allegedly discolor or blacken the skin of children that do not belong to them. Significantly, the Gypsies know how to disappear; for though the Colchester authorities sought the Gypsies out for questioning, they "could not be found."

The other important early English novelist, Henry Fielding, devotes a chapter (Book XII/12) of *Tom Jones* to a group of Gypsies celebrating a wedding in a barn. The chapter serves two purposes: 1) to add exotic color; and 2) to provide Fielding with space to air his views on political theory.[25]

Like Vicente, Fielding injects exotic color through an attempt to approximate a dialect. The King is the only Gypsy whose speech is reported. The King can neither read nor write. He refers to himself as "Me" instead of "I," as in "Me have honor, as me say, to be deir King."[26] "D" substitutes for "th." "H" is entirely absent, "have" is pronounced "ave." And also similar to Vicente's Gypsies, "z" is asserted: "suprize." Linguistically, Fielding is seemingly approximating pidgin, the language mix that occurred during the period of European expansion.[27]

Fielding capitalizes on Tom and his companion Patridge's excursion to the Gypsy camp to discuss absolute monarchy. The writer describes the Gypsies as a happy set of people, ruled by an absolute monarch. The Gypsies themselves decided on this form of government to ensure their survival and to halt fighting within the group. The King expresses to Tom the responsibility of the sovereign:

> for me assure you it be ver troublesome ting to be King, and always to do justice; me have often wish to be de private *Gypsy* when me have forced to punish my dear Friend and Relation; for dought we never put to Death, our Punishments be ver severe. Dey make de *Gypsy* ashamed of demselves, and dat be ver terrible Punishment; me ave scarce ever known de *Gypsy* so punish do Harm any more.[28]

The King decides on criminal sentencing. Important and in contrast to the European legal system is that the Gypsies reject punishment by the death penalty; to speculate, perhaps Fielding realized that the death penalty is the most potent and ultimate threat that Gadje culture can utilize to destroy Gypsy culture.

For these Gypsies, the purpose of punishment is to shame the criminal, which leads to his reform. In its finality, the death penalty offers no chance for any reform for the one sentenced.

Indeed, a situation occurs which places the King in the position of judge. A young Gypsy wife has seduced Patridge, while her husband stood by as onlooker. After an initial confusion where the King grants the Gypsies two guineas as reward for Patridge's action, the King decides in favor of Patridge and against the deceitful Gypsy couple, after learning new information that the husband had encouraged his wife to act as seducer. The King's verdict:

> Me be sorry to see any *Gypsy* dat have no more Honour dan to sell de Honour of his Wife for Money [...] me do order derefore, dat you be de infamous *Gypsy*, and do wear Pair of Horns upon your Forehead for one Month, and dat your Wife be called de Whore, and pointed at all dat Time: For you be de infamous *Gypsy*, and she be no less the infamous Whore.[29]

Jones is surprised by the verdict, to which the King replies:

Me vil tell you, how the Difference is between you and us. My people rob your People, and your People rob one anoder.[30]

This leads Fielding to interrupt the narrative for his views on absolute monarchy. Fielding thinks that there is only one "solid objection" to it, that it is very difficult in practice to find a man worthy of assuming the title of King. The person must display three qualities, moderation, wisdom, and goodness. Apparently for Fielding, the Gypsies are capable of having a King, for "they have no false honours among them, and that they look upon shame as the most grievous punishment in the world."[31]

GÖTZ VON BERLICHINGEN (1773)

Goethe's play *Götz von Berlichingen* dramatizes the life of this sixteenth-century free knight (*Reichritter*). Breaking with the dominant Classical French tragedy of Racine and Corneille, Goethe's work returned to the dramaturgical principles of Shakespeare — multiple scenes, multiple plots, with "elements of the grotesque placed side by side with elements of nobility, with representatives of different social classes."[32] One of these "different" social classes is the Gypsy camp that Götz enters in the final act.

Why a Gypsy camp? The obvious answer would be that as a work of the German "*Sturm und Drang*" period, the Gypsy camp adds a magical, supernatural, and one might add Romantic element to the play. In this interpretation, the Gypsies are not significant in themselves, but rather, for their injection of a magico-supernatural element at a crucial juncture in the climax to the plot.

However, before dismissing this scene as simply color, let us analyze Goethe's scene. What warrants a closer analysis is not only the poetic power of the language, but the existence of such a scene at all in the first great play by Goethe, whose literary presence through *Faust* will tower over nineteenth-century music. Furthermore, by privileging this short scene, we can continue to pile up a literary web of interconnected details on perceived traits of Gypsy life.

The scene in question is Act V, Scene 6. Again, the setting is the early sixteenth century. The Peasants War (1525) has seen 100 villages burned in Swabia, the province where Götz has his castle, at Jaxthausen. Goethe assimilates historical time in this fictional episode — the Holy Roman Emperor, Maximilian, who died in 1519, is here still alive. The scene opens:

> Night in the wild forest (wilden Wald). A Gypsy encampment (Zigeunerlager). A Gypsy woman (Zigeunermutter) by the fire.
>
> THE GYPSYWOMAN (Mutter): Mend the thatch over the cave-door, daughter. There'll be rain a-plenty tonight.
>
> (Enter a boy.)

THE BOY: A hamster, mother. There! Two field mice.

THE MOTHER: I'll skin them and roast them for you, and you shall have a cap from the pelts — You're bleeding (Du blutst)?

THE BOY: Hamster bit me.

THE MOTHER: Fetch me some kindling to make the fire burn up. When your father comes he'll be wet through and through.

(Enter another Gypsy woman with a child on her back.)

THE FIRST WOMAN: Did you make a good haul (Hast du brav geheischen)?

THE SECOND WOMAN: Little enough. The district is full of tumult all around us so no one's life is safe. Two villages are blazing (Brennen zwei Dörfer lichterloh).

THE FIRST WOMAN: Is that a fire yonder, that glow? I've been looking at it for a long time. We've got so used to fiery signs in the sky (Feuerzeichen am Himmel) lately.[33]

In less than half a scene, Goethe advances a vivid and stunning portrayal of Gypsies. He sets the Gypsy encampment at night, in a "wild forest." (Musicologists are well acquainted with the forest as a place of the supernatural through Weber's *Der Freischütz*, which occurs about forty miles to the West on the Neckar, on a thickly forested mountain near Heidelberg.) Goethe's qualification of the forest as "wild" sets the tone for our entering the world of the Gypsy encampment. Night encodes the signifier of darkness, and we can venture that this also encompasses what we have already seen as the European-perceived notion of Gypsies. The first image of the camp is that of a Gypsy woman by a fire. We learn in the first sentence of the dialogue, as the mother addresses the daughter, that the Gypsies live in a cave. The significance of the cave is that it shows that these Gypsies are settled, perhaps, or at least semi-nomadic, yet still amazingly primitive.

The son has caught some rodents for his dinner; through this line it is evident that these Gypsies must sometimes improvise for their dinner. The boy's bleeding wound from the hamster bite anticipates the bloody entrance of Götz. Yet the mother seems unconcerned, almost indifferent to the bite, ordering the child to fetch some wood for the fire. She is not uncaring, but rather shows the Gypsies' resilience, toughness and strength, and their ability to withstand pain.

From the second Gypsy woman (with a child on her back), the economic dependency of the Gypsies on the local population emerges. "Did you make a good haul" asks the first Gypsy woman. "Haul" is an effect of bringing-together, collecting, and gathering. In this passage, "haul" results from two activities, either begging or trading. In English, it is unclear which Goethe intends. But in Middle German, the verb "*heischen*" has the connotation of an asking for help, which suggests that the woman was begging. The woman's begging did not go well; as she notes, two villages are blazing. Finally, the supernatural enters, as in the "fiery signs in the sky lately." *Feuerzeichen*: literally, the sign of fire, a symbol of something to come. Indeed, the scene is engulfed in the spirit of fire, here, also an elemental sign of war. In any case, the "*Feuerzeichen*" refers to the comet that precipitates the death of the Emperor astrologically; for the Gypsies, the sign is ominous, as we will soon see.

The scene continues with the dramatic entrance of the Gypsy leader (*Hauptmann*): "Do you hear the Wild Huntsman" ("*Hört ihr den wilden Jäger*")? The translator of the English edition notes that this is a "folklore personification of the tempest, originally he was the god Wotan himself."[34] The dogs of the camp immediately respond by barking ("*Wie die Hunde bellen*"). The Gypsies interpret the hunter as the devil himself. The leader reports that the peasants are robbing among themselves, thereby granting the Gypsies the possibility of doing the same.

Götz's entrance into the Gypsy camp is equally dramatic. The great knight's enemies have wounded him; as he bleeds, he sees a fire with which he equates Gypsies ("*dort seh ich Feuer, sind Zigeuner*"). The great knight is bleeding profusely, and he implores the Gypsies for help. The Gypsy leader, after learning that the knight comes in peace, articulates his profound respect for Götz, "*ein edler Mann, an Gestalt und Wort*" ("a noble man in looks and speech").[35] In the leader's tent, a Gypsy woman binds Götz's wounds. Götz is surprised that the Gypsies know who he is; the Gypsy leader's exclaims their alliance such that "we'd give our lives and blood for you" ("*Götz, unser Leben und Blut lassen wir vor Euch.*" As the Gypsies try to protect Götz, the knight reflects on his fate:

> O Kaiser! Kaiser! Räuber beschützen deine Kinder. Die wilden Kerls, starr und treu.[36]

> O my Emperor, my Emperor! Robbers shield your children. Those wild lads, tough and true![37]

In a reversal of the usual order, Gypsies as robbers protect the child of the Emperor, Götz. The wild Gypsies remain loyal and truthful. Unfortunately, the forces of the *Bündische* overcome the Gypsies and capture Götz.

Goethe's Gypsy camp is remarkable for introducing the Gypsies into the early Romantic movement. The "wild" Gypsies partake of the poverty of life on the margins of the European towns, yet simultaneously never lose touch with the supernatural order.

GUY MANNERING (1815)

Sir Walter Scott set his historical novel *Guy Mannering* in mid-eighteenth-century Scotland, during a time when "the belief in astrology was almost universal."[38] Scott himself was an early Gypsy lorist, who had Gypsies living on his estate.[39] The book's second scene has the title character (an Englishman) wandering beyond the Scottish town of Ellangowan out to the castle ruins, giving the reader a perfect picture of early nineteenth-century Romanticism. There Mannering spies Meg Merrilies, a Gypsy whose song bewitches him:

> Equipt in a habit which mingled the national dress of the Scottish people with something of an Eastern costume, she spun a thread. [...] As she spun, she sung what seemed to be a charm. Mannering, after in vain attempting to make himself master of the exact words of her song, afterward attempted the following paraphrase of what, from a few intelligible phrases, he concluded to be its purport: —

> ' *Twist ye, twine ye! even so*
> *Mingle shades of joy and woe,*
> *Hope and fear, and peace and strife,*
> *In the thread of human life.*
> *While the mystic twist is spinning,*
> *And the infant's life beginning,*
> *Dimly seen through twilight bending,*
> *Lo, what varied shapes attending!...* ' [40]

At the ruins of the castle, Merrilies, dressed part-Scottish, part-Eastern, is spinning. As she does so she sings a tune that compares her activity to the vicissitudes of human life. Mannering, the concealed observer, is here also an early folk-song collector. Already in Scott's hero we have the prototype of the Gadje who becomes infatuated with the mysterious, closed world of the Gypsy.

Forgiveness occurs at the climax of the book (Chapter Fifty-Four), roughly a decade and half after the story's opening. Meg Merrilies exposes the crimes of murder and kidnapping by the captain and smuggler Dirk Haiteraik. At the same time her companions (including Betram, the kidnapped boy, now grown and come back to claim what is rightfully his legacy) lay in wait. In the ambush Haiteraik shoots Merrilies. After she is brought back to a hut in town (Kaim o' Derncleugh, the only place where the spirit will "free itself o' the flesh," 357),[41] she declares:

> That is Henry Betram, son to Godfrey Betram, unquhile [?] of Ellangowan; that young man is the very lad-bairn that Dirk Hatteraick carried off from Warroch-wood the day that he murdered the gauger. I was there like a *wandering spirit* — for I longed to see that wood or we left the country. I saved the bairn's life, and sair, sair I prigged and prayed they would leave him wi' me [...] I made another vow to mysell, and if I lived to see the day of his return, I would set him in his father's seat, if every step was on a dead man.[42] (my emphasis)

"Wandering spirit" aptly describes Merrilies's character as a Gypsy. After this speech, she turns to Dirk to confirm the truthfulness of what she has proclaimed, relying on the imagery of blood:

> 'Dirk Hatteraick, dare ye deny, with my blood upon your hands, one word of what my dying breath is uttering? Then fareweel! and God forgive you! — your hand has sealed my evidence. When I was in life, I was the mad randy Gypsy, that had been scourged, and banished, and branded — that had begged from door to door, and been hounded like a stray tike from parish to parish — what would hae minded *her* tale? But now I am a dying woman, and my words will not fall to the ground, any more than the earth will cover my blood!'[43]

The hand of Hatteraick has spilled the blood of Merrilies, while this same blood guarantees the truth of her words about his crimes. Nobody would believe what she says if she were to live, for she is the "mad randy Gypsy."[44] But as a dying woman, her words assume a truthfulness that is guaranteed by her blood.

Scott's Merrilies is thus a powerful force of goodness and truth, unacknowledged as such during her lifetime. But she emerges by the end of the book not as a beggar who once cursed the House of Ellangowan, but as a great heroine who saved Betram.

NOTRE-DAME DE PARIS (1831)

Victor Hugo's masterful novel reaches further back into history than Scott's, to the time of late medieval Paris. Landmarks and architecture dominate Hugo's Paris of 1482, especially the Place de la Grève and the Notre-Dame cathedral. In addition to serving as a place of government (city hall, the Hôtel de Ville), the Place de la Grève is also the site where punishments occur, including capital ones. A fierce abolitionist of his own day, Hugo calls attention throughout his novel to the bloodiness of the executions in the famous square that borders the magnificent gothic cathedral along the Seine. It is surprising, however, to learn that Hugo as a writer takes a dark view of Gypsies, associating them with the satanic and demonic.

The Gypsy "La Esmeralda" is the heroine of Hugo's tale. Like Preciosa, she turns out to not be a Gypsy at all, but rather to have been stolen by Gypsies. La Esmeralda's companion is her white goat, Djali. The two perform magical and sometimes acrobatic feats in the Grève to the delight of all, especially the sinister churchman Claude Frollo who watches clandestinely from the Notre-Dame's tower. Frollo is secretly in love with the girl.

Hugo's poetic description of Esmeralda reinforces all of the Gypsy stereotypes we have seen so far:

> As with her dancing and beauty, so with her voice. It was both enchanting and indefinable: something pure, resonant, aerial and winged, so to speak. It dilated

continually into melodies and unexpected cadences, into simple phrases scattered with sharp, sibilant notes, and leaps up the scale that would have defeated a nightingale but where the harmony was never lost, and then into gently undulating octaves that rose and fell like the singer's own breast. Her beautiful face followed each caprice of her song with a peculiar mobility, from the most dishevelled inspiration to the chastest dignity. At one moment she seemed a madwoman, at the next a queen.[45]

Hugo draws attention to Esmeralda's voice, "indefinable," "pure," angelic. Hugo is like Mannering, observing the Gypsy song, yet unable to comprehend it except through ambiguous description: "unexpected cadences," "sharp, sibilant notes" (sibilant=hissing), "leaps up the scale," "gently undulating octaves."

Gypsy music, perhaps as music itself, is thus indefinable, given to the unexpected, sharp (timbrally, we would add) yet admitting of gentleness. The broader point here is that writing about Gypsies is akin to writing about music. The voice expresses itself in the movement of the face, which changes from madness to the dignity of a queen. Finally, the song must be capricious and free, like the Gypsy herself. In fact, Esmeralda does not even understand the words of her song, "for the feeling she put into the song bore little relation to the meaning of the words":

> *Un cofre de gran riqueza*
> *Hallaron dentro un pilar*
> *Dentro del, nuevas banderas*
> *Con figuras de espantar*
> *Alarabes de cavallo*
> *Sin poderse menear*
> *Con espadas, y los cuellos*
> *Ballestas de buen echar.*

Arab horseman (*Alarabes de cavallo*) immediately transports the reader to Moorish-Spanish-Gypsy Andalusia. Later in the book Hugo describes her character and wanderings thus in a significant passage on the Gypsies, from the point of view of her "husband" Gringoire:

> Gringoire had managed to find out that as a young child she had traveled all over Spain and Catalonia, as far as Sicily; he even thought that the caravan of zingaris to which she belonged had taken her to the kingdom of Algiers, a country situated in Achaia, Achaia itself being bordered on one side by lesser Albania and Greece and on the other by the Sea of Sicilies; which is the route to Constantinople. The Bohemians, said Gringoire, were vassals of the King of Algiers, in his capacity as chief of the *race of white Moors*. What was certain was that La Esmeralda had come to France when she still very young, via Hungary. From all these countries, the young girl had brought back shreds of weird dialects, songs and alien notions, which had turned her language into something as motley as her half-Parisian, half-African costume.[46]

In this wonderful passage, wandering, traveling, and the nomadic life define the Gypsy lifestyle above all. Through Gypsies, Hugo can indulge in a kind of virtuosic display of geographic exoticism: Spain, Catalonia, Sicily, Algiers, "Achaia," Albania, Greece, leading to Constantinople. Amazing is that the Gypsies here become a "race of white Moors." As Moors, their traveling comes to divide their cultural heritage: we might say, following Hugo, "half local and half other" (compare to the above description of Meg Merrilies). Esmeralda came to France via Hungary, yet she knows certain Spanish songs, as we have seen, and speaks in motley language. Again, language surfaces as a topic in describing Gypsies.

But though she has lived as a Gypsy, as a beautiful baby Esmeralda was stolen from her mother (who actually is the penitent locked in the cell of Tour-Rolland in the Grève, Paquette de Chantefleurie). Or perhaps exchanged, for the Gypsies left a deformed baby in her place:

> In place of her [Paquette's] sweet little Agnes [i.e., Esmeralda] so pink and fresh, who was a gift from God, a sort of hideous little monster [the hunchback, Quasimodo], lame, one-eyed and misshapen, was dragging itself across the floor squealing. She hid her eyes in horror. [...] It was the monstrous child of some Gypsy who had given herself to the devil. He looked about four years old and spoke a language which certainly wasn't human.[47]

The Gypsies played a trick on poor Paquette, exchanging her child, an angelic "gift from God," for a monster, a deformed beast begotten of the devil. If we read the above passage with Cervantes in mind, we see a pattern: if a beautiful girl is stolen and hence raised by the Gypsies, she remains honest and virtuous (by implication, unlike other Gypsies), while successful adapting to Gypsy occupations — especially music and dancing — indeed, beyond what is possible for a Gypsy. Furthermore, with the exchange of babies, Hugo stages a stunning reversal: the orphaned and horrifyingly disfigured creature Quasimodo is now the child of a Gypsy.

But the world will never know the true identities of Esmeralda and Quasimodo. Instead, Esmeralda will hang as a Gypsy. But before this, Claude Frollo, the black specter pursuing Esmeralda, begs her to come with him:

> Alas, you watched unmoved as I wept! Child, do you know that these tears are lava? Is it really true, then? That we feel no pity for the man we hate? You could watch me die, and laugh. But I don't want to watch you die! A word, a single word of forgiveness! Don't tell me that you love me, simply tell me you are willing, that will do, I shall save you.[48]

Frollo wishes that Esmeralda will pardon the wrongs he has done to her. The priest begs pardon/forgiveness from the Gypsy, who withholds her word. Instead, when the soldiers finally catch up with her (after a brief reunion with her mother), she goes to the gibbet. The scene is a bloody one, as her mother bites the hand of Provost Tristan, the hangman, as he carries Esmeralda to the top of the ladder to her death.[49]

LORCA'S *GYPSY BALLADS* (1927)

Unlike the other works with which we have been dealing, Federico García Lorca's *Romancero gitano* is a difficult and abstract work to analyze. Seventeen ballads on the Gypsy-Andalusian theme make up this work. Most scholars seem to agree though that the main opposition running through the poems is that between the *Gitanos* (i.e., the Gypsies of Andalusia) and the Spanish Civil Guard.

However, a study by John Crosbie tries to problematize the absoluteness of this opposition. Crosbie argues that critics have "idealistically interpreted the conflict of Gypsies and Civil Guards as symbolic of a hopeless, irresolvable — in short, absolute — tragedy."[50] To summarize, he identifies what he calls a "counter-structure," where the Gypsy–civil guard as a positive-negative opposition is dissolved, where the meanings of these symbolic terms become ambiguated. Crosbie then shows that though the "dominant structure" of the opposition (Gypsies-Civil Guard) is usually on the textual surface of the poems, still, the counter-structure consistently works to undermine it; thus, the poems contain their own "immanent critique." Another way of putting this would be that because of the high level of abstraction, symbolic terms mutate into their opposites, thus entailing the possibility of multivalent interpretations.

I would tend to agree with Crosbie, while not settling on any ultimate meaning for Lorca's work. Some interpreters have seen the collection biographically: the *Gitanos* represent Lorca as a homosexual, while the civil guard stands for the repressive structures of middle-class society. However, I think that main point is that without the *Gitanos* in all of their multivalent and enigmatic equivocality, the poems are structurally not possible. Specifically, they are poems *about* Gypsies, carrying the dissemination of this signifier. Hence the idea that the Gypsies are *merely symbolic*, put forth by Crosbie, cannot be upheld.[51]

Because there is not enough space to interpret the individual poems here, we will focus on two poems. The second poem, "*Preciosa y el aire*," revisits Cervantes's Preciosa. Though Preciosa turned out to have been a Gadje stolen by the Gypsies, in Lorca's view her appropriation by the Gypsies has held. Yet the poem tells quite a different tale — the attempted rape of Preciosa by a mythical figure, called St. Christopher:

> *Niña, deja que levante*
> *tu vestido para verte.*
> *Abre en mis dedos antiguos*
> *la rosa azul de tu vientre.*
> *Preciosa tira el pandero*

y corre sin detenerse.
El viento-hombrón la persigue
con una espada caliente.

Come here, my child, and let me look
While I lift up your clothes
Let my old fingers open wide
Your belly's bluish rose.
Preciosa throws down her tambourine
And runs in headlong flight.
The great man-wind with burning sword
Gives chase with all his might.[52]

Preciosa had been out playing (*tocando*) when the wind (St. Christopher) spied her. She runs in fear, throwing down the tambourine (*el pandero*). The old wind has assumed, mistakenly, that Preciosa is an easy woman, symbolized by the music of her tambourine. But like Cervantes's Preciosa, her sense of honor drives her to protect the dignity of her sexuality.

Crosbie provides a solid interpretation of poem eleven, "*Prendimiento de Antoñito el Camborio en el camino de Sevilla.*" Crosbie writes that when Antoñito surrenders to the civil guard, he "ceases to act as a true Gypsy should." [53] His "Gypsy credentials" are withdrawn; it is asked who Antonio Torres Herdia is, without his willow wand ("*sin vara de mimbre*," the willow wand is a water symbol; the equation "water = Gypsies" remains in the dominant structure of Lorca's work):

Antonio, ¿quién eres tú?
Si te llamaras Camborios,
hubieras hecho una fuente
de sangre con cinco chorros.

Tony, what kind of man are you?
If you were a Camborio real,
You'd have made a fountain of blood from which
Five jets shoot up and fall. [54]

The five jets refer to the five soldiers of the Civil Guard who have arrested Tony. Tony has not fought back, therefore, what kind of a Gypsy is he? A "real" Gypsy would have shown his dagger (*cuchillo*), and drawn the blood (*sangre*) of the soldiers. As such he is no longer a Camborio:

Ni tú eres hijo de nadie,
ni legítimo Camborio.

You're not the son of anyone,
And no Camborio at all.

Tony loses his family name, he is no longer to be called "son" ("*hijo*"), no longer a Camborio. Indeed, in the next poem ("Muerte de Antoñito el Camborio") he will die at the hands of his four cousins, offended by the insult to the Camborio family name; ironically, as Tony dies, he calls out to the poet, "Federico García Lorca" to summon the Guard for him. Blood is powerfully present in his death in this poem, especially the line "*Tres golpes de sangre tuvo*" ("Three pulsing beats of blood he had").[55]

THE VIRGIN AND THE GYPSY (1940)

As *Götz* was one of Goethe's first works, this is one of D. H. Lawrence's last. Already the title juxtaposes two opposing stereotypes, the whiteness of the virgin and the blackness of the Gypsy. Indeed, Lawrence's first description of the Gypsy is that he was one of the "black, loose-bodied, handsome sort."[56] When the group of young people including the virgin, Yvette, pulls up in their car to the side of the Gypsy wagon, she noticed the Gypsy's "complete indifference to [Gadje] people" like her companions; upon meeting his eyes, Yvette thinks "He is stronger than I am! He doesn't care."[57] This is not only freedom, but a mode of non-attachment to the concerns and conventions of English (Gadje) culture.

Yvette notices the Gypsy's otherness through her sense of difference, for Lawrence implies at the opening story that she has inherited her mother Cynthia's wildness. "She-who-was-Cynthia," as the vicar calls his departed wife, had left her husband (the Vicar) and her two girls, Yvette and Lucille, for a younger man. Cynthia stands for the protest against all that is comfortable, boring, complacent, and secure in bourgeois life. [58]

Yvette and the three other girls, including her sister Lucille, get their fortunes read by the Gypsy's wife. After hearing the other girls' fortunes, Yvette decides she will not have hers read. The Gypsy woman insists, and takes Yvette into the caravan for privacy.

As she enters the caravan, she feels the eyes of the Gypsy man, with his "pariah's bold yet dishonest stare." Lawrence writes:

> Of all the men she had ever seen, this one was the only one who was stronger than she was, in her own kind of strength, her own kind of understanding.[59]

The Gypsy's strength and power allows Yvette to realize what she really is, how she understands the world.

Yvette's misappropriation of some fund money ("the affair of the Window fund") for the church leads to a spiteful reaction from Aunt Cissie (who hates who Yvette is) and the vicar, who is desperately trying to hold onto his daughter's love. Yet Yvette exerts her power over her father like Cynthia:

She only looked at him from that senseless snowdrop face which haunted him
with fear, and gave him a helpless sense of guilt. That other one,
She-who-was-Cynthia, she had looked back at him with the same numb, white
fear, the fear of his degrading unbelief, the worm which was his heart's core.[60]

Lawrence sets up an opposition between Cynthia, Yvette, and the Gypsy on the one
hand, and the vicar and his family (Aunt Cissie and his mother, called the "Mater").
The former have liberated themselves from the stale, stuffy, and hypocritical world of
English society, and of a false Christianity. The vicar becomes terrified with dread and
guilt when anyone "*knew* his heart's core was a fat, awful worm."[61] With her freshly
discovered self via the Gypsy, Yvette is able to control her father. In similar fashion,
the Gypsy is capable of exerting his power over Gadje culture.

After the Gypsy man comes by the rectory selling his candlesticks, he was "gone
like a dream which was only a dream."[62] In fact, the Gypsy's virile nature has pene-
trated the deeper layers of Yvette's consciousness:

> the feeling that she had been looked upon, not from the outside, but from the
> inside, from her secret female self. She was dressing herself up and looking her
> most dazzling, just to counteract the effect that the Gypsy had had on her, when
> he had looked at her, and seen none of her pretty face and her pretty ways, but
> just the dark, tremulous, potent secret of her virginity.[63]

Lawrence's description of how the Gypsy perceives Yvette is also how the Gypsy perceives reality, not as the appearance, but as the essence, like the Kantian thing in-itself.
The English boys see Yvette's charms in terms of the trophy of a potential wife, whereas the Gypsy has no concerns for future realities, he sees her in the here-and-now.
Lawrence beautifully and powerfully evokes the mysteries of the holiness of female
virginity: its "dark, tremulous, potent secret." As a secret, virginity separates the female from the world of commerce, of the social contract; it encloses the female self in
its most essential purity. The virgin acts *in* the world and not *of* it. Coincidently, this
is why the Gypsy can see into, inside the secret of the virgin: for this enclosed, secre-
tive, other space is also the space of Gypsy culture, in its protective defense from the
ways of the gadje.

Yvette feels the ultimate contrast to the power of the Gypsy in the smile of Leo:

> But instead of penetrating into some deep, secret place, and shooting her there,
> Leo's bold and patent smile only hit her on the outside of the body, like a tennis
> ball, and caused the same kind of sudden irritated reaction.[64]

Yvette's rejection of Leo's offer of engagement is her rejection of white society. She is
irritated, impatient with the surface aspects of her own culture, where people do not
try to reach out to the other. Their feelings remain suppressed, while what little

emotion they do give is so superficial that Lawrence compares it to a tennis ball. A tennis ball provides the perfect metaphor, for unlike a harder ball, a tennis ball does not hurt when it hits you. It is harmless, and can symbolize the leisure activity of the Western middle- and upper-classes. Leo's smile is comfortable, like a relaxed game of tennis, with elements of competition (he wants to win her over), but without any intensity or ferocity.

The Gypsy has awakened in Yvette the longing for sex. She rides her bike out to his caravan; he invites her in, and as she ascends the stairs of his caravan to "wash her hands," a car drives up and interrupts. But she discusses sex with her sister Lucille:

> 'Yes!' she said vaguely. 'Yes! Sex is an awful bore, you know Lucille. When you haven't got it, you feel you *ought* to have it, somehow. And when you've got it — or if you have it' — she lifted her head and wrinkled her nose disdainfully — 'you hate it.'[65]

At this point in the story, Yvette is confused about her sexual desire for the Gypsy.

Water as a symbol appears in the story, as it does also in Lorca's *Romancero*, but here as the content of a dream that the old Gypsy has:

> 'Be braver in your heart, or you lose your game [...] Be braver in your body, or your luck will leave you. And she as well: Listen for the voice of water.'[66]

Of course, water does come, in the form of a massive flood in which Yvette almost dies. But in this surreal section of the work, the Gypsy saves Yvette. He helps her go up to the second floor. She gets into bed quickly to warm herself, but the cold is unbearable. She begs the Gypsy to warm her, for she will die of shivering:

> The Gypsy nodded, and took her in his arms, and held her in a clasp like a vice, to still his own shuddering. He himself was shuddering fearfully, and only semi-conscious. It was the shock.[67]

After this they fall asleep, and when Yvette wakes, the Gypsy has disappeared and instead a policeman stands over her.

Thus their love remains unconsummated. She never tells anyone of their experience together, but she receives a note from him, in which he signs his name "Joe Boswell." Lawrence ends the story: "And only then she realized that he had a name."

CONCLUSION

By investigating the historical configurations of Gypsies in literature, we see that as Other, Gypsies were the obvious target of racist stereotyping. Yet at the same time and complicating this negative marking, the Gypsies' status as "exotic Other" helped to codify a discourse practice that could be manipulated in any number of ways. In terms of the musical reception of Gypsy music, one hypothesis is that this discourse practice served as a positive reference point when Europeans were trying to understand the mystique and power of itinerant Roma musicians; today, this discourse practice is subtly and expertly exploited by marketers and promoters of Gypsiness. We will add that at the opposite end of the political spectrum, these literary stereotypes have become fuel for Roma-rights advocates as already seen in Diane Tong's thesis, and in the engaged political writings of Ian Hancock, especially his *Pariah Syndrome*.

As writings about Gypsies contributed to solidifying their place in the European psyche, so too did they in part prepare the way for Gypsy music's rise to notoriety in nineteenth-century musical circles. Liszt was well versed in the literature on Gypsies, citing Cervantes, Hugo, and Borrow specifically in his chapter called "The Gypsy in Literature." He also mentions the universal recognition of what were stock characters in nineteenth-century theatre and opera; Liszt writes:

> In quoting the Zingaro of the Spaniards, the Meg Merrilies of England, the Esmeralda of Paris, the Zemphira of Russia, the Preciosa of Weber, the Vielka of Meyerbeer, and others, we do no more than mention names known to everybody and probably more familiar to us than the Biblical characters were to the Scotch puritans.[68]

The literary-artistic encounter with these characters thus became a vehicle for propagating the code that we are associating with Gypsiness — the interplay of emotion, freedom, and spontaneity.[69]

The nineteenth-century identification of these codes with Gypsy musical practice happened as part of a gradual development, which was seemingly accelerated at mid-century. In Hungary, this was due to the aftermath of the War of Independence (1848), in which Gypsy musicians played a huge role in healing the wounds of defeat. Commenting on a poem from this period, Bálint Sárosi says that:

> It is difficult for us to understand today this magic power to cure everything which the Gypsy violin playing verbunkos music and Hungarian songs possessed — of which magic power, incidentally Széchenyi had written earlier and Liszt was to write later. Patikárus (chemist) for example, is reputed to have got his name — even before the War of Independence — by "curing" a melancholic nobleman with his violin.[70]

Here, one of the central aesthetic premises of nineteenth-century music, that music expresses, communicates, and translates the innermost feelings of the soul, is identified as a principle trait of Gypsy music.[71]

In France, another mid-century phenomenon ended up becoming the most lasting Gypsy legacy of the nineteenth century. This was Prosper Mérimée's novella,

"Carmen" (1845), immortalized in Bizet's opera comiqué (1875). We have intentionally avoided dealing with Mérimée in this chapter, in part because the topic of Carmen and Bizet's opera (especially its reception) would require a sustained
investigation in its own right. But we shall offer a short digression, based on Susan
McClary's recent interpretation.[72]

McClary tries to engage with Carmen through the prism of recent postcolonial
and feminist theory. One of her theses concerning Mérimée typifies this style of theory:

> Virtually all of the elements that compose the structure of the story are intimately
> linked to questions of control and mastery, as the major narrative strategy aptly
> illustrates. A Frenchman begins the story with learned, controlled discourse
> about history and local color, then surrenders his control to another tale told by
> a different narrator (foreign, violent, uncivilized).... Violence erupts, forcing the
> Frenchman to reassert mastery. He does so by attempting to reweave the torn fab-
> ric with yet another learned discourse, this time upon the nature of language in
> general, and of Romani in particular.[73]

Though her main point is well taken, even if it is non-original in its theoretic formulation, the thesis is so general as to become virtually applicable to any instance of narrative writing. Writing itself *is* a form of mastery, whether through narratives or not;
Derrida speaks of "the metaphor of writing which haunts European discourse," where
the repression of writing serves as the "mastering of absence."[74] And there is the following paradox: if Mérimée's text is in fact the attempt to assert masculine control
and authority, what allows for its easy reversal and embracing by feminist and gay theorists, as noted by McClary?[75] Why is the image of Carmen so empowering to those
who are quick to suggest Mérimée's deficiencies as author, his entrapment in the colonial and sexist project of a dominant and dominating French culture? Against her
own position, McClary seems to hedge on both Mérimée and Bizet as authors; both
would seem to also "grant power, courage, and integrity to the character of Carmen,
while they portray José as lacking in moral fortitude."[76]

However, the most glaring and stunning oversight of McClary's treatment is
her omission of a significant source of Mérimée's Carmen: Pushkin's Zemphira, in
his poem *Tsygany.* We shall deal directly with Pushkin in Chapter Seven, when we
turn to one of the operas based on it, Rachmaninov's *Aleko.* But in this context, note
that Mérimée and Pushkin had a profound mutual influence; Pushkin's *Songs of the
Western Slavs* are based on Mérimée's *La Guzla* (1827). *La Guzla* was one of
Mérimée's hoaxes, by "Hyacinthe Maglanowich," of ballads that were supposedly
authentic and which deceived scholars. Mérimée later translated Pushkin's *Tsygany*
into French; thus the figure of Zemphira would serve as the most immediate literary
source for his Carmen.

To conclude, literary Gypsies provide a compelling context for viewing the reception of Gypsy music. Whether or not literary conventions were ethnographically true, the associations with Gypsies and music began early — already in Vicente's *Farsas das Ciganas*, and continuing with Cervantes. Indeed, Sárosi notes how in the fifteenth century Gypsy musicians were already said to have received money for their playing.[77] At least in the case of music, literary conventions were accurate depictions of real activities. Finally, as signifiers, we have tried to suggest that "Gypsies" and "music" function in ways that dovetail with one another: ambiguous, malleable, unstable terms, at once suggestive of nature's purity — virginal, untouched space — and of the power beyond nature, the fiery signs which prophecy the ominous future in Goethe's *Götz.*

This mystical approach to a reality that recedes from rational codes is to what we turn next: improvisation, considered by many to be the hallmark of Gypsy music-making.

Chapter Three

A Nineteenth-Century Tale of Two Others: Gypsy Improvisation and the Exotic Remainder

In its central Lisztean formulation, Gypsy music is synonymous with the freedom of improvisation: "Bohemian art more than any other belongs to the domain of improvisation, without which it does not exist."[1] The free element of "Gypsiness" in Liszt's *Rhapsodies* can be interpreted as a conscious yet somewhat vexed attempt to recapture the composer's experience of what he considered as Gypsy improvisation (described in Chapter Six). Because improvisation became so prominent, so fetishized, so ritualized in the marketing of Gypsy music with and after Liszt — a commercial aspect we also identify as "Gypsiness" — it, too, warrants in-depth and sustained investigation.

Yet in terms of our main theme, the Lisztean formulation presents a dilemma. Namely, was his search for "real" Gypsy music an attempt at legitimization of the phenomenon? Or rather, was Liszt's experience of what we are calling Gypsiness part of a larger program, a general tendency for the demand for greater performance freedom — symbolized by what was understood as improvisation — within the codes of Western music culture?[2] Related, can we speak of the substance of Gypsy music "in-itself," or does Gypsy music only exist, in part, through the visibility of the Western imagination, from the traces of Gypsiness? For Liszt, it would seem to be the former in both cases.[3] However, his discourse as well as the aesthetic direction of his own music leads us to the complications and difficulties tied to the latter. Might we conceive of Gypsiness as a significant element in the drive toward greater subjectivity in Western music?

Improvisation has a long and illustrious history in Western music and performance practice. Many famous composers are known to have been adept improvisers. In some cases, public improvisation served as one of the rights of passage for a composer. When Beethoven arrived as an enfant terrible in turn-of-the-century Vienna, part of the way he established himself was through the "direct expression" of improvisation. Furthermore, Maynard Solomon notes that Beethoven worried about his extemporizations, that other pianists in this highly competitive scene might steal the "peculiarities" of his style.[4]

There exist numerous genres that sought to encode the freedom of improvisatory traces, including toccatas, fantasies/fantasias, preludes, cadenzas, and variations.[5] These genres help indicate that the history of improvisation is tied to the imagination, to flights of fancy, as it were. As one well-known example, Carl Czerny's method for piano improvisation employs the word *"fantasieren"* in the title: *Systematische Anleitung zum Fantasieren auf dem Pianoforte.*[6] Incidentally, as the student of Beethoven and the teacher of Liszt, Czerny stands at the crossroads of the reevaluation of improvisation, a topic we will consider in the conclusion of this chapter.

In perhaps the most rigorous formulation, Apel defines improvisation as "the art of performing music as an immediate reproduction of simultaneous mental processes, that is, without the aid of manuscript, sketches, or memory."[7] His conception aims for absolute purity, in its demand for an *immediate* reproduction of some inner process, without any resorting to mnemonic devices. For, the economy of memory names a calculation that is outside the activity of improvisation. However, Apel's ideal definition seems impossible, in practice, to realize. Thus he recognizes a more "restricted" sense of the word: the introduction of unnotated, ornamental details into written composition. Furthermore, as Paul F. Berliner has recently confessed, identifying precisely what we mean by improvisation becomes more difficult and problematic the more closely we try to pin down exclusive properties.[8] But for Apel, writing in the 1940s, the "great art of improvisation is lost, since it is no longer practiced by the composers and *survives* chiefly among organ virtuosos." We shall return to the idea of another possible "survival" for improvisation in the conclusion.

If Gypsy music has been identified or at the very least associated with improvisation from the start, the slipperiness of this latter concept has perhaps blocked a fuller appreciation of the function of Gypsy music in Europe since the nineteenth century. Moreover, what remains unclear in the history of improvisatory practices — especially with regard to Romanticism — is the extent to which the concept itself changed, and along with it the ontology of music. Thus, before we consider improvisation within the wider context of nineteenth-century Romanticism, it is necessary to establish some broad understanding of both exoticism and nationalism, and their interplay.

EXOTICISM AND MUSICOLOGICAL DISCOURSE

Musicological discourse invokes exoticism as a broad aesthetic and social platform for understanding the perception of the Other in the nineteenth century.[9] Commonly at stake in this writing on exoticism is the ethical question of representation as mis-appropriation. Does the musical representation of the East (David, Saint-Saëns, Gilbert and Sullivan, Rimsky-Korsakov, et al.) betray, in a negative way, what is being represented? Is there an inherent racism or racial agenda in the colonial (re-)marking the Other? Can a seemingly benign fascination with the East be used to justify imperial and colonial aspirations?

Dahlhaus writes that it was not the substance of exoticism that matters for historical understanding, but the function:

> The crucial point is not the degree to which exoticism is 'genuine,' but rather the *function* it serves as a legitimate departure from the aesthetic and compositional norms of European music.... It is not so much the original context as the new, artificial context which we should examine if we want our analysis to be historical — that is, to pursue the aesthetic and compositional significance of the phenomenon in the nineteenth century. To do otherwise is lose ourselves in comparative anthropology, which can do nothing more than establish various degrees of corruption in the music or style quoted (my emphasis).[10]

Although Dahlhaus's main point is well taken — that we should investigate why exoticism served as a legitimate departure from compositional norms, and not the authenticity of these exoticisms — still, the status of what constitutes a "norm" has never appeared as shaky as it does now. Dahlhaus's "norm" is the canon of great composers; and yet, could we imagine these figures, from Schubert to Liszt to Dvořák to Brahms to Mahler, without their departures and deviations from this so-called "norm?" Moreover, it would seem that deviation itself is always already a part of this norm. Georgina Born has signaled this attempt to erase difference in musical modernism as the construction of "aesthetic *autarchy* and self-enclosure, through the negation or denial of reference to the other musics and cultures."[11]

In any case, a musical culture's need for the alien milieu of exoticism depends on both self-consciousness as difference and historical distance.[12] As is well known, it was during the nineteenth century that the canon of musical works as a museum began to stabilize.[13] A musical division of labor became possible, separating composition from performance; virtuosity was on the rise as public performance became competitive and professionalized. While the reception of musical works was becoming autonomous through disseminated interpretation, at the same time pieces were uprooted from their immediate surroundings and context. This detachment created an atmosphere of heightened awareness of what art *is*. Indeed, after his discovery of the phenomenological movement of consciousness toward higher degrees of self-consciousness, Hegel in his *Introductory Lectures on Aesthetics* made the prediction that because of its reliance on sensuous forms for its presentation, art was surpassed by philosophy and religion.[14] But for most writers , art, and especially music, would become religion, a tendency represented from E.T.A. Hoffmann to Schopenhauer to Hanslick. Finally, toward the end of the century it was in an intellectual environment of cultural inadequacy, laziness, decadence, and finally what Nietzsche would call the "disease" of European civilization, nihilism, that exoticism found its place, reconfigured along with nationalism, folklorism, and realism as mass-marketable styles.

The history of Gypsy music (*Zigeunermusik*) in the nineteenth century encapsulates the turbulence of the hegemonic society's encounter with Eastern Otherness. Unlike most of the Eastern-Oriental music that was essentially imagined, Gypsy music occupied a significant niche in Central European culture — it was paradoxically an exoticism that was neither alien nor foreign to European space, an "exoticism from within" as it were. Furthermore, we can assume that numerous prominent composers had some contact with the cosmopolitan (or, displaced) Gypsy bands of the day — certainly names like Liszt, Brahms, Verdi, Sarasate, Bizet, and Rachmaninov.[15]

Unlike other Orientalisms, however, the difficulty in theorizing the appropriation of the Gypsy Other remains the dependency on improvisation. Bellman interprets improvisation somewhat cynically, following Sárosi, as the activity of business; we might say in this conception it is external to performance.[16] At the opposite extreme, as in the writings of Liszt, for example, improvisation only occurs in the interior space of the soul. The quotation which began this chapter, "Bohemian art *more than any other* belongs to the domain of improvisation..." (my emphasis), should be interpreted in this spiritual, perhaps psychological, way. Liszt goes so far as to argue that Gypsy emotions in music are impossible to reproduce by a European player, even by a "musician who from childhood has been most familiar with their art."[17] Contained in Liszt's quest for genuine, authentic Gypsy emotions are the *cinders* (in the Derridean sense of trace; see the conclusion to this chapter) of how Gypsy music once figured as a strand of the exotic; what follows is an attempt at an inventory of improvisation as a disappearing sign of this exoticism.

THE EQUATION I+V=E

In Chapter One we proposed the equation "Improvisation plus Virtuosity equals Emotion" (I+V=E) as a shorthand way of articulating, quickly, the simultaneous *Ereignis* and appropriation of Gypsy music, something we are calling "Gypsiness." We will now try to introduce improvisation as a gathering principle of the reception of Gypsiness as the Other, where improvisation serves as either a perceived and marked element or as an actual performance gesture.

We shall also have to deal with improvisation in terms of subjective agency, which will only work to complicate our problematic. But our approach in this chapter will be schematic, necessarily, in the desire to preserve the ubiquity and yet paradoxical handiness of improvisation as a concept. For, what remains of improvisation, even as we try to deconstruct it? Missing from any deconstruction of improvisation is the "what is to come" of improvisation. To describe this "coming," this unpredictability of improvisation, we shall use the term "remainder," as how is it possible for improvisation to remain.

But before going much further, a qualification. Improvisation has a broad stylistic meaning, social context, and history extending well beyond Gypsiness. We will have to deal with these wide parameters, and, as we shall see, with problems of subjective confirmation and verification associated with improvisation. Further, although there are other genres or styles of improvisational music — jazz and blues, among others — what distinguishes improvisation in Gypsiness is its conflation in the listener's mind with a *natural* virtuosity.[18] That is, a listener grasps improvisation in Gypsiness as part of a wider set, one that binds together freedom, nature/the natural, and emotion. In so doing, Gypsiness loses its uniqueness, for within this wider set Gypsiness might not be very much different than say "Africanness" in jazz, or "Mexicanness" in the Hollywood Western.[19]

As a promise of the exotic Other, Gypsiness extends an invitation to improvise. An invitation can be either accepted or rejected; what matters, however, is the opportunity granted by the asking. In this respect, Gypsiness can be thought as a temptation, seducing the player to respond to the musical material and *at the same instant* the situation of time, place, and community. By inserting itself into a musical context, sometimes as a violent intrusion, Gypsiness divides consciousness of the instant moment. This "instant" is an inner moment of an impossible temporality, where the player experiences divided time (see "Heterogenetic Improvisation" later in this chapter).

Traditionally, for music to be considered improvised, the player must evoke the impression, whether real or illusory, that the music is original or unique to the very moment of its sonic offering, and dependent on the situation. In the case of a preexistent melody, song, or even work, under the state of improvisation the player adds something new, invented on the spot, immediately, to the performance of X (where "X" stands for the quasi-work). This process is sometimes referred to as the act of "spontaneous creation," and as we shall see, signifies a realm that is *in principle* beyond representation, language, and knowledge (Apel even says so much).

If our hypothesis might appear straightforward at first glance — the necessary role of improvisation in Gypsiness — still, the articulation of improvisation involves an array of experiential difficulties. By sharpening the paradoxes and problems of improvisation, we will try to come closer to our goal of understanding what kind of a substance Gypsy music was understood to be for composers and audiences alike.

POSTMODERN MUSICOLOGY AND THE REVALUATION OF IMPROVISATION

What has the overture to postmodern criticism in the New musicology done to musicology? Although positivist studies continue, New musicology has shown the limits of musicological concepts, and thrown many terms into a problematized zone. Indeed, a cursory glance at recent national meetings of the American Musicological Society show that remaining positivists have conceded, perhaps begrudgingly, that an intellectual paradigm shift has occurred.[20] Famously, in 1979 Lyotard termed these postmodern, postindustrial shifts "incredulity toward metanarratives."[21] Meanings once thought stable now shift in the infinite sea of possibilities of language games; the Enlightenment fiction of a guaranteed truth passing from sender to addressee is revealed to be conditioned by the power to control the means of information and the politics of authority. Further, there is Anderson's revelation that modern culture, nation, and identity follow from a conscious effort of "imagining" these structures, itself dependent on the retrieval of information via the dissemination of print culture.

As a wider array of topics have become appropriate, even in vogue, for musicology via postmodernism, the conceptual space has opened for a re-consideration of the role of improvisation in the nineteenth century. Gypsy music, so we shall argue, locates one place where the decision to improvise remained, and the fallout remains glaringly present — though not noticed as such — in the encore presentations of today's concert hall.

Coinciding with the postmodern turn is a greater recognition of the mythical opposition between improvisation and composition.[22] At the broadest level, improvisation and composition have much in common: both use an existent, defined, idiomatic musical language or style, share a historical and social context, and employ technical approaches which are, as it were, "pre-planned." As stated by a practitioner, the guitarist and author Derek Bailey maintains that the "really important" part of improvisation consists not in this comparison between composer and improviser, but the "accidental, the coincidental, the occasional" — what we will call the mystery of the Event — that "happens between people, between the players."[23]

HETEROGENETIC IMPROVISATION

Improvisation institutes a pure performative situation. At its definitive core, the player creates through improvisation the limits for a new musical universe where the unpredictable, unexpected, and unforeseen exist in an equilibrium and tension with the ordinary and stable. The entire logic of improvisation rests on the positing of the "un-." What is the unpredictable, in the case of a musical statement? Can a musical phrase be unpredictable? Is it possible? The desire for the surprise entails that the emotive platform of improvisation remains freely and spontaneously bound to a reality firmly entrenched in the moment. Here we refer to the aporias of temporal categories, the breaking-apart inherent in the presencing of the present.[24] If the essence of Gypsy music cannot be determined, precisely and exactly, it is because of this "un-" at the heart of the un-predictability of improvisation. The difficulty in theorizing improvisation expresses the commonality linking improvisation and Gypsy music, of performance in-itself.

"Heterogenetic improvisation": the divided interval where improvisation originates out of a moment of otherness while identifying with itself.[25] The equation I+V=E articulates this pure *coming* of improvisation as a mode of alterity — improvisation is always thought *in relation to*, as a modality of, as embedded in an equation, never as in-itself. The stakes of the equation are the stakes of performance itself: the risk involved in all music-making, that the listener will be unaffected. Not bored or uninterested, for this would name an affected state; rather, completely uninvolved. Improvisation as a heterogenetic art, where the impossible division of time is embraced and acknowledged, grows out of this desire for a purely involved performance, a symbiosis of listener and sound, via an identification with the same with its unpredictable mutation.

However, what does it mean to say that a practice, an improvisatory art form, is "unpredictable," when in fact improvisation, especially as studied and analyzed by (ethno-)musicologists and theorists, can be proven to be based on rules, strict rhetorical codes, and highly sophisticated sociological contexts for listening and appreciation? An assumption here is that no one has yet figured out *in theory* what the practice of improvisation actually is. Nor will anyone ever. And it is not our intent to solve what is really a problem of semantics concerning improvisation, rather, we will use the assumption that improvisation remains inadequately theorized to probe those discourses (academic and commercial) which use improvisation as a predicate of Gypsy music.

ANXIETY OF IMPROVISATION

Since the early nineteenth century and particularly after Beethoven, there has been much anxiety in Western art-music circles around improvisation. Liszt's careful attention to improvisation is defensive in nature, as if he knows he is one of the last great practitioners of it.[26] But as composers tried to compose everything into the score, they slowly began to realize that something approximating the experience of improvisation (what we have expressed as the embracing of the divided moment of time) should enter somehow into their music. One hypothesis: that composition appropriated the ideals of freedom and spontaneity once drawn from the performative excitement generated by improvisation, and included these, paradoxically, in the very concept of composed musical structure. It is the nineteenth century's familiar tale of the triumph of the composer and work over the performer and event. Indeed, "improvisatoriness" was written into composed music, as in the phenomena of composed cadenzas, and other approximations of improvised music (usually coupled with virtuosic implications) in nearly any genre.

As another possible set of hypotheses: perhaps it was this *anxiety of the unknown* that has led to the marginalization of Gypsy music, blocked a full ontological and aesthetic investigation of improvisation by musicologists, and lastly, contributed to the historical triumph of the teleological, progressive, and evolutionary view of Western art music (as in Adler and Schoenberg) used tacitly in the bias toward a Germanic canon.

MYSTERY

The history of mystery is also that of secrecy, of what is out-of-sight and hidden.[27] In principle, mystery precedes and eludes attribution, predication, and designation; in religion, mysteries can only be "known" paradoxically only through faith (belief). Musically, the mysterious refers to the event of improvisation, the decision beyond calculation. Beyond calculation means that improvisational choices should be in principle, once again, spontaneous, free, and risk-taking.

But in characterizing improvisation as mystery, the related concepts "free" and "spontaneous" must be interrogated. Both are complex ideas, and lead to massive philosophical paradoxes when their causality — that every event can be shown to have a cause — is taken into account.[28] Thus if we continue to privilege these terms as leading threads (as in the secondary literature on improvisation), at the same time we must try to determine how these terms can actually transfer their semantics into musical activity. In fact, mystery can be used to denote the limits of these concepts.

Returning to Liszt, we sense this with his *poetic affinity* to improvisation:

> For the Gypsy, art is not a science that one may learn; or a trade which one may practice. [...] It is a *mystic song* — a language which, though sublimated, is clear to the initiated.[29]

This is the Romantic aesthetic of art, that art is an innate language that cannot be learned. Obviously Liszt is not only speaking of the Gypsy here, but of his own experience of music.

For the world-music industry, it is the capacity for and illusion of mystery that unites improvisation and Gypsy music, especially as both of these categories relate to the (post-Western) imagination. To follow what has become cliché, after an experience of live Gypsy improvisation, something unfathomable emerges.[30] Improvisation expresses the emotions of the Gypsy fiddler's soul at that moment (*ex tempore*), but not through rational, technical, or representational means; rather, the means of the improviser are mysterious, mystical, and outside of representation.[31] As substantiation for this, one need only look at the contradictions and misunderstandings surrounding the marketing and reception of this music in the media. In a press review of Taraf de Haïdouk, we find this confusing remark: "with influences from the south and east, Romanian music has a more Middle Eastern sound than most 'Gypsy' music, although the recent mixings of Gypsy and klezmer traditions often produce similar results."[32]

"Gypsiness" in music can be thought from the side of the mysteries of seduction.[33] Exemplifying this, Liszt describes the process of arranging Gypsy melodies for piano (in his *Rhapsodies*) as follows:

> The pleasure of transferring to our instrument the eloquent apostrophes, the lugubrious displays of feeling, the reveries, effusions and exaltations of this wild muse seemed to become more and more seductive.[34]

The apostrophes, the "lugubrious displays," reveries, effusions of this wild muse speak volumes about the aesthetic tenets of Romanticism as understood by Liszt, but they also indicate what he thought improvisation to be: the wild muse. It is like madness, beyond reason and control. As wild, improvisation is outside of the written page of composed music. Paradoxically, Liszt sought tried to inaugurate a compositional style that appropriated this wildness for the *Rhapsodies* (see Chapter Six).

Improvisation as mystery leads to the direct pondering of the essence/core of Gypsy music, which as we shall see has undergone a recent surge in popularity via the world-music industry and by Roma themselves.

IMAGES OF GYPSY MUSIC

One strategy for understanding a historical phenomenon is also to become aware of its current unfolding.[35] For example, take the contemporary world-music industry; here, producers latch onto the Romantic stereotypes of Gypsy music and exploit it accordingly. Improvisation figures massively in numerous CD liner notes, showing the term's continuity and permanence. Again, though Gypsy music shares at least the perception of an improvisational aspect with numerous world musics, what remains specific to Gypsy music is that it is a trans-national, and perhaps an a-national, phenomenon. This makes studying the interrelationship of Gypsy music and improvisation an even more difficult one than other more specifically nationally based musics (that is, music with stricter territorial limitations).

The question of national attribution derives in part from contemporary tensions involved in the politics of nationalism (state sovereignty) versus the international aspirations of an open, capitalist marketplace for global corporations. Under the covert influence of nationalism, some folk enthusiasts seek to deny the Roma's role in the creation and preservation of national musics, especially in the case of Hungarian-Transylvanian repertoires, and now Moldavian (Csángó) ones.[36] In contrast, the music industry has no problem in dealing with national attribution. And the industry embraces the Roma "diaspora" (more on what is involved in this concept in Chapter

Eleven) and markets "Gypsy" compilations spanning sometimes as many as fifteen countries, such as *Road of the Gypsies*, (1996) or now even the *Rough Guide to the Gypsies* (1999).[37] With these types of compilations, improvisation is ripped out of its regional and national context, and deferred indefinitely to Gypsy music.

The image of this wild, seductive (equals sexy, perhaps even sexual), improvising Gypsy has appeared also in films intended for an intellectual and international audience, most notably *Latcho drom*, *Underground*, and *The Red Violin*.[38] We will only note here how powerful and striking the graphic image of improvisation is articulated in these and other films.[39]

This was also the package promoted in *The Gypsy Caravan* (1999). *Caravan* was the most important, so-called "outsider-conceived" Gypsy event ever to be targeted at American audiences, who, unlike Europeans, have had less direct contact with the phenomenon. This staged production of Gypsiness brought together six allegedly "Gypsy" music groups from different countries — Rajasthan, Russia, Romania, Hungary, Bulgaria, and Spain.[40]

With such CDs, films, and staged events in mind, it seems that since the 1990s, one could argue that the ghost of Gypsiness culled from Lisztean discourse is circulating with a worldwide intensity not seen since the late nineteenth-century. Furthermore, and more difficult to determine, is to what extent current Gypsy bands have latched onto this specter of Gypsiness.

Economically, if the terms of contemporary music-marketing in popular music reduce down to a dialect of stasis versus movement (rest versus restlessness), improvisation commonly represents the movement, really the restlessness of the dialectic.[41] It is the marketing of pure desire,[42] the quest for something new, and the search for a fresh meaning; our argument will try to take up these enigmatic terms and try to align them with the aesthetics of Gypsiness.

IMPROVISATION AND MUSICAL COMPETENCE: THE WESTERN CANON

Moving back to the problem of improvisation in Western art music, we run into the monolithic structure of what defines musical competence: the Western canon, or what we can call the "imagined community of musical works." We do not have space here to reconstitute the origins and history of this massive organization of music into this museum. The edifice of the concert/recital hall is an abstraction, an artificial atmosphere for passively "receiving" music, without participation (only so-called "active" listening, without dance, singing; only clapping remains, what is this?). But simply put, a canonic approach to music history places little emphasis on oral music, insofar as oral music resists codification and reproduction at a historical distance. And improvisation, a non-written art which by its ephemeral definition is unstable, shifting, and ceaselessly changing, has no proper place in the canonic conversation with the past.

With the advent of what Dahlhaus has called the "work concept," improvisation has withdrawn from the prestige it once enjoyed in even the highest artistic circles (Bach, Mozart). Dahlhaus famously writes that:

> This is not to say that 'events' are irrelevant, merely that the emphasis falls on understanding works — which, unlike the relics treated in political histories, are the goal of historical inquiry and not its point of departure. The concept 'work,' and not 'event,' is the cornerstone of music history. Or, to put it in Aristotelian terms, the material of music history resides not in *praxis*, or social action, but in *poiesis*, the creation of forms.[43]

Improvisation takes the side of the event, it is momentary, fleeting, absent in its very presence. Music history's material resides in work, in the creation of a form (*poiesis*). Music historiography can rest when work (in both senses of the word) is finished. Although Dahlhaus's work on work is more complex than can be indicated in our context, with improvisation in a Gypsy-music context we will be carving out the opposite path for a music historiography than the one proposed by Dahlhaus here.

If improvisation has fallen by the wayside for composers and performers, there is little doubt, as we have seen with Dahlhaus, that this has infected music historiography. According to this view, musicology avoids non-permanent structures, and anything that emphasizes an ephemeral, fleeting glimpse of musical production.

The outlook for improvisation is even more dire for professional Classical performers, where a thorough and in-depth commitment to the standard repertory is required for professionalization. Conservatories demand that music students become proficient in benchmark pieces, and with good reason. Orchestral auditions, especially the ones for the higher-paying and more prestigious organizations, require that the applicant be over prepared to play the standard pieces asked for at every audition. Of course, and this is the main point, a Classical performer would never be asked to improvise in order to show musical competence. The only spontaneous area of an audition might occur if the applicant were asked to sight-read, which coincidently seems to be the closest remaining activity to improvisation left for a Classical player.

Furthermore, when some composers of the avant-garde of the 1950s and 60s once demanded orchestral players to improvise, the results were unsatisfactory for many. (Aside: who is to blame? Were Foss, Stockhausen, Ligeti really the ones responsible, in that their "sonic" expectations for improvisation were never based on a real notion of freedom internal to the concept of improvisation as an Event (*Ereignis*), but instead asked for a freedom within a certain musical language which they were inventing?)

Yet with the opening of new possibilities and trends now available for Classical musicians, it is significant that groups which reject the standard repertory have simultaneously embraced improvisation. An excellent example of this trend is the Kronos Quartet, who have latched onto to the mystique of improvisation (appropriately enough, in a "Gypsy" context!) as a viable mode for marketing.[44]

BELLMAN AND THE *STYLE HONGROIS*

If musicology has resisted both Gypsy music and improvisation, how do these terms function in Bellman's *The* Style Hongrois *in the Music of Western Europe*? Quickly, what remains under investigated in his account: the significance of the force of the *idea* of Gypsy music, something we are calling "Gypsiness in music." As another way of formulating it, "Gypsiness" refers to a set of ideas, real and imagined (and this mixing is precisely the difficulty), that manifest around Gypsy music.

Bellman defines the *style hongrois* as "a combination of Hungarian popular song and dance repertories with the performance style and interpretive traditions of the Gypsies."[45] It "represents the first wholesale and conscious embrace of popular music associated with a lower societal caste by the composers and listeners of more formal, schooled music." Bellman places the *style hongrois* in the typical art-historical narrative of origins-maturity-decline. The style begins in Gluck, Haydn, Mozart, and Beethoven, reaches maturity from Schubert through Liszt, and declines around the figure of Brahms. For Bellman, Brahms was the last great "speaker" of this musical dialect.

But after studying in some detail artistic and technical approximations of Gypsy music, Bellman argues that the topic is essentially a late nineteenth-century phenomenon, as its found prominently in the music of Liszt and Brahms. Its most significant appropriation into Western music was the figure of Hungarian popular music (*a la hongrois*), as in Liszt's *Hungarian Rhapsodies* and Brahms's *Hungarian Dances*. Bellman then attempts to unravel the nineteenth-century context for Liszt's notion of Gypsy music. To date his remains the only serious treatment of Gypsy music in nineteenth-century Western art music.[46]

Against Liszt, Bellman writes that the motivation for Gypsy *style hongrois* performances was always "*commercial*" (my emphasis): "In the Gypsy performance tradition, the soloist looks into the customer's soul, perceives and understands his personal sorrows and concerns, and expresses them on his instrument."[47] Central to this process is improvisation, in that the performer must react, on the spot, to what he sees in the eyes of his customer. Indeed, we can add that this connection with "seeing" is part of the etymology of "improvisation," which literally means the ability to fore-see.

Significant in Bellman's narrative is the idea that Gypsy music allowed improvisation as a musical topic to re-enter Western musical thought at a time when it was increasingly untenable. We can speculate that Beethoven, known as a great improviser himself, perhaps sealed the fate on improvisation by introducing a new artistic and metaphysical standard for what a work meant. Again for Dahlhaus, improvisation forms an "opposing category" (*Gegencategorie*) to composition.[48]

Yet as a performative act, improvisation is outside of representation, notation, and composition. What does it mean to say that improvisation was part of the *style hongrois*? Bellman might maintain that the purpose of the *style hongrois* was really to approximate Gypsy Improvisation. What matters is above all the perception that a Liszt rhapsody contains improvisations, moments of "improvisationness," and hetero-improvisationally oriented mystical displays.

What begs to be asked and remains to be seen after an encounter with Bellman's text: did Gypsy music change, alter, transform the notion of improvisation in and for Western art music? Part of the answer to this question might be indirectly ascertained via a detour, one though the field of ethnomusicology.

TWENTIETH-CENTURY REEVALUATION: FROM GYPSY TO ROMA MUSIC

The most recent ethnological explanation of Rom (Gypsy) music is by Carol Silverman.[49] The title of her Garland encyclopedia entry places "Gypsy" in parenthesis, literally marking the word. The move from Gypsy to Roma is congruent with the political strategy for Roma-rights begun in the 1990s. Silverman articulates the political situation of the oppressed Roma as follows:

> A nomadic lifestyle, often enforced upon Roma through *harassment* and *prejudice*, gave them opportunities to enlarge their repertories and become multimusical and multilingual.[50] [my emphases]

Harassment and prejudice are what sedentary culture inflicts upon the nomad. Out of economic necessity, the Roma became multi-musical, and were able to "*creatively interact*" with local, settled repertoires [her emphasis].[51] But as the nomad, they were outsiders, at once beyond the laws of settled culture, but still held to them, especially, one might add, the law of the death penalty (a law not found in the Roma's *kris* [literally, the judges], the "justice" system).

Silverman also notes the unifying project of the Roma-rights movement. The purpose of this transnational movement is to make Roma aware of their shared ethnicity. We can describe this transnational awareness as a kind of nationalism without a nation.

She then organizes Roma music according to place, emphasizing the nation-states in which Roma live, or "relationships to music of the coterritorial peoples."[52] In terms of European Roma she refers to the "*propensity to improvise*," without further explanation.[53] The "propensity to improvise" operates as a universal, across music cultures.[54] In uniting displaced Roma musicians, settled and nomadic, this idea of the "propensity to improvise" reinforces the myth, unintentionally, that there is a single, unified Roma music culture.

The world-music industry reflects these two organizational types in its marketing Gypsy-music CDs.[55] Type one emphasizes the country of origin, as in *Hungary and Romania: Descendents of the Itinerant Gypsies, Melodies of Sorrow and Joy.*[56] The second emphasizes the Gypsy as a universal category, across cultures: the best example would be *Road of the Gypsies.* These are compilations, usually consisting of tracks taken from the first category of CDs. In her reference to improvisation, Silverman's article follows the idea of a "Gypsy route" organization.

EUROCENTRISM TO THE PERFORMATIVE (EXCUSES)

If musicologists have tended to neglect improvisation, ethnomusicologists, though perhaps with some reticence, offer more lively engagement with the topic. Bruno Nettl edited recently (1998) a collection of essays on improvisation, and Ali Jihad Racy published an article in *Ethnomusicology* (2000) titled "The Many Faces of Improvisation: The Arab Taqasim as a Musical Symbol."

In a famous article from 1974, Nettl raised the issue of how improvisation functions within various music cultures. Comparing the attitudes of Persian, Arabic, and South Asian musicians, he showed that these musicians' own conceptions of improvisation vary greatly. His Persian informant denied that improvisation was in fact happening, while the Arabic musician said that the same phrase never happened the same way twice.[57] And beyond these radically contrasting statements, Nettl concludes that what we commonly take for an improvisation is really "a rendition of something that already exists," which he calls a "model."[58] What Nettl signals is not only the idea that improvisation is a loaded signifier with various cultural nuances, but that it is sometimes Eurocentric. That is, it functions as a vague, general, and misleading idea that the West imposes indiscriminately on unwritten music. Nettl's article also raises the following epistemological question: how do we know, actually, when someone is improvising?

Though there are many ways of dealing with this question, here we will appeal to Paul De Man's theory of the excuse. The excuse is a performative speech-act that, as we will see, shares a common feature with improvisation: the verbal dimension of its confirmation. For an excuse, there exists no external verification as to its truth; the purpose "is not to state but to convince, itself an 'inner' process to which only words can bear witness."[59] Now, what complicates the discourse of improvisation is that structurally, improvisation functions in the same manner as the excuse. Namely, we do not know whether someone is improvising, we must take their word for it. A performer could, hypothetically, memorize what he calls an improvisation, and we would have no way of knowing to the contrary.

If an ethnomusicologist might have difficulty knowing whether a musician is improvising, what is it like for the amateur listener? Built right into the concept improvisation is the potential for misrepresentation, which could easily lead to the artistic manipulation of an audience.

RACY'S SUMMARY OF DEFINITIONS OF IMPROVISATION

As a kind of summation of the state of current understanding improvisation, Racy's article contains an excellent twelve-point summary of the "perspectives" of improvisation, as: 1) intuitive art; 2) art of practice; 3) highly creative; 4) highly personal/individualized; 5) inspiration; 6) power; 7) the musical idiom itself; 8) merger between the familiar and the novel; 9) involving the audience directly; 10) sense of the mystical or emotional transcendence; 11) freedom (!); 12) the natural.[60] Racy neatly summarizes some of the main aspects of each of these interpretations and functions of improvisation.

Racy then considers the Middle Eastern art of *taqasim* (singular, *taqsim*). In this instrumental and vocal practice, the "ability to improvise modally is generally considered a trademark of good musicianship."[61] A *taqsim* is self-contained and in a specific *maqam* (melodic mode), in which it is begun, developed, and resolved according to a plan. But the performative goal of *taqsim* is *saltanah*, an ecstasy that is realized through focus on and expression of the *maqam*. Racy concludes with a table of "symbolic poles" that show the ability of a taqsim to alternate between different realms of significance, such as community-individuality, tradition-innovation, and expectancy-surprise.[62]

Racy also analyzes some famous musicians who were known for providing very different kinds of approaches to the problem of taqasim. Among them are two Gypsies, the *buzaq* players Muhammed Abd al-Karim of Syria and Matar Muhammed of Lebanon. Racy writes that these musicians show that the "public may correlate their distinguished musicianship with the distinctive social or ethnic backgrounds, or even physical traits."[63] This seems to be a kind sociological theorem about Gypsies, that the public correlates their musicianship with their ethnic background.

Although Racy's approach yields nothing specific on the relationship of Gypsiness and improvisation, he provides an excellent model for how to situate a context for improvisation, by analyzing the relationship of a specific performance practice to its own music culture. We shall try this approach now, with Taraf de Haïdouk.

IMPROVISATION AND MYSTERY IN THE MUSIC OF TARAF D HAÏDOUK

Improvisation and mystery will now be approached using three examples of Gypsy music, all taken from recordings of the Romanian group Taraf de Haïdouk, which means "Band of Brigands."[64] Taraf is from the village of Clejani, about thirty miles outside of Bucharest.[65] On tour their number varies, from nine to as many as twenty musicians. After the fall of Ceausescu's dictatorship in 1990, Western producers handpicked the best musicians of the village. They include the older generation, who preserve the traditional style of Romanian ballads, and younger musicians who try to incorporate "Bulgarian," "Turkish," "Serbian," and other influences into their music (again, these terms — Bulgarians, Turkish, Serbian — remain in quotation marks in the context of their appropriation). Two recognizable virtuosos neatly represent these two poles: the violinist and singer Nicolae Neacsu, the elder statesman of the band, and the violinist Georghe "Caliu" Anghel, the fiery showman of the group.[66]

Surprisingly, a survey of their three CDs shows few moments of extended improvisations.[67] This might be due in part to the influence on the part of the producers, who know that audiences want shorter and knowable songs. Indeed, one of them, Michel Winter, admitted in an interview that "when we put the group together, we had to convince them to do their own music and not to try to make some Western music. The first gigs, they wanted to play 'The Lambada' and big tunes that everybody knows."[68] In trying to convince Taraf to play indigenous music, the thorny issue is raised of how to present traditional music torn from its village context, where music is inscribed within the events of the life cycle: birth, celebration, marriage, mourning, and death. And though most of us would perhaps prefer to hear Taraf's own music, artistic autonomy seems obliterated when producers dictate reportorial choices.

Nevertheless, in trying to understand Taraf's music, it is not correct to say that even their music is simply composed. Instead, we can use the idea of "improvisatoriness" to characterize at least their recorded music. This category is in-between composition and improvisation. "Improvisatoriness" means that the performance imparts the *impression* that the music is improvised. It can be thought of as the variation principle of oral music. But the impression of improvised is also partly due to the nature of Taraf's heterophony, where individual techniques and approaches blend and clash.

Furthermore, the effect of improvisatoriness produces what we will call compositional mystery. Again, mystery denotes music's ability to generate ambivalent and equivocal meanings through seemingly precise means. It also throws into question the process of music decision-making; who decides, on what, and how, in a performance?

We will first analyze Neacsu's rendering of an old style *hora*, a type of Romanian dance, called "Hora din caval" (caval is a wind instrument). The violin assumes the role of a wind instrument, sometimes approximating a speaking voice, by seemingly whispering. As a dance tune, the form is simple, with two sections, which we can label A and B. The melody is also fairly straightforward, focusing on the note G and the scale of G natural minor. However, each time Neacsu varies the tune, rhythmically, ornamentally, and especially through his characteristic version *ponticello*; his ponticello undulates constantly, so that the timbre fluctuates. Note that this fluctuating timbral effect is used by Middle Eastern violinists when they want to imitate the nasal sound of the nay, a type of wooden flute. Improvisatoriness is massively asserted with each variation of the tune, throwing into ambiguity the national origins, "Romanian," of what is heard. Finally, through the speaking of his violin, Neacsu seems to be telling us something, but what it is remains beyond our knowing.

The second example is "Sirba," which also means dance, but with the explicit meaning of incorporating variations. Caliu begins this with the standard cliché of improvisation, playing over long-held chords, here, with the accordion closely imitating him. His virtuosity is always asserted. The mystery in this example is his seemingly mystical union with his chosen instrument, the violin. Caliu's sound offers more polish, clarity, and technique than Neacsu's. He uses speed effortlessly to show the power and grace of his playing. Caliu's approach to improvisation exerts a confidence in its ability to guide the listener. But precisely what he is saying seems overcome by the sheer intensity of his personality, and his inner attachment to and love of the violin.

The song "Tot taraful," which means "the whole band [taraf]," is one of the greatest examples of Gypsy music undergoing renewal in the 1990s. The song is on their third CD, "Dumbala Dumba." It is an instrumental fantasy lasting about seven minutes. As such, "Tot taraful" is the most extended and complicated piece to appear to date on a Taraf CD (*caveat*: on the *Latcho drom* CD is a tune called "Rind de Hore" which does share the basic principles of "Tot taraful"). The basic elements of Taraf's scoring are present: the violin–driven melodies, the bass countermelodies that mark off the time, and an accordion and cymbalom that plays with both. For the European listener, the piece falls within the familiar Hungarian-romungro (city, café) tradition of stringing melodies together creating a potpourri, though here with Middle Eastern-flavored transitions. A casual listening to the song might give the impression that the band is improvising, but in fact, on a careful listening, one can hear that the song is masterfully composed. And surprisingly, there is only one space for an improvisation over an ostinato, where the cymbalom plays a brief solo.

Indeed, Taraf's cymbalom player Ionica comments on Taraf's message to the world in the following quotation:

> At last I understand why the Taraf de Haïdouks is so successful in the West. The West has lost its own folklore and people are saturated with electronic music, they want something more natural.[69]

His point is an obvious one, that the West has become technologically so sophisticated that we no longer have folk, or what he calls "natural" music. Of course, this is also largely false, as witnessed by the recent attention given to folk revival bands in America and Europe in the last decade. Yet the cult of the natural can easily be grafted onto Gypsy music. In this view, Gypsies represent the "noble savage." Their music functions as a bridge to the innocent and lost world of the primitive.

Still, why is Taraf so successful? The answer might be in their positing of desire. As Hegel maintains, in desire one recognizes that "something other than self-consciousness exists";[70] in contemporary social terms, Taraf's music (and many other Gypsy and world-music bands) challenges the self-certainty of the Western economy as human progress. Taraf's music seethes with a ferocious intensity that seems lost in the administered reality of the West. Yet the true force of this intensity is perhaps its ability to disappear, close up, and vanish into the mystery or "mystic song" of Gypsy musical space.

CONCLUSION: THE EXOTIC REMAINDER OF THE GYPSINESS IN THE CONCERT HALL

Appealing to present-day groups like Taraf might appear to be the best approach for uncovering how Gypsy improvisation functioned and appeared in the nineteenth century. Historical documents will not aid us, for numerous reasons:

1) The proper testimony for this phenomenon has disappeared, and was never available in the first place; 2) Gypsy musicians were illiterate; 3) in the hyperbole of Lisztean celebration and genuine veneration, Gypsy music was employed as a trope, in part, for narcissistic reasons; 4) definitively, we will never experience it; its absence situates its very presencing today — at once evocative of the postmodern paradigm of musical studies, where musicology slips into the investigation of performance practice; and 5) because of exotic marginalization with an attendant commercial success, the spectacle of Gypsy music was always inseparable from the marketing.

Despite the irrevocable loss of the pastness of the past, in the best of all possible worlds, fieldwork of a contemporary performance practice might yield stunning insights for understanding the historical context. That is to say, any tension between ethnomusicology and musicology would be overcome in a hermeneutic vision that attempts to get at the past through conscious work on the present.

However, there are risks involved in fieldwork aimed at historical orientation. Two in particular will concern us for the rest of this book: 1) what can be called hypostatisizing the object; and 2) the entangled assimilation of the present with the past, and vice-versa. The first risk can create issues within a subject matter or topic which previously did not exist. We will deal specifically with this in Chapter Eleven, in the discussion of my fieldwork on Taraf. The second risk has to do with historical unfolding itself, or, the problem of anachronism, and can refer to what Dahlhaus has termed the "non-contemporaneity of the contemporaneous."

Therefore, instead of a transition to a history that appeals to fieldwork, we will situate the moment deconstructively through a quotation by Derrida:

'cinder' renders better what I meant to say with the name of trace, namely, something that remains without remaining, which is neither present nor absent, which destroys itself, which is totally consumed, which is a remainder without remainder. It testifies to the disappearance of the witness, if one can say that. It testifies to the disappearance of memory. When I keep a text for memory, what remains there is not cinders apparently. Cinders is the destruction of memory itself; it is an absolutely radical forgetting, not only forgetting in the sense of the philosophy of consciousness, or a psychology of consciousness; it is even forgetting in the economy of the unconscious by repression. Repression is not forgetting. Repression keeps the memory. Cinders, however, is an absolute non-memory, so to speak.[71]

What we have been saying in this chapter is that Gypsy improvisation, or Gypsiness in music, is a cinder, something "that remains without remaining." Its divided temporality — the non-memory which Apel uses as its condition — is the trace of a musical language that cannot be a language. Paradoxically put, Gypsy music (even the traces of what Bellman assimilates to the *style hongrois*) was known as a language only precisely because of its ability to deny itself the status of language, its mystical ability. When this process becomes ritualized, fetishized, in the totem that is the spectacle of capitalist marketing, the non-memory is complete.

As a final strategy, we will assemble the fault lines of Gypsiness and improvisation via the contemporary violin recital.[72] Here every contradiction to which we have referred is not only relevant but glaring. Yet we will not attempt a sociology of this institution, rather, we take notice of the cinders surrounding the recital, the encore.

Traditionally, the encore is not relevant to the recital. It is not printed. It is not even necessary. The newspaper might mention that it occurred but rarely reviews it as a serious part of the evening. Yet for audiences, this is the moment of moments, where the artist reveals his true personality. Many performers will even speak, announcing what they play, at this juncture of the evening.

Music Example 1 "Hora staccato" by Dinicu-Heifetz

In the early nineteenth-century virtuoso recital, it was expected that a performer would freely improvise something at this point — indeed, a reputation was guaranteed for a young virtuoso who exhibited mastery of improvisation. An open question we will pose: can we consider these virtousic displays as the opening of the public space for Gypsiness? Answering such a question is speculative; however, the links between Beethoven-Czerny-Liszt would lead us to venture a "yes."

If we consider late twentieth-century performance practice, Gypsiness exists, definitively, in the encore. This names the exotic remainder of Gypsiness. Anxiety disappears as the performer settles into Wienawski's "Legende," or if we were in Central Europe, a piece imitating the Gypsy fiddler like Dinicu's "Hora Staccato" (see Music Example 1) which functions as a substitute for the mystery of improvisation.

Chapter Four

Nomads and the Rhizome: Becoming Gypsy

As a possible way of dealing with the semantic field of the Gypsy as nomad, we propose to utilize Deleuze and Guattari's theory of "nomadology." However, because their theory is difficult to assimilate if one is not familiar with the technical terms of their thinking, and to our knowledge has never been dealt with American musicological literature, we will begin with one, counterintuitive idea: "that the nomad does not move."[1] To quote from their text:

> The nomad distributes himself in a smooth space; he occupies, inhabits, holds that space; that is his territorial principle. It is therefore false to define the nomad by movement.[2]

"Smooth space" denotes open land, as in the desert, as opposed to sedentary space, which is "striated, by walls, enclosures, and roads." Here movement means to go from one fixed point to another. The nomad's movement is not fixed spatially because he does not stay at a point. Rather, if we say that the nomad "moves," we mean this as a temporal occurrence, as in the nomad's *speed* or rate of movement.

What they are saying is a Zen aphorism, that in moving one stands still. The nomad occupies the space of movement itself, and in being occupied, that space ceases to move. The nomad's body fills the smooth space, paradoxically "absolute movement," a "swirling movement."

Deleuze and Guattari oppose the nomad to the migrant, who goes from one fixed point to another within the space of sedentary culture. The migrant resettles in a new territory. In contrast, the nomad experience is instead *"deterritorialization,"* (an important technical term in their text) because there is no attempt to resettle.[3]

Here, what we can call the "deterritorial principle" means the distribution of goods and people across open land. They stress "distribution" because the etymology of the word "nomad" is from the Greek *"nomos,"* which means law, as in the distribution of the law to the people. Pursuing etymology further, we can add that distribution contains the Latin root "*tribuere.*" This means grant, give, bestow, and is also where we get our word "tribute." As a process of exchange, distribution involves the event of giving, of the gift.

Before going on with their ideas, I wish to return to the suspended point from my treatment of Silverman. Again, I have said that her account of Roma nomadism as the result of harassment is too straightforward. Harassment certainly figures into some Roma movement, but we do not know to what extent it mingles with human agency, or choice. After all, this is a culture which readily valorizes the nomadic lifestyle.

THE NOMADIC NARRATIVE OF THE GYPSY MIGRATION

We can only speculate on why the Roma left Northern India, and to what extent they became the "Rom" as the result of their wanderings; again, we emphasize the word "speculate": there will never be a scientific confirmation establishing with certainty why, when, and how they migrated. The most recent proposal is that they were a warrior class that became cut off from India after years of battling Muslim forces. This view was endorsed and included in the notes to *Gypsy Caravan* in an essay "Origins of the Romani People" by Ian Hancock,[4] himself a Roma who is a linguist and professor at University of Texas in Austin and also among the most outspoken of the Roma activists.[5] Why would Hancock endorse this myth? I use the word "myth" intentionally, because there is no hard scientific evidence whatsoever, again, not even linguistic, that is not open to conflicting interpretations in order to support his view.

We can summarize his description as follows: The Aryans of India came under attack by the Muslim general Mahmud of Ghazni in the eleventh century. To defend themselves they raised armies from the non-Aryan population. The non-Aryans included Lohars, Gujjars, Tandas, and Rajputs; the fight against Islam took these "Indian troops, the early Roma" (Hancock's words) further and further westward.[6] Thus for Hancock, Roma were warriors, and they began their migration in the context of war. We must confess that we are extremely sympathetic to Hancock's view; pragmatically, its obvious strength is to empower the Roma people in their struggle for international recognition of their rights; and philosophically, there is a tantalizing connection here with nomadology: Deleuze and Guattari devote much space of their nomadology to an analysis of the war machine. In short, war is only possible as a nomadic uprising against the State apparatus.[7] What is any nationalism, after all, without war? War establishes the current international system of state boundaries.

Much of the rest of Roma migration is also mired in myth; even the surviving documents of the dramatic Gypsy entrance into Western Europe in the fifteenth century — sometimes called the "Great trick," as some of the Gypsy groups identified themselves as penitents from "Little Egypt" — is open to conflicting interpretations.[8] In short, despite the Roma as warrior theory, we do not know with precision the historical reasons for the Roma diaspora, and for their nomadic lifestyle. Harassment certainly figures into these reasons, but we do not know to what extent it mingles with human agency, or choice.

And today, Roma nomadism is becoming rarer, perhaps disappearing. As is well known by those who study the Roma, many Roma groups have been settled for centuries. From slavery in Wallachia (southern, present-day Romania) to laws against nomadism in nearly every European state at some time (most notably under Maria Theresa and Joseph II of the Austro-Hungarian Empire), the settlement has been forced. Recently in the Czech Republic smaller cities debated, violently, whether or not to build concrete walls around high-rises where Roma lived.[9]

Because they have settled, Roma now are not only nomadic, but are migrant. Again, a migrant moves from one fixed place to another. Contemporary Roma migration occurs within a bewildering range of possible causes, in what the diaspora literature calls the "global migration crisis." Three hotspots of the crisis are particularly relevant for the Roma — the Soviet Union, Eastern Europe, and the Balkans.[10] One aspect of this crisis is that many migrations are involuntary, the result of conflict, war, and civil war. This is the category of the refugee. In 1999, Roma were among waves of refugees who were brutally forced out during the crisis in Kosovo.[11]

For Deleuze and Guattari's nomadology, the Roma reality of nomadism, migration, and refugee status would denote a "fuzzy aggregate," an indefinite assemblage. Furthermore, Gypsiness in music, which in the nineteenth century meant the carefree attitude of the suffering Gypsy fiddler, has perhaps recently undergone a broadening to include migrant categories such as the refugee. In other words, Gypsiness in music today has become an intensely politicized category, and a much broader one than in the nineteenth century.

THE RHIZOME AND GYPSY MUSIC

The rhizome is a significant concept of Deleuze and Guattari's *A Thousand Plateaus*. We will quickly try to summarize some of their main points. The rhizome refers to weeds, whose roots are distinguished from real roots in that they possess bulbs and tapers, which serve as reserve food deposits. These rhizomatic roots can grow above or below ground, and are in constant reorganization. In animal terms, the pack is the analogue to the rhizome; one could add to this that the pack seems even more chaotic in its organization than the rhizome, in that it reconstitutes itself from moment to moment. For Deleuze and Guattari, the rhizome can assume diverse forms, and its surface extension is unpredictable.

The organization principle of the rhizome is the opposite of the tree, whose roots seek a fixed order. Culturally, the tree as a metaphor expresses itself in the book. In this conception the book is the product of sedentary culture, whose goal is an explication of the world in the terms of binary logic. The concept of the tree dominates Western reality, which culminates in the control of phenomena through the imposition of the word "to be."[12]

In contrast, the rhizome *"ceaselessly* establishes connections between semiotic chains, organizations of power, and circumstances relative to the arts, sciences, and social struggles."[13] We emphasize the word *"ceaselessly,"* because in terms of analyzing these connections, the work is always unfinished. That is why the logic here is associative. Anything can relate to anything else; again, Deleuze and Guattari seem to be advocating a sort of chaos theory. Furthermore, there is no stable position or point within these connections, there are only multiplicities (as opposed to the unity of "to be"), which are described as an assemblage of lines. A multiplicity can be thought as the principle of non-unity: there is nothing that unites a subject or object, instead of a point, there is a "line of flight." (For Deleuze, the concept of unity is the "power takeover in the multiplicity by the signifier.")[14]

Finally, these multiplicities are collected into "plateaus," which are always already connected to each other through rhizomatic stems. A plateau assembles the multiplicities, or these lines of flights; it can be thought of as the larger organizing principle in Deleuze and Guattari's system. The plateau of historiography is thus a sedentary activity, that is, it occurs within the apparatus of the states.[15] We might add to this the idea of nationalism. The opposite plateau is what they call "nomadology," the logos (discourse) of the nomad.

We can next compare the growth of trees and rhizomes. Tree logic is reproductive, it represents systems by *tracing* (a technical term). A tracing imitates, it tries to represent the codes of something without alteration. Yet the danger with the tracing is its redundancy, it organizes according to its own rules, destroying that which it attempts to model. Tree logic seeks points and roots, organized according to hierarchies.

In contrast, rhizomatic logic produces a *mapping,* a new construction of the real, one that is "open and connectable in all its dimensions." Deleuze and Guattari use the image of the orchid and the wasp, which together form a rhizome: "the orchid does not reproduce the tracing of the wasp, it forms a *map* with a wasp."[16] That is, wasp and orchid fluctuate, constantly mutating through the performative. In other words, they relate to each other through lines, through multiplicities or variables, and there contact is always either decreasing or increasing. Lines are important here, for instead of a concentrated point, the line can bind, or separate; Deleuze and Guattari call the will to leave a territory the "line of flight."

Finally, these rhizomes, maps, and lines of flight are collected into "plateaus." The rhizomes of a plateau can be broken, the stems can be separated and regenerate in another place along the plateau; the pack can be disrupted, only to reform in another way. Thus a plateau can be thought of as the larger organizing principle in Deleuze and Guattari's system. The plateau that describes nomadic culture is what they call "nomadology," the weedlike logos (discourse) of the nomad.

Now, before seeing how Deleuze and Guattari's theory relates to Roma music and improvisation, I would like to reformulate the problem of the previous chapter: how can we think the relationship of Roma music and improvisation, if we are rejecting the idea that either of these are stable, unified signifiers?

We think that nomadology can explain this relationship of non-universals. For, nomadology allows us to say that Gypsy-Roma music can be improvised, while interpreting neither of the plateaus of Roma music and improvisation as fixed universals. Nomadology allows us to respect the particularity of a music culture, and its relationship to other organizations of meaning. Improvisation is rhizomatic, by definition, it is never stable, even when recorded and analyzed as text. To reiterate, as we have argued using de Man's ontology of the performative of the excuse, we have no external evidence to ever really know if improvising is occurring.

Furthermore, we suggest that Deleuze and Guattari's theory of nomadology provides a theory to explain what Gypsiness in music might mean. We might begin by imagining its categories as plateaus. Thus some of our plateaus would be improvisation, Gypsy appropriations in Western art music, so-called Roma folk music, Gypsy pop music, and Roma appropriations of local musics.

What connects these plateaus is that they are continually re-creating themselves, escaping easy classification. Again, any connection from one plateau to another is possible. With nomadology we can construct new relationships among the plateaus of Gypsiness in music, without having to combat charges of historical anachronism.

Finally, nomadology explains the historical and geographically breaks of Gypsiness in music. These breaks have so far impeded a full understanding of the power of this phenomenon. Again, Gypsy music has relationships to Classical, to folk, to pop, and to world-music genres. Yet sometimes, music we call "Gypsy" is hypothetical — by what right can we call the music of the Rajasthan desert nomads (the group "Musafir," a Farsi [!] word which means traveler) who now live in Belgium "Gypsy"? Yet the disruptions and eruptions show how Gypsiness in music is rhizomatic, reconstituting, re-imagining itself with each new cultural contact.

And insofar as Gypsies identify themselves as transnational, beyond nation-states, they create new cultural connections. In an unpublished paper I show how commercial Gypsy music manipulates symbols of nomadic culture; in this respect, Roma music works with *associations*, producing new lines of flights within the cultures with which they interact.[17]

So, if we take these two plateaus, Roma music and improvisation, the question remains: what lines of flight connect these plateaus? I will address this in the conclusion.

GYPSINESS, AMERICA, AND THE NOMADIC LOGIC OF IMPROVISATION

We have been dealing with nomadology because of our argument that neither musicology nor ethnomusicology have constructed a wide-enough framework to deal with the shifting nature of Gypsiness in music, Roma music, and improvisation. Furthermore, we have suggested that Deleuze and Guattari's theory of the nomad may provide a theory to explain some of the current and political implications of Gypsiness in music. I would like in this conclusion to propose another way of highlighting the relevance of the nomad for improvisation.

We will approach this indirectly. Again, we saw earlier that the nomad exhibits deterritorialization. To reiterate, this concept signifies an open-ended, unceasing movement, with unending variations and mutations through time.

Now, for Deleuze and Guattari, of all the arts music is a unique case, in that it articulates the deterritorial principle to a higher degree than the other arts. I will give one example of this process cited by them: Schumann's setting of children's songs. At the level of the child, songs are what they call "refrains," which are territorial, they relate to the earth; the musician, like Schumann, takes these refrains in order to deterritorialize music, which means to open music up to new sonorities, new combinations of sound, indeed, to the cosmos.[18]

Though in itself there is nothing new or surprising in how they deal with Schumann's settings of children's songs, what is new is the relationship that Deleuze and Guattari propose between music and nomadism. Namely, both music and nomadism contain the same essential element, that of *movement through time*; whereas sedentary culture manipulates space and landscape, nomadic culture is a temporal happening like music. Thus perhaps Liszt's search for what we have been calling Gypsiness in music was in fact his search for music itself. In the late nineteenth century, Gypsiness in music occurred against the social and intellectual backdrop of the enlargement of the Western world domination through colonialism, the critique of divine human creation with Darwin's evolutionary theory, and the attack on Christian morality (or any morality, really) by Nietzsche. It was a time of a re-evaluation of values. For Liszt, Gypsiness bridged the gap between human and divine; it was a sign of God's musical gift to the artist. This gap was becoming increasingly unbearable for Western thinking since the Enlightenment, and Gypsiness and improvisation were ways of relieving some of the pressure.

Improvisation is not cited in *A Thousand Plateaus*. But it is perhaps a better example of the "deterritorial" principle than composed music like the Schumann example, since improvised music is not fixed in writing. Improvisation can thus be used to describe how nomadic music culture *deterritorializes* musical models. This is the nomadic logic of improvisation, and I think that it counts as an aesthetic principle of at least professional Gypsy music-making.

But if we push this further, I think we are led to something startling: that one of the central ideas of Gypsiness is not merely that Gypsies improvise, but that music *as music*, music itself, is improvisation. In my violin lessons with Caliu or his son, Robert, they would repeatedly say "improvisation," with a smile. Any playing of the tune could possibly become an improvisation.[19]

Today Gypsiness in music is increasingly entangled in late or postindustrial capitalism. To give an example, *Gypsy Caravan* referred to on page 52 was a staged production that toured America, again, with six allegedly "Gypsy" acts. Because the bands touring are actually sedentary Roma, we can analyze this event commercially, as a producer's attempt to market Gypsy nomadism as emotion, virtuosity, and improvisation, (a confusing aggregate) and sell it to an American audience.

However, in contrast to this commercial reading of *Gypsy Caravan*, this event can be interpreted as an example of the emerging relationship between Gypsy music and America, one perhaps begun in 1993 with the release of *Latcho drom*. America is the new context, the fresh territory, across which Gypsiness will try to move.[20] Gypsiness has discovered a new context, and will transform itself in reaction to American demands. As is well known, Americans usually look to jazz, blues, and rock bands to find improvisation; we can speculate that at least some Americans will increasingly turn to Gypsy music for this. This is already the situation in Europe, where today, a significant strand of European jazz is Gypsy ("*Sinti* jazz" for the Germans, "*musique manouche*" for the French), the musical offspring of Django Reinhardt and Stéphane Grapelli's hot jazz of the 1930s.[21]

But why America? What is the significance of America? I will quote from *A Thousand Plateaus* on America:

> Everything important that has happened or is happening takes the route of the American rhizome: the beatniks, the underground, bands and gangs, successive lateral offshoots.... America reversed the directions: it puts its Orient in the West, as if it were precisely in America that the earth came full circle; its West is the edge of the East.[22]

America's tradition is its own non-tradition, of its abrupt reversals of position. On the issue of deconstruction in America, Jacques Derrida notes that deconstruction's political aspects — the "frontier" between the political, the economic, and the academic — "is original to the United States; to envision the stakes involved, one need only read what is said about deconstruction in the *Wall Street Journal*, the *New Yorker*, or *The New York Review of Books*."[23]

As ethnomusicologists continue to frame their Roma-music fieldwork around constructions of transnational, regional, and local identities of Roma, a deconstructive view would question the idea of identity itself as a myth-making, and as a remainder of the colonial project. And this, at least for us, is what "America" might have to contribute to Gypsiness in music: the continued contact between deconstruction from an *American* problematic (a political and economic strategy) and Gypsiness, in order to displace the ethnographies of Roma music as colonial discourse, no matter how "locally grounded" (a presumptuous formulation in our view) they may be in reality.[24]

Though I think that the improvisation within *Caravan* was minimal, and when occurring, constrained, American audiences encountered the *myth* of Gypsies as improvisers with this show. Yet again there is the unverifiable aspect of improvisation; but how can we defend the idea that improvisation was minimal? That I went to four performances of Caravan? How can I prove this statement? Again, when I asked Caliu about improvisation, he told me that the all Gypsy music is improvisation, and that everything he does is improvisation. Reflecting upon this later, I thought of Nettl, when he was told by the Arabic musician nearly the same thing, when Nettl knew from his own experience that much of the time, this musician was actually playing formulas.

In any case, it is safe to say that Caravan audiences experienced the illusion of improvisation, perhaps in much the same way that Liszt encountered it with the Gypsy violinist and band leader János Bihari. Again, it was backstage, after the event, when bands who before Caravan had never heard of each other tried to play each other's music that improvisation occurred.[25] Here, in this "imaginary community" on tour within the borders of America, Gypsiness itself was re-created, showing that even under sedentary constraints, Gypsiness reverts back to a nomadic aesthetic to locate music — locating, in Deleuze's terms, the becoming Gypsy Caravan.

Chapter Five

Brahms's "Hungarian Dance no. 5" and the Dynamics of Exaggeration

Even Gypsy music, whose characteristic scales have become influential among several surrounding nations in the Balkans, though it is not as foreign to our ears, has been unable to penetrate the wall separating folk music from art. Whenever Brahms incorporates such a melody in a composition the structure will not surpass the implications of a set of waltzes or of a quadrille.

Arnold Schoenberg, "Folkloristic Symphonies," in *Style and Idea*, 163

In my performance I repeat an entire section, the way a Gypsy might improvise on the cymbalom. It's almost impossible to put down a Hungarian Rhapsody the way its creator felt it, or the way a Gypsy might improvise, and to which Liszt might listen and be impressed by it.

Hungarian pianist Ervin Nyiregyházi, *Nyiregyházi Plays Liszt*,
Columbia Records LP

A small number of pieces in the Western orchestral repertory have become warhorses without anyone knowing their original versions. Arguably the most popular is Brahms's "Hungarian Dance no. 5," originally for piano four-hands.[1] Yet the picture of Brahms presented to students of music history refuses to acknowledge the significance of such works, instead presenting Brahms as a sober, monumental, intellectual — in a word "serious" — composer.[2] Emerging as secondary in such characterizations is the Hungarian or even "Gypsy" side of Brahms. In this chapter, we shall reverse this tendency, and argue for Brahms's forays into Gypsiness as a necessary element of his style.

Broadly speaking, we might posit this compositional desire for a non-German substance to other composers in the Germanic legacy of composition. Bach, considered by everybody to be the "Godfather" of German music, becomes unthinkable without the *Italian* concerto, or his numerous French overtures/suites. Indeed, it seems likely that what we call "German" music might turn out to be a hybridity of competing national or marked styles.[3]

By the later half of the nineteenth century, composers began to respond to the aesthetic demand for deeper subjectivity in their music. Gypsy music fit perfectly into this paradigm shift. It was perceived as a repository of emotional states, quickly alternating between grief and happiness. In terms of representing subjectivity, what was attractive about Gypsy music was its *immediate* response to sorrow or joy. Because this music could react on the spot to emotional turbulence of both the listener and performer, another strategy for reading Gypsiness would be as the constellation of a musical environment demanding immediacy or presence.

These moments of immediacy are central to Western art music; less noticed is that these moments challenge the ideal of musical completeness. Theorists understand musical completeness as organic unity, positing a work where material and form are integrated across levels (in the Schenkerian sense) of analysis. However, missing from such conceptions are the immediate and so-called surface aspects of the work. In a sense, unity and immediacy generate a dialectic. As the work becomes immediate, paradoxically it is also never fully there in a temporal sense; emotionally and cathartically something else lingers after the performance. Instead of bringing the work to completeness, the category of the immediate-emotional has the effect of deferral, causing the listener to experience art as a smokescreen. Other aspects of the work outside of the "immediate" recede, concealing themselves behind or even below barriers of consciousness. Finally, the immediate-emotional brings attention to the fact that all artistic presentation is *mediated* by something other; classic twentieth-century sites of mediation would be perception, the unconscious, and gender/ethnicity; today, we might perhaps posit cyberspace, the media, and hyperglobalization.

However, the main stumbling block for reintroducing the immediate-emotional is not organic unity per se, but the notion of music history as the onward march of technical — melodic and harmonic, to a lesser extent rhythmic — progress from the nineteenth to the twentieth centuries. Schoenberg's "emancipation of the dissonance" would represent the *telos* in this interpretation, where dissonances are freed from the strict rules of voice-leading.[4]

This fictional narrative of progress is the really the triumph of German music as the model of music "in-itself" by some music historiographers. Other musics, especially "national" and "exotic" styles, receive predicates that qualify the music as a substance that is no longer "pure." For example, in the nineteenth century, Smetana and Dvořák represent the Czech national school, while Glinka and Borodin (and others) the Russian one; by contrast, German composers from Beethoven to Brahms seem to escape this nationalistic determination, despite the existence of numerous nationalistic/political elements in their music (to mention only one area: music inspired by military models).

Already in this allegedly pure Germanic musical heritage is much corruption. One major fault line in this heritage is what I call the "Viennese contamination."[5] This names the idea of heterogeneities at the core of "Germanness." Pause for a moment on the triads Haydn-Mozart-Beethoven, or Schubert-Brahms-Mahler, the Central European composers whose works are the so-called "meat-and potatoes" of the concert hall, what would their music be without what Adorno's calls Viennese "laxity," or Austrian humor, or the waltz, or folk music for that matter? Can we think away the environmental effects of light, popular kitsch on their music, despite the empirical impossibility of ever having direct knowledge of the precise nature of this kind of sonic influence?

In a recent article,[6] Michael Beckerman proposes the idea of the Hapsburg empire as an "impossible fiction," a "universe of competing and symbiotic ethnicities, rapidly changing nation states and gradually less stable economic classes." Relevant is also his interpretation of Franz Lehár as the quintessential Hapsburg composer, whose *The Merry Widow* can be interpreted as an "unrelieved Hapsburgian polyglot shimmer," with his "Tempo di Mazurka" made up of little bits of Czechness, Gypsiness, and some Magyarness thrown in. The point is that if we push Beckerman's idea, the aesthetic effect of this "polyglot shimmer" might reach to some of the "serious" works (symphonies and other works based on sonata principles) by the heavyweight composers who worked in the realm.

MELODO-RHYTHMIC ANALYSIS

Musically the *Hungarian Dances* are about the melodo-rhythmic, a feature commonly held up as the *Bild* of Gypsy music, and that this is perhaps nowhere in evidence more directly than in no. 5. As a corollary, the concentration on melody has been negatively interrogated by musicologist and theorists. Further, it is this focus on melody that locates the aesthetic of the *Hungarian Dances* within the expressive world of Gypsy music.

Now, in Dance no. 5, let us try to determine how Brahms builds into the melodic structure a sense of whimsical, of the illogical, directly into the well-known opening theme (see Music Example 2). Already the tag ending's sixteenth notes (labeled as "a") propels us ahead, causing us to experience the time as rushed, similar to an adrenaline burst due to an excess of emotional torment (note that this is also a standard czárdás move). The lower range of the theme is essential to the opening, giving the mood of intensity and darkness, perhaps foreboding. The restatement of the theme ends with

Music Examples 2-7   Brahms, "Hungarian Dance no. 5" (excerpts).

a sequential idea with sixteenth notes (see Music Example 3, "b"), pulling downward, again, and hurrying the musical intent.

   When the theme is re-stated the fourth time in the higher octave (m. 25), a sense of the frenetic enters via ornamentation. Namely in the theme's first measure ("c," see Music Example 4), the C-sharp rises through the arpeggio of F-sharp minor to a C-sharp (instead of A), screaming in this upper range an ambiguous content that we all seem to understand as a modality of intensity, and in fact indicates the kind of ornamentation to be expected from the stereotype of a Gypsy fiddler's improvisation in a restaurant.

The B section (starting at m. 33) continues the rhythmic contrast hinted at in A; gentle syncopations (labeled "d," see Music Example 5) are exactly what a listener versed in *verbunkos* or more specifically *czárdás* would expect; but the *poco ritard* (m. 41, marked *piano*), often played as an exaggerated, massive *ritard*, again, draws us deeper into the world of Romanticism, here the language of sentimentality and of the heart. This phasing in-and-out of tempo via the *ritard* signals musical immediacy — as if we are re-experiencing the emotional pysché of Brahms well over a century later. I think, furthermore, that it is this kind of emotive gesture, built into a piece that is principally *about* the beauty of melody (here, without the distractions of musical formal devices, including counterpoint, variation, and development), that communicates directly to audiences' ideas about the encoding of emotion in music, and has contributed also to the worldwide popularity of this piece.

With the *Vivace* (see Music Example 6) we step into the domain of the cymbalom,[7] for Brahms and Liszt the Hungarian-Gypsy instrument that accompanies, and also an instrument easily approximated on piano as Liszt had shown nearly twenty years earlier in his own *Hungarian Rhapsodies* (discussed in Chapter Six).

Once again, the section is pasted onto what preceded, with no preparation, fully developed. This follows the procedures of what Dahlhaus would call the *Hausmusik* of the nineteenth century, domestic music-making for the lower middle-classes.[8] Characteristic of this music is the absence of formal music devices, and a kind of pseudo-virtuosic surface. Indeed, the continuation of the thirds into the second measure of this section (labeled "e") gives the impression of this kind of surface. This passage intensifies the emotional instability — that there is no focus to the mind when emotional turbulence exists. Then, abruptly and mirroring the first *poco ritard* at m. 41, Brahms gives another *poco ritard* (m. 61, see Music Example 7), where the melody for the first time gets the A-sharp that defines F-sharp major, with its upper-neighbor and lower-neighbor tones shining on it. It seems as though he reserves this significant note for the contrasting section. We can never prove in any empirical sense where the tradition of swelling in the strings in fact comes from, but it is likely that this is a Hungarian-Gypsy performance gesture invoked by Brahms through the *crescendo* marking.

COMPARISON OF RECORDED PERFORMANCES

Since Gypsiness names a performance practice, any treatment of it should include some variety of aural analysis. As we shall now see, investigating aspects of recordings of the Fifth Hungarian Dance yields stunning insights into the multivalent folds making up Gypsiness, and indeed, about Gypsiness per se. This kind of work constitutes a phenomenological subdivision of the field of "Classical music" fieldwork. The choice of recordings is bewildering. Our method, therefore, will be to choose four currently available CDs that reveal *different* aspects of the score. We begin with what seems closest to the score.

But we must at the same time be wary of the concept of "score." What is close to the score? What is near? Nearing, for that matter? Musicologists have long been aware that *exact* duplication is impossible; however, a new twist on this old trope is that authenticity is itself impossible to realize. And it has been clear for a long time that what is closest to the letter of the score might turn out to be furthest from it. As an ideal, closeness may be the furthest category for thinking music.

Further, "live performance" is itself a signification, a partially fictional construction of the textual field. It is invented through interpretive means. There is no way of knowing its possibility, except as a trace of text. In this sense, even if analysis of form, process, or tonality is displaced by performance analysis, at heart it, too, presents troubling aporias for thinking.

As one example, for a performance to be "live," living, it must also be capable of surviving *beyond* the performance itself. Its trace resonates beyond the possibility of its own sound. And if this is so, then, how can we still speak of *live performance*? Or living performance? Is not all performance both alive and yet dead on arrival? Can we name what performance is? Moreover, what is the experience of the performance? In the Event (*Ereignis*) something also slips away, falls out, escapes, from what Heidegger argues is our impossible attempt to master the present. This remainder of the Event can be summoned by technology, in this case, the recording process. The remainder also indicates the *standing reserve*, that which waits for us to use, in the ordering of using it up. In this complex process, the live performance exists while always disappearing from the scene. If nowadays all performance exists within the space of the possibility of recording — what does this possibility entail for the concept of performance?

In one rendering, the recording can instigate what Husserl calls the phenomenological bracketing (*epoché*). Here, the world of the natural standpoint becomes suspended; everything experiential falls away. We focus on the recording in-itself and what it says.

A final problem that we cannot forget to mention is technological. It concerns microphone placement and the final mix-down (editing) of the recorded takes. How do these processes alter and inform our perception and listening of these works? Research in the future might be oriented toward the conditions of capturing sound: sound engineers, their musical background/training and aesthetic viewpoint, and the recording equipment and techniques they employed.

I. Budapest Symphony Orchestra, Conducted by István Bogár[9]

We start with the standard orchestral arrangements of the *Hungarian Dances*. Brahms himself arranged the First, Third, and Tenth in 1885. The selection of the arrangements for the dances by Bogár is standard, and can actually serve as a bench-mark for other recordings. This particular recording was done in 1988 at the Italian Institute in Budapest, and reveals a competent rendering of the Dances.

Bogár takes the quarter note at about 144, and his *accelerandos* and *ritards* seem standard, in that they do not jolt the listener. The string section is lean yet powerful, playing with much precision. The B section has a slight speed up, which works well, in order to set up the subsequent and massive ritard. The *Vivace* section (C) has the usual string swells. Here the quarter note is set at 152.

One key aspect lacking from what we are calling a "straight" recording is emotional energy. Admittedly, emotional substance cannot be measured. But the overall clarity and drive of this performance does not lend itself to emotional identification: as listeners, we do not lose ourselves listening to this.

Perhaps one reason for this coldness is that in effect, this CD proposes a vision of Brahms that we noted at the beginning of this chapter: serious, dry, possessing sympathies for yet never overindulging in a Gypsy style. Also, in 1988, Hungary was still behind the Iron curtain, and there might be questions of competing in the capitalist marketplace, against the bigger, more well-known European orchestras. That is, orchestral reputation might have been at stake; what went was the emotional exercise of Gypsiness.

II. The Magic of the Budapest Gypsy Orchestra

This CD released on Hungarton in 1997 begins with the "Hungarian Dance no. 5."[10] The CD directly instantiates Gypsiness; that it places Dance no. 5 first should not be seen as arbitrary. The other Hungarian Dance on this CD is no. 1. The most serious and substantial piece on the CD is an arrangement by Farkas of Liszt's Hungarian Rhapsody no. 2. As an aside, it seems impossible to know who "Farkas" is, since it is a common name. In Gypsy circles, it might mean the primas Andras Farkas; yet playing on this CD is a László Kecskeméti Farkas. Other kinds of pieces on the CD are typical restaurant pieces, along with operetta tunes by Strauss and Lehár. The artistic director, László Berki, arranged many of the tunes, including Brahms's "Hungarian Dance no. 5."

Before turning to the tune, we will first focus on the orchestra. To quote from the liner notes on the history and *raison d'être* of the group, founded in 1985 in a "non-profit character" (?!):

> One of the main goals of the establishment of this concert gypsy orchestra, being unique world-wide, was to *raise Gypsy music to a new musical and artistic height* that had never been heard before and by this to create a new sound on the stage and in the concert halls that offers the audience an extraordinary experience not only by music but the scenery as well. (my emphasis)[10]

I think the point needs restating: the raising of Gypsy music to new artistic levels occurs through a "new" sound on stage and in concert halls, that is, by the correct context. The factors for this improvement are many. First, the concert hall offers an opportunity to increase the audience size well over the size of any restaurant. Second, the frame of the concert hall (this seems to be what is meant by scenery) obviously symbolizes the prestige signaled by the raising of the artistic level (this seems to be what is meant by scenery). Third, and most significantly, the concert hall allows the Gypsy orchestra the same venue for reception as even the most hallowed orchestra of Europe.[11] Yet the Gypsy Orchestra is not aiming for competition with the major orchestras. Judging by the traditional nineteenth-century costumes, complete with red vest still in vogue for the restaurant musicians, the Gypsy Orchestra enlarges upon its Hapsburg Restaurant heritage. In a sense, it is turning this Restaurant tradition into serious music, a modality of absolute music as music-to-be-listened-to, in-itself, without the food or drinks.

In addition to their CD liner notes, their Web site offers the perfect *Bild* of what is involved in Gypsiness. Their Web site provides a stunning scene of Gypsiness.[12] A pop-up, made with Macromedia's Flash player, is encountered on first opening the page. Scrolling over the orchestra while *holding* a left-click (not a common web surfing technique!), four different songs can be heard, from left to right: 1) László Berki, "Summer in Paris"; 2) Vittorio Monti, "Czardas"; 3) Grigoras Dinicu, "Fly my swallow"; and 4) Johann Strauss, "On the beautiful blue Danube." While playing, blue notes swirling left-to-right wiggle their way upward from the orchestra. The setup of the orchestra is telling: no music stands or conductor, overwhelmingly strings, with a big cymbalom flanked by two smaller ones at the center stage, framed by two primas standing before the orchestra. The string presence is also noted in the alternate name of the band: 100 Gypsy Violins.

One of their pages has a stirring description of the group; note that the capital emphasis is native to the site:[13]

> The BUDAPEST GYPSY SYMPHONY ORCHESTRA, also called HUN-DRED GYPSY VIOLINS, is the Only Gypsy Symphony Orchestra in the World with 100 musicians from BUDAPEST playing famous hungarian and international gypsy music from SZENTIRMAY, MONTI, FERRARIS, BERKI, DINICU to classical pieces from BRAHMS, BERLIOZ, KHATCHATOURI-AN, LISTZ, Johann STRAUSS. [*sic*]

> Each concert is an unforgettable experience, comparable to listening to 100 PA-GANINIS.

Surely, this is a marketing ploy; yet the economy of this marketing orients us toward a real context: Gypsy musicians' ability to generate income at a difficult time. In

Budapest, the work situation is not the best for musicians; according to cymbalom player Kalman Balogh (who once played with this orchestra, in the 1980s), the city is full of excellent musicians somewhat desperate for work.[14]

The first notes played by the Budapest Gypsy Orchestra evoke a bygone time and place. The tempo is slow, beyond the measurement of a metronome: for immediately, the *accelerando* loses any sense of timekeeping. The slowness of this recording works to transports us back to a legendary past: it is as if the musicians are haunted by some tune from the past, and they are struggling to reignite it under their fingers. The effect is powerfully inebriated; and if there is anything such as the existence of *authenticity* in Gypsiness, it is in recordings like this one that it can be gleaned. The repeat of the A section (preceded by a rare and silent fermata) lingers with astonishing grace; then speeds up, into a gloriously halting B section: it is as if the concept of slowness was being reinvented. The C section provides the fast release, as the primás circles around the rest of the orchestra with a lighthearted ornamentation over the cymbalom's percussive pounding. The return of the A gives the standard clarinet fireworks.

Unfortunately, after this, the limitations of Gypsiness are revealed: it is as if there is no room for anything else to happen, as the playing becomes absolutely consistent and standardized in relation to itself. Even if it takes improvisation as its ideal, Gypsiness in the orchestral setting cannot offer development. Paradoxically put, its excitement at variation, at emotional nuance is possible only in that these variables are predictable and expected. Because of its predictability, Gypsiness, in the aspect of a large-group reduplication, can be compared with the consistency inherent in the finest orchestral playing.

III. Sándor Lakatos: "König der Zigeunergeigen"[15]

The primás Sándor Lakatos (1924-94) stands at the head of one of the great dynasties of Gypsy bands.[16] Information on these family-organized bands is difficult to gather; still, this statement by Dork Zygotian adequately summarizes the phenomenon:

> Large professional orchestras comprised of Gypsy musicians began to appear in the first half of the nineteenth century. History records the popularity of those led by the famed Czinka Panna, Ferenc Patikarus, Laci Racz, and the semi-mythical Czermak. Band members were often related, giving rise to family dynasties of Gypsy musicians which endure to this day, such as the Balogh, Berki and Lakatos families, many of whom have branched into jazz, winning international recognition.[17]

The Lakatos family, under Sándor Deki Lakatos (Jr.?), has at least ten titles on the esteemed Hungaroton Classic label, including: "Gypsy Magic," "A Souvenir from the Balaton,"[18] and the sparkling "Dance the Csárdás!"[19] This last CD features ten-minute potpourris, strings of tune virtuosically woven together: a typical example is "Good Evening>Little Boy, Big Dog>What a High Inn>Little Well, Water Well>Wooden Fork, Wooden Spoon, Wooden Plate>I Never Stole in My Life>Poke it Out>Soldiers March on the Highway>Gypsy Tent>There are Only Two Girls in the Village." About half of the tunes are anonymous, and were originally vocal numbers. They are simple in their structure, allowing for improvisation and variation, and as such each tune is repeated a number of times before letting go into the next. Sometimes it only takes the crying out of a motive to signal the transition. Without the proper for-knowledge of the tunes, it sometimes is difficult to know which tune is being played at a given time: indeed, for a non-Hungarian audience, despite the titles, are we in the realm of absolute or perhaps quasi-absolute music? In any case, what binds the tunes together is the rock-solid four bar phrase structure, underpinned with a steady accompaniment and clear and redundant harmonic progression. As the prelude for the climax, the procession halts, and the tempo undergoes a sudden speeding up; this is the moment where virtuosity is unleashed with furious and ferocious intent.

The Lakatos approach follows in the small ensemble tradition, which they are partly responsible for, of the Budapest restaurants — two violins, a cello, bass, cymbalom, and clarinet. This instrumentation epitomizes the idealized Hungarian-Gypsy sound for their local and international clientele. Note that many Hungarians openly despise this style of "tourist" music, calling it music from the "wax museum." Against this, however, the same critics hold up the Lakatos family as ideal interpreters. Furthermore, no one denies the technical ability of the musicians in these restaurants, only that the music can come as background wallpaper.

Sándor's unique yet stylized version of the Hungarian Dance is realized through the bow. The tempo is, once again, slow (ca. 72), and though he uses vibrato, what accomplishes the sonic event is the heaviness — borderline pressing, yet with masterful grace — of the bow on the string. We lack any kind of vocabulary to describe the bowing gestures aimed at *espressivo* in this context. An entire treatise should someday be devoted to the articulation and attack of Gypsy bowing.[20] Indeed, a powerful way to think about ornamentation is not only to refer to the glissando and vibrato often thought as the essence of Gypsy-style playing, but rather in the attack strategies of bowing articulation, from that exact moment when legato to *spiccato* are instituted.

The transition to the B section features a perfectly instantiated accelerando, and one with a heightened lessening of bow pressure. This is often referred to as the "magic" of the Gypsy style of bowing — it is simply not formally present in Classical schools of bowing, except through imitation of what was called the Gypsy "café" school of playing (see especially Fritz Kreisler).[21] The B section emerges as lightening fast (albeit with the usual *ritardandos*), ca. 176, with intonation not present on any other recording of which I am aware.

In the C section, Lakatos adds in fermatas that give the effect of cutting the phrase into antecedent and consequent. Once again, the musical reason for such a sharp break is perhaps for the achievement of maximum contrast. For, when the A section comes back, its slowness feels even more pronounced (in fact, it actually is slower).

Unlike the version from the Budapest Gypsy Orchestra, the return of the A and B does not suffer from staleness. Lakatos achieves the freshness through an ecstatic approach to the material: the ornamentation through an upward glissandi effect at the re-transition to the repeat of the B speaks with a poetic force that is entirely befitting of the König.

IV. Iván Fischer and the Budapest Festival Orchestra[22]

Fischer (b. 1951) is today one of the preeminent conductors coming from Hungary. Along with Zoltán Kocsis, he founded the BFO in 1983. Fischer's interpretations focus on bringing something new and original to the score, sometimes to the chagrin of orchestras he is conducting.[23]

Fischer represents the new breed of the Classical musical establishment. The essence of this movement comes down to the reinvigoration of standard works through an attempt to get *closer* to their sources. Indeed, the CD jacket contains this remark:

> A refreshingly new look at one of the most enduring success stories in music history. With partly new orchestral arrangements [by Fischer himself], *bringing the music closer to its Gypsy sources* (my emphasis).

Here Classical music is in step with trends in the world-music industry, in that both are marketing "source" as the main purveyor of authenticity. Examples from recent CDs (the principle material site for the reception of music) can be multiplied at length of this turn toward the "real." The concept of "source" also translates into an original configuration; something at its origins (what Heidegger would call "*Ursprung*," the fundamental leap, versus "*Herkunft*"). Furthermore, this notion of source locates the essence of musicological inquiry: to discover the origins of a thing, before it divides and multiplies, separating from itself. The source is Being (*Sein*) as Being: a thing in its purity, untainted by later reception.

Fischer's own commentary shows that he is a conductor passionately interested in the historical circumstances of the music he is playing. In a conversation with him after he conducted *The Miraculous Mandarin*, I asked him about the source material of the Fourth movement of Bartók's *Concerto for Orchestra*. He not only gave an impromptu answer, but went into considerable details about Bartók's atypical quoting of a Hungarian song; for Fischer, this was a nationalist

gesture in the best sense — pride, and not chauvinism. And for Fischer, Shostakovich was simply not present in the movement (something I find hard to believe).

Fischer is keenly aware of the problems of origins concerning Brahms's *Hungarian Dances*. He notes the central paradox in the first sentence:

> To call Brahms the composer of the *Hungarian Dances* would be an exaggeration,
> but it would also be wrong to say that he simply "arranged" this music for piano.

He goes on to cite the debates in the press over the origins of the dances, and of Béla
Kéler's accusations of Brahms's intellectual theft. But Fischer seems content with Geiringer's explanation, holding that Brahms "raised" nineteenth-century popular music
to a higher level.

Fischer's recording is orchestral, yet he employs Gypsy musicians: József ("Csóc-
si") Lendvay and son on violins, and Oszkár Ökrös on cymbalom.[24] Incidentally, this
mixing of classical orchestral players with traditional or "folk" musicians is a powerful
trend in the classical music scene.

Overall, the mood of Fischer's version captures the refined, nineteenth-century
spirit of Hungarian popular song, what we will call its aristocratic splendor. The added cymbal crashes are perfectly placed in the B section; the intimate quality of the
strings on the slow down to the B is also well done. The giving over of much of the
melody to the winds becomes evident especially in the C section, which emerges with
a delicate, graceful quality. What Fischer's orchestration, with its contrast of wind and
strings, has effectively accomplished is the recontextualization of Brahms's piece, here,
into the world of operetta; for example, the overture to Strauss's *Zigeunerbaron*. In
Strauss, the orchestral sections sometimes function as choirs, and frequently play in
isolation from one another.

But once again, the unfortunate aspect of Fischer's rendering is orchestral limitations — in the repeats of the A and B, for example, nothing really happens: this is
a static example. Thus, I would argue that Fischer, at least in this example of what he
himself acknowledges as the most popular of the twenty-one dances, has not lived up
to his claim of bringing the music closer to "Gypsy" sources.

MUSICAL EXAGGERATIONS, GYPSINESS, AND AUDIENCES

We have tried to indicate how the twists, turns, and surprises of the melody of the
fifth "Hungarian Dance" appeal to a sense of primitive emotion, impulses, and perhaps barely checked primal urges. What Deleuze would call the passage to the "deterritorial principle," the nomadic uprooting of fixed places. In the Western concert hall,
this Dance can be experienced as the direct articulation of ecstatic immediacy in

music. Listeners encounter this music as the opposite extreme of the Austro-Germanic symphony — marked by "development" and "motive." Furthermore, the Dance usually occurs, appropriately enough, as an encore (i.e. not written into the program) to an evening of symphonic music, perhaps Beethoven. The conductor might even announce from the stage that it is none other than Brahms who wrote the music, reinforcing the audience's preference for the masters.

Yet to problematize this reception for a moment: what do audiences think they are hearing? What do they know about this music? The title of the piece marks the music as "Hungarian," but what is "Hungarian?" My sense of this is that audiences interpret this piece as a mode of "exaggeration" of pure musical style.[25] That is, as an analogy, the fifth "Hungarian Dance" is to art music what Dinicu's "Lark" is to Gypsy restaurant music: not something "real" in-itself, but a fantastic, marked, pseudo-virtuosic showpiece which calls to music as display, bragging, and exaggeration (music as an impressive rhetorical strategy).

What I mean here by exaggeration can perhaps best be approached through a literary example. Kierkegaard's analysis of seduction serves as an excellent point of comparison: when Faust seduces Margarete, it is through hyperbole and linguistic exaggeration, through the *promise* of earthly love beyond God. In a remarkable passage, Kierkegaard assumes Margarete's inner voice:

> God in heaven, forgive me for loving a human being more than I loved you, and yet I still do it; I know that it is a new sin that I speak this way to you. O Eternal Love, let your mercy hold me, do not thrust me away; give him back to me, incline his heart to me again; have mercy on me God of mercy, that I pray this way again![26]

Faust has implanted in Margarete a burning desire for sexual consummation; she cannot defend herself from this desire. Faust exaggerates to Margarete, he knows that the completion of his seduction will not alleviate his desire, for it is actually full presence that he seeks (summarized in the lines *"verweile doch, du bist so schön"*). Lingering, the moment that stays, this is what musical exaggeration seeks: it does not want to leave. This is precisely what we heard in the string swells of the *poco ritard* of the *Vivace* (see Music Example 6).

Still, Brahms's calling of the piece "Hungarian" has effectively continued to throw many people off the track of obvious elements of what I propose is really "Gypsiness." As indicated in Chapter One, I define Gypsiness as the set of ideas, both real and imagined, about the substance, really performance of Gypsy music. We have summarized this in the mock equation I+V=E, where again "E" stands for the emerging emotion, "I" for improvisation sparked by the moment, and "V" for the athleticism of a sparkling virtuosity. With each of these elements, what is important in performance is their exaggeration, not that they are actually present. I think that this equation and its exaggeration through seductive qualities *in* the music explains to a great extent the astounding success of the *Hungarian Dances* when played by orchestra.

Still, perhaps only emotion (E) and virtuosity (V) are actually felt (whether imagined or not, or in the musicians or the listeners; this is beside the point) in any performance of a Western "work" in that in this music culture, the principle of improvisation (I) has been neglected since Beethoven. Yet even the event of emotion in Gypsiness is beyond and outside the abstract machinery of the serious music. Pure, undiluted musical emotion as energy/force, as close to sexual desire as music ever gets; this was also the aesthetic goal of late or high Romanticism. A kind of musical Ecstasy (to shift the signification of the "E").

Yet the difficulty remains that the dance trace in Brahms's *Hungarian Dances* is not *Tanz* in the sense of the "Deutscher" of Haydn (*Deutscher Tänze*) or of Mozart (as in its insertion in the overlapping dance strategy in the Finale to Act I in *Don Giovanni*). One way of delineating this trace, which we will maintain is not dance in any prior received sense of the word, is to insist on the figure of desire as sexual immediacy, experienced as undiluted melody via temporal variety. Furthermore, we may ask: what is a dance as a work, and one attenuated by "Hungarian" that seems possible only with reference to what is absent, to Gypsy and Gypsiness?

DIALECT(IC)S OF MUSIC HISTORY

The *Hungarian Dances* cannot exist without their dialectic partners found in the opposing genres of the multi-movement sonatas forms. Tied to these latter forms are the claims of nascent Austro-German nationalism, which sought an experience of music that was ethical, moral, and above all thoughtful. Musical composition as the intellections of *Geist*, as work (*Werk* in all its ambiguities), where Beauty merges with the Good in Platonic hypostasis.

Thus to understand the phenomenon represented by the *Hungarian Dances*, their difference as Derridean *différance*,[27] one must simultaneously grasp their jettisoning by the moral and aesthetic strategy of the philosophy of music. This aesthetic history of the work is now viewed by champions of musical progress, by musicologists and philosophers (Lydia Goehr et al.) whose subtext is a music history as first the triumph of the work as formal complexity (Viennese structural preoccupations) and later harmonic expansion/revolution (from Beethoven to Schumann to Liszt to Wagner to Schoenberg to Webern). Music outside of nationalism, of ethnicity, of body, of sexuality, of dance. Pure music, absolute music, boundless context, endless melody. And when music gets mixed up with literature, program, or text (Berlioz, Liszt, Wagner), it can be always defended on philosophical grounds for its latent musical content and energy.

In the twentieth century it was the ideal of folk music for artistic circles that presented the first challenge to the hegemony of the composed work. But Bartók's and Stravinsky's folk-inspired music were criticized by both Schoenberg and later Adorno.[28] Indeed, Adorno's resolute dismissals of commercial music, of jazz, of popular music, of folk can be read as Steppenwolf-like, as the conscious rejection of what one really desires. Despite Adorno's protest Stravinsky has now been fully accepted by the establishment. And there exists today a growing musicological and analytical camp of Bartók enthusiasts and defenders, chief among them Elliott Antokoletz, who are analyzing his music with an analytical rigor previously only granted to a few major composers, justifying his promotion to the title of major composer.

The writing of history thus presupposes a massive and perhaps overwhelming philosophical heritage. What is music supposed to do? What is its purpose? What is the end of music? Since at least Hanslick, who relies on Kant, such questions are ascertained within a theory of perception. How does the mind perceive a "musical" (read: conscious) sonic event? Hanslick's famous answer is "*töned bewegte Formen*," or "forms moved in sounding." Every paradox of *Geist* is summoned here: form as the thoughtful application of mind (*Geist*) on a content (melody, emotion) that turns out not to exist, or only exists through formal procedures of mind. A strange alliance here, and perhaps a circularity, between formalism and historiography: the "important" composers in the West turn out to be masters of structural detail.

What is at stake here, behind and in front of these discourses on musical language: the history of musical decision, of what constitutes a compositional choice, of the consciousness organizing musical events into structure.

With the melodic impulse and Gypsiness of the *Hungarian Dances*, music historiography deconstructs itself around the figure of arrangement, of what Schoenberg calls the potpourri of musical ideas. Pasting themes together, *cutting* them up, without any musical logic, without *Geist*, the absence of work: those features that are not "developing variation," escaping the purview of musicology are also the ironic features of musical language or "dialect" that most easily speak to and aurally "touch" audiences.

IMMEDIACY AND ETHNOMUSICOLOGY

If there exists a constant and built-in imprecision in the historiography of Western music, one that I have tried to show through the prism of Brahms's Hapsburg, Hungarian-style Gypsiness, this imprecision also shows up in ethnography. Again, the goal of writing up the other is to preserve authenticity, the full presence and immediacy of the Other as a unique face, to use the language of Levinas.[29]

Bartók tried to capture "pure" folk music as authenticity by preserving as many possible variants of each melody he notated, as if a statistical average would tell us what the tune actually is. Yet when writing about musical influence, Bartók sometimes, perhaps unconsciously, reverts to a Hungarian nationalist perspective:[30]

Therefore, if we analyze the 'Rákóczi March' we find in it elements originating from the Arabic-Persian 'long melody,' Eastern European-Hungarian elements, and ornamental motives of Central European art music: quite a collection of the most heterogeneous elements! Nevertheless, the way they are transformed, melted, and unified presents as a final result a masterpiece of music whose spirit and characteristics are incontestably Hungarian.[31]

Fascinating about this passage is that Bartók speaks first as an ethnomusicologist, cobbling together a nice assortment of heterogeneous source elements, then abruptly, he switches gears into the language of high Romantic nationalism, that the spiritual ground of the March is actually, "incontestably" Hungarian. Strategically, a complete reversal of Liszt's idea that the "Rákóczi March" is not really Hungarian, but actually Gypsy. My point in highlighting this passage is not to argue or introduce new evidence about the obscure origins of the "Rákóczi March," but rather to show how slippery, and really arbitrary, the discourse of authenticity and national attribution actually is.

How can we ever know what the "Rákóczi March" is? Only through musical immediacy, through the emotional turbulence of performance.[32] And this also negates the primary goal of ethnomusicology, to represent scientifically/objectively the musical utterance/act/signified in its cultural context, in its social significance, as if this were to analyze what it *really is*. Is it ever possible to do understand phenomena like the "Rákóczi March," when our own language is always already disseminated, caught in the infinite regress/play of signifiers?

The statement of "whateverness," as the philosopher Giorgio Agamben puts it, the idea that a predicate is part of a set but not really: pure singularity can never belong to a set, it can never be identified.[33] Yet it exists *as such*, hence the term "whatever" to denote its being. Does not all music exhibit "whatever being," significant in its relationship to the totality of possibilities, yet never determined as such by these possibilities? Might this describe the relationship of immediacy to the *Hungarian Dances*, despite any ethnomusicological protest to the contrary?

Whatever-being indicates the contemporary classification of a phenomenon like Gypsy music. In an unpublished paper[34] I have tried to understand why Gypsy CDs get put into a Gypsy music bin, an anomalous area found in the World Music section of CD stores like Borders or Tower for at least the last decade or so (I will return to this in the final chapter). In this bin we find mostly Eastern-European and sometimes Russian music; where is flamenco? Flamenco has its own bin, we find out, over next to the Spanish section. Though it might be perhaps seem at first banal to study such commercial phenomena, still, it seems to mask something deeper in the West's understanding of Gypsy music. American and I would suggest West-European audiences turn to Gypsy music for exotic reasons of experiencing the music of the sensual, dark other. Gypsy music is one way among others to satisfy this need for abandonment of the social premises of enforced whiteness in the bland social reality of the "administered world."

I would argue that the existence of the Gypsy music bin taints any search, on both a meta- and grassroots level, for a "real" Gypsy or Roma music. For the signifier is already displaced, thrown out into what Deleuze calls the "smooth space" of nomadic territory.

Take Tony Gatlif's 1993 film *Latcho drom*, analyzed in Chapter Ten. Without language, without discourse, without plot, without external narrative, Gatlif presents eight scenes of Gypsy life, from Rajasthan, to Upper Egypt, to Istanbul, to Bucharest and then Clejani, Romania, to Hungary, to the Slovakian-Polish border, finally to France and Spain. In each of these scenes music performance emerges as the unifying thread. We watch gradually as the *kemache* becomes the violin, how the vocal cry gets less erratic, how the cymbaloms become guitars, how the musical act changes from desert to village to the raw edge of urban life. As if the Gypsy diaspora contained within itself half of the entire content of world-music history, in a single, poetic, and filmed vision. I insist on this *filmed aspect*: filming becomes the truth, *aufgehebt*, of music today, in a postindustrial dawn (we could follow the metaphor of light and fire in metaphors of Gypsiness) obsessed with visual images, with the spectrums of web banners, with anything that can be seen or shown visibility.

How does fieldwork, or even ethnomusicology, account for such commercial products of late capitalism? I pose this as an open question, to be discussed in Chapter Eleven. My suspicion, again, is that these products call into question the endeavors of fieldwork, by displacement, by spectral visions of Gypsiness, especially as now there is a burgeoning consciousness of "Roma-ness" throughout the world, as witnessed by the successes of outreach of various Roma-rights organizations. Roma have never been more aware of the connections of various Gypsy groups, sometimes separated by centuries. Again, these connections are taken for granted in films like *Latcho drom*, CDs like *Road of the Gypsies* and even in some recent ethnographic writing.

I am not trying to suggest that fieldwork on the Roma ceases, but rather that its epistemological stance toward its subject changes. For the strategies of promoting Gypsy music have become the smokescreen for many things that I have mentioned at the beginning of the chapter, and should be understood as a marketing: as a funnel of musical expression that aims at immediacy in emotion through any available means.

INTEREST AND STRATEGIES OF ADVOCACY

What other composer, besides Liszt, has been an open advocate for Gypsy music? Who has championed its cause? Who takes an interest in Gypsy music when writing music history?

Yet again, what is the *interest*, however, behind a pure consideration of music *as* music? Why are we interested? Why study, investigate, analyze music — what motivates our projects? Is there a hidden economy? Can we imagine — is it possible — to have a discussion of music that *remains* above this economy, perhaps beyond, any interest calculated as debt, outside of music? Recalling Kant's claim in his aesthetics, that the interest in the beautiful should be disinterested, what would this means in economic terms, applied to music? Do we not sense an interest, motivated by commercial gain, for any discourse on music?

We began with Brahms's fifth "Hungarian Dance," but what is the interest for writing such a piece? Adorno would see this piece as yet another instance of bourgeois trash, the forgetfulness of mass culture; he would not view it worthy of musical interpretation except only insofar as it exhibits the cultural contradictions inherent in capitalist economy.

My interest in Brahms's fifth "Hungarian Dance" is that I see it as an articulation of Gypsiness in music, again, exemplified in the immediacy of the mock equation "I+V=E." Yet the equation does not exist in Brahms unless we are advocates of Gypsy music. However, as an advocate, I am well aware of the cultural contradictions of Gypsy music, of its commerciality and marketing, yet simultaneously its qualified reality, authenticity, and mystique. In advocating a dissemination of Gypsiness in music, I am trying to displace and loosen notions of hierarchy, ranking, and musical progress in Western music history, and also of "purity" in folk music research. As the deconstruction of Gypsy music continues, however, I am not proposing immediacy, exaggeration, or Gypsiness as stable/closed categories; rather, I believe a very different Brahms, not to mention a host of other nineteenth-century composers that we will turn to in the following chapters, as well as present-day Gypsy music, will emerge as these categories continue to evolve.

Chapter Six

The Poetics of Gypsiness in Liszt's *Hungarian Rhapsodies*

By the word "Rhapsody" the intention has been to designate the fantastically *epic* [Liszt's emphasis] element which we deem this music to contain. Each one of these productions has always seemed to us to form part of a poetic cycle, remarkable by the unity of its inspiration, eminently *national* [my emphasis]. The conditions of this unity are fulfilled by the music belonging exclusively to the one people whose soul and intimate sentiments it accurately depicts.... These pieces do not recount facts, it is true. But those who know how to listen will easily catch from them the expression of the states of the soul, forming a compendium of the *nation's* ideal [my emphasis]. That nation may be one of Pariahs; that is no concern of art.

Liszt, Gypsy in Music, 337

Every serious musician should be able to turn himself into a Gypsy, if only the short time it takes to play a Hungarian rhapsody by Liszt. For this is the territory of the Gypsy *par excellence.* Then he will know intuitively what Liszt meant by 'tempo rubato' or 'quasi recitativo'; he will know that bar lines are not important events in the life of a piece of music to be triumphantly demonstrated by vicious and unnecessary accents, but merely facilities for reading, accents being a means of expression, only to be used as such (and very often in opposition to the beat); that 'fast' and 'slow' are relative terms dependent on musical judgment, not on the sporting standard of what is physically possible — all this and a lot more.

Louis Kentner, "The Interpretation of Liszt's Piano Music"

During the Romantic era, the performative of Gypsiness became recognized stylistically as an alternative site to Western performance practice. Perhaps nowhere is this more adequately illustrated than in Liszt's *Hungarian Rhapsodies*. Indeed, the *Rhapsodies* are a site for locating the turbulence of Liszt's own search for a national identity.[1] As such he worked this out through his synthesis of a Hungarian-Gypsy art music, where the world assumes a specifically *national* understanding. Ironically, what was intended partially as a vindication for Gypsy musicians ended up becoming a lightening rod for rallying Hungarian national sentiment, at the expense of Gypsy music.

In short, we shall argue that the nationalist fallout from the debates over Liszt has essentially shifted attention away from the nuanced yet powerful impact of Gypsiness on Western music and thinking. It also seems to have a set a pattern, in that controversy or debate seem to erupt whenever Gypsy music reaches a heightened profile or visibility in the public sphere. Despite the existence of the genre of rhapsody before Liszt, Liszt was the first to establish a connection between the idea of the national and rhapsody.[2] And this proved to have important consequences, as witnessed by the rhapsodies of a host of other so-called "national" composers, including ones by Bartók and Enescu, and indirectly in the genre of the ethnically inspired national dances as in Dvořák, Grieg, Granados, and others.

Liszt's formulation of Rhapsody at mid-century constitutes the first rigorous attempt to bridge the aesthetic chasm separating Western art music and Gypsy music. This he accomplished in two ways, first, the publication of the *Hungarian Rhapsodies* (numbers one through fifteen appeared in two versions between 1847-1853), and then in his book, *Des Bohémiens et de leur Musique en Hongrie* (1859), published later in English as *The Gypsy in Music*. Haunting the book is the question of authorship; most commentators have held that Princess Caroline Sayn-Wittgenstein composed large portions of the book.[3] Originally conceived as a preface to the *Rhapsodies*, the book provides the philosophical justification for these works.[4] Liszt's task is to explain how the national substance of the *Rhapsodies* becomes possible through the interpenetration and imbrication of two distinct cultures, the Hungarian and the Gypsy, the former as audience and the latter as players. Dialectically, Michael Beckerman has proposed that Liszt composed his *Hungarian Rhapsodies* as a "fundamental argument against Germanness, the opposing realm, in which improvisation, virtuosity and emotion are, if not banished, carefully subordinated to the grand intellectual design."[5]

The negative reception of Liszt's ideas from the Hungarians has provided the mould for the critique of Gypsy music ever since. Writing in the early 1860s, Lajos Újfalussy held that Gypsy musicians do not possess their own national music; instead, they prey upon their host country, be it Spain, Wallachia (what is today Southern Romania), or Germany, among others.[6] In terms of this dependency on other music cultures, it is not hard to determine how Gypsy musicians are open to marginalization: "not even the best Gypsy dared to present himself as a composer" (Újfalussy). To be sure, in these nationalistic debates the central critical concern was over the Hungarian origins and provenance of the melodic material that Liszt had dubbed as uniquely "Gypsy"; this would persist in the criticism of Bartók, discussed in Chapter Ten.

Yet another of Liszt's opponents, Sámuel Brassai, also criticized the Gypsy manner of performance. He maintained that Gypsy ornamentation was no more

> than the crumbs picked up from modern European virtuosity, of which crumbs the irregularity so much extolled by you [Liszt] originates not in the independence of the idealized Gypsy character but from the imperfections of amateurish study, and which is to be experienced in every so-called 'natural' whether he is Gypsy or not...[7]

It is interesting that this kind of criticism is rarely encountered in the political correct world of today; if anything, the imperfections of amateurish study are used to buttress the search for greater authenticity in the approach to alleged "folk" material.

The reception of Liszt's *Rhapsodies* is rife with contradictions. For example, Claude Rostand wrote in 1960 that:

> In fact, these *Rhapsodies* are not Hungarian at all; they are pure Gypsy music, just as are Brahms's famous Dances. But Liszt did not know this. By his time, genuine, native Magyar music had almost entirely disappeared, or at least it only existed in the depths of certain parts of the countryside. This is what two musicians, Béla Bartók and Zoltán Kodály, were to show at the beginning of the twentieth century when they unearthed authentic Hungarian melodies and rhythms, whose appeal is very different from the Gypsy music that had exclusively inspired the conception and indeed the instrumental style of Liszt's *Rhapsodies*.[8]

Of course, Rostand is bothered that Liszt did not call the *Rhapsodies* "Gypsy," and that Liszt saw Gypsies as possible only within the space of Hungarian culture. But Rostand has essentially misunderstood Liszt — "Hungarian," again, was a tribute to the audience, to those who "adopted the Bohemians as national musicians."[9] Liszt thought that without the Hungarian environment, Bohemian music would never have achieved the state of development that it reached. If anything, Liszt did understand the *Rhapsodies* as Bohemian — nowhere in the *Rhapsodies* could we imagine such as an emotionally charged indication for a Hungarian label as "*im trotzigem, tiefsinnigen Zigeuner-Stil vorzutragen*" of "Rhapsody no. 7" ("To be played in the Gypsy style, defiant, and yet melancholy"). Furthermore, we might ask of Rostand, what is "pure" Gypsy music in the Romantic context? It is not clear that anyone — even Gypsies themselves — would see the Hungarian-Gypsy style of the *Rhapsodies* as exemplifying "pure" Gypsy music.

In contrast to Rostand stands Jonathan Bellman's view of the *Rhapsodies*. As we have already noted, Bellman's perhaps most significant contribution to the matter is his musical lexicon for understanding the *style hongrois*. Again, he defines the phenomenon as the "specific musical language used by Western composers... to evoke the performances of Hungarian Gypsies."[10] Following Sárosi,[11] however, the "musical materials" of the style "are almost exclusively Hungarian in origin";[12] the Gypsy side denotes the mere "performance characteristics" of it.[13] Thus, in Bellman's opinion, "for all his good intentions, Liszt was of course quite wrong about the origins of the music [*Rhapsodies*]; as we have seen, they were unquestionably Hungarian."[14] Bellman also seems to disapprove of the performance tradition of the pieces themselves:

> What today can, in unsympathetic hands, seem to be his trashiest compositions are really those that came out of the deepest part of him: the effortless virtuoso, the wanderer, the disappointed bearer of nameless griefs, the self-styled Gypsy.[15]

However, what do we really know about the ethnic provenance of the verbunkos as source and origin for the *style hongrois?* What can we know, given that no recordings of Hungarian-Gypsies exist during this time, as Bellman acknowledges?[16] How can he and Sárosi, for that matter, be so sure about the propriety of what is largely an oral, popular repertory? We would argue that the discourse which determines the propriety of "national" music is problematically linked (whether consciously or not) to vested interest in the national apparatus. Namely, whoever and whatever possess the right and means to research will also be in control of the outcome. In terms of this dynamic, Hungarian musicologists perhaps feel compromised by the Austro-Germanic claim to superiority in music, as buttressed by greater institutional power. Beginning with Bartók and Kodály, the Hungarians tried to stake their claim in the hierarchical ordering of the musical world; they perhaps realized that they must first establish Hungarian music as a pure, original, and real national style. And we can question the concept underneath of this musical politics of propriety: for, what is the concept of a "musical language" as a national one? Does music admit of national (ethnic) utterance? And, what would it mean to "speak" for the nation, through a musical work? On the surface, discussions like Bellman's recall a nineteenth-century orientation — languages have been thought to express the essence of a national "spirit" since Humboldt's influential and groundbreaking work on the topic in the early part of that century.[17]

Thus the even deeper philosophical questions remain: is it possible in a musical work to speak for the nation, beyond the individual? What distance separates the individual from the collective, and how does music bridge this gap? If the myth of nearness and its corollary, the obliteration of distance, are what constitutes the nation, then what are the specifically musical consequences of this contraction of the parameter of space?[18]

One avenue for investigating these kinds of question is the figure of the virtuoso, he who brings the culture closer to its own music.[19] He possesses the power to give the music to the audience because he "possesses" the music, as it were. The virtuoso also the reinvents his instrument in the process, marking a dynamic moment in the history of a particular instrument. Now, the problem of Liszt's virtuosity is that it is caught up in ontological questions about the status of music, especially what amounts to as his own virtuosic discovery of Gypsiness. Liszt's understanding of this is how musical composition is realized: either is it determined by formal rules (what we have seen as "Germanness"), or through the poetic idea (*poetischen Gedanken*). Gypsiness, insofar as it is can be understood as a subtype of program music, falls on the side of the poetic idea. We can trace this search for the *poetischen Gedanken* in Liszt's first attempts at a synthesis of virtuosic piano music with the Hungarian-Gypsy impetus.

THE CONTEXT OF THE *RHAPSODIES*

The 1840 series of pieces called *Magyar Dallok* ("Hungarian National Melodies") were probably based on melodies that Liszt heard at Gypsy camps during his 1839-40 trip to Hungary.[20] Here, Liszt first formulated the idea of a Hungarian music that would eventually crystallize in the *Hungarian Rhapsodies*. The *Rhapsodies* (nos. 1-15) represent the final phase of the project, and anticipate the next set of compositions for piano based on thematic transformation, especially the B minor Sonata.

In his last two years of touring as a virtuoso Liszt visited Hungary, Transylvania, the Ukraine and Turkey; the enthusiasm over these appearances marks Liszt at the height of his powers.[21] Politically significant in Hungarian speaking areas was his performance and improvisations on the "Rákóczi" March (mentioned in the previous chapter in connection with Bartók), a tune that represented Hungarian national aspirations, to the dismay of the Saxon aristocrats of Transylvania.

Liszt heard numerous Gypsy bands on his tour. He frequently requested to have Gypsy musicians brought to him, and notated popular melodies he heard in a sketchbook.[22] In Klausenburg (Transylvania, present-day Romania) Liszt gave four triumphant concerts, consulting with Count Sándor Teleki on who were the best Gypsy musicians.[23] Count Teleki in his *Memoirs* provides an insightful glimpse into Liszt's search for Gypsy music:

> One evening they were chatting when Liszt turned to Teleki and said, 'I would like to hear some Gypsy music. Tell me, who is the best Gypsy musician in Hungary now?'

> 'Károly Boka in Debrecen, or Laci Pócsi at Sziget,' Teleki replied.

> 'But isn't there anyone here?'

'Of course. They are very good, but they are German Gypsies playing from the notes, and you are already familiar with them. You need the "uncivilized" sort, because the Gypsies who play from notes are partly *Künstler*.'

'When I visit you at Koltó will you send for an "uncivilized" band there? I would very much like to hear them.'[24]

Walker uncritically accepts such accounts/stories as facts. Memoirs as a genre are notoriously full of hyperbole and the tendency for exaggeration and even deletion, especially when such texts contain reminiscences of talks with famous personages. And note that Teleki's memoirs were not published until 1879, more than thirty years after this discussion allegedly occurred.

In any case, the startling opposition that emerges from this alleged request on Liszt's part is the one between the uncivilized musician versus *Künstler*. The pianist Louis Kentner notes the distinction in German of "Musiker" versus "Musikant":

> The German language has a subtle distinction unknown to English: a 'Musiker' is simply a musician (he could be a composer, conductor, instrumentalist or singer); a 'Musikant', however, is one who is not, strictly speaking, a concert artist but more like an entertainer mainly concerned with the lighter kind of music, a player in a band, a *Gypsy fiddler*, a bar pianist — all these come under the heading 'Musikant.' Not using the term in any pejorative sense, it could mean a musician not spoilt by too much erudition (or too little knowledge), ardent, instinctive, earthy, untamed, a savage with savage rhythm still in his blood, and a natural-born aptitude for his instrument — the Hungarian Gypsy or the Negro jazz player for instant — the naturalistic yet sophisticate 'Musikant.' Now, if all Musiker had a little of the Musikant in their make-up, the world of music would be a better place to live in.[25] (my emphasis)

For Liszt, Gypsy bands lose their passionate soul, their uncivilized essence, when they become educated — in Kentner's terms, it is better for them to remain Musikant.[26]

Teleki could have learned of this opposition from Liszt's own book. There Liszt writes about the "civilized" musicians who encounter Gypsy scales, and he refers to Beethoven and Schubert as "civilized."[27] Indeed, it is because of the encroachment of civilization that Gypsy music has declined:

> By way of punishment for the fault they had committed in giving themselves up to a sordid interest the Bohemians were gradually compelled to sacrifice their art and mix up the passionate accents of their adorable melodies with romances, cavatinas and pot-pourris in order to secure and retain their listeners.[28]

and later on:

Our Bohemians, therefore, once having entered the universal forum, could no longer dispense with playing Meyerbeer and Donizetti; Strauss and Lanner. Soon, no doubt, we shall hear them giving some Mendelssohn, Schumann, Berlioz and Wagner at their concerts. They, the immediate children of fantasy and pure inspiration, will now dispose themselves to recite productions due to reflection and thought![29]

The decline of Gypsy music is when it is out of its element. It becomes something else, taking on the light or trivial music of civilization: cavatinas and potpourris of opera tunes. For Liszt this is the trade-off of art for money, in that light music secures and retains casual and amateur listeners (similar to the cry raised by Schumann against the philistines). From performances of Meyerbeer and Donizetti, Liszt predicts that Gypsy bands will soon turn to Mendelssohn and Schumann (composers who for Liszt are provincial, at this point in his career), Berlioz and Wagner. Musical performance then becomes dry recitation, part of thinking and reflection, and loses its fantastic inspiration, its magical response to the moment.

THE ILLUSION OF WISH-FULFILLMENT

Because of his national "homelessness," Liszt's attraction to the Hungarian-Gypsy figure is neither nationalism nor proto-nationalism *per se*, but rather a case where *wish-fulfillment* impacts the construction of reality. Freud writes that what is "characteristic of illusions is that they are derived from human wishes."[30] They are not errors (e.g., Aristotle's belief that vermin come from dung). Illusions come close to psychiatric delusions, though illusions need not be in contradiction to reality or false.

Wish-fulfillment can be a driving force of a nationalist statement, yet it need not be. The essence of nationalism comes in the form of a qualitative judgment, where it is asserted that a given culture or race is superior to or better than, in any sense, some other. This is not what occurs in Liszt's vision of Hungarian-Gypsy music. Rather, it is the composer's wish for a direct, immediate, pure music, one not mediated by conventions or artifice: pure emotion, virtuosically transmitted. Romanticism, yet with a *national* impetus; hence the communicative essence that we are calling Gypsiness, once again a magic trick where Improvisation+Virtuosity=Emotion.

In his early Hungarian pieces (marches, fantasies) from the 1830s and 1840s, Liszt's conception of "Hungarian" was heroic. However, it was not the kind of heroism as exhibited in the complicated Beethovenian sense of triumph of the will over suffering. Rather, Liszt sought the direct manifestation of the heroic via the related category of the revolutionary-military, where content emerges as a pure triumph. Perhaps what made this coupling of categories so immediately attractive as art was the economic and social importance granted to the soldier through the Napoleonic wars. The officer-soldier was no longer disparaged; as a professional path it offered the chance for upward mobility to ambitious members of the peasant classes (see Stendhal's *Red and Black*). As further evidence for this, Hungarian music contained such strong military associations that its principle dance (the *Magyar*, the "Hungarian) later became known in German musicology as *verbunkos*, a translation for the German *Werbung*.[31]

The trip Liszt made to Hungary in 1839-40, culminating in his acceptance of the ceremonial "sword of honor," has already received much critical attention and derision from biographers.[32] What is usually noted about this trip is the psychological significance that Liszt's native Hungary from then on assumes. Expanding on this interpretation, we will signal the existence of a number of overlapping factors that impacted Liszt at this time: military aspirations for a Hungarian nation by the nobility (culminating in the failed 1848 revolution), Liszt's own search for a national identity, and encounters with Gypsy music. Whatever the relationships of these categories are, there is no doubt that they became conflated during the 1840s, culminating in the 1846-47 Hungarian tour, and finding a final realization in the *Rhapsodies*.

THE TRANSCENDENTAL STUDIES COMPARED WITH THE *RHAPSODIES*

As a point of comparison for the *Hungarian Rhapsodies*, let us take another set of pieces, the *Transcendental Etudes*, an early set Liszt dedicated to his teacher, Carl Czerny. Incidentally, we could also have chosen the *Paganini Studies* and would achieve similar results in the comparison. Like the *Rhapsodies* and other works from the early periods, Liszt continually revised the *Transcendental Studies*; though most were probably fixed by the late 1830s; Liszt's 1851 version is the definitive one today, and the one that bears the programmatic titles.

The notions of revision, renewal, and reformulation are themselves major elements in the unfolding of Gypsiness, especially when they are encoded as a deconstruction of the principles of Western art music. It is the opposite of the Romantic-Modernist myth of the composer who, working in isolation for perhaps years, reaches a definitive, immutable, and perfect rendering of an idea, substantiated in a work.

The aesthetic of revisionism is part of the ongoing, fleeting activity of the virtuoso. Furthermore, insofar as the virtuoso changes the culture's relationship to an instrument, he raises the technical level to the point that it can never go back (one thinks immediately of Paganini's *Caprices* but also Beethoven's *Hammerklavier*, both treasured by Liszt). This dynamic relationship of the virtuoso to his instrument repeats itself on the level of composition, which must be continually renewed.

With the exceptions of no. 4, "Mazeppa," and no. 9, "Ricordanza," these *Studies* do not possess the communicative power of the *Rhapsodies*. (The figure of Byron's and

Hugo's *Mazeppa*, a Polish count punished for amorous transgressions, exerted an enormous influence on the composer, as also seen in the tone poem of the same title.) In short, though Liszt's *Etudes* are masterworks in their own right, still, they do not seem to reach the profound, emotional, Romantic depths of the *Rhapsodies*; in their defense, as studies, perhaps they were never intended to. Indeed, the mechanical and predictable content of the *Studies* lies within the conventions of Western art music; they do not show the desire of what we have designated as wish-fulfillment. More specifically, there is neither a *national*, nor a Gypsy element in these studies, nor is there a personal desire on Liszt's part to create something beyond performance *as* performance. The "Prélude" (no. 1) clearly shows the keyboard as what it can be (see Music Example 8). In this music we hear gestures, figurations, with definite musical content (such as the rising chromatic line), but if this music conveys passion, it does so only in the act of performance.[33] Even the "Eroica" is lacking in national substance. The music at *Tempo di Marcia* lacks the dramatic military aspect of the forward movement of soldiers (see Music Example 9).

MUSICAL CONTRADICTIONS AND POETICS

Liszt's poetics reveals the force of creation as renewal. This takes on many guises in Liszt's oeuvre: 1) arrangements of symphonic works (Berlioz's *Symphonie fantastique*), or lieder (Schubert), or operas (*Don Giovanni*); 2) the reworking and sometimes republication of his own pieces; 3) pieces based on landscapes, monuments, or definite geographical locations (*Années de pilgrimage*); 4) literary-character studies (Mazeppa, Faust); 5) non-commitment to traditional forms, or their rethinking (B-minor sonata); 6) pieces based on national tunes (Hungarian czárdás, melodies, rhapsodies).

Music Example 8 "Prélude" no. 1 from Liszt's *Transcendental Studies*, measure 13-15.

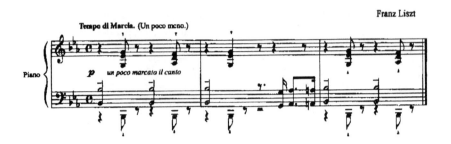

Music Example 9 "Eroica," no. 7, "Tempo di Marcia," from Liszt's *Transcendental Studies.*

However, there are ontological distinctions within each of these categories that reveal differences in approach to *poiesis.* We cannot reconstitute here each of these differences, which would be a massive task. But to focus on one: the rhapsodic as revelation. Revelation means the power of uncovering, but also of preserving what was once covered.

What Liszt achieves in the *Rhapsodies* can be called "poetic music beyond poetics."[34] Poetics as inside and outside, at once but not (n)ever. This is the truth of the poetic: to reach outside of the poetic, which can only stand for static, representational truth. A correspondence that cannot be conceptualized nor ever present (see the next section). The *Rhapsodies* are paradoxically the power of musical language that brings language into its own (*Eignen*), an appropriative event (*Ereignis*) that cannot be reduced to a predicative statement. We shall try to bring this into clarity through the idea of contradiction, where saying receives itself through its opposite.

Carl Dahlhaus argues that the poetic category "thrives on its own contradictions."[35] The contradiction concerns the location of the poetic within the two broadest areas of aesthetic debate during the nineteenth century, on the one hand that over the primacy of vocal versus instrumental music, on the other between program versus absolute music. Without going into the details of these debates here, the point in understanding Liszt is to grasp the "similarities of conception between absolute and program music than to stress their opposition."[36] The idea of poetic, for Dahlhaus, is thus negotiated by Liszt not through the "literalization" of music; rather that the "composer succeeds, as it were, in picking up the *thread* of a major work of literature."[37] Pushing this idea, which Dahlhaus applies to the *Sonetto 47 del Petrarco*[38]: what happens when a composer picks up a *thread* from something considered "minor" by adherents of technical progress in music, a substance like Gypsy music?

Here, precisely, we experience the turbulence of thinking the *Rhapsodies* as poetic music that reveals while knotting, which is exactly the way Liszt conceived of this music.[39] Because so many commentators are stuck worrying over whether or not Liszt is truly a "great" composer (a non-issue for us), the ontology of his music is simply overlooked and missed. If we can convincingly trace the process of aural binding and tying in pieces like the *Rhapsodies*, we will understand the musical revolution around the contradictory figure of the poetic that constitutes nineteenth-century Romanticism.

CREATION CONTRA THE VIRTUOSIC PERFORMATIVE

We have tried in the previous section to use hyperbole, the instability of the deconstructive nerve, to expose the poetic as something not within itself, as contradiction itself. This turns out to be the revolution that has been called Romanticism in music, which in fact has never ceased.

Insofar as Romanticism entails a re-thinking of the performative, the significance of virtuosity increases. The discourse of this virtuosity was from the beginning masculine and, surprisingly, moral; Liszt writes:

> The words virtuosity and virtue have both their origin in the Latin *vir*; the exercise of one as much as the other being an act of masculine power. Whoever has not the faculty of engendering an ideal type, fruit of the transports of love for ideal beauty, can neither be virtuose nor virtuous.[40]

Liszt's argument is a form of popular Platonism, where the idea of the Good and the Beautiful "can never radically detach one from the other."[41] Thus the goal of the virtuoso is to enact this equivalency, so that the listener may realize that every beautiful deed (or performance) is also a good one.

Historically Liszt is perhaps the first virtuoso who justified his approach to performance through writing. Susan Bernstein tries to relate this dichotomy of performer/author in Liszt to the "Homeric" question of the nineteenth century, as in Nietzsche. The debate in Homeric studies is on whether or not there is a single author, "Homer," or if this is not a convenience for naming the rhapsodes, the performers/quasi-creators of the epics. Her point is well taken, and relevant for Liszt, since he himself picks up on the image of the rhapsodists and Homer.[42] Yet her own discourse deconstructs itself precisely around the question of the analogy of language and music:

> The untranslatability of reading in this context reasserts the heterogeneity of language and music, despite the many parallels that have been drawn here. On the one hand, the relationships poet/rhapsode and composer/virtuoso are in fact different versions of the *structure instituting* the standard of authorial original and the subordination of execution and reproduction. At the same time these terms have their own specificity; it is important to retain a sense of their difference and to not thoroughly reduce the relation composer/virtuoso to a literary model.[43]

What and who are *instituting*? What is a "structure" in this context? We should pause for a moment on what Bernstein has signaled out in her remarks concerning what appear as structural parallels of these categories of production. Instituting also goes beyond originality and reproduction; it is a form of founding, of granting, and of comporting. It also *transcribes*, which is precisely the mode of composition Liszt is attempting; in this he differs from the rhapsodists.

In her attempts at a poststructuralist reading of Lisztean production, Bernstein wants to interpret the relationship of music and language in multivalent ways, and perhaps too quickly: a distinction between language and music, yet a structuring that sublates (*relève*) a version or representation of their difference for their identity. Indeed, she has hit on a massive issue, which is to name the bind, the tying, or "structure," but she then leaves it without probing. What is structuring? Again, what allows these categories to emerge in the first place?

She continues her argument by setting up the obvious opposition of the virtuoso and his counterpart, the composer. On the one hand she remains sympathetic to Liszt's arguments against Wagner, who represents the composer:

> The proper characteristic of the virtuoso is to have no proper characteristics; the proper quality of extension in time is to efface itself toward the meaning that has prescribed it.[44] For Liszt, the performance is essential and of equal rank with composition, similarly enjoying the status of autonomous art.[45]

Yet she is then equally capable of criticizing Liszt:

> Liszt's claim for the legitimacy of his *Hungarian Rhapsodies* is grounded in their popular and traditional origin. Unfortunately for Liszt, he unwittingly outlines how their presentation, meant as mere editing and repetition, has usurped the position of origin to which he attaches himself…. For the performing position to which he hands over the power cannot be sustained in print; what the virtuoso gains, the author has lost, even if the author is himself the virtuoso he describes.[46]

Bernstein here assumes that the author of a text does not perform. The written word is rigid, fixed as the property of the author. In a previous passage Bernstein also condemns "authorial originality" and the "values, property, and propriety it *institutes*."[47] In contrast, the virtuoso's performance is not text, but the "contradictory moment of productive repetition."[48]

Bernstein's privileging of performance over composition through the characters of the virtuoso and the composer is simply a reversal of the over-emphasis on composers and works in approaches to the Western canon. Further, composition and the written text are neither so rigid nor non-fluid as she thinks: these structures are also open to shifts in interpretation and in value. The whole idea of structure can admit of instability, something imposed on property to grant it a value/price. On the other hand performance is not necessarily as destructive to composition as she thinks;

performance innuendos can be extremely repetitive, part of the same "structural" and mechanistic grammar as composition.

LEGITIMACY AND NATIONALIST WHITEWASH

Despite a kind of musicological upgrade (in stock-market terms, from hold to buy) in recent years, Liszt is still considered by some to be an illegitimate composer. Charles Rosen writes:

> The least respectable side of Liszt is to be found in the Hungarian Rhapsodies: even more than the opera fantasies, this is what has given him a bad reputation, and it is from the fame of these works that his most earnest admirers feel that he must be rescued.[49]

To be fair to Rosen, he goes on to say that passages in the Tenth Rhapsody are "dazzling and enchanting," and that "the real invention concerns texture, density, tone color, and intensity."[50]

Yet this question of legitimacy continues to haunt Liszt studies. Though all seem to agree that Liszt's importance to Western music is deserved, especially because of his overhaul of keyboard technique, still there are doubts about the content of his music. And a significant content is what is found in the *Hungarian Rhapsodies*: nationalist ideas, and Gypsy music. Bartók writes that "it is only these slighter works [the *Rhapsodies*] that have received what is after all only a *national whitewash* [my emphasis, what Bartók means here is Gypsified versions of Hungarian popular songs]; the principle works... are happily exempt from this influence."[51]

ROMANTIC RETREAT VIA GYPSY MUSIC

Liszt retired from performance at age 35 in 1847 at the height of his pianistic powers. This he did because he had grown tired of catering to the public, and wished to preserve the legacy of his own playing.[52] But this is also a major strategy of Romantic mythology, what today we would call a marketing/public-relations strategy: the creation of mystique through withholding oneself. And if Liszt's withholding of his phenomenal keyboard abilities had the effect of increasing his public aura, then we can expect to find traces of mystical retreat in his *Rhapsodies*.

Restated, the publication of the *Rhapsodies* produces the following paradox: Liszt's personal retreat from public performance is not compatible with his triumphing of Gypsy music, and especially its communicative nature. Liszt makes it clear in *The Gypsy in Music* that his *Rhapsodies* represent a "Bohemian Epic," one where the Western listener can experience Gypsy music as Liszt had heard it on his travels in Hungary and Transylvania.

Beyond questions of legitimacy, thus, the problem of the *Rhapsodies* becomes how to understand Liszt's withdrawal from public performance, his personal *resistance* to his own virtuosic power. Only his memory serves to preserve the time when he once performed them, and when he heard Gypsies in their camps. A sweet nostalgia, a love for a time that once was, helps bring us closer to the *Rhapsodies* as legitimate retreat from pianistic performance.

TRANSFORMATION OF WORK

Development, transitions, motives — all the processes of *Gang* — determine the contemporary and academic mythos of representing musical thinking. Neither melody nor a tune nor a rhythm can compete with how a composer *works* or *executes* the material. This is the Protestant work ethic in music, exemplified through Beethoven: the signing of the work with the hand that has labored, that has suffered, to achieve a work that bears the mark of the divine mind. In theological terms, divinity can be reached through the intensification of work in a work. In German, the assimilation of *Werk* (the product) to the fetishism of *Arbeit* (the process of working or labor involved in the act of production).

In their relationship to the works of the past, the role of the musician becomes one of preservation, conservation, or protection. Inherent in these concepts is a religious conservatism: the inner sanctity of the musical work must be upheld from the Philistines.[53] Liszt's was the first generation to try actively to preserve earlier works as part of what would become the musical museum; it is not coincidental that Liszt would later turn to religion. Religion and work converge in the activities of both performance and composition: these latter activities are no longer opposites (again, see the passage from Nietzsche quoted in footnote 26).

Liszt's *Rhapsodies* are the translation of the metaphysical ideas of the work into the what for him was the realm of Gypsy music. Despite the fact that in Liszt's arranging of themes the potpourri is the privileged form, Gypsy music is now accorded all of the protocols granted to thematic process applied to a motive, and becomes *work*.

WHEN COMPOSITIONAL TECHNIQUE WENT PUBLIC

Liszt was fully conscious of the ontological distinction of his own music from the previous musical models, exemplified by Beethoven. He writes:

> Bei der soganannten klassischen Musik ist die Wiederkehr und thematische Entwickelung der Themen durch formelle Regeln bestimmt, die man als unumstösslich betrachtet, trotzdem ihre komponisten keine andere Vorschrift für sie bafassen als ihre eigene Phantasie, und sie selbst die formellen Anordnungen trafen, die man jetzt als Gesetz ausstellen will. In der Programm-Musik dagegen ist Wiederkehr, Wechsel, Veränderung und Modulation der Motive durch ihre Beziehung zu einem poetischen Gedanken bedingt.[54]

So-called "classical" music demands the return and thematic development of themes through formal rules, which one views as unchangeable, even if compositionally there are no other instructions except one's own Fantasy, requiring of them to fulfill formal arrangements, which one now sets forth as law. [my translation; excerpt]

Classical music poses no relationship of thematic processes with anything outside of the processes; famously, the music is allegedly self-contained. It fantasizes a relationship only to itself. We might add that it leaves no trace of its dependency on a world or things in the world. Of course, this fictional transparency can be rigorously deconstructed precisely around the point of its own resistance to deconstruction.

But extending the implications of Liszt's thought even further: at some point, the techniques, rules, and procedures that constituted the craft and ability of a composer became legitimate in their own right. Detached from any scene of content *in* the world, these procedures became the substance of music *in-itself.* Motives were manipulated not to show anything about the world, but as the expression of what music *does.* We now understand this is as the idea of absolute music, which turns out to be nothing other than an ideology about music as a self-contained entity, or something "natural," if one accepts it.

Liszt recognizes absolute music as a historical phenomenon, something that happened *to* classical art music. By proposing the *poetischen Gedanken,* Liszt is the one who protests against this rigid notion of pure, abstract compositional technique, detached from the world, as the true source of music. For Liszt, the triumph of absolute music would represent a huge historical mistake and misunderstanding of what music is. Unfortunately this is precisely what happened in the construction of the Western canon, and it subsequently led to the prejudice against Gypsy music. As one example among many is Schoenberg's criticizing of the Gypsy element in Brahms. We can hypothesize that for Liszt, the greatest poetic thought is the melody that burns from the violin of the Gypsy.

RHAPSODIZING: *HUNGARIAN RHAPSODIES* NOS. 1-3

Gypsy music emerges from the first few notes of the First Rhapsody (see Music Example 10). The *recitativo* melody begins on G-sharp and descends to F-sharp. Though it is in E major, still, at this point of the piece, we do not know what key we are in. After homophonic passages that are about rhythmic transformation, with emphasis on the sixteenth-dotted eighth sequence, the *recitativo* appears two more times. In its last playing before the song proper begins, the tritone C/F-sharp is outlined in the outer voices (see Music Example 11); to approximate Gypsy-style accompaniment, the C-natural half-note on the downbeat serves as a passing note.

Music Example 10 "Hungarian Rhapsody no. 1" by Liszt, measures 1-3.

Music Example 11 "Hungarian Rhapsody no. 1," measure 23.

This passionate introduction to the *Rhapsodies* contains all of the elements we associate with Gypsiness: an improvised melody expressing anguish of an undetermined specificity; this is done through the rhythmic fantasy of a virtuoso musician. Note that an amateur could "play" these notes, but without intuitive musical understanding of the equations of Gypsiness, he could not give them the energy required to express the melancholy aimed for by Liszt. In short, this articulates precisely why Liszt was required to preface these works with his book: this is the reinvigoration of Western music.

The Second Rhapsody, dedicated to a connoisseur of Gypsy music, Count László Teleki, is the most performed of the set. Again, it is in the opening bars, before the *Lassan*, or the slow section of the piece, that Liszt realizes the impetus for Gypsiness (see Music Example 12). The *Lassan* is wistful, capricious, and pure nostalgia (see Music Example 13). We do not really know where it is heading, until the opening is reintroduced. The third playing of this material, with the melody in the bass, leads to the *Friska*, the faster follow-up to the *Lassan*. The privileged texture here is the tremolo, beloved by Liszt in his early works (most famously in "*La campanella*").

"Rhapsody no. 3" begins in the parallel minor to B-flat, again, with the melody in the bass. To get to the subdominant, the usual concern of "folk" style writing, Liszt uses an ambiguous chord, spelled D, G, B, F-flat (see Music Example 14). The F-flat

Music Examples 12 and 13 "Hungarian Rhapsody no. 2," measures 1-3, and "Lassan."

resolves melodically, by half-step, to the E-flat sonority of the subdominant. To use VI to arrive at IV is standard. However, it is the motion that makes a passage like this so harmonically potent: the D- and B-naturals come directly out of D- and B-flats. This raising by half-step, *unprepared*, of the harmonic impetus is yet another appropriation of Gypsiness. The D in the bass as the leading tone of E-flat is what is significant: the G can be thought as an added pitch in anticipation, a common-tone connector, to the E-flat. Thus to speak of a VI sonority is perhaps completely out-of-place in this context. This is confirmed when Liszt wants to move to the dominant, he simply states an E-natural in the bass.

A delicate cymbalom texture comes to the fore at the *Allegretto*. Idiomatic for the cymbalom is that the melody descends. The first note on the off-beat is always dissonant — Brahms also will use this in his own "Hungarian Dance no. 5." Here Liszt uses the augmented second called for in his book (D, C-sharp, B-flat, A). The lower tetrachord of the scale also relies on this interval (F-sharp to E-flat) (see Music Example 15).

IM TROTZIGEN, TIEFSINNIGEN ZIGEUNER-STIL VORZUTRAGEN

"Rhapsody no. 7" states an oxymoron of Gypsiness, defiant yet melancholy (see Music Example 16). To our knowledge, this is the first occurrence of "*Zigeuner*" as an

Music Examples 14 and 15 "Hungarian Rhapsody no. 3," measures 1-4, and measures 33-34.

expressive articulation indicating the emotional path of the piece. In the second part's *Vivace* the rhythmic energy is pure defiance (see Music Example 17).

However, what attracts the listener to Gypsy music is always already the realm of the melancholy: this is the power of music itself, as stated by theorists of the seconda prattica and understood in the laments of the early operas. The gestures of a violin solo on the first page realize the melancholy.

The timbre of the cymbalom is not difficult to imitate on the piano. Both are hammered instruments, capable of producing percussive explosions. But the violin cannot be appropriated by the piano. Liszt tries, however, and this shows his deep commitment to Gypsy music as Gypsiness.

THE VIRILE/VIRTUOSIC POWER OF THE *RHAPSODIES*

Virtuosity is a male signifier, the power of seduction itself. Liszt was conscious of this, writing that (we have already seen part of this quotation on page 99; here we now insert it into a fuller context):

> The words virtuosity and virtue have both their origin in the Latin *vir*, the exercise of one as much as the other being an act of masculine power.... He must know how to impose respect and admiration for the beautiful; and should be the author of good works or actions — whether these belong to art or morality makes no difference; as these are but two aspects of the same thing, two sexes of the same species.[55]

Music Examples 16 and 17 "Hungarian Rhapsody no. 7," measures 1-4, and *Vivace*.

Virtuosity is predicated on a patriarchal version of sexual difference, that the male has the faculty to "impose respect and admiration for the beautiful." Yet while upholding a masculine version of virtuosity, Liszt wants to collapse sexual difference, as in art and morality being "two aspects of the same thing, two sexes of the one species." The "same thing" turns out, in the next paragraph, to be the human soul.

Liszt then defines the virtuoso:

> Musical works which have been dictated by inspiration are, fundamentally, only the touching or the tragic *scenario* of feeling, which it appertains to the executant to cause, by turns, to disclaim, sing, weep, sigh, or adore; as also to pride himself and take pleasure in the accomplishment. The virtuoso is therefore just as much the *creator as the writer;* for he must virtually possess, in all their brilliancy and flagrant phosphorescence, the written passions to which he has undertaken to give life.[56]

What is new with Liszt is the idea that the performer is the equal of the composer. But the reasons why turn on what music is, in its essence: a *scenario* of feeling. Music as a scene of feeling, a place where feeling happens.

Digressing for a moment, this is what underlies the nationalistic response to music: music's power to evoke emotions. This gives the illusion that music can identify the collective. This process is always a step beyond what music is, music as sound. It is the appropriation of music, whose repercussions are still being determined. For music, as a vehicle of feeling, can be understood in any number of emotional-charged political situations: nationalistic program, or, as a major player (= moneymaker) in the entertainment industries. The full implications of this massive appropriation is today only beginning to be understood, especially as global industries push music further into marketplace. Gypsy music provides a great site for thinking about how this appropriation occurs, and of how nationalism dovetails with mass consumerism.

To return to Liszt, during his performing career he had the problem of how to handle his many female admirers. His virtuosity, the exhibition of his male power, was no small factor in attracting women. Nietzsche, an acute commentator on the sociological place of women during the nineteenth century,[57] makes the following remark on the effect of music on women:

> Almost everywhere one ruins her nerves with the most pathological and dangerous kind of music (our most recent German music [= Wagner]) and makes her more hysterical by the day and more incapable of her first and last profession — to give birth to strong children.[58]

Liszt must have felt the dangerous side effects of his music, and its effect on women. With his turn to Gypsy music in the 1840s, the power had truly unfolded, and perhaps explains why he stopped performing.

LETTERS

The force of letters in forging the reception of European musical works has not received the attention they deserve. Many musicologists assume that letters are secondary to the canon of works or to the winds of stylistic change. But for a moment, let us imagine the opposite: that the letters are primary, and the work, secondary.

From Galatz, 17 July 1847, Liszt wrote to his estranged wife, the writer Marie d'Agoult:

> It concerns a Preface or Postface to my *Rhapsodies hongroises*, for which I would of course give you a good many notes and instructions. I greatly value this work, and it is *absolutely necessary* for the deep and inner significance of this series of compositions to be made eloquently clear to the public...[59]

Liszt knew that the works would not be received correctly by the public. The idea of "necessary" will determine Liszt's relationship to the *Rhapsodies*.

With this in mind we shall look at a letter on Milton's *Dante* that he wrote to Princess Caroline, while still in the first year of his love affair with her:

As for *Satan*, I would willingly say of him what you said about the *necessity* of Hegel. It isn't great — for Satan gets excited, does things, discourses, battles, reasons, becomes a diplomatic negotiator, etc. [...] he suffers and doubts [...] it seems to me that this conception of him would be more in accord with our poetic feeling of today...[60] (29 January 1848)

Before this passage Liszt approves of Milton's conception of earthly love, and here he identifies with Satan, as the principle of the "poetic feeling of today."

Thus here we will finish tying our knot, around the following threads of Liszt's life: *Rhapsodies*, virtuosity and its withdrawal (including Satan's withdrawal from the world), prefaces (writing), poetic idea as structure, and necessity. All of these came to head in 1847 on the most important trip of Liszt's life, his trip that brought him into countless contacts with Gypsies. And Gypsiness constitutes the final device that ties all these elements together: it is what allowed Liszt to communicate his necessary poetic idea of the substance of their musical force to the wider European public.

Chapter Seven

Gypsies and *Vol'nost'* in Russian Music: *Aleko*[1]

It is dusk and the young Gypsy clings to his lover, Zemfira. They both hope to remain until daylight, despite the dire tragedy that this might bring. She knows that if her husband, Aleko, were to discover the betrayal, he would kill them. This reality intrudes upon her deepest fear as Aleko enters, who immediately — without thinking — stabs the Gypsy lover, and then Zemfira.

During the double murder, the psychological condition of the Russian character Aleko is cataleptic. He is numb, overwhelmed, and blinded by passion. Before this Aleko had tried to accept the ways and laws of Gypsy culture, especially the demands of its active and aggressive sense of responsibility. Yet the passivity (more on this below) and zombie-like state of mind of Aleko stand in conflict with his appropriation of a sensual and erotic Gypsy persona.

Despite the political marginalization and persecution of Gypsies in Russia, Gypsy culture is a substantial element and source for Russian literature and music. Even today in the former Soviet Union, Rachmaninov's one-act *Aleko* remains one of the most common and popular operas in the repertory. Audiences of all ages seem to relate to the dramaturgy bridging Russian and Gypsy cultural stereotypes, and musically, to the melodic pathos and harmonic fluency. But beyond being a mass-audience favorite, *Aleko* is based on the one of the canonical texts of Russian literature, Pushkin's poem *Tsygany*.

READING PUSHKIN'S *TSYGANY*

Like much of Pushkin's verse, the first lines of his *Tsygany* are common expressions in Russia:

The noisy crowd of Gypsies
Wandering in Bessarabia
Tonight tonight, above the river
They spend the night in the torn tents
Their night is joyful as freedom itself
And peaceful is slumber under the sky (lines 1-6)[2]

"Bessarabia" is the old name for the region of Moldavia, and it immediately imparts an exotic flavor to the text. The word translated as freedom is "*vol'nost*." Pushkin wrote a separate poem titled "*Vol'nost*" which he dedicated to anti-government forces (the so-called Decembrist coup, an anti-czarist event that took place in 1825). "*Vol'nost*" contrasts with "*svoboda*." This latter term refers to the abstract or philosophical concept of freedom. Pushkin yearns for *vol'nost* through his imagining of the noisy Gypsy camp — for him, the essence of Gypsy camps is noise.

Commenting on Pushkin, Alaina Lemon signals "*volia*" at the end of the poem as the key concept. She understands *volia* as free will or freedom — as, for example, when the old man admonishes Aleko: "You want '*volia* [free will/freedom] only for yourself." Lemon continues: "*volia* is the ideal inherent to Gypsies that Aleko cannot grasp."[3] She is partially correct, no doubt, but she overlooks the complicated Latin etymology of the root *vol* as it unfolds in the Russian language. *Volia* alludes to the general term for open space (perhaps wilderness), locating a place away from civilization. It is not free will. The latter is abstract and has a peculiarly Christian heritage, and again, is captured by the Russian word "*svoboda*."

The young Gypsy Zemfira brings a dissatisfied non-Gypsy, Aleko, to her camp. She tells her father that she found him in the desert:

'My father, I am bringing a guest.
Beyond the barrow in the desert I found him
And I enticed him to the tabor for the night.
He wants to be a Gypsy as we are,
He is chased by the law.
I will be his girlfriend.
He is ready to follow my footsteps.' (lines 42-50)

Tabor designates both the nomadic camp and the social organization of the Gypsies. *Zazvat'* means not only to invite by calling, but also to conquer someone's heart, as in a seduction. It is the word in the Russian translation of the *Iliad* to describe how the sirens entice the sailors to come. Aleko is persecuted for a crime, the nature of which is irrelevant for this story; it leads him to try to escape from his life into the imagined freedom of Gypsy life. This is what Zemfira represents for him, a way out of his life in civilization. *Podruga* is literally a casual girlfriend, not a lover or wife. From this aspect of Zemfira's phrasing, we already understand that she will not commit herself, fully, to Aleko.

Pushkin joyfully returns to the noise a little further on in the text. With the sunrise, the energetic joy of the tabor takes off:

Husbands, brother, wives, girls
Old and young they all go;
Shouts, noise, Gypsy refrains,
The dance-bear's growl and his chain's
Impatient jangle,
Bright and mixed colors of the rags of the clothes
The nudity of children and elderly men
Dogs barking and howling,
The bagpipe's garble, coach axles screech
Everything is squalid, wild, and disharmonious,
But so vivid and unsettled,
So foreign to our dead pleasures,
So far from our useless lives,
Which pass as the monotonous song of slaves. (lines 80-93)

Pushkin contrasts the free, noisy, boisterous life of Gypsies to the dead, static, and monotonous life of "us" — the poem's listeners, who are non-Gypsies. Pushkin himself is a non-Gypsy onlooker, longing for the noise of the Gypsy refrains (*Pripevy*). He employs a classically metered Russian, which has been compared by Russian literary critics to Byron's English or Ovid's Latin. Pushkin never loses his artistic refinement (as one finds for instance in Tolstoy or Dostoevsky's realistic imitations of peasant and lower-class speech). Yet Pushkin's lexicon is wider than any previous Russian poet, which makes it possible to describe his subjects quite realistically.

Pushkin's portrayal of Aleko involves a crucial aspect of the stereotype of the Russian character, what can be called "heart laziness." This translates "*serdechna len*" (line 129). To understand this term, we can refer to what the French literary critic Maurice Blanchot calls passivity:

Passivity: we can evoke it only in a language that reverses itself. I have, at other times, referred to suffering: suffering such that could not suffer it [...] and then there the passivity which is beyond disquietude, but which nevertheless retains the passiveness of the incessant, feverish, even-uneven movement of error which has no purpose, no end, no starting principle.[4]

Aleko's passiveness, his heart laziness, leads him to the Gypsy way of life, and also, makes him a toy of his passions. Intensely, he suffers without knowing from what he suffers. Furthermore, for Pushkin, this passive facet of the Russian essence aligns the Russian to the Gypsies. As an aside, this perhaps could be used to explain why Russia has had a love affair with Gypsy culture since at least the early nineteenth century.

Aleko lives the Gypsy life for two happy years with his beloved Zemfira. Then there is a tragic turn in the plot. This is signified by Zemfira's song about leaving an old lover for a new lover, "Old man, terrifying man." She hates her overbearing and jealous lover, and she denies his love for the love of another. She will die for the new love: stab me, burn me, I defy your wrath. Zemfira has, in fact, found a new lover, a young Gypsy. Aleko does not approve of Zemfira's song, and tells her so. Zemfira responds by saying that I am not frightened of you, and in fact I am singing about you (beginning at line 285).

Zemfira has grown tired ("*postyla*") of Aleko; my heart ("*serdtse*") longs for freedom (again, "*volia*," related to "*vol'nost'*," lines 314-315). That same night, Aleko dreams of his former life, and cries out. The dreams terrify Zemfira, who calls out to her father. At this point, Aleko no longer trusts Zemfira, and he tells her father that she does not love him.

The Old Man's advice to Aleko is that a young woman's love is free and playful. It cannot be owned. He himself learned this lesson from Zemfira's mother, Mariula, who forsake and left her husband and baby daughter for the love of a Gypsy from another tribe (*tabor*). But Aleko cannot heed this advice, and his hot passions overtake him with a jealous rage as he stabs Zemfira's new lover and then Zemfira. The Old Man then tells Aleko to leave the *tabor*:

> *Depart from us, proud man.*
> *We are wild, we don't have laws,*
> *We don't torture, we don't punish,*
> *We don't need blood and screams,*
> *We don't want to live with a murderer*
> *You are not born for the wild life,*
> *You want freedom only for yourself,*
> *We will be terrified by your voice,*
> *We are meek and kind souls,*
> *You are mean and bold,*
> *Depart from us,*
> *Forgive us, and let peace be with you.* (lines 510-520)

In the eyes of the Gypsies, Aleko is proud in the narcissistic sense (*gordyi*). The Gypsies, by contrast, are humble and good-natured. They have no formal law, yet they do not endorse assassination. Restated, the Gypsies do not fall under the rule of law, and yet paradoxically, they assert a way of life that obeys a certain order. Aleko did not understand the idea of an order outside of law. He is a murderer, and the Gypsies have no punishment (*kazn'*, or execution), no torture (*terzanie*) for dealing with this kind of transgression. Finally, Aleko's crime of passion asserted itself from his personality, in which an inner meanness (*zlo*) resides.

Yet in the poem's epilogue, we learn that Pushkin does not think that the Gypsy way of life leads to happiness. The poem ends:

> *Everywhere fatal passions*
> *And there is no defense from the Fate.*

These lines summarize Pushkin's worldview, one that is permeated by fatalism. There is no escape from our passions, whether we are Gypsy or Russian.

ZEMFIRA'S SONG[5]

Before publishing his *Tsygany*, Pushkin published three small fragments of the poem, among which we find Zemfira's song, "Old man, terrifying man." Then, the song was republished in the widely read magazine *Moskovskii Telegraf,* along with the melody. The editor says to the reader: "This is wild melody of a song that the poet heard in Bessarabia." Zemfira's song was sung everywhere, and when it became dramatized (the premiere was on 9 June 1832, St. Petersburg) it was already the center of the play, much as we have seen in Vicente's *Farsas de Cigana* in Chapter Two.

RACHMANINOV'S MUSICAL LANGUAGE AND THE AESTHETIC OF GYPSINESS

Early on Rachmaninov became fascinated with Gypsies; his first attempt at opera, the fragment "Esmeralda," was based on Victor Hugo's *Notre Dame de Paris.* Commenting on Nemirovich-Danchenko libretto for *Aleko,* one of Rachmaninov's biographers, Maria Biesold, writes:

> The dramatic conception of *Aleko* is without doubt inspired by [Mascagni's] *Cavalleria rusticana* and Nemirowitsch-Dantschenko's Russian version of it. The Gypsy life in *Aleko* is comparable to the Sicilian village life.[6]

But comparing *Aleko* to Mascagni's opera de-emphasizes the force of Pushkin's poetry. The great Russian director who wrote the libretto for *Aleko,* Nemirovich-Danchenko, cannot be counted as a representative of verismo. Along with the director Constantin Stanislavski, he believed in the recreation of a human life as the spirit of acting:

> our art demands that an actor's whole nature be *actively* involved, that he give himself up, both mind and body, to his part. He must feel the challenge to action physically as well as intellectually, because the imagination, which has no substance or body, can reflexively affect our physical nature and make it act.[7] [my emphasis]

This, rather, was the direction of art, really the aesthetic atmosphere of the theater, in which Rachmaninov developed as an artist.

It appears that as Rachmaninov was finishing his degree at the Moscow Conservatory, he and two other candidates were handed the libretto as their final examination project.[8] The other candidates were Lev Konius and Nikita Morozov, whose works were neither published nor performed[9]. Rachmaninov says in the *Recollections told to Oskar von Riesemann* about how easily and quickly he composed *Aleko*:

> On the following morning I began my work, which I found very easy. I took the libretto as it stood, and the idea that it might be improved never even entered my head. I composed, as it were, under high pressure. Slonov [his friend who lived with him and his father] and I sat at my writing desk facing one another. I wrote without once looking up, and only passed the completed sheets across the table, when the kindly Slonov kindly proceeded to make fair copies of them in his neat hand.[10]

Though composers are notorious for fabricating accounts of the compositional process, it does not seem to be the case here, given the pressure he was under; from this description it appears that the youthful Rachmaninov wrote his opera in a kind of "white heat" of inspiration.

We will propose two ideas as a prolegomena to our analysis of the harmony and form as present in his opera: 1) Rachmaninov must have had some prior experience and real knowledge of "Gypsy music"; 2) on the other hand, the work itself is not inspired by any "real" Gypsies, but rather by the composer's own tonal imagination in its relationship to the so-called "oriental" music of Russian composers. In other words, Rachmaninov's musical language does not borrow *directly* from actual Gypsy music that surrounded him. His use of mode, like the tetrachord D, E-flat, F-sharp, G (known in the Middle East as a *hijaz* tetrachord, but referred to by theorists in Eastern Europe and in Russia as the "Gypsy scale," [*tsiganskaya gamma*, in Russian]), relates (at least for a Russian composer at this time) to the general idea of exotic, Eastern, or "oriental music," and overlaps with a notion of "Gypsy." Indeed, Vladimir Stasov, the famous Russian critic responsible for naming the composers in Balakirev's circle the "mighty handful" (*moguchaya kuchka*), had already recognized a strain of "orientalism" as a distinguishing feature of the Russian national school.[11] We can cite Balakirev's own piano fantasy *Islamey (orientale fantasie)* and Rimsky-Korsakov's *Scheherazade* as two among many examples of this exotic strain.

Yet Rachmaninov's own Romantic, emotive, expressive musical language, often thought as the essence of Russianness in music, borrows heavily from the communicative/intervallic structure (modal path)/musical rhetoric of Gypsy music. Rachmaninov's music does not rely on Gypsy tunes, rhythms, or harmonies *per se*, yet without Gypsy music as a sonic ideal, Rachmaninov's music would be different as we know it.

Thus, in a sense, Rachmaninov displays through his harmony an insider's knowledge of the emotional effects of Gypsy performance, while his tonal language extends what was previously understood as an oriental style.

Because of this appropriation, we rely on the term "Gypsiness" to try to describe the aesthetic of this harmonic language. Inherent in this ideal is the non-directionality of nomadic culture, the perpetual spacing and movement of the *tabor*. Generally, it these ideas that separate Gypsiness from the more sedentary cultures of the Orient.

RUSSIAN MUSIC, ORIENTALISM, AND GYPSINESS

Geoffrey Norris mentions the music of Rimsky-Korsakov, Borodin, and Tchaikovsky as immediate musical influences on the youthful Rachmaninov.[12] Although many connections to these and other composers such as Glinka, Anton Rubinstein, Arensky and Balakirev can be made, we will here only provide a couple of indications of the musical exoticism of the learned Russian musical environment of Rachmaninov's youth.

Rimsky-Korsakov's *Scheherazade* is a piece which employs recognized exotic elements based on the Arabic *Thousand and One Nights*. Here, the idea of the "Orient" is transformed into the musical language of a Russian composer. The famous passage (see Music Example 18) introducing the violin soloist very near the opening of this work captures the spirit of "Arabicness" as imagined by a Russian. The composer wants the essence of Arabic taqasim, the soloistic, improvised form of this music. He does this rhythmically, through the oscillating triplet figure. The harmony is where he really departs from European, classical structure, but at the same time, it is also where he departs from Arabic taqasim, which would only admit of a drone, here, over an A (the "maqam" or mode of this passage would be A, B, C, D, E, F-sharp, G, which does not exist as such in Arabic music). Harmonically, what Rimsky-Korsakov does is expand the subdominant, A minor, resolving into E major with no reference to the dominant. (This is perhaps why "exotic" or "oriental" can be thought as impossibly heterogeneous yet necessarily part of at least two traditions).

Yet there is a crucial difference: that the exotic substance of *Scheherazade* lies *outside* of Russia, unlike Rachmaninov's Gypsies, who constitute an exotic substance *within* Russia.

As a second reference, we would like to look at the *Polovtsian Dance* by Borodin (see Music Example 19), from *Prince Igor*. The melody is probably taken from a Tartarian folk song. It is impossible to use a Western harmonic tonality to set this tune. Although the chordal arsenal used by Borodin is familiar — triads, seventh-chords, and their inversions in a context of a drone on A — the chordal movement is nothing short of astonishing, and probably unprecedented. The melody can be thought in B minor, yet against the A drone it assumes a transcendent meaning, beyond any

Music Example 18 Rimsky-Korsakov, violin solo from *Scheherazade*, measures 14-18 (reduction).

original context of folk music. The final chord is an F-sharp minor 6/3 chord (with the A in the bass). It is well beyond the immediate topic of this chapter, but we should say that what we are dealing with is a so-called "intermittent folk mode." This refers to a mode with two or more centers. With B, the other center would traditionally be F-sharp; however, with the addition of the A, what Borodin has done is added another center to this mode, in effect making it triple-centered.

Music Example 19 Borodin, *Polovtsian Dance*, at rehearsal A.

What unites Borodin with the aesthetic of Gypsiness is the notion of additive tonal centers. The universe of alternative tonality is open to transformations of the harmonic substance. What justifies the use of an alternative tonality is, simply put, a non-consciousness of what the content of the mode is supposed to be. It is *vol'nost'*, the abandonment of rules: as long as it feels and sounds right, no objection can be made.

ALEKO'S "CAVATINA"

Our analysis focuses on the center of the opera, with the most conspicuous number, the "Cavatina" (no. 10 in the piano/vocal score). "Cavatina" comes from the Latin "cavare," which means to hollow out, to engrave; a short song in simple style without repetitions. In *Aleko*, the "Cavatina" follows this path. It is introduced by a short introduction in recitative style; the body proper begins at the *Meno mosso* (m. 37).

In nineteenth-century Russian music it was Glinka who established the genre of cavatina. For example, the Cavatina of Antonida from Glinka's *Life for the Tsar* became a kind of standard for this genre, and it served as a model for many Russian composers to come including Borodin, Rimsky-Korsakov, Tchaikovsky. Although the "Cavatina" of Aleko has a ternary outline (the B section at m. 55, the recapitulation at m. 65), the music presents a powerful and uninterrupted flow, as if it were written in one breath, as one big wave. Indeed, as our analyses will show, the dynamic character of harmonic flow distinguishes this piece from most of the earlier cavatinas, and will characterize Rachmaninov's most essential achievement in building what we call continuous lines of development. One way this can be described is as the line which exceeds the normal length of breath (the standard criterion for the length of musical phrases) and which in turn renders the listener breathless.

I. Melodic Ambiguity

First, to the melody. Melodic considerations pervade and perhaps over determine Gypsy music. Rameau's notion that melody comes from harmony is completely out-of-line when speaking of this topos. Yet the opposite is not entirely true either, namely, that the harmony comes from melody. Their relationship is difficult to conceptualize, but it seems clear that there is an additive approach to the appropriation of Western harmony in Gypsy music. Or, bricolage, as Levi-Strauss might say.

In terms of collecting folk music, Bartók wrote:

> It also became gradually evident that the slight alterations occurring verse by verse — especially in the ornamental notes of the melody — are not the result of unsureness on the part of the singer, or that he is 'poorly acquainted' with the melody, but that this variability is one of the most characteristic, integral peculiarities of folk melodies; indeed, a folk melody is like a living creature: it changes minute by minute, moment by moment.[13]

Though an ethnomusicologist operating under the assumptions of poststructuralism might want to question Bartók's method of collecting folk melodies, still, what Bartók has to say about the variability of melody, its breathing of life, applies unequivocally to Gypsy music, and we will add, to Rachmaninov's melodic line.

In a sense, the impossibility of grasping melody is similar to the difficult of understanding art: both revert to a materiality that conceals, escapes, and folds in upon itself when we try to get inside of it.[14] This has proved to be somewhat embarrassing in the analysis of melody, and perhaps explains why much analysis ends up trying to avoid melody (we could add rhythm, or timbre) and privileges more rigid, graspable topics, such as form, counterpoint, or harmony. When a melody is investigated, it is broken down into motive. This exploding of the melodic substance has the positive effect of rendering a hierarchical structure, yet not without bending, twisting, and torturing the melody itself.

Rachmaninov's "Cavatina" provides no melodic basis for defining the form. Music Example 20 from the end of the A section of Aleko's cavatina shows this unpredictability of the melody. Aleko's vocal part is loose, not aligned with the

Music Example 20 Vocal line from Aleko's "Cavatina."

accompaniment definitely, which gives the *vol'nost'*: the *tabor* is asleep, his heart trembles, and he is tortured by sadness. As audience we empathize with his character.

II. Subdominant Subterfuge?

In a recent monograph on Rachmaninov, David Cannata discusses the equivocality of the harmonic complexes of the composer's early music. He speaks of "double-tonic," and "tonic-subdominant strategies," concepts which we think are valid, but which are in need of more refinement in terms of close analysis of tonal function; we will call attention to the overwhelming presence of the subdominant, to the point where it seems to override the tonic-dominant relationship.[15] We think that this lends support to our thesis about the Gypsy element in Rachmaninov's musical language.

In Figure 1 we provide a graphing of the harmonic structure. A quick glance at the figure shows that there is a heavy concentration of subdominant harmony. However, because the subdominant is reached by unorthodox means, we use arrows to show large-scale functional anomalies. According to both functional and Schenkerian logic, the subdominant cannot serve as a goal for a harmonic progression. In this case, we use the term "functional streak" to describe the line of escape from the rules of inferential tonal hierarchy. The arrows in the figure show the connections, sometimes violent, between statements of the subdominant.

Figure 1's progression begins in m. 38 with a very short statement in C minor. Already in the next measure a strange chord, I4/2, appears. What is important about this chord is that it is the first move away from tonic, going toward the mediant. Indeed, the mediant also plays a significant role in Aleko's "Cavatina" and in fact, occupies a greater portion of this piece than C minor. After a short re-visiting of C minor in m. 42, the key does not return until its recapitulation (m. 65).

The next harmonic event is the oscillation between A-flat/D (mm. 42-43). This could be interpreted in two ways: 1) something within C minor; or 2) an event in its own right. If it is this latter, which we suspect that it is, then it recalls the work of Erno Lendvai, Boleslav Javorsky (among others) who have suggested different ways to

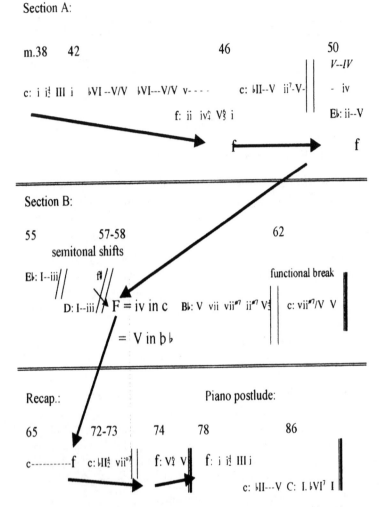

Figure 1 Local goal chords in the tonal plan of Aleko's "Cavatina" by Ildar Khannanov.

interpret such tritonic pairing of harmonies. Traditionally, this oscillation of A-flat and D is a form of pre-dominant preparation; however, as suggested by the work of these twentieth-century theorists, it can also be an independent element.

Our reason for suggesting that the oscillation is *not* a pre-dominant structure is the following: instead of going to C minor, the following progression brings us to F minor, which is where the first statement ends (m. 46). By such means Rachmaninov gives his listener a taste of what will unfold as a virtuosic display of the subdominant. We can call this harmonic "subterfuge." For example, in m. 47 he starts to go to C minor, but after reaching the dominant, he abruptly shifts to the subdominant (m. 50). Here, though, the F becomes a pivot in the modulation to the mediant. In the B section of the cavatina Aleko remembers the brighter side of his affair with Zemfira. To express the inner ecstasy of the text, Rachmaninov executes what we have already signaled as a virtuosic treatment of the subdominant. In order to do this, he introduces what can only be described as seismic semi-tonal shifts, which, we will add contribute to our idea of *vol'nost'* and Gypsiness. The most impressive is the apposition of F-sharp minor and F major (mm. 57-58). And the composer continues this cycling downward by fifths by turning F into the dominant of B-flat minor (beginning in m. 58). Paradoxically, even though a V4/2 chord of B-flat minor shows up (m. 62), the tonic triad of B-flat minor never appears.

The recapitulation ends on F minor (m. 76), prepared by a closing with two chords, flat II and VII (a diminished-seventh chord) in C minor (mm. 72-73). All of a sudden, a cadential 6-4 chord in F minor appears (m. 74). Astonishingly, in F minor the vocal part ends (m. 78). What happens next is an orchestral postlude which plays the main theme in F minor, and then, as if to finish the "academic" requirement of the opera, Rachmaninov returns to C major (m. 86 to the end).

But how do we interpret the prevalence of the subdominant? The subdominant can be expanded, according to Schenkerian theory, but that is not the case in our cavatina. Rather, the subdominant plays an essential role, in a way subverting the function of tonic-dominant. Now, to finish our argument: that Rachmaninov's emphasis on the subdominant, within the context of an elliptical harmonic language, is more than a simple programmatic reference to Gypsiness and Gypsy musical rhetoric, it informs his formulation of harmony itself.

THE SIGNIFICANCE OF GYPSINESS FOR RUSSIAN STUDIES

The importance of Gypsies to the burgeoning nineteenth-century Russian artistic imagination has been well documented in literary examples, from Pushkin, Tolstoy, and Dostoevsky. In musicology this topic has received little attention, despite some efforts to discuss Gypsy source material in Stravinsky's *Histoire du soldat*.[16] The intent here has been to investigate a striking example of Gypsy music in Russian art music, the "Cavatina" from Rachmaninov's *Aleko*. Though hardly known in the West, this work was frequently performed throughout the twentieth century in Russia, and is one of the key sources to understanding the significance of Gypsy music in Russian music.

Finally, we have tried to show how Gypsiness can be added to the list of "oriental" or exotic elements that can be found in nineteenth-century Russian music. This idea can probably be expanded to include the twentieth century, as certain composers (Shostakovich) were known to be well acquainted with this music. Essential to

Gypsiness as it is understood in Russia is the idea of *vol'nost'*, as we have seen in Pushkin's *Tsygany*. Thus, as with other exoticisms, Gypsiness can be interpreted as a device that allowed Russian composers to explore their own intuitive grasp of harmonic events as they heard them, apart from what they took from the West. In Rachmaninov's music, these events are, summarizing once again: subdominant subterfuge, semi-tonal shifts, and breaks in tonal-functional inference. Finally, our findings in analyzing early Rachmaninov allow us to suggest that other heterogeneities to be found in this period of Russian music, as in Skryabin, should not be held to Western notions of harmony or form.

Chapter Eight

Gypsy Pleroma: Janáček's *Diary of One Who Disappeared*

Since she [Kamila Stösslová] was Jewish and dark-skinned, Janáček, often referred to her as his 'Gypsy,' both the source for Zefka in the song cycle, and a model for Emilia Marty.

Michael Beckerman, *Janáček Studies*, 122

The correct understanding of the concept of *alteration* is also grounded upon [recognition of] this permanence. Coming to be and ceasing to be are not alterations of that which comes to be or ceases to be. Alteration is a way of existing which follows upon another way of existing of the same object. All that alters *persists*, and only its *state changes*. Since this change thus concerns only the determinations, which can cease to be or begin to be, we can say, using what may seem as a somewhat paradoxical expression, that only the permanent (substance) is altered, and that the transitory suffers no alteration but only a *change*, inasmuch as certain determinations cease to be and others begin to be.

Kant, *Critique of Pure Reason*, 217

Pure singularity: neither the empiric individual that death destroys, decomposes, analyzes, nor the rational universality of the citizen, of the living subject. What I give as a present to the woman, in exchange for the funeral rite, is my own absolutely proper body, the essence of my singularity. The woman receives it in the night, however, long or short. But what she receives, as pure singularity, immediately passes into its contrary. The feminine burial (place) guards nothing, unless there is an instance — for example the name called proper — that tries to hold itself, that stretches itself between the opposites or the equivalents, even though they annul each other.

Derrida, *Glas*, 143-144

In the tradition of the song cycle, from Beethoven's *An die ferne Geliebte*, to Schubert's *Winterreise*, to Schumann's *Dichterliebe*, the distant, unattainable lover does not appear in the narrative or poetic substance. The feminine lover withdraws, as it were, reinforcing the isolation, gloom, and desperation of the thwarted male voice. But she remains present in her absence, in that the cry of the male lover calls only to her image.

Outside of Czech music circles, Janáček's 1917 song cycle *Zápisník zmizelého* (*Diary of One Who Disappeared*) is not well known. From the title, one might guess that Janáček intends to recast the idea of unrequited love through the private intimacy of the diary. Instead of following this tact, however, Janáček chose a narrative that turns the traditional one of its head. Namely: the distant beloved not only appears, with *her own voice*, in Janáček's cycle, but she is successful in her seduction of the male protagonist, Jan. Furthermore and perhaps more significantly, the one who seduces turns out to be an outsider — non-Moravian, a dark-skinned Gypsy.

Indeed, the title of Janáček's song cycle *Zápisník zmizelého* for tenor suggests another way to conceptualize Gypsiness: its ability to make something vanish through a fundamental alteration. As we shall see, Jan's singularity is raised up through a process of *Aufhebung* — *woman as Gypsy*. And woman, as a vanishing interval of distance, will have a peculiar, necessary, and privileged relationship to the singularity of Gypsy music, reconfiguring its essence as a permanent structure.

As becomes immediately apparent to understand the idea of disappearance in music crossed with a Gypsy theme, given Janáček's musical setting, requires a philosophical orientation. Gypsy music implies, for the temporality and historicity of music, that there can be no permanence in music. And does this not define the case with all so-called ethnic or folk musics, even with what (once was) "art" music? Can there ever be such a "thing" as musical permanence?

How is it possible to disappear? Here we are caught in the paradoxes of thinking Being: that even modes of non-existing are dependent for their expression in language on the verb "to be." Disappearing entails reappearing, the making way for a new spacing/configuration, the hammering away of old idols.[1] What is an appearance? How does something appear, on the scene, only to disappear/reappear? Or, to follow Kant who recoups for transcendental idealism the concept of Aristotelian substance, is everything in Being simply an alteration of what already is?

But to ponder Janáček's confrontation with a Gypsy *topos*: what kind of a musical style engages his response to the subject of disappearance? The common answer involves showing how Janáček's musical language appropriates modality, *altering* while *preserving* it (another way of naming *Aufhebung*), and how this results in a hyper-modal approach based on Moravian/Czech models.[2] Yet this hyper- or quasi-modal musical language exists only in the equivocal space of what we will call *stylistic virtual reality*. Here the boundaries of so-called folk/village versus art/composed musics become indeterminable. When a phenomenon such as "Gypsy music" is added to the dichotomy of folk versus composed, the chaos of indeterminacy intensifies.

Reformulated: Janáček's "Gypsy" style cannot be categorized according to the nationalistic predicative associations as they have been developed in historical musicology and in ethnomusicology. That Janáček's music is "Czech," for example, denotes a stylistic shorthand that breaks down at close examination. Bohemia and Moravia under Hapsburg rule included Jews, Germans, Gypsies, and Czechs — could there ever have existed a purely isolated, self-contained ethnic-musico phenomenon as "Czech?" If Czech (or any other) peasant music turns out to have a modal basis, can we ever be certain that this is really an isolated, unconscious, natural phenomenon (as folk music was for Bartók)? A part of some natural evolution? Alternatively, might modality be a musical process learned from "advanced" musical thinking, a heritage from the top down, emanating according to processes impossible to know from the learned cultures of the Middle East and especially the former Greek empire?

GYPSINESS AND THE CENTRAL EUROPEAN TRADITION

As we have tried to show with Brahms, Liszt, and Rachmaninov (the latter, as a Russian, an honorary member of our hypothetical "Gypsy" inspired Central European school), there was a primal attraction on the part of these composers (and others) to the Gypsy worldview expressed in the performative demand of music-making. Gypsies performed music *beyond* entertainment, in excess of and in spite of performance, in an age dominated by amateur music and the art-religion of the bourgeois concert hall. In this configuration, as functional (ritualistic) yet artistic, Gypsy musicians appeared on the scene in the same way "peasant/folk music" would appear later to twentieth-century composers from Bartók to Stravinsky. In the terms of Benjamin: the idea of Gypsy music exerted an *aura* beyond the superficialities of the bourgeois life, while embracing its codification into a stereotypical style.

And yet, it is only in the twentieth century, with Janáček, that the musical problem of Gypsiness *as* Gypsiness arises: its identity as a concept (an analytic proposition to use Kant's language) becomes the basis for a synthetic proposition, in that something is joined to it. We could say that Janáček *adds* something to the concept of Gypsy music. He does not appropriate the common associations of Gypsy music, as in its fundamental stereotyping in popular- or folk-song ornamentation or in string arrangements. Rather, Janáček uses Gypsiness in its appearance on the Central European scene to depict not emotions in general, but the specificity of his personal emotional state as pure *desire,* unknowable yet paradoxically thinkable. (Liszt, by contrast, uses Gypsiness to depict general observations of music as an emotive platform, universally situated.)

At this point, we stand in need of a kind of proof never before attempted in the history of music: a transcendental deduction. Despite its non-existence in the literature, every musicological utterance would seem to require it. Namely, we need to be able to show how a concept can relate to music material in order to make musical experience (performance) possible. With some irony and knowledge of the impossibility of its own possibility, we present:

INTERLUDE: THE TRANSCENDENTAL DEDUCTION OF GYPSINESS

For Kant, a deduction is the necessary logical operation to prove the validity of "the mode of our knowledge of objects in so far as this mode of knowledge is to be possible *a priori* [independent of sensibility]"; this kind of purely philosophical knowledge Kant calls "transcendental."[3] Now, the purpose of a transcendental deduction is to show how the objects of sensibility (the manifold) as given through the intuitions of time and space, or "appearances," can relate to the categories of the understanding (the purely formal, synthetic terms of thinking, all of which presuppose original and analytic apperception — the term "I think"), and thereby render experience possible. For Kant, the transcendental deduction is the most difficult operation of philosophy as a science, and as such he made two significant attempts at a deduction of his pure categories of the understanding.

Insofar as Gypsiness denotes a way of understanding a phenomenon, we can call it a category (note that strictly speaking, in the Kantian sense, empirical concepts can never rise to the title of the transcendental). As a category, Gypsiness is an operation of subjectivity, in that it shows itself only through the application of the understanding and the imagination. This implies that Gypsiness is not something found *in* the object, but is a relationship, subjectively determined.

Thus, to follow Kant's logic of the transcendental deduction, we can ask the following: how is it possible for Gypsiness, as a concept, to relate to any musical object or phenomenon (as a work)? Can there be a deduction, transcendental or otherwise, that allows us to use the term "Gypsiness" as an original, *a priori* judgment (or any kind of relation) concerning a musical happening?

Now to repeat our original thesis (see Chapter One), we have proposed that Gypsiness contains the values of emotion, virtuosity, and improvisation, as given by the equation $I+V=E$. Here Gypsiness denotes a way of synthesizing an appearing musical object (what Kant calls the *schematism* in its relationship to the pure category) in a way that these *subjective* values (the equation) determine and validate the musical process and ultimately performance. Thus in this way — as a subjective power of judgment derived from the understanding and imagination — Gypsiness would denote the purest *formal category* of the conditions for the possibility of emotive performance in Western music.

GERMANNESS IN MUSIC

Opposed to Gypsiness is what we might call "Germanness in music."

Germanness denotes the values of intellect, developing variation (in Schoenberg's sense; we use this term because it anachronistically summarizes for Schoenberg's camp the values of music as given through the heritage of the Viennese triad), and form (structural coherence), summarized in the mock equation:

Developing Variation + Organic Form = Intellect (DV+OF=I).

These values reach their historical *kairos* in Adorno's *Philosophie der neuen Musik*. However, what has escaped music historians including Dahlhaus and even a philosopher of Adorno's stature is that Schoenberg's values are subjectively determined: they are not given or dictated by the musical material.[4] They, too, stand in need of a transcendental deduction and are not *facts* as some would have it.

Germanness in music has as its driving aesthetic the idea that intellectual operations (motivic manipulation, development, growth, the variation principle) represent the highest goal of compositional technique, and that advances in music are based on pitch manipulations.

Thus taken together, Gypsiness and Germanness form the dialectic playfully driving the history of music since at least Beethoven. Analysis, as institutionalized in professional music theory, has neglected Gypsiness in favor of Germanness. In short, the reasons for this are based on the principle of quantification: analysts perceive pitch and rhythm as quantifiable parameters. Gypsiness, in contrast, operates according to mystique.

JANÁČEK'S MUSE

Janáček's final years saw a creative outburst that is incomparable to many composers, writing no less than four major operas in his final years, leaving perhaps the greatest such legacy from the twentieth century. Chronologically prior to this outpouring was *Diary*, a quasi-dramatic work for tenor and alto (and offstage women's chorus), written near the end of World War I (1917-18).[5]

The intense work coincides with Janáček's falling madly in love with Kamila Stösslová, the beautiful wife of an antique dealer. While Kamila appeared to have remained faithful to her marriage vows and withstood Janáček's fervent advances, Janáček's passion only grew stronger. As is well known, this passion inspired much of the composer's late work beginning with *Diary*, where the ideal of forbidden love determines the pathos of the compositional style. Janáček even placed a picture of his creative muse Kamila on the original title page of this piece.[6]

However, Janáček had encountered the texts that he would set as *Diary* in the Brno newspaper *Lidovy noviny* (Peoples Newspaper) in May of 1916, just before he met Kamila. Like most readers, Janáček assumed that the texts were real and not by a poet. It was only recently discovered that Ozek Kalda was the anonymous writer. Kalda wrote concisely in the Valachian village dialect, similar to Janáček's native Lachian. This linguistic peculiarity would have certainly attracted Janáček, whose lifelong interest in "speech melody" has been carefully studied by generations of musicologists.

This is how the newspaper set up the "diary" as nonfictional prose:

> Some time ago, in an East Moravian highland village, J.D., a law-abiding and industrious youth, disappeared from home in a mysterious way. At first an accident or even a crime was suspected and the imagination of the villagers was kindled. Some days later, however, a diary was found which disclosed the secret. It contained several short poems which eventually provided the key to the mystery...[7]

Newspaper publication guarantees that the line separating fiction from non-fiction becomes non-distinguishable: no matter what a reader might make of the alleged "village poetry," the fact that they are found in the newspaper medium seals their status as quasi- documentary truth.

We can also note the semantic contrast between village and city life. For Janáček's generation, village life represented a repository of truth; encroaching urban environments threatened the sanctity of this village life.[8] However, the city plays no role in the tale of the *Diary.* Rather the corrupting force is the nomadic life of the Gypsies.

Thus Kalda's writing is not a discourse on peasant life per se, but on the peasant encounter with Gypsies. Though in the early twentieth century there does not seem to be many Gypsies living in Moravia, still, most of the positive and negative associations that had been building in Europe over the centuries must have been present there.[9]

Jaromil Jires's film (again, the category of film is unavoidable) *The Lion with a White Mane* proposes exactly what Gypsies came to mean for Janáček: the positing of sexual desire and fulfillment. With a director's eye for colorful scenery, Jires proposes, perhaps with some element of truth, that Janáček had in fact visited a Gypsy camp. The theme of *dark* (the word cannot be overemphasized) Gypsy love with its built-in transgression of Czech social taboos paralleled Janáček's sexual passion for a much younger and married (= according to societal taboo, unavailable) woman. Jires depicts this in a swirling, surreal scene where Kamila merges with a Gypsy girl in Janáček's imagination.

Gypsies as the source and yet erasure of an imaginary style: this is the real power of Gypsiness, its ability to reflect the mind of the artist, as we with some irony tried to prove through a transcendental deduction. A truly vanishing style, where nothing is at stake (the political marginalization of the Gypsies) and yet everything matters (the turbulence when thinking of taking leave from the economic security of

Moravian agricultural life). We will also liken it to the deconstructive moment, where image and poetry exist only through the erasure of the one who writes.

Broadly put, *Diary* locates the converging of two interests for Janáček the *melos* of real speech as the model for melody, and actual/real love as the source of artistic inspiration. It is commonly assumed that real-life interests, as we are calling them, can be found in the work. Yet again, it is only through an imagined entity of what the text is about, Gypsies, that these two interests first become intertwined. Janáček's love for Kamila falls into the blurring of real-life and unconscious, dreamed desires. But if *Diary* is any indication, it certainly seems plausible: "it's too bad my Gypsy girl [Zefka] can't be called something like Kamila."[10]

A nationalist interpretation might not worry about the status of peasant appropriation by Gypsies in Janáček's work, because from this perspective, the work need not be interpreted, strictly speaking, as something "Czech." Yet because nothing political hinged on this work (the work was discovered by Janáček's student stuffed in a desk drawer, apparently forgotten), Janáček was free to explore his emotional landscape and psyché as an inner conflict. Through his dark, forbidden Gypsy muse, Janáček was able to explore his entire historical being as a man.

NARRATIVE OF THE CYCLE

In terms of the narrative it is the protagonist, Jan,[11] who vanishes into the milieu of Gypsy life. At the end of the cycle, Jan bids farewell to his native country, "for there can be no return from the life I'm beginning." Once he leaves his Czech village life to begin life with the Gypsies, in effect he is barred from returning.

Immediately we are reminded of Pushkin's Aleko. However, unlike Aleko, Jan leaves "civilized" life not because of his dissatisfaction therein, or a longing for sensual freedom (*volja*) that is only possible outside of an urban setting, as we saw with Aleko; Jan leaves because of his passion for a Gypsy girl. Restated, whereas Aleko meets Zemfira after he has left his previous life, Jan's reason for leaving is his desire for Zefka. Finally, it seems that Janáček would not have been drawn to a character like Zemfira, who betrays her non-Gypsy husband for a youthful Gypsy lover; Janáček's Zefka appears as a devoted wife and mother. (This transposition of the family into the Gypsy world stands in need of further analysis; see Forgiveness, Pleroma, and *Aufhebung* later in this chapter.)

MODALITY, MORAVIANNESS, AND GYPSIES

We have already mentioned that Janáček's artificial use of modality occupies what we are calling a stylistic virtual reality.[12] We shall now explore what this might mean, drawing on specific examples from *Diary*.

If Janáček is using the idea of Gypsies as a pretext for creating his own vision of what Moravian folk music might be, this is nowhere more urgent than at the Lydian onset of the cycle (see Music Example 21). Volek has commented that the "most complicated and original Lydian minor mode [centered on E] appears immediately at the beginning of [song] 1 — like a sign of the modal saturation of the whole work."[13] What complicates the modality of this passage is the vocal melody's C-sharp and D-sharp, for Volek, components of the major scale. However, we can question the positing of a major (ionic) in this context: the assertions of major intervals at scale degrees six and seven do not necessarily imply the major scale. Indeed, heard against the background of the minor Lydian tetrachord (E-F#-G-A#; note the augmented second), the C# and D# seem to be associated with the A#. This is confirmed when the melody descends to the A# in measure six; the rising perfect fourth of A#-D# is emphasized in measures 10-11(foreshadowed in m. 6 vocal/m. 7 piano) (see Music Example 22). This rising fourth creates the tension that Volek attributes to the clash of Lydian minor and major. The tritone symmetry of E-A# is destroyed with the emphasis on the D#.

Speculating for a moment: would a meditation on a purely Moravian theme have led Janáček to such an original modal language? Might we suppose that it is the Gypsy theme that allows or frees Janáček to create a new modality? For, what is heard in Janáček's modal appropriation can be understood as an *erasure* of the line between Gypsiness and Moravianness: Janáček mirrors the complete absorption of Jan into Gypsy life with the invention of a modal style beyond mode. In other words, Janáček is using the theme of forbidden Gypsy love as a way of initiating a broader confrontation with the implications of the effect of artificial modal directionality on Western music.[14]

The "supernatural" element enters in the piano part of the third song (see Music Example 23). The pitches F#-G-A#-B-D-E (Phrygian major; note the augmented second G-A#) are used for a text with an expressionist orientation: glow-worms and Gypsy eyes penetrate Jan's dreams under the moon.

Yet the difficult question remains: is there a precise, exact correspondence between the sonic reality of the mode and the text? Of course, such a question can be asked of tonal pieces in traditional song cycles; yet somehow, the question seems more urgent in the context of modality. Is there a level of *specific penetration* in terms of modality that reaches beyond the generalities of the tonal language?

In song number six, the pounding of the rhythmic ostinato over a Mixolydian seventh (B-flat) creates the perfect imagery of the heating up of the peasant's blood when he notices the Gypsy girl waiting for him (see Music Example 24). The unexpected B-natural at bar four distances the music from the world of the peasantry. The heterogeneity of what to call such a event of tonal (referring to *tonos*) slippage can only

Music Examples 21 and 22 Janáček, *Diary of One Who Vanished*, no. 1, "One day I met a Gypsy girl, measures 1-2, and measures 10-11.

Music Example 23 *Diary*, no. 3, "... twilight glowworms," measures 3-5.

be accounted for through recourse to the semantical juxtaposition of the unexpected Gypsies in Jan's landscape.

BENEVOLENT INTRUDERS?

Yet who are these Gypsies? Are they understood by Janáček as intruders to the otherwise peaceful landscape of the Czech landscape? This would be one way of reading the interruption of Jan's monologue by Zefka, to which we now turn.

Music Example 24 *Diary*, no. 6, "Hey, there my tawny oxen,' measures 1-5.

Immediately preceding the introduction of Zefka's voice is a homophonic exposition on Jan's acceptance of what his path in life will be (song eight). After a statement that cadences on A-flat major, Janáček moves back to E Lydian. The modal instability of this E Lydian is pronounced, however, in that it quickly mutates into a lyrical chromaticism (see Music Example 25). The transcendence of this line is reflected in Jan's

Music Examples 25 and 26 *Diary*, no. 8, "Don't look, my oxen" measures 9-13, and no. 9, "… handsome one," *Un poco meno mosso*.

first denial of Zefka, in a tight range, an intense reply to the tender beckoning of Zefka in the next song (see Music Example 26).

But the real "intrusion" or surprise of the piece does not occur until the so-called Gypsy "prayer" of Zefka. The surprise is the three altos that Janáček introduces into the texture, who function like a Greek chorus in their commentary role (see Music Example 27). The purpose of this interruption is to set the atmosphere for Zefka's song about the sad plight of the Gypsies, condemned to wander by God.

The piano introduces the choral intrusion, focusing on three-note cells in the ambit of thirds (see Music Example 28). Though the thirty-second note rhythm of the figure tries to indicate that Jan at this point remains undecided, the chorus

Music Examples 27 and 28 *Diary*, no. 9, "Drei Frauenstimmen," and three-note cells.

completely gives away the fact that the Gypsy has succeeded in her seduction at a distance. Indeed, in Zefka's song (song ten) which follows *attacca*, the figure returns (accompanying her recitative), and then full-blown with the chorus and its motive. The climax occurs when all three of these elements are combined (see Music Example 29).

Though these passages perhaps have more to tell us about "Moravianness" than anything specifically Gypsy, the intensity and directness propels us to reconsider what Janáček is proposing in this cycle.

Namely, what is the status of female agency, especially considering that we *hear* her voice and its echoing commentary (the female chorus)? Some possibilities: 1) as an unwanted stranger darkening an otherwise "normal" tale of running away from home; 2) as a radical mutation/violation of the semantics of the song cycle as handed down from the nineteenth-century tradition; 3) as an empowerment to the voice of woman in music; and 4) as a benevolent intrusion, where we experience the intrusion as disruption, breaking the flow of Jan's simplistic narrative, yet the disruption breaks the cycle of distance, creatively rendering the truth of woman's power as seductress.

What seems clear is that whether one views the feminine and likewise Gypsy intrusion as negative or positive, a subjectivity enters the drama that is somehow more alive and realistic than the flat character (at least up to now) of Jan. The benevolent grace of her entrance is that she ignites a fire in the heart of the protagonist: that though he will suffer in the Gypsy life, his reward is the purely erotic and faithful heart of a Gypsy wife. If there is one possible criticism of Janáček's narrative, it would consist in the fact that Jan's life does not seem to vanish; rather, he has been transformed through a once-distant woman.

Music Example 29 *Diary*, no. 10, "God all powerful," Tempo I.

WOMAN AS DISTANCE

Yet the original seduction by the Gypsy Zefka occurs at a distance — she waits at the border of the field, to catch the eye of Jan as he plows. Zefka says nothing to him, patiently waiting for the inevitable moment when he will approach. We refer to Derrida's commentary on Nietzsche's treatment of the subject of woman, which in the interest of space we present in an abridged form:

> A woman seduces from a distance. In fact, distance is the very element of her power. Yet one must beware to keep one's own distance from her beguiling song of enchantment. A distance from distance must be maintained...Perhaps woman is not some thing which announces itself from a distance, at a distance from some other thing. In that case it would not be a matter of retreat and approach. Perhaps woman — a non-identity, a non-figure, a simulacrum — is distance's very chasm, the out-distancing of distance, the interval's cadence, distance itself, if we could still say such a thing, distance *itself*. Distance out-distances itself.[15]

Woman disarms the touchstone of philosophy, the term "truth," for in her distancing (her essence) which veils/covers, woman proposes the moment of the "untruth of truth."[16] We could add that woman's distancing violates the principle of contradiction, what Kant calls "the universal, though merely negative, condition of all our judgments in general."[17]

But what interests us here is the thinking of woman as Gypsy? Gypsy woman: what does she name? If distance is an out-distancing, what kind of distance is indicated by the song of the Gypsy, possible only through its reverberations in the off-stage chorus? The echoing occurs from off-stage, never on the scene, throwing into permanent disarray the fictional status of the work as a song cycle.

For Janáček, the seduction by Zefka cannot be untruth or non-identity — rather, these terms apply to Jan's previous farming life, as in the ox and its cart. Woman, from a distance exercises a power to mold a man's being. Through her closeness to earth (song eleven), Zefka transcends the settled life of the non-Gypsy in the dialectical process of Hegelian *aufheben* through pleroma, the excess of love beyond calculation.

FORGIVENESS, *PLEROMA*, AND *AUFHEBUNG*

The figure of Zefka can be compared with Mary Magdalene, the prostitute who loved Jesus. Through their disruption of the reciprocity of the oath, both Zefka and Magdalena are the promise of a transcendent forgiveness outside of and beyond the law.[18] In the house of the Simon, Mary anoints the feet of Jesus with an oily balm: Jesus says "for this reason I tell you that her sins, her many sins, are forgiven her, because she loved much. But one who is forgiven little loves little." Derrida comments that "the extreme of love inundates, the *pleroma* always gives cause for action."

In his love of Zefka, Jan's actions go beyond (*aufhebt*) the law. He steals from another woman, his sister, not knowing whether or not the act is wrong. Jan's love for his sister remains within the confines of the law — he has not yet experienced pleroma with regard to his natural family. Only through his new Gypsy family is he capable of freedom, where an act is no longer subject to the rules of the law, but is motivated by pure love.[19] Thus Jan steals, but his conscience remains mute.

PARALLEL WORLDS: THE ROLE OF THE PRESENT IN THE *MAKROPULOS AFFAIR*

In Act II of the *Makropulos Affair* (the Czech word "*vec*" can also refer to "thing" or "case"), the plot digresses to the old man Hauk-Sendorf's devastating memory of a youthful affair with the beautiful *gitana* Eugenia, while he was in Andalusia. In terms of the perception of Gypsies around the time that Czechoslovakia was formed (1918), Michael Beckerman writes:

> Far from being a harsh, disturbing or sinister presence, the Gypsies at this time functioned as what we might call 'orientalism from within,' an exotic symbol of freedom, passion and improvisation.[20]

Beckerman analyzes Hauk's "madman" scene as containing three kinds of music; his example 6.2 exemplifies the sonic world of the Gypsies, especially with the castanets.[21]

Beckerman quotes the three worlds of music to show that "musical time tends to be innately circular, or rather spiral, since it can only have meaning by referring back to itself."[22] The problem, of course, is that if the audience can possibly *hear* only the present narrative action, how does a composer write in a previous time's music (a reminiscence) while music from the present is playing?

At this point, we can ask: why Gypsies at this point in the opera, and why the Gypsy dance? The obvious answer is local color, an "exoticism from within," presented through the reconfiguration of Emilia Marty as Eugenia Montez, a seductress in line with Zefka (= Kamila). Though this is plausible, on another level we can ask, why Spain? Beckerman argues that

> Although its castanets immediately suggest Spain, the dance does not derive from any proto-Iberian style but is a musical dialect Janáček has used many times before.[23]

Music Example 30 Janáček, "Gypsy Dance" from *Makropulos Affair*, rehearsal nos. 48-49 (reduction).

He bases his view on the concept of musical dialect on modal process — the use of the so-called "Lydian minor" (i.e., a minor third and a raised fourth). Music Example 30 is a reduction of the passage in question.

In spite of what Beckerman says, the phrasing and rhythm do seem to suggest a flamenco guitar. Furthermore, in terms of the temporality of the scene in question: Gypsies would denote the present, and an impossibly deferred one. For Beckerman, this locates an *imaginary* present.[24] Whether it is impossible or imaginary, the central point is that the Andalusian Gypsy atmosphere depicted on stage is culled from Hauk's memory.

Yet no matter what the level of clashing of past and present timeframes might be, the "Gypsy Dance" (again, the marker Janáček uses for Hauk's flashback to Andalusia) seems unmistakably in the present for the listener, foreshadowing and enveloping the portrayal of sex as Marty becomes *la chula negra* for Hauk one more time, sending him spiraling downward, once again, into madness. Paradoxically, the sexual reliving (relieving) of the experience of the past action becomes for the audience more a living, alive, or enlivened vehicle than the "present" as given via the operatic action.

This temporal vortex created through the mixing of past and present is what the artistic vehicle of Gypsiness became for Janáček. It is also a play on a purely emotional turbulence at once *beyond* the codes of Czech and Gypsy culture. For, even in old age Janáček, like Hauk, cannot seem to escape the inspired memory of a dark Gypsy seductress, real or imagined, but so necessary to his work.

Chapter Nine

The Specter of Bartók: From Hungarian Musicology to the Folk-Music Revival

Investigating the historical appropriation of the aesthetic of Gypsiness in Western art music, we must take into account the seismic shift in the valuation of Gypsy music. Again, as initially sketched in Chapter One: for Liszt and other nineteenth-century composers, Gypsy music as Hungarian national music was an exotic language, treasured for its rhythmic flexibility, melodic fluency, and evocative performance gestures. Beginning with Bartók and then spreading to other twentieth-century Hungarian composers/(ethno)musicologists, Gypsy music became a problematic phenomenon. In Bartók's estimation, Gypsy music represents a contaminated, mass-audience tourist-traffic music. Furthermore and with larger implications, Bartók refused to equate Hungarian music proper with especially urban Gypsy music.

Though this last point has begun to become recognized in circles outside of Hungary, its ramifications are less well understood and explored. Especially when we take into consideration the broader narrative, in which composers such as Bartók, Janáček, and Stravinsky enjoy iconographic status as great Modern masters whose musical languages cannot be separated from the folk-music traditions of their native Eastern Europe and Russia. Indeed, for some time now, views about Bartók's music have been crystallizing around two ideas, in order of significance: 1) compositional procedure *vis-à-vis* symmetries, golden section et al.; 2) his discovery and subsequent integrational appropriation of peasant music. Substantiating this later idea for students, we find that music history textbooks frequently reproduce a picture taken in 1905 showing a young Bartók recording the peasants with a phonograph.

Like all generalizations, the tenet about the peasant/folk music influence on his compositional style, propagated by the international musicological machine, must be deconstructed, and rigorously.[1] I will do so along two lines: 1) a spectral gesture, where we imagine Bartók's ghost hovering over both performances of his music, and statements by performers and musicologists made *in his name*; and 2) the questioning of what "peasant" actually means, and its later reintegration and conflation with the stylistic series verbunkos (later czárdás)/Gypsy/Hapsburg.

This chapter investigates the aesthetic and epistemological underpinnings of Bartók's discourse, focusing on his ideas about peasant musical creation, and his critique of Liszt and Gypsy music. This topic has received limited and only recent scholarly attention; appropriately I will try to indicate areas that are in need of further analysis. After this we will look at ways in which Bartók's notion of authenticity continues to fuel Hungarian folk music and study, culminating in a reading of the Hungarian group Muzsikás's recent album and performances in the United States.

BARTÓK'S ACHIEVEMENTS IN MUSICAL FOLKLORE

Bartók's fieldwork sought to uncover the given nation's real or pure folk music.[2] Urban music represented a mixture of multi-national influences, a tainted source, and hence could not be taken as a true symbol of the nation's music. Rather, the vast, collective memory of culturally isolated peasants formed a massive storage bin for the nation's authentic folk music. Furthermore, because of encroaching urbanization and industrialization, Bartók believed that peasant music was on the verge of extinction, and that his generation was witness to its "final hour."[3]

In terms of Hungarian musicology, Bartók's thinking exerted a powerful re-evaluation of his nation's belief system. The main feature of Bartók's system is that he substituted the peasant for the Gypsy fiddler as the repository of the Hungarian nation's musical life. In contemporary Hungarian circles, this view still holds, though ironically mediated with a realization of the significance of Roma (Gypsy) village string bands in keeping alive the ancient Hungarian tradition.

WHO SPEAKS FOR THE PEASANT?

But first a reservation: there seems a certain amount of presumptuousness to the notion that the music of peasants can be preserved by researchers, whether they be amateur musicians or professionally employed ethnomusicologists. What grants Bartók, or any other researcher, the right to "speak for," as it were, the peasant? What are the hidden politics and class interests behind such schemes of representation? Bartók could respond that he understands the difference between an "authentic" and "non-authentic" folk tune, an issue that a peasant could not possible be conscious of. Moreover, as we shall see, Bartók's approach assumes that an uneducated peasant, by definition, has no real knowledge of what music they are singing.

It is precisely a point like this, however, which re-affirms a central difference between Eastern European/Russian (formerly Soviet) ethnomusicology and American/Western European ethnomusicology, in that recent poststructural trends in the latter traditions have problematized the search for "authentic" musical events interpreted by a non-judging, objective consciousness. Every moment constitutes a "final hour," in that at every moment some event is lost forever.

TWIN SOURCES OF MUSICAL CREATION

Within Bartók's writings on folk music is a theory of musical creation that is in opposition to Western aesthetics. What led Bartók to his theory was his valuation and advocacy of peasant music. In this respect Bartók was truly in the forefront of ethnomusicological (or, "comparative musicological") knowledge during his time.

For musicologists of the late nineteenth and early twentieth centuries, there was an unspoken assumption that great music issued only from great composers. Indeed, the essence of music was defined in circular fashion by great music of the Western canon; most "primitive musics," for the *Musikwissenschaftler* of this time period, would be called "music" only for lack of a better word. Peasant music would fall into the category of primitive music, or what we might call pre-musical process.

The idea of "greatness" was founded on the cult of the genius, whose two greatest representatives, Bach and Beethoven, came from German-speaking lands.[4] Furthermore, "genius" was understood in the nineteenth century in its Kantian formulation. In the *Critique of Judgment* Kant states that "genius is the innate mental predisposition (*ingenium*) through which nature gives the rule to art."[5] For Kant, the source of great art (and not science) is ultimately nature, defined vaguely as a power (*Gewalt*, also the German word for violence) whose energies are channeled through the genius.

Bartók's idea remains Kantian in spirit, especially with the grounding of art in natural processes, yet he adds another source for artistic creation: the collective body of the peasantry. Acknowledging this collective source shows willingness on Bartók's part to revise the standard Western interpretation of musical creation. Perhaps, too, lurking here is a variant Marxism, with its appeal to the collective body of the working class.

How, then, do peasants create? Bartók's answer is psychological:

> [P]easant music... is nothing but the outcome of changes wrought by a natural force whose operation is unconscious in men who not influenced by urban culture.[6]

The crucial aspect of the force is that its operation is unconscious, a product of nature, a formulation with a clear Kantian heritage. The urban life of the city contaminates men, and prevents the natural creative force that we all possess from realizing itself. Startling in Bartók's formulation is its appeal to an abstract, natural force, which seems a secularized version of the "divine gift" of man's reason as found in the Thomastic heritage, and that the life of the city would effectively cancel out this divine light.

AUTHENTICITY IN FOLK MUSIC

We can summarize some of Bartók's criteria for determining a folk tune's authenticity:[7]

> 1) Peasants must inhabit a given and defined geographical region over a relatively long and stable period of time (what he calls the "law of the locality"), and the researcher must encounter the tune in its native environment (13); the tune must be sung by a majority (13), in order to determine:

> 2) A melody must "undergo various changes and begin to branch out into variations" (10);

> 3) A performance of the tune must exhibit the "uniform emotional pattern of the peasants";

> 4) The informant must be uneducated (an "absolute restriction," 13)

> 5) The scale used is the pentatonic; though this scale may utilize the two tones of the diatonic scale, in a passing role (61).

Famously, Bartók was one of the first to compare peasant music with the masterpieces of Western art music:

> Correspondingly it [peasant music] has in its individual parts an absolute artistic perfection, a perfection in miniature forms which — one might say — is equal to the perfection of a musical masterpiece of the largest proportions. It is the classical model of how to express an idea musically in the most concise form, with the greatest simplicity of means, with freshness and life, briefly yet completely and properly proportioned.[8]

In his description of a peasant aesthetic, Bartók also provides an indication of his own neo-classical leanings: a perfection in miniature, mimicking on a smaller scale the proportion or symmetry of the large work. This compact beauty is the ideal of conciseness, defined here as the simple. For a work to be good, it must be simple, which we interpret as direct, without artifice: further down, Bartók will use the word "clarity": peasant music, like the best Classical music, presents the material clearly, according to the "transforming" principles of true art.

To summarize so far, Bartók's logic admits of only two figures who can create, to the exclusion of the town-dweller: on the one hand, the peasant, on the other, the "individual genius": "the creative impulse of anyone who has the misfortune to be born somewhere between these two extremes leads only to barren, pointless, and misshapen works."[9]

BARTÓK'S NEGATIVE APPROPRIATION OF GYPSY MUSIC

At first glance, it seems that for Bartók, Gypsy music would fall into the category of barren works, because most of the tunes produce a mixture of "exoticism and banality."[10] Bartók observes that

> The music that is nowadays played 'for money' by urban Gypsy bands is nothing but popular art music of recent origin. The role of this popular art music is to furnish entertainment and to satisfy the musical needs of those artistic sensibilities are of a low order.[11]

And yet, despite Bartók's seeming damnation of Gypsy music/Hungarian popular art music, a mass commodity article for lowly tastes, he still feels its worth above the

> onslaught of the jazz and salon orchestras; we wish that they [the Gypsy bands] may continue to cling to their old repertory with its original physiognomy, without the admixture of waltzes, song hits, jazz elements, and what not.[12]

This passage has not been taken into account in recent years, in that many still assume that there is a final or definitive demarcation in Bartók's thinking separating Gypsy music from peasant music (more on this below).

Thus to determine exactly where Gypsy music fits into Bartók's thinking is not as simple as it first appears, and requires a complex and patient amount of analysis. How do we reconcile Bartók's mature defense of Liszt, for example, with some of his critical takes on what inspired Liszt? (We will examine this extremely tricky matter in more detail below.) And more and more, it seems that musicologists are finding Gypsy material as a potent source in Bartók's own music.[13]

The idea of "negative" appropriation is here relevant, which we will define as putting something to use to make fun of it, a mode of musical satire. And yet, in the act of negative appropriation, the interpretive effect of the musical process on the listener becomes amazingly complex, in that listeners (especially once the work becomes torn from its original timeframe) do not know the context for the appropriation. Thus what began as negative can be heard, later and out-of-context, as positive!

For clearly, if Bartók values what must be traditional traces in peasant life and music to such a high degree (indeed, it would not be too strong a statement that his encounter with village life completely and forever changed his belief system and life), there is nothing conflicting in his statement concerning Gypsy music and jazz; but still, there is always the vexing problem of how to explain the existence of numerous elements associated with Gypsiness and its performative in his mature work, especially the *Rhapsodies*, the verbunkos movement in *Contrasts, Music for Strings/Percussion/ Celeste*, the Second Violin Concerto (duvo accompaniment), the Sixth String Quartet, and the *Concerto for Orchestra*. In short, the works that today he is most famous for are unthinkable without reference to their Gypsy components.

Now, to interpret these in a way that is congruent with Bartók's writings (the essay review "Gypsy Music or Hungarian Music" was, after all, written in 1931), there remain stunning reasons why Bartók would denigrate Gypsy music as a valid source of inspiration. First, Bartók's critique of Gypsy music has symmetrical parallels with German-centrist critiques of Bartók's (and other composers from the formerly Hapsburg lands, including Janáček's) own music. Take Adorno's criticism of Bartók, for example, that Bartók's own music represents artistic backsliding because the source material is outdated *vis-à-vis* the historical destruction (in fact, deconstruction) of tonality. For Adorno, Bartók's (and Stravinsky's) choice of peasant music as the basis for a new art form is a historical wrong turn.

Second, there is the rather complicated phenomenon of expanding Hungarian nationalism at the turn of the century. Judit Frigyesi has analyzed the sociological context of the popularity of the urban Gypsy during the nineteenth century.[14] It seems that the proud Hungarian gentry class, some of whom were actually broke by this time, took pride in writing popular songs, that they would then have the Gypsy bands play. At a certain point, probably by the mid-nineteenth century, the performing and improvisational facility of Gypsy bands led to the widespread belief that these were tunes of Gypsy origin. And in addition to this question of musical property, the upshot was that this Gypsy music became the symbol for the Hungarian nation/people, the repository of the nation's soul. One factor standing in the way of the public acceptance of Bartók's "scientific" attempts (more on this below) to found peasant music studies were pre-conceived ideas, really myths, about what actually constituted Hungarian music. Thus because of his opposition to the Hungarian gentry's brand of nationalism, it was only natural for Bartók to oppose Gypsy music. Yet he was still patriotic enough to realize that the real stranglehold over his country's artistic and political aspirations was the Hapsburg Empire, and the German language hegemony it represented. This is why, precisely, he held up Gypsy music (even after the establishment of Hungary after World War I) against the waltz, for example; one wonders what he means by jazz and song hits (Tin Pan Alley?), but this is an area which could be resolved in new research.

BARTÓK CONTRA LISZT

The title of Bartók's first opus number, the *Rhapsody* for piano and orchestra (1904) already reveals the composer's debt to Liszt. This is to be expected, especially given the fact that nearly all non-German composers (and some German ones, too, perhaps) — so-called "nationalist" composers and even French ones — are unthinkable without Liszt.

For the philosopher Philippe Lacoue-Labarthe, Wagner is one of the great watershed figures in the history of music, in that he changed how to think about music more than any composer in history.[15] Whether or not Lacoue-Laborthe's thesis about Wagner is in fact correct, something seismic does seem to occur to the concept of music in the late nineteenth century. It seems no small coincidence that the two philosophers who re-evaluated music's position within the arts are nearly contemporaneous to Wagner and Liszt — Schopenhauer and Nietzsche. Indeed, Nietzsche's philosophy would be unthinkable without the context of Wagnerianism, itself owing huge debts (still largely unexplored) to Lisztean thought and aesthetics.

In the essay Bartók wrote in 1936, "Liszt Problems," we must insist on the use of the word "problem" in the title. What is a problem, and especially when applied to a composer? How can a composer's music possibly be a problem?

One problem that Bartók identifies with Liszt is the reception of his music, that audiences are opposed to the most difficult of Liszt's music, while accepting the "insignificant and outwardly brilliant works [by which he means the *Hungarian Rhapsodies* among them]."[16] But how does this constitute a problem, for Liszt? Or is it really the author Bartók's problem, the writer of the text on Liszt? Is "problem" a construction of writing and representational strategies, rather than of musical performance or display?

After considering why Liszt's works are imaginative but never perfect,[17] Bartók considers the book on Gypsies. Bartók first excuses Liszt for making the mistake that Gypsy music is of Gypsy and not Hungarian origin; for in Liszt's day, there was no such branch of science interested in musical folklore.[18]

But then, beyond the limitations of the science of his day, it was in fact Liszt's tastes which led him astray:

> One sees that the classical simplicity of the peasant melodies [We can question this point. Bartók is referring to the structure of the melodies, how they are organized formally; yet as sounding phenomena, these are anything but simple. Furthermore, why simple? What is so simple this about this style?] did not interest him [Liszt] (if indeed he was ever able to hear them at their most beautiful) and for this again we must blame his period, the nineteenth century. Liszt, like so many of his contemporaries, was fascinated by frills and decorations, show and glittering ornamentation, than by perfectly plain, objective simplicity. This explains why he placed the extravagant, over-loaded and rhapsodic [again, this word seems so overblown, so necessary, so wonderfully arrogant every time Bartók employs it] Gypsy music-making higher than the peasant performances.[19]

Although Bartók is usually concerned with appellation and what we have been calling the issue of musical property, in this passage he instead hones in on what really bothers him about Liszt's preference for Gypsiness in music. For Bartók's protest/resistance to Lisztean gestures are really against what Michael Beckerman has recently called the "polyglot shimmer of the Hapsburg music" (mentioned in Chapter Five). Beckerman pins the polyglot shimmer to the favorite and most popular operetta composer of this style, Franz Lehár, but finds traces of it in composers such as Mozart, Schubert, Dvořák and Mahler.

Bartók's sets up an opposition that bristles as a manifesto for early twentieth-century modernism: classical, simple, peasant, objective, and plain, versus frill, decoration, glittering ornamentation, extravagant, over-loaded, and rhapsodic. This opposition can be reduced to the traditional philosophical privileging of essence (peasant) over accident (Gypsy).

Simply reversing the opposition only leads to a re-engagement with Bartókian metaphysics, what we can call his ontologizing of the peasant. If we take the side of the Gypsy, this does not defeat Bartók's metaphysical position. To argue with a metaphysical position is merely to set up another metaphysics; instead, we will follow Heideggerian procedure and take a step back from the debate.

DECONSTRUCTING BARTÓK

We can begin to deconstruct Bartók's position from the following passage, upon which his entire metaphysics rests:

> As for the origins of such music [pure folk music], this factor would be as difficult to determine as it is difficult to determine the origin of vegetable or animal species or life. Another comparison is the following: folk language and folk music have very much similarity in their appearance, life, and function. We cannot trace the origin of the single words and grammatical forms to their absolute source, to the very invention of these words and forms. And, in a similar way, we cannot indicate the very source of the single tunes of pure folk music.[20]

On first reading, such a passage seems a fairly straightforward statement of the "problem" of folk music research (again, this passage is taken from another essay with "problem" in the title: "Some Problems of Folk Music Research in East Europe").[21] The basic idea is that musical transformation (and continuity, one might add) rests on a process of barely perceptible changes to a pattern that becomes established, generation after generation. In this respect, music is like a language in that both seem to exhibit the force of change in similar ways.

But then, why hold on to such formulations as "pure folk music," especially when the "absolute source" cannot be determined, as Bartók is willing to grant? By his own admission it is impossible to prove an origin by observation; a state of origin can only be arrived at by deduction from what is present. And yet in any treatment of purity, the pure concept must stand as absolute, without *any* amount of indeterminacy; there can be no hedging, no empirical messiness, no exceptions around its borders.

Someone wanting to defend to Bartók against such a rebuttal would say that he is only pointing to a difficulty, a problem, in his search for the oldest layers of folk music. He is not thereby engaging in philosophy. By "pure," he merely indicates only uneducated, village, isolated music in a quasi-natural environment. For, the argument would continue, music does exist, at a certain historical point, at a stage similar to birdsong: in this, its pure, natural state, before becoming a part of the contamination of urban, planned life. We might formulate what Bartók is searching for in his idea of pure folk music this way: music untouched by a consciousness of music-making, or music as pure doing separate from knowing.

However, what Bartók calls pure folk music does more than merely postulate an old-style of music. Again, Bartók establishes a hierarchy of what he values in music, where the oldest, uneducated layer of peasant music is equated with nature, which exhibits an unconscious power of creation on the same level as the individual genius. One cannot wish away the metaphysical standpoint of Bartók's position, whether or not he intends it in that fashion.

Simultaneously, Gypsiness in music — ornaments, frills, filler, schmaltz, Hapsburg polyglot shimmer — are all condemned as impure music, unworthy of serious, systematic, scientific study. This locates where the deconstruction of Bartók's position begins: around his establishment of a rigid hierarchy based on a metaphysical conflation of source, purity, and origin, identified as the uncontaminated folk music of the peasant, and his deflation of the ornamental. Again, none of these links can be established with certainty, while at the same time and by definition these concepts require recourse to the notion of the absolute. And the absolute is unattainable in terms of empirical research. Thus within this spacing of the conceptual array of Bartók's pseudo-scientific and philosophical justification of peasant music, we can begin to see how frail his aesthetic privileging of a natural, unseen, and barely perceptible musical transformation is.

SCIENTIFIC COLLECTING

Bartók's published transcriptions are what today would be called descriptive transcriptions, in that they aim for the closest possible level of detail. As for playing these transcriptions, a musician would basically have to ignore much of what Bartók notates in order to get something to sound. In short, these are difficult transcriptions, multivalent, and unyielding. They seek to be purely representational, intending to show *exactly* what is sounding on the phonograph. However, in their privileging of pitch and to a certain extent rhythm, they essentially ignore timbre, background sound, overtones, imprecisions (what for Bartók might have been mistakes) in the performance. Yet no notation is ever exact. We might ask why he publishes in this rigid and difficult style? In a word, for legitimacy: to provide an objective, unreachable, scientific basis for his advocacy of the music that fascinated him.

Furthermore, Bartók did not leave us with any indication that he was interested in having future generations perform these tunes; rather, his instinct was one of scientific preservation, like an archeologist storing flora and fauna in a vast archival warehouse. His idea of collecting is based on the idea of reproduction:

> The amateur work of old [by which he means collecting efforts in the nineteenth century] was replaced by *scientific research*. Even if the first collectors had intended to, they could not have produced satisfactory results from the scientific viewpoint, for they lacked the essential of instruments — the phonograph. Present-day researchers work with a variety of measuring and fixing instruments: they are thus able to give the most faithful reproduction possible in the form of a "snapshot" of each melody. But having the best material equipment is not enough: the equivalent *intellectual equipment* is just as important. In fact the folklorist possesses an erudition that is virtually encyclopedic.[22]

An assumption here is that a given melody is capable of being reproduced. A sound recording device can "measure" and then "fix" the sounding phenomenon. Fixing and measuring are the essence of a scientific product, the "result" also being indebted to technology. The new technology makes possible measuring/fixing in ways that were impossible in the nineteenth century.

As we enter the new millennium, we know that so-called historic recordings can sometimes raise more questions about what we are hearing than they answer. What does Jascha Heifetz's recording of Mendelssohn's E minor concerto tell us about his playing? What standards do we hear by, in order to gauge or to measure his performance, especially as we lose touch through remastering (cleaning up) and digital technology with the original means of the sonic fidelity of the recording? Further, the standards of what constitutes proper taste might turn out to be not of Heifetz's choosing, though we try to sit in judgment. History, taste, aesthetics, personal philosophy, and finally cultural context intersect in ways that make hearing an impossible category by which to determine what something is.

When we hear the early recordings that Bartók or others like his counterpart Brailoui in Romania made, we cannot presume to know what we are hearing. That is, no context is fixed for us as a yardstick of truth as we experience these recordings. Recording technology has produced a distance and vanishing from the material that is unprecedented in history. The material exists in what Heidegger has called the "standing-reserve" (*Bestand*), where it waits for use, ready for use; yet we have not yet adequately thought through the implications of an archive of stored sonic memories.[23]

And Bartók is well aware of the limitations of technology, that "having the best material is not enough: the equivalent intellectual equipment is just as important." What he means here is that the person must be an expert in linguistics, phonetics, choreography, customs, sociology, the history of settlements, and an expert musician. And he knows that such a person never has nor never will exist.

"Intellectual equipment" indicates the interpretive level, something that in Bartók's view exists as something added on to the objective level of scientific research. Research fixes and measures, while interpretation alters according to the inadequate level of knowledge of the measurer.

Though we will leave this matter of science at this point, it would be instructive to trace all the texts in which Bartók invokes the concept of "scientific research" to justify his own fieldwork or methodological approach to criticism.

THE PROBLEM OF SCIENTIFIC INTERPRETATION IN ROMANOLOGY

As such, my argument is that scientific folk-song collecting is impossible on the very grounds by which it claims to be possible: its completeness. Empirically, musical material, as Bartók himself observes, is like a living creature, breathing and changing from moment to moment.

Let us take Bartók's idea about "intellectual equipment" and apply it to a fledgling and relatively young field of Romanology (the study of Roma groups and topics). What a scholar (s)he would be! Someone, a linguist, conversant in the dialects of Romani, who in addition knows the hundreds of languages and dialects of all the various countries that Roma live in; someone with comparative anthropological and ethnomusicological credentials on at least four continents, in a bewildering (and as of now, unknown) number of local contexts. And this is not even to mention the massive and centuries-old dissemination of the signifier "Gypsy" across popular and so-called "high-art" cultures. Not even to mention the massive political difficulties in studying the Roma: the politics of identity coupled with legal advocacy issues.

GYPSIES AS PEASANTS

In Frigyesi's writing, it is assumed that there is a clear separation of peasant and Gypsy music. She tries to note transference in what was valued as a Hungarian national essence, from Gypsy "weeping-rejoicing" to peasant coolness (non-emotionality) in Bartók's thinking. Though she herself does not seem to buy into this distinction completely, she argues that for Bartók it was a definite dividing line.

And Bartók does seem to position his theory in terms of the dynamics of musical property. This idea entails that the act of creation entitles the person or group to the privileged status of group ownership. When given an ethnic bias, musical property is extremely difficult to disentangle from ideas about nationalism. Thus Bartók argues that Gypsy musicians play repertoire that is not the property of Gypsy culture. Specifically, Gypsy bands play music composed by the dilettante composers of the Hungarian nobility. Because it was beneath the dignity of these aristocratic gentlemen to perform in public, they hired the Gypsy bands to do so.[24]

To prove his theory, Bartók had to retrieve what for him was authentic Hungarian music. This triggered the fieldwork that Bartók carried out in the first two decades of the twentieth century, which has proved to be the foundation for later Hungarian musicology.

For Bartók, fieldwork meant recording and doing on-the-spot notation of melodies. As he was concerned about the contamination of peasant life and music, the only informants were those who had spent their entire life in the village. He cautioned against mining districts or areas where there might be "tourist traffic," and did not allow educated persons as informants.[25]

But I would still question how rigid the line is between peasant life and music and the sense of Gypsy style, as Bartók sets up this distinction. Namely, perhaps Frigyesi is claiming that the distinction in Bartók is based more on the development that Hungarian musicology would take later in the century. But as we shall see in the next section, Bartók was not so secure in the separation of peasant and Gypsy, hedging on it in ways that later Hungarian researchers would seek to erase.

BARTÓK-MÖLLER POLEMIC

In 1997 Benjamin Suchoff published Bartók's ethnomusicological writings for the first time in English, specifically those which could not be included in the earlier *Essays*.[26] The edition contains a polemical exchange between Bartók and the German ethnomusicologist Heinrich Möller, carried out in 1931-32 in the journal *Zeitschrift für Musikwissenschaft*.

The exchange is significant in many ways, and here I will note two points: 1) Bartók gives a more refined and sharper version of his views on Gypsy music in this published polemic than is presented, say, in his *Hungarian Folk Song*;[27] 2) though both authors claimed victory, the main points of the debate remain wide open, unresolved, and pertinent for the contemporary world-music scene.

Bartók argues that Möller's collection of Hungarian folk songs titled *Ungarische Volkslieder* is faulty from a "scientific viewpoint."[28] Bartók's main complaint, to summarize quickly, is that the popular art song is not adequately differentiated from the peasant folk song, and that even within these larger categories the proper sub-types are not represented. And even worse (at least for Bartók), Möller apparently has privileged the popular art song, which Bartók hardly feels is worthy of serious study (for a particular song that was disputed, see the song "Nem volt párja a faluban," in German as "Ohnegleichen war Andreas Kerekes"). Finally, Möller has made possibly the most damning mistake of all in Bartók's eyes, which is that he incorrectly designates the new Hungarian popular art music as "Gypsy music."[29]

Möller's preface to his edition contains the following crucial argument against what Möller calls Bartók's "theory," which Suchoff also quoted in his Preface to the

1997 text of Bartók's writing. Because of the importance of the passage, we will quote it in its entirety (again, this is Möller's prose):

> Modern folk song specialists tend to underestimate the Gypsy flavor — in fact, they would rather not count the Gypsy-influenced tunes and the popular art songs among the Hungarian folk songs at all. This theory attempts to limit the term folk tune to the narrow concept peasant tune, in the not easily proved assumption that the result would be "pure" folk music. However, *never and nowhere have the peasants been the only source of folk songs or exclusively carried on its traditions.* The tradition has rather been carried from one place to another and through the ages by traveling folk more than by any other class, and in Hungary these people were Gypsies. It is therefore quite impossible to separate "pure" and Gypsy-influenced Hungarian folk music.
>
> Separation of the so-called peasant song from the rest of Hungarian folk song would not be very profitable even it possible: for the peasant-song concept is historically, socially and stylistically just as relative and indefinite as that of the folk song in general; peasant tradition is no more reliable than Gypsy tradition; both assimilate and deform in conformity with certain conventional rules of which it is hard to say whether the peasant or the Gypsy stereotypes are the artistically more valuable ones.[30]

When I first read Möller's passage, I must confess to be completely taken aback. For here was a succinct statement of what might be wrong with Bartók's "theory." Bartók's thesis about the peasant origins of the oldest layer of the Hungarian folk song is really that, a hypothesis, in that it is pre-scientific: it is Bartók's proposal for what accounts for the existence of a layer of music material that exists only the countryside. As such, his proposal is reasonable in that it explains why the peasant material does not make its way into the cities, and it does possess an inner logic that remains tantalizingly compelling. This is perhaps why Bartók's theory has been persuasive in terms of its reception by the Hungarian musical and especially folk establishment.

However, as Möller forcefully stresses, "never and nowhere have the peasants been the only source of folk songs or exclusively carried on its traditions." There can be no scientific justification for Bartók's theory, in that prior to the recording techniques of the twentieth century, an oral tradition is impossible to know as such. Again, apropos Möller: "peasant tradition is no more reliable than Gypsy tradition." Möller's essential argument that it is the traveling people — in the case of Hungary, Gypsies — who carry the tradition of the folk song is an updating of the ideas of Liszt. But it, too, is still only on the level of theory, and one like Bartók's that is not possible to "prove" scientifically (see both Bartók's and Möller's difficulties in trying to come to terms with the so-called Gypsy scale, the scale with augmented seconds, called "Gypsy" in many countries, including Hungary, Russia, and Germany).

Bartók's response to the passage is also indicative of the fact that Bartók thought he could provide a methodology that would differentiate Hungarian peasants from Gypsy peasants living in their midst. Again, it is necessary to quote the text from Bartók:

> There remains the possibility of a designation like 'Gypsy performance.' Yet there is a catch here, too. The mode of performance customarily designated the 'Gypsy way' will be encountered in its purest [again, the necessity of a notion of purity infects Bartók's thinking everywhere] form in the city Gypsy bands. The further we move from the urban cultural centers, the simpler this 'way' becomes until, finally, we find a *Gypsy performance in remote villages that is in no way different from peasant performances* [this is truly an amazing concession on Bartók's part!]. Thus it seems that even the mode of performance depends not on race but seemingly on the environment. This leads to the conclusion [what follows is rather a non-sequitur] that even the so-called Gypsy-style performance is of Hungarian origin [for political and really nationalist reasons, Bartók latches on to this term, apparently disregarding that what he is calling Hungarian would be better termed as a Hapsburg style] and is a mode of performance of the Hungarian gentry class. A non-Hungarian will only ask: Why do Gypsy bands play in this way? The question is incorrect in view of the fact that Hungarian gentlemen do so (on the piano, the dulcimer, the violin) and to a considerable extent, but exclusively within the family circle; that is, without remuneration, for it was considered disgraceful for a Hungarian nobleman (it is well known that until the last century the gentry class was composed solely of Hungarian nobles) to earn money by playing in public.[31]

First, Bartók concedes that Gypsies can and do play music in the peasant tradition of the villages. Second, Bartók refuses to acknowledge that the tradition of Gypsy performance of the Hungarian popular art song (to concede this term to Bartók, for the sake of argument) has its origins with Gypsies.

In terms of this second point: it is impossible to know with certainty, and to prove empirically, where the style of verbunkos performance actually came from. One of the first great names, however, that is associated with this style is János Bihari, the Gypsy fiddler and bandleader who was among those responsible for Liszt's passion for Gypsy music.[32] And to use a non-historical argument, the style of verbunkos performance (what Bellman labels as the *style hongrois*), as described by Liszt in terms of ornamentation and improvisation, seems to share Gypsy performance characteristics as found in Russia, France, Turkey, and Spain. Thus given the existence of the bandleader Bihari and the fact that some of performative gestures of verbunkos seem to be an aspect of Gypsy music in other countries, it seems highly probable — though not absolutely certain — that at the very least, Gypsies have something to do with verbunkos performance gestures, the "weeping-rejoicing." Lastly, though we cannot empirically refute Bartók, it seems improbable to believe that the Hungarian gentlemen of Bartók's day could perform in the style or mannerisms of professional Gypsies.

THE RECEPTION OF BARTÓK IN KODÁLY'S FOLK MUSIC OF HUNGARY (1956)

Turning to the reception of Bartók's ethnomusicological research, his original collaborator and to certain extent inspiration in the field Kodály was among the first to reaffirm the central significance of Bartók's work for the younger generation of scholars. At first Bartók's "theory" seems to have received little general attention, and even was unacceptable (as Möller argues) to the Hungarian scholar community. Kodály adds in his preface that

> ... unfortunately Bartók's study only reached a small circle of experts, and the public hardly at all. Generally speaking, Hungarian folk music is still identified with Gypsy music ...[33]

Perhaps it would be better to substitute the word "convinced" for "reached," for it would not seem to be the case that writings coming from Bartók, a famous composer and personality, would only "reach" a small circle of experts.

Kodály's position is much more defensive than Bartók's: the first few pages of the Preface are dedicated to a refutation of the identification of "Hungarian" with "Gypsy."

And Kodály references the so-called Gypsy scale, which was a part of the debate between Bartók and Möller which we did not mention, in the following way:

> Gypsies falsify the folk songs they play by introducing the augmented intervals of this scale, which was never used by peasants. It should be emphasized, however, that the Gypsy scale by no means predominates in Gypsy music, and that modern major and minor are much frequent.[34]

On the one hand, he is against the scale in that it falsifies. Kodály here exhibits a biased, prescriptive approach to ethnomusicology, in that he judges the material he works on, instead of trying to describe his observations. Furthermore, he reverses himself in a strange fashion that the Gypsies do not really use the scale that often. What is going on in this kind of discourse?

Gypsies follow, they do not create: this is a common trope in Hungarian musicology:

> Gypsy composers follow faithfully in the footsteps of other native and assimilated Hungarians [why are not Gypsies, especially as most actually speak the local language, numbered among the assimilated? There seems much prejudice

lurking in this writing]. The most prolific, Pista Dankó, is even strongly under
the influence of indigenous Hungarian peasant music. He wrote more than 400
songs to contemporary Hungarian texts, whereas other Gypsy composers con-
fined themselves to the wordless and instrumentally conceived *czárdás*.[35]

As is obvious, it is startling how much attention Gypsies are receiving in a book titled
Folk Music of Hungary. And now we are starting to get contradictory information, in
that we learn that Dankó, a Gypsy composer, is writing under the influence of the
equivocal "indigenous Hungarian peasant music." How could this be? Gypsies were
supposed to only follow in the footsteps of the Hungarian gentry, at least according
to Bartók.

Kodály's book develops the classification of "authentic" Hungarian tunes begun
by Bartók and continued at the Hungarian Academy of Sciences. His bias of equating
"old" with "authentic" is everywhere in evidence, and he shows in greater detail than
in Bartók the Asian basis of Hungarian melodies. Kodály compares to the music of
the Chuvash and Mari what is allegedly the oldest stratum of Hungarian music, pen-
tatonic melodies with the "fifth shift" (the repetition of the melodic phrase at the interval of fifth; refer to the song "Szolo hegyen keresztul," see Music Example 31). It
is thought that these Asian tribes came from the same region as the ancient Magyars,
from whom the modern Hungarians descended.

Kodály's slant toward the nation is made more explicit than in Bartók. In the
concluding chapter of his book we learn why he wrote the book when he did:

> It will not be long before the educated class in Hungary will be able to restore the
> folk tradition they have adopted and shaped into artistic form: restore it, that is,
> to the national community, to the people that become a nation.[36]

His point is that the educated, by whom he means scientific researchers like himself,
will deliver the true, peasant music of Hungary back to the middle.

Yet the idea of a restoration is in considerable tension with the very essence of
"peasant music" as they conceive it. By definition, peasant music exists in its village
environment; it cannot be brought to the urban areas of the "national community."
The idea of brining the peasant music forth, to a public, seems a curious development
in Kodály, and one that most likely came out of his substantial work in music education.

Like we have seen in Bartók, Kodály's music too shows the marked influence of
Gypsy music: Bálint Sárosi in his book *Gypsy Music* mentions *Háry János, The Spinning Room,* and particularly the *Dances of Galánta* and the *Dances from Marosszék*.[38]
The descending augmented-seconds (G#-F) at the close of the phrase confirm a Gypsy impetus of the line (see Music Example 32).

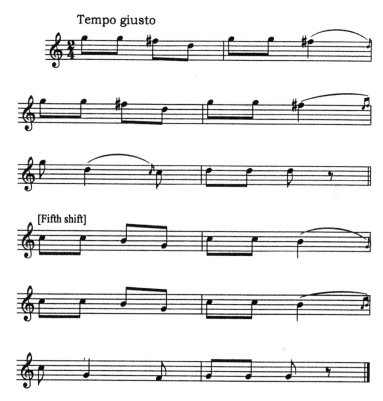

Music Example 31 Folksong from Kodály, "Szolo hegyen keresztul."

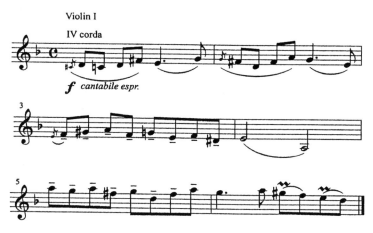

Music Example 32 Kodály, *Dance of Marosszék*, violin I, measures 6-11.

SÁROSI ON GYPSY MUSIC

> They [the Hungarians] generously conferred the title 'Gypsy music' even on mu-
> sic learnt, note for note, from a score, if it appeared on a 'Gypsy' programme.
> Over the course of a century and a half the epithet 'Gypsy' became imbued with
> respect within the profession, even among musicians who otherwise would not
> have taken kindly to being considered Gypsies on the street; it meant musician
> (or, as the famous Bihari was known in the first half of the nineteenth century,
> Hungarian folk music). It is quite a different story in this case of other peoples
> where the recognized masters of musical entertainment are likewise traditionally
> Gypsies. In the case of the Turks, the Greeks, the Albanians and the Romanians,
> the music played by Gypsy musicians is called 'Turkish,' 'Greek,' 'Albanian,' or
> 'Romanian,' respectively. And this entirely as it should be [...]"[38]

An ethnomusicologist trained in his native Hungary, Sárosi published in 1971 his
book *Gypsy Music* (*Cigányzene*) which still is astonishingly the only such book devoted entirely to the topic. Because we cannot possibly review this carefully researched
and detailed book, we will confine the discussion to a couple of points which we have
been following.

But first, a short digression. The quotation cited above is from a Sárosi review of
Alan Antonietto's articles on Gypsy music.[39] It explains that in Hungary, and only
Hungary, is the term "*cigányzene*" (Gypsy music) associated with the music of the host
country, whereas in the other countries, the music receives the predicate of the nation.
Why so much confusion, then?

This mistake seems to haunt twentieth-century Hungarian ethnomusicology, a
confusion I will conflate with the specter of Bartók. It is incredible how much this
idea bothers Hungarian writers; Sárosi writes:

> The Gypsies have no common musical language, there is no common melodic
> treasury, or way of making music which is identical with all the Gypsies scattered
> throughout the world. So does Gypsy folk music exist at all? It does exist but it
> is generally different in every country, and everywhere it displays many features
> in common with local folk music.[40]

This statement would be an extremely offensive one for any Romani-rights advocate.
A Rom might justifiably respond: "why do we want to misrepresent our own culture
and have it sort of given away to others... we are willing to do everything to please
others and not defend that which is our own heritage."[41]

The difficult task is to find a way of talking about Gypsy music that avoids both
the potentially offensive innuendo of Sárosi, while not putting forth the idea that the
Gypsy musical heritage is another repository among national repositories. Indeed, a
Roma activist might consider this entire book a futile exercise in misrepresentation,
especially in its employment of the word "Gypsy"; while the point of the book is to

try to avoid making any representation as such, but rather to deconstruct the discourse practices that have led to some of the confusion of what constitutes Gypsy music or Gypsiness in the first place.

Other comments made by Sárosi show further his ethnographer's distaste for the idea of Gypsy folk music (as distinct from urban music):[42]

> The Gypsies have no true traditional epic songs. Their few ballad-type stories sung to the melodies of the slow songs (among the best known is the story according to which a Gypsy girl, for the sake of her lover, gives her brother the meat of a poisonous snake to eat and kills him) have not yet crystallized into a traditional form. (31)

> One *lack* in Gypsy folk music is that they do not have any children's songs; but what is even more surprising, they do not have any ritual songs — songs connected with various festivals or customs. (my emphasis, 33)

> The old Spanish Gypsies do not have any connection with Hungarian Gypsy folk music similar to those described above. Their relationship to what they generally sing as their own — *flamenco* music [Sárosi's emphasis] is approximately the same as that of the Hungarian Gypsy musicians to their repertoire: *it is not originally theirs.* (DM's emphasis, 35)

Summarizing quickly: Gypsies have no "true, traditional" epic songs, they lack children's songs, have no ritual songs, and their repertoire "is not originally theirs." These are strong, categorical statements, and like all such generalizations, are open to question.

Concerning Liszt, Sárosi seems in agreement with the Hungarian public before him who were "scandalized by this 'plundering treatment' from Liszt."[43] Sárosi mentions many of the participants in the Liszt "controversy," although even the best respondent, Sámuel Brassai, did not "manage to find an objective tone with regard to Liszt."[44] Brassai accuses Liszt of merely looking in the mirror, "we know that his piano playing…the principal element, the chief resource was the ornament."[45] Sárosi also and rightly pins the highly negative and charged Hungarian reaction to Liszt on the failed Hungarian revolution of 1848-49.

Then Sárosi defends Liszt on grounds similar to Bartók's defense of Liszt:

> From Liszt's word — even though with not quite unequivocal clarity — it is possible to feel that in the music of the Gypsy musicians he is thinking primarily of this [performative] part of the process of creation which is repeated again and again with every new performance. In this respect the creative role of the Gypsy music cannot be doubted (since for example in performing a song composed by a 'whistling composer' they add a lot of different things to it — orchestration, harmonization, ornamentation, variation… which the composer could not even have imagined originally).[46]

And like Bartók, Sárosi seems to have a certain liking for the Gypsy orchestras of the Budapest cafés. He notes that in the early hours of the evening (before the "sparkling effects of the alcohol"; when the "engineer with his family, the Circus official, the old woman pensioner, etc." are present) Hungarian popular songs are hardly heard; instead "old verbunkos melodies [the stereotype of this kind of music], operetta medleys, international light serenade music, waltzes, and tangos."[47] Then, with consumption of alcohol the Gypsy responds to the altered circumstance:

> He [the Gypsy] is in full vigor when most of his audience can scarcely use their legs any longer [because of alcohol]. This is when the most dazzling variations are to be heard. From then onwards the proportion of *Hungarian songs* in the program increases.[48]

Apparently Sárosi approves of the Hungarian turn to the evening, which accompanies the "revelling guests" — the simple worker, the tradesman, the relative from the country — versus the "dining guests" with their preference for light international music (again, the series is incredible and bears repeating: "the engineer with his family, the Circus official, the old woman pensioner"). The social types that Sárosi sets up seem right out of a communist textbook, as both the "simple worker" and the "old woman pensioner" enjoy their entertainment proper to their societal role.

THE HUNGARIAN DANCE-HOUSE (TÁNCHÁZ) MOVEMENT

Frigyesi has traced the aesthetic and history of the Hungarian Revival Movement.[49] Fascinating about this movement as she describes it is that it was not part of right-wing nationalist sentiment, but that it constituted in the 1970s an "avant-garde opposition of young people against the conception of art in general."[50] The definition of a "real revival group" is that it has an "authentic peasant repertoire," which means that it learned its songs directly from a peasant ensemble.[51] Indeed, in ways that were impossible for Bartók and Kodály's generation, these "young, long-haired hooligan-looking students" were able to play with the village musicians. Finally, as these bands did their best to preserve something of a village performance context, they rejected the concert hall for the communal dance house.[52]

The slant of Frigyesi's article is toward "intellectuals:" "the musical and 'cultural' rules of revival music are determined more by the aesthetic awareness of the educated middle class."[53] These educated ones are the bridge between the peasants and the broader public in the transmission of the "authentic peasant repertoire."[54] It is surprising that Frigyesi retains this kind of rhetoric while she chastises Bartók earlier on ("*even* Bartók could not see entirely clear in this matter [concerning Gypsy string bands]."[55]

What does this movement have to do with Gypsies? Because most of the string bands of the small villages are Gypsy ensembles, it means that the revivalists are actually learning what they consider to be Hungarian music from Gypsies. This latter implication is not stated nor developed in Frigyesi's article, perhaps because of some empathy for the revivalists.

But perhaps the most problematic aspect of Frigyesi's interpretation is her privileging of authenticity. We read that "members of the revival movement turned toward authentic performance."[56] And this was in opposition to both the "purified Hungarian folk songs" (by which she means a dry, academic rendering) and the popular version of urban Gypsy music; "it turned out that the most authentic performing style sounded the most modern." Why is *popular* Hungarian-Gypsy music not regarded as authentic?

MUZSIKÁS: BACK TO BARTÓK

Frigesyi's views on the Hungarian revival movement may have been true at one time, however, since the opening of its borders and coming European Union membership, the remnants of the revivalist movement or *tánchaz* are caught up in exactly what Frigyesi says was not at their origins: a Romantic idea of the past, and a positing of ethnic identity with some anti-Gypsy slant.

While on tour for their *Bartók Album*, Dániel Hammer (the bassist) began his pre-concert lecture at UCLA (30 April 2000) with the following negative statement: "we do not play Gypsy music." And then he continued with the typical critique of Liszt (who has become the usual suspect), and the glorification of Bartók and Kodály.

Why such a strongly combative attitude? In Hammer's defense: he wants to distinguish what is a village, peasant music from the urban, restaurant music that most Western audiences quickly assume is a hallmark of Hungarian music, and of course, dominating this latter scene are Gypsy musicians (Romungro, the most assimilated [read: "Hungarianized"] of the Roma living in Hungary).

However, how do we ascribe ethnic origins to an oral, village tradition? The easiest way would be to identify an isolated ethnic group and then to study their music. But in Transylvania, more specifically the Kalotaszeg region that Bartók first focused on, there are Jews, Gypsies, Saxons, and now Romanians living among the Szekely, the ancient Hungarians who live there.

Can we ever say with absolute certainty that this melody belongs to the Hungarians, that it is a purely Hungarian tune? And Romanians are currently involved in fieldwork in Transylvania, too, and were in the time of Bartók. Furthermore, as the recent nationalized fueled clashes in Cluj show, the entanglement of diverse ethnicities makes this region a highly politically charged atmosphere for research. The conclusion would be that it becoming increasingly impossible to know with certainty

Music Example 33 Bartók, "Dance from Máramaros," violin I (excerpt).

what is purely "Hungarian," "Jewish," "Roma," etc., in this region of the world. For it is the Roma musicians who are now the main performers in the peasant tradition that has had such a powerful effect on Bartók's thinking and composing.

Muzsikás engages in precisely those things that Frigyesi says were not at the origins of the *tánchàz* movement, romanticization and nationalism. This is not only about music, but addresses the very idea of how to exist in the world: "Bartók became a different person from his encounters in the village."

The stage set-up was remarkable, in that the famous picture of Bartók and the peasants loomed on a painted canvas backdrop (the same picture that has found its way into numerous textbooks). When I first entered the hall and because of the reflection of the light I thought I was seeing a ghost. And Bartók watched the proceedings in other ways: during the concert, they actually played tape recordings of Bartók's fieldwork! After this they played Bartók's arrangement of it for two violins (see Music Example 33), they then gave a czárdás arrangement of it.[57]

This is a highly conscious and mediated approach, a performance that performs a double relationship to the past: first to Bartók, the composer, second to the music that influenced Bartók but that we receive via Bartók's publication. This pulling together of the past is enormously complex, and because of their bias against urban Gypsy music (which they do not explain to the audience) it becomes a contaminated play on authenticity. In that Transylvania has pretty much been tapped in terms of what the European and American markets can bear, performers and folkloric acts have begun to venture further out, to ever remote regions like areas in present-day Moldavia where the ancient Csangos people live, who apparently speak one of the oldest surviving Hungarian dialects.

Chapter Ten

Gypsiness in Film Music: Spectacle and Act

A significant arena for the debate over the value of Gypsy music concerns what can be called "musical property." Do Gypsies create their own music, or are they dependent on the music of their host country? Further, in this sense of belonging, to whom does music belong? Nowhere has this been more controversial than in the two places where Gypsies have flourished as musicians: Andalusia (a place that looks south, to the African continent) and Hungarian-speaking lands (which includes Transylvania, today part of Romania).

What we will consider under the topic of Gypsy film music is actually a series of questions around questions of (intellectual) property, ownership, and what ties these two together, a notion of self (here, the one who owns). What is proper to Gypsy music? What does it mean to "belong" to a tradition of music-making? Who creates music? Can music be owned?

With these questions I am not interested in the arena of international copyright laws, of the legality issues of the music and film industries, though these areas certainly form interesting (relevant is Marx's idea of interest, of a capitalistic, market, or class interest) and complex avenues for reflection.

Instead, my interest is the deconstruction of a certain discourse practice, our ways of relating to films as the possibility for discovering a "truth" about self or society. This discourse practice is the *international distribution* of films, a process that on the level of global boundaries challenges the governmental notion of the controlled, policed, and unified nation. And I think there is perhaps no better example of this challenge to governmental policies as the Western idea about the nomadic Gypsies, a "people" (nation) who persist without a state (a legally defined territory of land with fixed boundaries).

And yet, here is the danger of what is sometimes referred to as a romanticism in any attempts at understanding Gypsies: in the discourse of film (and fictional

-documentary practice, we might add), Gypsies have a shared history, shared nation, and a shared *bond* (in the sense of binding, tying together) that if, when compare to the lived situation of Roma groups throughout the world, can be called nothing other than a massive misunderstanding, a catastrophic fiction with real political consequences. That is, film purports to give us Gypsies, and especially Gypsy music, when in fact, like Liszt's *Hungarian Rhapsodies*, what it gives us are one-sided Western stereotypes about Gypsies and their music, while simultaneously forgetting the sometimes harsh political and economic reality of Roma life. And yet when Roma are involved in the making of these films, and other Roma might identify with these films (as Roma musicians obviously cherish Liszt's *Rhapsodies* and especially Brahms's *Dances*) we have to wonder about the boundaries between art and reality. In fact, it is in another Gypsy film (Carlos Saura's *Carmen* (1983), featuring the non-Gypsy flamenco guitarist Paco Pena) that we find a merging, a complete mapping of art onto reality pushed to the point where both are implicated in each other.

The reckoning that the aforementioned questions turns out impossible to answer indicates the deepest level of what can be inaugurated as the first deconstructive moment in Western art music: the event where the unity of Western music is forever destabilized, and not through a circumscribed and circumscribable delimitation through the exotic Other; rather, the invasion, the *deterritorialization* (after Deleuze) of Western space through what is simultaneously inside and outside of the West, Gypsiness in music.

To articulate these reservations, especially the process of representing Gypsy music through film, we will appeal to two concepts, indicated in the title — spectacle and act.[1] As it has come to be analyzed since the 1960s, here spectacle will refer to the state of global capitalisms under the unnamable, or the network of communications gathering what is sometimes called the "world": the interconnection, the optical *interface* of machines via digital, silicon technology; an electro-magnetic matrix that is an irreducible multiplicity. Note that the mass media smugly defines this as a "global village." More than ever, computer codes underlay the digital representations of the society of the spectacle, where the simulacra, the representation of the represented, exist on the level of authenticity, more real than the real. Advertising, marketing, and packaging are what encapsulate the reception of these products of screen, from television to film to the Internet. These products and their wrapping (the recent transformation of the logic of wrapping would require a whole analysis of its own, beyond the scope of what is possible in our context) challenge the essence of the activity of the self, the idea that the self *acts* or *performs*, initiating an alteration of some kind in the world.

For, in this screening of the spectacle, who is responsible for the activities of the meta-productions of filming, screening, and distributing? Who defines discourse and its possibility? In politics, who is responsible for bombings, for police actions, for war itself? The emptying of the responsibility of self (depersonalization) has led to the feeling of apathy and powerlessness in the face of digital inter-facing, sometimes summarized as the experience of "Generation X," though obviously felt beyond this boundary of age. Paradoxically, because of the enormous economic transformation unleashed by these new technologies, Generation X, and now we can add Y, have led to an intensive gathering of wealth, whereby people attempt to appropriate the means of the latest internet and wireless technologies as a buttress against homelessness (one is always "connected").[2]

PREDICATION AND PROPERTY

Property is about the truth of possession. Possession as a fundamental right of man, transcending all conditions of community.

Following a recent turn in Continental philosophy, Agamben investigates predication in terms of belonging and set relationships. He reformulates the question concerning the meaning of man as a paradox — a radical, exposed singularity that belongs to a set and yet remains singular, apart from the set. Navigating the boundaries of ontology and ethics, Agamben writes:

> Because if instead of continuing to search for a proper identity in the already improper and senseless form of individuality, humans were to succeed in belonging to this impropriety as such, in making of the proper being-thus not an identity and an individual property but a singularity without identity, a common and absolutely exposed singularity... then they would for the first time enter into a community without presuppositions and without subjects, into a communication without the incommunicable.[3]

Describing the condition of this new singular existence, or "whatever-being" (being-such in the condition of belonging), is an affirmation of a new relationship toward Being, a "coming community." In his vision of "whatever being," we are freed from choosing between our own ineffable individuality and the fact that we belong to a set (being red, being French, being Muslim). Singularity is reclaimed, as it were, in the sense of "belonging," of a belonging not in terms of belonging to this or that set, but of belonging in-itself. This belonging is, in turn, the condition of desire, as whatever you want as exposed singularity (singularity apart from the set).

The coming community contrasts with civilization under the disaster of nihilism. Nihilism can be defined as the loss of meaning within traditions, of "differences of language, of dialect, of way of life, of character, of custom, and even of physical particularities of each person."[4] Agamben confirms his thesis by noting trends in advertising. In advertising or the "marketing of the spectacle," what is experienced as "real" is the representation of the product/thing. We watch television, and become convinced we need certain items and services to live, or greater quantities and types of food to eat.

The state of existence under the spectacle becomes "homelessness" (continuing in the wake of Heidegger), a state where "man" loses shelter and his own ability to experience language and more specifically his own death, both of which are negated in global mass culture. The "real" becomes speed, the matrix of communication devices and what is referred to as a widening of communicative space, as in "broadband." With the desiccation of language, the ideal of "knowledge" in post industrialism becomes the database, where facts are stored up for future retrieval. Databases are growing exponentially, toward the final goal where every "thing" will become available online, ready-for-use.

THE IMPACT OF FILMING ON GYPSY MUSIC: THE EVENT

More than any other event in its musical history, film has bestowed, granted, and institutionalized the idea of the existence of Gypsy music. It has brought Gypsy music into its own proper, so to speak.

Gypsy music existed prior to its filming, and yet, *how* it existed in the Western imagination was as a *marginalized music*. Liszt's *Rhapsodies* tried to institute a scheme of legitimation for a national music, and of one pariah nation, Gypsy, paradoxically not named in the title of the *Rhapsodies*. Instead, "Gypsy" would be deferred to Lisztean prose, in his curious book (originally, as we have noted, as a preface) about the *Rhapsodies*.

When the ethnology of Gypsy music occurred, begun by Bartók and Kodály and continued by researchers first in Eastern Europe then in the United States, it thematized Gypsy music as a regional music, an isolated music, something limited by a border, non-universal and strictly local. It was also dependent on other nations, especially the Hungarian and Romanian. And despite Bartók's idealization of the peasant, "local" does not escape the pejorative sense of provincial, non-urban, remote (one recalls Liszt's stunning and biting critique of Schumann's music as provincial, which means removed from the times, from what is occurring in intellectual circles).

But film radically changed all of this. Now the bands cherished by Liszt, the restaurant musicians (called Romungro, a term that refers to Budapest Gypsies who have become Magyarized, losing their Romany language) whose repertories so bothered Bartók, could be experienced outside of their milieu, by international audiences. In its early configuration, from *Golden Earrings* (1947, with Marlene Dietrich as a self-fashioned Gypsy) to *Love in the Afternoon* (1957, starring Gary Cooper and Audrey Hepburn), Eastern-European Gypsies were presented as primarily performers, as musicians, and in the latter film, as barely competent drunks.

Yet these initial efforts at Gypsy music in film do not lead us out of the fundamental debate over Gypsy music: Gypsies as creators versus Gypsies as thieves. In the former argument, Gypsies create national musics for their hosts, as in Hungary, Spain, Russia, and Romania (even France, where Gypsies practice "hot jazz," could be added to this list). In the latter, Gypsies are parasitical to national traditions, stealing musical ideas and repertories of their hosts and neighbors. This idea of Gypsies as thieves also receives a strong reinforcement in literature, and is clearly motivated by racism.

With director Tony Gatlif's 1993 *Latcho drom*, this debate over Gypsy music is at once erased, and yet new horizons — political, and especially the politics of identity — are simultaneously opened up. Gatlif unpacks eight, tightly woven scenes of Gypsy music-making, without explanatory notes or commentary to propose the thesis that Gypsy music as Gypsiness is the quintessential world music. Moreover, with *Latcho*, the usual logic for consideration of a musical topic is reversed, according to the strictures of dissemination in a globalized setting. To understand the topic of Gypsy music as a world music, Gypsy music in film assumes a kind of privilege over Gypsy music in other scenarios, say on CDs, or in economies — live concerts, restaurants, even in the village.

Pausing on this idea for moment: this is revolutionary in terms of how we understand music in its exposure to the world. Namely, in stylistic and historical analysis of film music, one usually turns to something called "the music" first, then to how the sounding phenomenon coordinates with the filmic image. In this hierarchy, music in its instantiation in image would always remains secondary to the purity of the "music itself."

However, film calls into question this notion of the "music itself," which is always already equivocal. How is music identical to itself? Is there one music? Film music challenges the autonomy of music, and shows the heterogeneity implicated and implicit in any notion of music. We can find precedents for this in the nineteenth century with its attendant idea of "program," as we have already seen in Liszt's "poetic idea." Music merges with idea, with nation, with expression, with emotion, with virtuosity. (In Liszt's estimation, sonata process and thematic development are formal elements of the composer's workshop that historically, should never have gone public. Musico-historical event becomes giant compositional misunderstanding!) This eventually caused Wagner to theorize and instigate his *Gesamtkunstwerk*. As an aside: the history of film music begins not with actual film music, but with Wagnerian music drama. Film music presents the ultimate triumph of Liszt's and Wagner's philosophy; in Wagnerian terms, it is the "future of music." As such, one conclusion would be that film music allows for the permanent displacing of the sounding phenomenon called the "music."

A THEORY ABOUT GYPSY MUSIC REALIZED VIA A THEORY OF FILM MUSIC PSYCHOLOGY

In film-music theory, the music serves as an emotional repository for the image, which is usually privileged in terms of the meaning of the film. However, Roy Prendergast quotes Copland that music "can play upon the *emotions of the spectator*, sometimes counter pointing the thing seen with an aural image that implies the contrary of the thing seen" (my emphasis) and Prendergast adds that "the ability of music to make a psychological point in film is a subtle one, and perhaps its most valuable contribution."[5] Composer Leonard Rosenman argues that the "musical contribution to the film should be ideally to create a *super-reality*, a condition wherein the elements of literary naturalism are perceptually altered."[6]

Analogously, as we have seen, Gypsiness in music is a way for a composer to have immediate access to the emotions of the listener. And this, too, in ways that might counteract the actual musical content. The Gypsy passage in *The Red Violin* provides a perfect example of this: Corigliano has composed Gypsy music with a precision and anxiousness that supersedes any of the emotional qualities of live Gypsy improvisation. And yet Corigliano captures the attention of the spectator, perhaps in ways that using actual Gypsy music could not replicate. He does this through the idea of improvisation. Thus non-Gypsy music (the actual content) carries the listener's emotional energy into what Rosenman's "super-reality," what we will reformulate as the hyper-space of aesthetic hallucination.

Latcho drom, in its portrayal of the act of Gypsy music-making, produces the spectacle and event of Gypsy music that allows for it to unfold in its proper. The proper as an event (*Ereignis*) articulates its identity, political strategy, and economic success in the global marketplace. The strategy becomes one of heightened cosmopolitanism as producers of Gypsy acts accentuate the "road" of the journey to the West.

However, this process is not simply a reappropriation for the Roma of what is "rightfully" theirs. The political order becomes much messier and more complex. For once Gypsy music is in-place, assuming its fixed identity as a world music, it becomes open to the same deconstruction and political critique, as to the alleged ontology of any other music, Western or otherwise. This could occur in the guise of a distortion of history or misrepresentation of prejudice. Yet this also names the difficult challenge for thinking Gypsiness today, to preserve while overcoming the spectacle (again, the process of *Aufhebung*) while leaving open the possibility for a new call to action against the flattening procedure inherent to contemporary political discourse.

APPROACHES TO SOUND AS IMAGE

The three films chosen for analysis here — *Latcho drom*, *The Red Violin*, and *Black and White in Colour: A Portrait of a Gypsy Singer* — articulate similar yet vastly contrasting universes in terms of sound as image. All three conceive of sound as an independent element, one that translates into an optical play that is paradoxically free from a determinate imaging/mapping. That is to say, the image, what is *essential* to the definition of film itself, whether static (the photogenic, the play of light) or in motion, takes as its content not the "viewable" represented quantity (a desert land-scape, or a scene in an auction house in an urban, British setting), but rather the sonic force of Gypsy music (this, indeed, is a feature shared with other films about Gypsy music, most recently *Underground* and Gatlif's *Gadjo dilo*).

However, what separates each of these films is their relationship to economy and marketing. *Latcho drom* falls in the tradition of successful, award-winning interna-tional cinema, where *artistic* or *visionary* portrayal makes socio-political claims about reality that attempt to alter, shape, and re-form our relationship to that same reality. The director of such films emerges as a figure parallel to the composer. The American marketing of such films is aimed at upper-East-side-styled intellectuals, viewers who attend so-called art house releases on a regular or limited basis. If these types of films are economically successful, it is perceived as accidental to the film. That is, the pur-pose of artistic films is not to make money, but to propose a thesis or a series of hy-pothesis about the way we perceive the world in order to change it. In short, to create a philosophy. Paradoxically, we can summarize that the "non-marketing" of such films enjoys a marketing niche specific to their status as "art."

The Red Violin is our example of a mass-audience film, a major release by a major studio, Universal Studios. In style, sequence, and impetus it is derivative of *Latcho*, but this non-original quality is a typical sign of a major release. I do not hesitate to caution, however, that even as a box-office success, this film does not speak to a true majority of the American population, as say a Spielberg mega-release does. Nor is it calculated as such. *The Red Violin* is rather a perfect example of the transposition of art film values into the arena of the mass-audience spectacle. As such, it retains the *touches* of a film like *Latcho drom*, though without their intellectual justification. It is art film clothed in a Hollywood guise, in other words.

Black and White in Colour: A Portrait of a Gypsy Singer (1998) falls more on the side of *Latcho drom*, but in its choice of theme (the Roma singer Vera Bile, enormous-ly popular in the Czech Republic, Slovakia, and Western Europe) and its genre (doc-umentary, more or less) it will never reach the audience that *Latcho* commands. To be brutal about it, we do not feel the power of the director's gaze and vision as we do in *Latcho*. In this sense, it is less interesting *as* film than *Latcho*. But what *Black and White* depicts that in fact gets lost in the cinematography of *Latcho* is the portrayal of the harsh reality of Roma life in Eastern Europe, even though the Roma depicted have the opportunity to become successful Gypsy musicians.

VERA BILA: I AM A ROMANY WOMAN

During Vera and her band Kale's triumphant trip to Paris as presented in the film, the French media person asks Vera, in the spirit of an interview, "What does it mean to be a Rom? What is the Romany spirit?" Vera answers: "I don't know. One can't just state it. I am a Romany woman so I am a Romany woman." Without the political posturing of the Euro or American star, the Rom singer Vera Bila innocently states that she is a "Romany woman," when asked what it means to be Rom. The onlookers from the French press smile, sympathetically yet ambivalently, at what they have just heard: yet as film viewers, we are left to ask, what kind of response was this to Vera's non-response to the question?

Coming from the formerly communist Czech Republic and lacking formal education, we could say that Vera simply does not understand the question. The interviewer's question purports to be political correct, speaking, perhaps, to the racism that the Roma encounter on a day-to-day basis. Yet the idea of a "Romany spirit" is itself in line with stereotyping, the basis for racism; that the Roma are distinguished, different in "spirit" from their neighbors. But Vera remains innocent in this questioning and the violence of its interrogation, simply because her identity is not an issue for her. It is neither thematized nor thematizable as such.

The producers feel the same way, writing in the film's press release:

> A vivid portrait of Vera Bila, a Gypsy singer acclaimed in the international music world. The film explores Romany culture and what it means to be part of a marginalized minority group. Without sentimentalizing, it questions the prospects for mutual understanding.

I would emphasize the phrase "without sentimentalizing." Read: no apologies for the bittersweet reality we are about to present — this is how it is for the Roma. One of the co-producers and husband of the director, David Charap, states in an interview that the film has taught him "documentary truth. It is very common in documentaries today to distort, to sentimentalize but I think this film within the constraints of film making process inevitably entails has managed to capture something real and that is a big success." For him, sentimental refers to a kind of distortion. The director has written that "the camera is a detached observer, watching happiness, suffering, personal encounters, seeing life without sentimentality but how it truly is." Of course, the misleading idea of the camera as a "detached observer" avoids the complications of context and reception, where nothing is as simple as some would like it to be.

The director is Mira Erdevicki-Charap, a woman from Belgrade who is pursuing her career in the Czech Republic. Erdevicki chose Vera as a subject because

> of her music, which stems from traditional Romany songs but has changed to meet commercial standards. Somewhere along her path of adaptation, Vera has found a distinctive voice but also a certain cultural isolation.[7]

The other reason for her film is personality, that Vera and her band are "original and lively individuals." But who is this director to consider Vera's musical style as an accommodation of commercial pressures?

The intersection of identity and music when considering the Roma situation is nowhere as clean, as clear, as direct, as in film. The audience for Gypsy music, at least in its internationally staging, is shown well in the film. And yet, what does it mean to subtract "sentimentality" from a film? Is not music itself forcefully sentimental, especially as it exists as shared memory? The word "sentimental" itself means an attitude or thought prompted by a feeling. Is emotion, at least according to these filmmakers, something that distorts? Why do they believe that a camera, a "detached observer," can capture the real, an identity, a human voice?

The filmmakers found some kind of reality while making the film. Erdevicki says that "I have learnt from Vera not to get so fretted. They really live from one day to the next and so they can appreciate the joy of any one moment."[8] Here Erdevicki has struck on one of the major tropes in thinking about Gypsies: that Gypsies inhabit the here and now of reality. They live for the moment. This is why, for instance, they can be valued as performers.

VOICE AS MONEY

Vera's voice is the cause of much uproar, in terms of traditional popular music. Near the opening of the film, Vera sings:

> *No one loved her dark hair.*
> *One year passed, then another, then another*
> *She lived in the woods, in a little house*
> *Alone, with her old mother's tears.*

This kind of poignancy in song lyrics, combined with her unique and unusual voice, has brought Vera fame and fortune. A musical redundancy of the film can be mentioned in this context: this same song is played three times, in different settings.

Though Vera has achieved moderate fame in the Czech Republic, the singer still suffers in the Bohemian town of Rokycany. Her husband apparently does not work, and her son is put in jail because of a robbery. In most Eastern European countries today, it is not uncommon to find large numbers of Roma men in the prison system. Vera worries about her son's fate, and also about the family's money problems.

Money forms a theme that runs throughout the film. Vera earns all of the family's income through her voice. Her insecurity about money and finances stems from her own impoverished background, coming from a poor Gypsy village in Slovakia on the "edge of Europe."

THE THIRD WORLD OF GYPSY VIDEO

While looking for a wife for her son to marry, Vera and her husband make a trip to poverty-ridden Roma villages of Slovakia, where their families originally came from. "That is one of the saddest sights on the road to Europe." The houses have tarps barely covering the roof; the women wash clothes in a stream. They express fear at stopping, "One is afraid to stop here," yet they immediately correct themselves, "they won't do anything, they are people, just like us."

While gazing at the impoverished Roma, Vera feels that she and her husband share a "character that is more Czech than Romany." Namely, Vera identifies more with the Czech people than with her Romany roots. Yet she then feels a sense of nostalgia: "But the Romanies in Slovakia still have the same temperament. They have remained faithful to their origins." In other words, these are authentic, real Gypsies: to reinforce this, the camera shows us dirty, unkept children, dogs, and a cold, muddy village with shacks.

This scene presents a classic example of how members of a low-status group, when faced with the reality that they cannot exit from the group to which they belong, can choose to try to change the status of the group through a re-evaluation of its cultural markers. The idea of makeshift housing, of shanty-towns, can also affirm a way of life.

Why has Erdevicki chosen to show this side of Gypsy life? Her response would be that this is documentary, and there is no room here for sentimentality. Or, the camera as detached observer. Yet she does have a choice, as a filmmaker, of what to show. However, by jumping immediately to such a poverty-ridden landscape, without preparation and hardly any commentary, we get a good idea about how negative stereotypes are created in the first place, and how they persist in places like the Czech Republic.

Erdevicki then makes the typical move to soften our view of this landscape: she instigates a music video. Time and place are frozen in the universal soundscape; Vera sings: *By the water there's a Romany girl. I like her very much.* The Gypsy villagers respond with the refrain: *Mama, Mama, give me some water.* There is much dancing and rejoicing, and we see a man carrying an ax with a stump in it, snow falling, playing children, static stills of Gypsy faces, an old man holding on to Vera, women washing clothes, and then finally the global moment: children doing the wave. *By the water she sits alone and waits for me.*

How are we to interpret this break in the order of the documentary? I think the answer is clear: this is the film's response to the forces of the marketplace. This is what sells the material, especially in the Czech Republic and in the wider area of "world music": the music of the Gypsies.

To justify such a scene, Erdevicki then presents Vera with her father's traditional band, complete with cymbalom and violins. Vera remembers her youth, and how she would listen to Radio Free Europe, and especially the Beatles. Her father smashed her radio; he says of guitars: "I don't really like them." The irony is huge at this point in the film, for Vera earns money singing to guitars, and the "video" preceding this has little to do with the kind of music played by her father.

BLOOD AND *THE RED VIOLIN*: SONY'S WEB SITE

In our analysis of *The Red Violin*, we should never forget that red stands for blood. The violin painted with the blood of the maker's dead wife, who died giving child birth (see scene number 15, "Blood and Varnish"). The blood of the dead mother gives the violin a power, a mystery, and a perfect sound. On the screen we watch the cutting of her still hot vein, and the blood dripping into the mixture that is used to paint the violin.

No mention of blood is made at the Web site for Sony Classical.[9] However, the red on the page's border is unmistakably that of blood. Between these borders is the following text:

> A tale filled with passion, pageantry, tragedy, romance, adventure and intrigue, *The Red Violin* centers around a contemporary auction in which a priceless violin with an infamous past is placed on the block. As the bidding mounts, the story flashes back to signature chapters in the violin's history and the inevitable impact it had on all those who possessed it. From its creation in seventeenth-century Italy, to the court of imperial Vienna in the 1790s, to Victorian England in the late 1800s, to the People's Republic of China in the mid-1960s, the dramatic story spans continents and sweeps centuries. At the center of the story is a *dark secret* that is only revealed at the film's suspenseful and sensational finale. [my emphasis]

Of course, such a text is designed for marketing, to attract a video and DVD audience. What makes us want to buy the film is the last sentence's revelation of the existence of a "dark secret." This turns out to be a reference to the fact that the violin was painted using the blood of the dead mother. Also on Sony's Web site is an image that can also be found on postcards for the film: the back of a naked woman (showing her sacral crack) with violin F holes.

INTERLUDE, OR BACKWARDS FORWARD: DIRECTOR FRANÇOIS GIRAUD ON *THE RED VIOLIN*

Giraud writes the following about his film:

Long before we shot *The Red Violin*, I started to think about the score. It was clear very early on that the music process was going to be long, complicated and delicate, for many reasons: music plays a very important narrative role in our story; many characters are scripted with musical notes as much as with words; the soul of Anna Bussotti [the mother whose blood stains the violin] could not survive without her theme; the journey through three centuries and three continents could not possibly exist without music.... To begin with I worked with [violinist] Joshua Bell. I guess that first I needed a voice for my Red Violin, and he was the one to give it to me.... I believe that writing music for my movie was especially demanding, more so than for other films. And this is where John Corigliano comes in. From this vantage point, not only do I think that John was the perfect composer for *The Red Violin*, but I simply cannot think of anyone else who could have achieved what he did.[10]

The Red Violin is thus that rare film where music fulfills an important narrative function. We could say that the music has a starring role. Giraud even calls his film a "biography" of the violin, whose voice is Joshua Bell.

Furthermore, the fact that the score came first, *before* the filming, establishes beyond a doubt that music is privileged in this film. This is backwards for the normal methodology for film production. However, once the sound meets the image in the final visible product, the opposite perception emerges. As audience, the image takes on a power that overwhelms at any moment the sonic ideal.

What does Corigliano achieve in his score? His background music is masterful, providing continuity within a given scene (see scene 15, where the "dark secret" is revealed) and helping the film achieve a sense of unity, trans-scenically. However, according to a musicological standard of "authenticity," the source music (so-called "diagetic" music), by contrast, is a catastrophe. The divide in Corigliano's score between source and non-source music exhibits the difficulties and paradoxes involved in source integration for historical scenes.

I would argue that the power of source music is tied to its historicity. This means that when it is possible, the composer and director should employ some music from the actual time period under consideration. Cameron Crowe's *Almost Famous* (2000, set in 1973 America) obeys this principle, as does *Amadeus*, with remarkable results.

For the epics *Spartacus* (1960; starring Kirk Douglas, Laurence Olivier, and Charles Laughton) and *Cleopatra* (1962; Elizabeth Taylor, Richard Burton, and Rex Harrington) Alex North had no choice but to compose new music, because there is no surviving, ancient Roman music. However, the composer researched the topic intensely to achieve a historical orientation.

FRAMES

The Red Violin uses the classical film technique of twin framing devices to tell its tale: the predictions of an Italian fortune-teller in 1681 Cremona, whose narrative describes the fate of the violin (though she speaks to the wife of the luthier), and the scientific testing of the instrument in the present day. Temporally both the esoteric and scientific converge in the finale, where the testing ordered by Charles Morritz (nicely portrayed by Samuel L. Jackson) discovers the true source of the redness of the violin.

CONVERGING ON THE DEMONIC

The Victorian aristocrat, composer, and violinist Lord Frederick Pope is "*il diavlo*" (the devil). Preceding his scene is the fortune-teller's prediction:

> *and then...*
> *a man comes into your life*
> *a handsome man and intelligent*
> *He'll seduce you with his talent and worse*
> *in short he's the devil*

During this description fingering Pope as the devil, historically we recall Paganini. According to contemporaneous legends (though not the violinist himself), Paganini had sold his soul to the devil to achieve his violin technique.

Pope uses his demonic abilities on the red violin for sexual purposes, seducing his novelist girlfriend, Victoria, when he "feeling a composition coming on." He plays violin while they engage in sexual activities (signaled by the feminine moan). Unfortunately, these tastefully tasteless quasi-pornographic episodes show that we are in the realm of mass cinema. After Victoria's discovery that Pope has found a new mistress while she was on a trip to Russia, Victoria shoots the violin upon bursting in on the love-making composition, after which Pope commits suicide.

THEFT AND GYPSIES: CONFRONTING STEREOTYPES

In order to set up this demonic scene, there is a Gypsy passage, which is actually the centerpiece of the film. As we shall see in our analysis, this passage presents many of the negative and positive stereotypes about Gypsies.

The violin's possession by the Gypsies occurs as the result of theft, and in terms of the supernatural, the worst kind — grave-robbing. The film thus confirms one of the West's main and most persistent stereotypes of Gypsies, that they are grave robbers. The fortune-teller effectively sets up the Gypsy theft:

> *And then I see a time of life*
> *a time of lust and energy*
> *loosed across mountains and oceans, and time.*
> *Confusing madame, I know.*
> *But I see it. I'm certain*
> *Yours is a Lazarus soul.*

The chain of signifiers — lust, energy, rebirth, traveling through time and space — summarizes some other stereotypes about Gypsies.

After the violin is dug out of the grave, we hear a passionately played lament-cadenza in A minor by a Gypsy solo violinist (who in fact is Joshua Bell). Unfortunately Corigliano chooses to compose his own Gypsy dance, in a "pseudo" E Phrygian (E-F-G-A-flat). Gypsies are depicted as close to nature. The camera pauses for a moment during the cadenza on a snowy and desolate mountaintop in the Austrian Alps, giving us a transcendent moment of *cinemusic* (that is, visuals with no music). We see the Gypsy caravan, complete with wagon and horse, and cymbalom player. Ironically the film score uses an orchestral accompaniment, with strings and percussion, undercutting the power of the source music on the scene, in effect making the scene both source and non-source.

The Gypsy men are dark, with mustaches and unkept, long, and shaggy hair. The scene then cuts to a forest, where a Gypsy girl plays the red violin. The thread of the scene is the dance that does not change with the shifts in time and place and players. While the Gypsy girl plays, we hear the B section of the tune with an orchestral clarinet, which again, is not shown on the screen.

Night is shown next, as expected, complete with a fire. Gypsies whirl and dance as the scene intensifies. Contrasting to this is change to the meadow, a static pastoral where old women and men sit on a flowery hillside in the sunlight. Then the ocean scene of coastal France follows. Gypsies here have accordions (unheard, however) and now the sight of the clarinetist indicates that we have source music. The red violin now makes its way across the ocean and lone fiddler carries the tune. To frame the scene, Giraud cuts to the same mountain that opened the scene, however, now viewed through a barred window of the monastery and in the present time. A brief moment of *cinespoken* (visuals with spoken language) with the framed mountain serves to sober up the audience after the ecstasy of the Gypsy revel.

This Gypsy passage, given here in close detail, occurs rapidly. In a sense, this quickness as immediacy functions to display a major stereotype of Gypsy culture. As nomads without loyalty to the land, they occupy the here and now, the present, in opposition to the Western and Chinese cultural pillars of the film. They do not speak, unlike the other characters; the Gypsies of the *Red Violin* are eternally trapped in, deterred to, a kind of hyper-musical suspension of time and place.

OWNING A PRECIOUS VIOLIN

Enter Pope, who again, represents the demonic in music. The Gypsies are camping on *his* land. Confronted by Pope with this fact of ownership, the Gypsies are at his disposal and mercy, despite that they could easily overwhelm him. They do not, because they understand that the authority of the land belongs to him.

Pope takes from them the violin for his concert, in exchange for permission to use his land and also for entrance to the concert. The violin prior to Pope belongs to a Gypsy woman, though not for long. She knows as he plays his improvised "inspiration" that Pope's action has appropriated the possession of the violin.

Ironically, as it was through a theft that the Gypsies first got the violin, the re-taking of the violin from them constitutes another layer of theft.

During this scene, we can wonder: who can possibly own a precious violin? How, in fact, can such a violin be owned? Do the bidders in the auction think that it is possible to own the instrument? In fact, the longevity of the violin negates individual ownership: no single person can outlive a violin, and even an institution as powerful as the state (China) is unable to control the violin as property. A violin can even outlive a gunshot.

PAGANINI, GYPSIES, AND VIOLINNESS

What *The Red Violin* shows through Gypsies is the absolute intertwining of Gypsy culture and a phenomenon that originated in the nineteenth century with Paganini (approximated by Pope), which we will call here *violinness*. On the now-defunct and by invitation only Romani-rights e-mail group, called Romnet, there was even a flurry of messages at a certain point claiming that Paganini was a Gypsy. Without bringing any new documents forward, with really no basis for this claim other than the fact that Paganini seems to *fit* certain stereotypical imageries of a Gypsy violinist. We can ask: is this an anachronism — were the markers of Gypsy violin playing formed *after* Paganini? This represents the political arena of appropriation, expressed as pride in one's ethnic ancestors.

The Red Violin's Gypsy passage carries the violin to the end of the nineteenth century. This Romantic musical bridge coincides with violin-ness, where the violin is the ultimate *expressive* vehicle for *professional music-making*. Gypsies, of course, are precisely these professional music-makers. The intimate yet outward world of the violin was closed to the amateur, by the fact that the violin is difficult to play at a basic level. This contrasts with the piano, the instrument *par excellence* of the professional and the amateur. Indeed, one of the forgotten masterworks of the nineteenth century, Joseph Joachim's Violin Concerto no. 2 (1860s) attests to the cult of the violin as a difficult instrument, and its convergence on Gypsy culture.

LATCHO DROM AND THE ACT OF GYPSY MUSIC-MAKING

Gatlif describes his film *Latcho drom* (Romani for "safe journey") as "neither documentary nor fiction, but a 'musical film,' a setting of a happening/scene (*mise en scène*), with one continuity: the historical route of the Gypsies from India to Egypt."[11] As the tale of wandering and music-making unfolds, the Gypsies are portrayed as victims of at least one thousand years of persecution. This film was widely distributed and well received by newspaper criticism, seemingly part of a rekindling of interest in Gypsies.[12]

The text which opens the film presents a narrative summary of the Gypsies geographical trajectory and subsequent persecution, immediately posing the question of the relationship between Gypsy persecution and their alleged nomadic lifestyle: has the historical persecution of Gypsies necessitated their wandering, which in turn became a necessary component of their identity, or the reverse, does the persecution of Gypsies result from their unwillingness to accept the culture of settled and sedentary peoples? The eight *mise en scène* which follow make no real attempt to deal with what we might call the "origins" of Gypsy movement. And perhaps, rightly so, for a theory of "origins" is more proper to a scholarly or scientific analysis. Theory of this sort would serve to draw our emotional gaze away from the aesthetic import of the film, and from its urgent political dimension. Both the aesthetic and political offer a window into the phenomenon of Gypsy marginalization.

It is in this latter sense that *Latcho* aims to describe reality. And this ambiguates the film *as* film, "neither documentary nor fiction," and makes it a fascinating site for speculation. Within what I would call this "whatever" space between fact and fiction, some interesting issues are raised for criticism: how are we to separate our own, personal understanding of *Latcho* as an artistic statement from the intended political agenda?[13] In trying to come to grips with such a question, we see immediately that the film sharpens the tension between art and reality. Does art support a politics, necessarily, and further, how does art offer a critique of reality?

I will assume that the film *as art* does offer a political viewpoint, one that I will try to uncover as complex "socially symbolic act," defined by Fredric Jameson as a text "whereby real social contradictions, insurmountable in their own terms, find a purely formal resolution in the aesthetic realm."[14] The film's aesthetic dimension is clearly musical expression, wherein we experience the "authentic" Gypsy cry as a response to the pain of their social situation.

THE QUESTION OF GENRE

In Irene Kahn Atkins's terminology, *Latcho* would be a "backstage musical," where all the music is justified on screen *as* what the music is, music *as song, as dance, as ceremony.*[15] Yet our experience of the film is not that of a passive Western audience listening to a concert, nor of a "show within a show." We encounter an excess of music's meaning from the cinematic, whirlwind effect of the source sequences in *Latcho*. The excess is the illusion created by the film as an artwork, where we are cognitively displaced from mundane (everyday) reality, yet asked to focus on a real situation with political ramifications.

Let us pause on Gatlif's statement, that *Latcho* is "neither documentary nor fiction." It is precisely a negative point that informs our understanding of the film. The eight *mis en scène* are staged occurrences, cinematically interpreted by the cameras under the gaze of Gatlif. However, an overture to reality is made, in that we are experiencing what the filmmaker's believe are *real* Gypsies making music. This is perhaps the fine line that Gatlif is trying to negotiate, in his attempt to appropriate the real with a camera.

What are the conditions that make a documentary possible? Are not all documentaries impossible by admission of what they omit, the "facts" that are not included? Are documentaries, in effect, a kind of "staging" underneath the gaze of the director?

In his use of Gypsies on location, Gatlif has drawn out these conclusions to their logical conclusions. And the location shooting imparts to the film a truthful visibility that would not be possible in any other way. We feel the change in light, from the burning desert sun of Rajasthan, to the softer skies of Turkey, to the cloudy haze over Southern Romania: we sense the element of the place. Though "acting," as it were, the Gypsies in the film are in their element, inhabiting their own place.

We could compare *Latcho* to the cinematography for rock music. The genre of the rock-concert film, based on live footage, presents music from the point of view of the "ideal" audience. But closer to the staged effect of *Latcho* is the rock-music video. Here we watch real musicians perform, even though we sometimes know they are only acting the part; sometimes there is no context for the performance, and the producers mingle in added imagery. In this sense the image alters the sonic landscape. Yet despite this we still assume that we are granted an access to a dimension of the authentic song.

This leads to the following proposition: is the equivocal genre of *Latcho* only possible within the postmodern pasticcio of the 80s and 90s rock-music video? Would the film have been possible in earlier decades, when videos were mostly of concert footage (though with some psychedelic exceptions). With its blending of real elements with staged ones, *Latcho* mimics an ideal reality, but still a reality. And it does seem possible to classify the film as a kind of extended music video, perhaps a cinematized one.

THINKING GYPSY MUSIC

Latcho is *about* Gypsy music-making. The story is told through source music, that is, music that is visibly justified on screen, at least audible to the characters depicted. Atkins notes that in the source-music sequence, the other parameters of film — the visual, the dramatic, and the narrative — are "largely determined" by the causal chain emanating from the source music.

Latcho uses source music in precise ways in order to generate these parameters, and also one missed in Atkin's theory: reflection. At the moment of reflection, the combination of sound and image produce a philosophical position, either for the characters or the audience or both. We confront a subject matter, issues, as partners in a dialogue. Lastly, reflection ceases the time, suspending the perception of the movement of time. This entails that the dramatic action also ceases.

The case for the identity of Gypsy music across/through/between (all prepositions seem impossible in this context) cultures results from the singularity of Gypsy music-making in the Open of reflection. The basic argument of *Latcho* might be that the predicate "Gypsy" alters and yet paradoxically preserves the local tradition of music in a given region.

Yet how can we think the unity of the assumed predicate without violating the singularity of Gypsy as it relates to itself? Further, if we assume that Gypsy is a predicate, something that adds to the concept of "music," then we once again fall into the trap of introducing Western metaphysical baggage into the topic. The predicative modifier seeks to grasp the thing through the tyranny of possession. If "Gypsy" denotes a kind of possession, then it simultaneously will be dis-placed; moreover, the ethical responsibility of respecting a community and its right to exist will be lost.

EXOTICISM: RAJASTHAN, EGYPT, TURKEY

The film begins in the open expanse of the Thar desert in the westernmost region of Rajasthan. The songs and instruments used perhaps belong to the Manghniar tribe.[16]

Why are these people Gypsy? Surely it is only the framing context: in a film about Indian music using the same sequence, would we identify the tribe as Gypsy? (This is a huge topic that cannot be considered in detail here.)

Still, *Latcho* brilliantly situates all of the main cultural markers about Gypsies into this first scene: 1) traveling; 2) highly ornate vocal style in songs that deal with the pain of separation and distance; 3) devotion, ceremony, and religiosity; 4) ornamented dress style; 5) a preference for string instruments, both plucked and bowed (the kaimacha); 6) dance; 7) the significance of children for the transmission of cultural traditions in oral society; 8) a nearness to the four elements of water, fire, earth, and sky (something lost in postindustrial societies); 9) sensuality and sexuality; and 10) participatory music and music for listening (the gaze of performance).

The opening scene is the most energetic and colorful of the film. Part of the reason for this is that although the pain of separation is felt ("I will burn my horoscope for it has exiled me from those I love"), the pain of persecution has not been fully exposed. In this sequence the pure *jouissance* of the vibrant rhythms of life captures the audience. The sensuality of the dancer is exquisite. The boy sings that "Your fiancée is handsome," a reference to courtship, while other members of the tribe work, hammering spikes on anvils. The boy's song sets up a startling symmetry between work and dance. As the woman dances, one of the most beautiful images of the entire film, her girl counterpart imitates her. This mimicking is more than just a copy, it is the preservation of a way of life.

The boy singer's gaze of rapture on the beauty of the woman and her dance creates a distance. Our consciousness merges with the boy, as we experience the transcendence of the dance knowing that it is beyond comprehension and representation. The distance of the *voyeur* is echoed later in the film, especially in the Egyptian sequence. But this kind of on looking is necessary in the film, for it shows the predicament of the outsider trying to view the Gypsy/Other.

The climax of the Rajasthani scene is the elaborate ceremony, an approximation of the Hindu desert ritual of Holi. "I have prepared food," sings the master. The light of the day is the context for the voice of the boy, who also accompanies the work. The moon's emergence symbolizes the power of the night, and also the realm of female sexuality. These forces require their complement, the voice of the virile male. The sexuality of the situation continues in the lyrics of the song, "how can I sleep alone without you."

With the Ghawazi tribe of upper Egypt, we have a similar situation. Shouts of joy are heard in a field as the music happens. There is a male voyeur, who watches through an open window. As viewers, we wonder: why does the man decide not to go into the celebration? Is he not a part of this scene? The children learn the rebec and dance. The *mawwal* (Arabic vocal improvisation to a poetic text, also improvised) again for-grounds the pain of separation: "When I think of those I love so far away, I weep bitter tears." Who are the ones so far away? His family members? Or all the members of the Gypsy nation? (Again, like the Rajasthanis, it seems highly problematic that the Ghawazi are actually Gypsies.) Those who are "far away" then show up in boats, though we are not witnesses to the reuniting. Again, the climax of the sequence is the male's song with strong sexual overtones: "Dora, dora — you're as sweet as honey drinks passed around on trays/My beloved I see your image in the coffee dregs."

The final image from the banks of the Nile thematizes memory. The young *voyeur* now playing on the rebec recalls musically the beginning of the scene; he plays for hours, grooving until at least sundown. At this reflective moment of the film, any residual pain is overcome through the cathartic power of music.

The Sulukule quarter of Istanbul (a Roma neighborhood) presents the most bewildering overlapping of images that the film contains. The only presumably non-Gypsy source music occurs, the Muslim call to prayer. Source music is deftly employed: we hear the professional Gypsy *takht* (small ensemble) of the club, while we see a woman and girl selling flowers, a bizarre dancing bear (a typical Gypsy symbol in this area of the world), a boy shining shoes, and mothers calling children. The music creates a sense of urgency to the various activities of economy and domesticity. Finally the camera rests on the club, and we finally see that as a performance, music is also an economic activity.

The Turkish scene closes with the confirmation of the Gypsy closeness to the elements. A Gypsy man is selling telescopic views of the moon craters. Here the telescope can be interpreted to symbolize the Gypsy as an intermediary or bridge to nature. The Gypsy never loses his bond with the earth, even in this context of civilization. For the Gadje (non-Gypsy), the Gypsy offers the possibility of the rediscovery of the natural elements.

Finally, in these locales outside of Europe's borders the exotic origins of Gypsy tribes take precedence. However, we can problematize the "Gypsy" identity of at least the first two groups presented.[17] Why would the filmmakers try to manipulate us into believing that these are Gypsies, even as a quasi-documentary statement? What of the experience of the dynamics of each location? Music grounds itself in territory and in place. We hear the transformations in the musical utterance as the location changes. Even if we can accept the fact that we are not seeing "real" Gypsies, this music does not function like Gypsiness does in European territory.

Yet the film's statement that these are actual Gypsies playing Gypsy music becomes a socially symbolic act (following Jameson) in the face of such criticism. The film inscribes a narrative about Gypsies into the material, and probably to the annoyance of many scholars and activists, tries to the resolve the aporias and debates around the origins of Gypsies and musical property with an appeal made under the cover of the aesthetic realm, what we are calling Gypsiness.

THE "THIRD WORLD": ROMANIA, HUNGARY, SLOVAKIA

At a recent exhibit (2001) at the Guggenheim Museum in New York, Marjetica Potrc from Ljublana, Slovenia, set up photographs of makeshift homes, shanty-towns, and semi-permanent and self-made living structures that are quickly overtaking the world. Her caption for the photograph from Ljublana (probably of Gypsies) read that "Eastern Europe is alive and well." This celebratory attitude toward this location by the artist is completely relevant to the attitude that *Latcho* assumes. What gives observers from wealthier nations the right to judge? Who are we as members of the so-called democracies? There is an anti-materialistic thrust to such embracing of life in these poorer states by Western standards.

Returning to our commentary, the last image of Turkey is the view of the craters on the moon, from which the camera transports us to a boy walking in the muddy streets of Clejani, Romania.

The next music is immediately recognizable, and comes from another time and world. Nicolae Neacsu (one of the elder statesman for music from this village) plays violin and sings an epic ballad to the accompaniment of the cymbalom. His text mixes images drawn from folk ballads — "green leaves, wild violets" — with the story of the student rebellion in December 1989 that ended with the dictator's execution on Christmas Day of that year. This is the most specific political text of the film, and the song prepares us for the theme of persecution that will be unleashed in the following sequences.

The dictator Ceausescu has withheld "light." By turning off the electricity in apartment buildings, he denies the inhabitants the use of their lighting fixtures. But Ceausescu has also obscured what since the Enlightenment is the "light of reason," here, the ability of the self to determine its social dealings in the world. With the fall of the socialist state and the opening of borders to the material possibilities of capitalism, the need for reflection on one's existence in the world assumes a new urgency. This situation has led to massive insecurities in a country like Romania, where in the year 2000 the average wage was around $100 per month, a low salary by European standards.

The pain felt through Neacsu's song is of man's ability to create misery for himself, even amidst the stunning beauty of nature: "green leaf, a thousand leaves." Again, it is the Gypsy who is able to articulate the comprehension; the film reinforces this with the force of individuality, in whose Face we feel the buried potentiality of a kind of wisdom that is all-too-often forgotten in the West.

Neacsu's ballad becomes commentary (non-source), as the camera pans away from him and shows leaves falling, then flowers. Next is the image of the man eating bread, perhaps remembering the events related by Neacsu, in the giant empty square of *Piata Victoriei*, cars buzzing around him. Here memory plays an important role in the musical reflection. Linking the image of the man with the bread and Neacsu is the single listener, a young Gypsy boy. Neacsu's bardic cry becomes the voice of history, as the young boy learns of the trauma of his native country.

The Taraf de Haïdouks (*taraf* is the Turkish word for band, *haïdouk* is a Robin-Hood styled brigand) are presented as the virtuosos that they are. Their second CD, "Honourable Brigands, Magic Horses and Evil Eye" (the title and idea are the work of the producers, Michel Winter and Stephan Karo, not the musicians) was released in the same year as the film, 1994. Perhaps because of their critical success, and their high degree of professionalization (Clejani's wedding musicians are the most famous for the region south of Bucharest), they play with a different attitude than the other musicians of *Latcho*. In short, they manifest an authority that they are not anonymous; they are superstars of the burgeoning world-music scene. They perform beyond the camera, beyond the on-screen audience, directly *to us*.

A little girl on a train in the middle of nowhere, Hungary, sings of the miserable plight of the Gypsies: "the whole world despises us, we have been banished, we have been cursed... condemned to a life of wandering." The message of the film is now on the surface — that Gypsies are what they are because they are "condemned to wander," thereby setting up the train tracks scene which follows.

Here, despite their condemnation, the Gypsies can bestow light on the world through their musical talent. A little boy (Gadje) wishes to cheer up his presumably depressed blond-haired mother. Her blond hair is a necessary contrast to the darkness of the Gypsies. The contrast receives support from the train tracks, separating the world of the Gypsies from the rest of humanity.

The boy asks the Gypsies (who stand around the fire, a frequent and potent image in the film) to play. They mock the boy; again, the issue of money is central. Why would Gypsies play for only three coins? But they play and sing anyway, unable to resist the asking. As they do so, the boy and mother change their moods to intense happiness. Awkwardness becomes immediately apparent in the boy's attempt at dancing. The message is that the boy is not free like the Gypsies, and his attempt at imitation fails miserably.

The song "Auschwitz" sung with the gas-chamber buildings and ovens in Birkenau looming in the background completes the triad of the European third world. The song is heard twice, first by a chorus of women to the images of the barbed wire against snow, then by a camp survivor. The Holocaust serves as the ultimate symbol of human suffering and the tragedy of Nazi politics. The melody is actually from Czech lands (the woman holds a matches with the Czech president Vaclav Havel, who is outspoken against Roma racism in his own country), and the Romani text is about a blackbird (*"A me, mamo, adarig dzar"*). Strangely, the Romani text is mistranslated, and should read:

> In Auschwitz there's a large house, and they've put my husband there, he sits there and thinks of me. There's not any bread, and the guards are so evil.

Instead, the subtitles read:

> In Auschwitz we die of hunger, they have imprisoned us in a huge hangar...

Perhaps the filmmakers are here trying to raise consciousness about the Gypsy presence in the camps (it is estimated that at least 500,000 Roma perished in the Nazi system of camps centered in Auschwitz).[18] Since the film, we can note that through the efforts of Roma political activism they occupy a corner exhibit at the Holocaust Museum in Washington, DC.[19]

The film becomes surreal in Slovakia, where Gypsies are shown to live in trees. Here reality is stretched, for nowhere do Gypsies live in trees.[20] A Gypsy man laments the situation, "God has condemned us to wandering, we set out so far away." But we can ask, why the settlement in trees? Especially in a film that is semi-, quasi-documentary? Perhaps all that is meant is innocent, artistic license in showing that the Gypsies are close to nature, and we are to interpret the trees on the symbolic plane. In any case, the surreal nature of this scene produces the hallucination of what it is to be Gypsy.

CINE-POEM

Michael Beckerman has coined the word "cine-poem" in an effort to describe with more precision the kind of source music present in *Latcho drom*. Indeed, there are many levels to source or *diagetic* music, and we presently lack terminological to unpack these. Furthermore, the complement to source/diagetic would be non-source/non-diagetic, negative terms that do not address the power of music to shape a scene, especially when considering that most film music would fall into these latter categories.[21]

Beckerman defines cine-poem as film where the music takes precedence over the image, that is, where the image's purpose is to add to the meaning of the music. This may prove impossible, in actuality, in cultures obsessed with image and visibility. However, in a certain class of films where the subject matter is music, it might be the case that directors find visual imagery that they feel supports the primacy of the music's power to evoke, hence the realm of the poetic.

Finally, Beckerman argues that *Latcho drom's* real genre, given that we know that it is not documentary, is a massive cine-poem,[22] perhaps the first large-scale one.

MARGINS OF THE WEST: FRANCE AND SPAIN AND THE POLITICS OF BEING-GYPSY

Along with the Turkish scene, the French scene eschews vocal performance and subtitles. The scene calls attention to the situation of the Gypsies in Western countries, forced to the margins as they are in the neighboring lands of Eastern Europe. A harmless pastoral scene erupts into a scene of persecution, as two armed French farmers remove Gypsy squatters from their land. We can easily imagine this to be an everyday possibility for a nomadic group as they travel across private property. Property is power, as in the power to assume the authority of a police action beyond the police.[23]

Of all the scenes, the French is the most directly religious. The main justification for this scene seems to be to link it to the ceremony in the Thar desert, with which the film began; further, the guitar-driven hot jazz (*musique manouche*) prepares us for the energy of the guitar in the following Spanish scene.

Andalusian music will serve to summarize the tale of persecution and forced wandering. The boy sings that "we Gypsies lead a wandering life." The flamenco music is closest to a Western audience's sensibility, though with a sense of the predictable. The dancing and clapping, necessary ingredients of flamenco, in this context might seem forced and imposed, as does the theme of persecution, here sung by a woman:

Why do they spit in my face? What can I do if my skin is dark, if my hair is Gypsy black.... We've always been victims.

In a subtle reversal of gender roles, women and children are now the leaders. Is this an overture to political correctness? If Gypsy culture as Indo-European is patriarchal, why the sudden emphasis on the political power of women (furiously dancing and clapping), and especially the final image of such an angry one? It achieves a quasi-Faustian effect, as if the feminine represents the only possibility for redemption of the crimes and sins of the world. And yet an open question remains, as to whether or not forgiveness for the Roma can be (or is) possible.

The clapping becomes annoyingly obsessive, which may in fact be the intent of the filmmakers. The beauty of the wooden hand-clappers in the Rajasthani desert, with profound musical motivation, here loses focus and becomes the stuff of cliché; the hand-clapping, by contrast, is heard instead as accompaniment to song. Significantly, the clapping markets the film: on the CD cover, video cover and the photo book we encounter this image. The producers have taken a chance with the emphasis on this image, seemingly contingent to the film's deeper complexity. A stronger image that is more pertinent to the theme of the film is the singularity of the Face.

However, one aspect of clapping that does seem to possess a mythical power is that the activity of clapping involves the mystery of touching. How does one touch, who touches, and why? Touching bridges the centuries-old debate about how an immaterial substance, mind, can effect materiality, the body. Touching mediates the possible impossibility of these two distinct substances.

We take leave of the film with a quasi-defined idea of a persecuted people. Part of this is surely not a defect of the film, but rather a built-in problem of ethnography's encounter with the Other: how to write an oral culture, and in this case one that we are not sure even exists as a unity. And in this respect the political subject of the Enlightenment's narrative of emancipation is not available for consciousness. What differentiates Gypsies, again, from other oral cultures is that Gypsies occupy the space in which Western discourse practice occurs. This subtle aspect of Gypsy interaction is not sufficiently negotiated in the French and Spanish scenes. That is, it would seem possible at these points in the film to articulate concrete reasons for the historical persecution of Gypsies, and to show why the Roma are *raising their voices at this moment in history*, and through music. Why has the Romani rights movement emerged at this time, and not some other moment?

Finally, it is important to consider that there might be a certain amount of risk in emphasizing the persecution theme too strongly. For, if we perceive Gypsies as nothing other than victims, in a certain sense they too become assimilated into the mass, faceless humanity who partakes of this status. Up to and including the

Auschwitz scene, the singularity of Gypsy has integrity, as their situation on the margins of European prosperity is unquestionable.

But in the Spanish finale, the Gypsy cry of pain perhaps becomes overly fatalistic. We come to believe that the purpose of Gypsy is to suffer in a cruel world; the danger here is that we accept and see this as a kind of necessity.[24] A contradiction lurks here: that the passive suffering of the cry exists within a context of the dynamic musical explosion of the same cry. Here art as critique can misfire. Music as a powerful tool for conveying a political message is overly explicit in the last song, "*El pajaro negro*" — and it seems no coincidence that this is the song Gatlif composed himself for the film. (We assume that other songs are from oral traditions.) Gatlif fails to specify at this crucial final moment of the film how the transcendent power of the music can fuel resistance. The clapping and angry woman becomes over determined, as it this is how it is and it cannot be otherwise. Music can be a repository for pain, but another compelling reason for music's existence lies in its ability to transform consciousness through a dwelling in the here and now.

MARKETING GYPSINESS

Perhaps there are commercial reasons for keeping the content of the political resistance fuzzy: after the fall of the Iron Curtain, Gypsy music, as Other, simply put, sells. And part of the new marketing strategy is to depict Gypsies as victims. Angry women as such are part of this marketing, so obvious as an overture to the creative rage of female identity in our age of political correctness.

The idea of "Gypsy music" seems to assume a universal quality of *Gypsiness* in the musics played by Gypsies throughout the world, from communities along the Nile (which again, do not seem to be Gypsies), to the Sulukule ghetto in Istanbul, to the villages of Romania.

We stand as witnesses here, to the creation of a unique Gypsy identity before our very eyes: the visible construction of something new, call it a Gypsy/Roma *hyper-national identity*, without the call for a national territory, a "Romestan." Yet Gypsies are the keepers of a unified cultural legacy, despite their lack of a homeland, despite the various localities they inhabit (we can mention Australia, South America, and North America as other important locations for Gypsies).

As a final thought, we can posit the CD to *Latcho* as an empty reference amplifying the film.[25] Here the songs are given in their original languages, without any attempt at a translation. Only countries of origin are stated. Though the withholding of information seems to make the film as art work, it seems unnecessary as part of CD packaging.

Are we to listen to this music as "absolute music?" And why are the booklet's images overwhelming female — the dancer, the Spanish chorus of women, the little girl from the Hungarian train, the feet of the dancer?

POST-*LATCHO DROM*

The two directors who have most powerfully presented Gypsiness on film are Tony Gatlif (who is one-quarter Rom) and Emir Kusturica (a Muslim from Sarajevo, a controversially outspoken critic of the partitioning of the former and multi-ethnic Yugoslavia). *Gadjo dilo* and *Mondo* (and as of this writing, *Vengo*) are Gatlif's follow-ups to *Latcho drom*, and constitute his so-called "Gypsy trilogy." *Time of the Gypsies* is Kusturica's interpretation of the Gypsy mafia, while his *Black Cat, White Cat* (a satirical farce in the tradition of Fellini) continues this theme but transposed to a masterfully absurd level.

GADJO DILO (CRAZY STRANGER) (1998)

> It's a music which expresses the fear and pain of a people whose soul is hurt. That's why Gypsy music is beautiful. Otherwise it's 'anything goes,' full of false notes, the instruments are put together with whatever's on hand. But their music is the cry of pain, an ancestral pain which comes from the soul of a whole nation of people. That is its strength and its beauty. It is pure revolt, nothing is fabricated, all is unleashed. And that, in effect, is how I had imagined the film [*Gadjo dilo*].
>
> Interview with director Tony Gatlif

"Dilo" is the Romani word for crazy, but "Gadjo" means a non-Gypsy. Why then the rendering, "Crazy Stranger?" In general, like *Latcho*, this film hovers between documentary and fictional film. Without question it is one of the most poignant films imaginable on being a guest/outsider in a small village, in this case a Romanian-Gypsy one. Because the film's tale thematizes the relationship of Western and Gypsy cultures, we will it analyze the narrative of the film in close detail.

Gatlif opens his film with a young French man walking on a deserted, snowy, and muddy road in rural Romania. With a stunning attention to capturing the moment, the camera shows the Frenchman pulling out a hunk of hard cheese, in exasperation, as he leans against a stone marker. There is no music, only the sound of a bitter wind.

With his back to the camera, the first music we hear is the tabla (Indian drum) of contemporary global pop: then, to a strong bass, the Frenchman whirls and spins in the road. The song is called "Disparaitra (Disappears)," and is sung by Rona Hartner, the Romanian actress who portrays a beautiful Gypsy woman. Written by Gatlif, the song has a fascinating text, naming words in a number of language (including French, English, and German). The first series is people/Gypsy/disappears/world. He continues to spin on one leg, and then we gain the perspective of the Frenchman spinning, as the landscape spins. An accordion enters; the voice returns. The sun sets as the scene closes.

Next scene: Gypsy girls in a wagon are laughing at him and taunting him: "bite the cock," "lick my pussy" is what they sing in Romani, when he asks for "*lautar*" (musician). He is passed by a truck, with policemen (armed with machine guns) holding a beaten-up Gypsy boy between them. Gatlif subtly and forcefully articulates the topic of Gypsy persecution and oppression by unsympathetic police forces in Eastern Europe.

As he gets drunk with an old Gypsy man whose son Adrian has just been arrested, we first learn why the Frenchman has traveled all this way: for music. He plays a tape of a Gypsy woman (the legendary but probably mythical "Nora Luca"), in hopes that the Gypsy man knows whom he is hearing. The old man replies that these kinds of songs are everywhere around here. "God why have you abandoned me": the Gypsy man cries out in song, in a scene at dawn as he drives a horse and wagon back to his house.

While the Frenchman sleeps in the home of the old Gypsy, Gatlif employs a device he used in *Latcho drom*: Gypsies peer at the man through a window, the window serving as a framing device, indicating the separation dividing cultural worlds. The Gypsies who look in are draped in vibrant colors.

The little kids first proclaim: "he's a *Gadjo dilo*." "Gadjo" is repeated as they stare at him. "Who is this crazy guy?" and "Look at him, he's a bum," while the crowd stares at his tattered shoes. "Maybe he's stolen from my brother's house," then, in emphatic terms: "maybe he's put a curse on the house, maybe he's come to bring us bad luck."

As he walks down the street, a Gypsy man shouts: "what's that *Gadjo* doing here?" Another: "his bag is full of chickens." Again, what Gatlif is doing with this scene is turning around Gypsy stereotypes — Gypsies are accusing the Gadjo of what the Gadje usually accuse the Gypsies of doing. Gypsies objectify him, looking upon him with anger.

The Frenchman enters a bar, demanding a coffee. Again his tattered shoes are an issue, but his ten-dollar bill gets an immediate response.

When the old man returns from chopping wood in the forest, he is angered to learn that the Gypsies allowed the Gadjo dilo to leave. But the Gadjo then returns with food for the old man. As he speaks French, the Gypsies think he can speak Romani. "This is the man I met last night!" When the Gadjo dilo says the name "Nora Luca," the old Gypsy replies, "Of course I know her, she's my girlfriend."

What this exchange shows is what I have experienced in my own fieldwork in Romania. Namely, that Gypsies as hosts want you to be satisfied. You are their guest, and as a host it is their duty and honor to please you and make sure you are happy. If Gypsies can do this by agreeing with you, or telling you what you desire to hear, then they are satisfied too. They rejoice in the joy and smile of the other.

The scene cuts to the old man's house as he invites musicians. "Moi, Stéphane." The old man introduces himself as "Izidor." Gypsies crowd into the house. Again, this is exactly how I experienced it in Clejani: a great clamor and always numerous Gypsies in any room I occupied. The Gypsies want to understand him, so they go and get Sabina. The old man: "luck has sent him to me."

Sabina leans against the doorway; the image of her face, head covered with a bandana, gets the sounds of the cymbalom, probably source music as we can hear "Nora Luca's" voice on the tape machine that Stéphane carries with him. "Come translate what he says." "No way" is her response, and the girl struggles with the old Gypsy in a scene that we see through the eyes of the Frenchman, looking out through the door of the house.

They then clean up the Frenchman, as they think he is dirty. They are extremely worried about his shoes, and many Gypsies present shoes to Izidor. The old man returns to his house, and finds his son sleeping there; the old man steals the shiny black shoes (symbolizing the gangster world) for Stéphane. As they go into town, Stéphane thinks that they are going to see Nora Luca.

As they ride through village streets, the camera presents poignant views of Gypsies walking through the streets. The two men sit together, without a common language, yet with a bond beyond language.

They re-enter the bar and order vodka. "He's from Paris, he lives with us, so he can learn Gypsy." The barman asks if "Paris is beautiful." Izidor yells "he doesn't speak Romanian. He only speaks Gypsy. He has only Gypsy friends in Paris." The barman: "are there Gypsies in Paris?" Izidor (with or without irony): "there are Gypsy colonels, captains in the army, lawyers. French people and Gypsies live in perfect harmony. In France, no one calls Gypsies thieves." The audience is respectful and enjoys Izidor's speech: "Everyone loves them; they repair everything on earth: radios, televisions, they make saucepans, wagons...no one works as well as they do." A Romanian man responds: "you should be there too. You and your whole family." Yet this bar scene shows the relative respect of Romanians for Gypsies, as they leave without altercation.

As they drive back, a scene of linguistic appropriation ensues, as the Frenchman shouts French while Izidor imitates, culminating in "Le Pen's a motherfucker." When they return, the Gypsy women have fixed the shoes of Stéphane. He then tries to leave. "I can't stay. I can't spend my whole life here." "Don't go my son." At this point a familial substitution has occurred: for Izidor, Stéphane has become son.

Izidor plays for Stéphane his violin, showing off by playing behind his back. The smile of the face of Stéphane is an authentic reaction to what he is hearing; when I watch this scene I have numerous images of the same while in Clejani. You are hypnotized, barely aware of your surroundings while you listen to the sounds of the fiddle. One problem with this scene, however, is that the bow strokes that we see are not coordinated with the music. But the look on Stéphane's face is worth everything, his smile full of rapture as the Gypsy stares into his eyes.

An old light fixture hangs in his house; they must rig up an illegal electricity connection to secure power to the house. A Gypsy woman sets a flowered tablecloth for the guest; I can confirm that this is how it was for me, exactly. I would eat alone, with a table set up especially for me, with crowds of people around, staring at me eat. Here he eats alone: "Eat, there's enough for everyone," but I think Stéphane at this point does not believe him.

When they get a light bulb to work, they shout for joy. The camera cuts immediately to a contrastingly snowy scene. The quickness of Gatlif's camera work throughout this film is amazing and nothing short of virtuosic. Again language surfaces as an issue, as a Gypsy boy teaches the Frenchman words, even dirty ones. We see Sabina gathering wood, as snow falls. The Frenchman gazes at her, quizzically. She swears, and he tries to help her. She then bites him. The little boy asks: "Do you like Manole's daughter? She is a slut who left her husband in Belgium. No one wants her anymore. She's a whore." Sabina thinks that the Frenchman is from Belgium, a country she hates (for reasons that we do not yet know, but can imagine).

The bite is significant for at least two reasons. It is the first time that Sabina and Stéphane touch, foreshadowing their relationship. Furthermore, the bite is an ambivalent gesture: the violence intended by the bite is also the sign of sexual desire. Does she react so violently to Stéphane because of her desire for him? And does the bite seduce Stéphane? She lifts up her skirt, baring her ass, shouting "kiss my ass, you dirty Belgian!"

In the style an outdoor village meeting, Gypsy men shout xenophobic speculations about the intentions of the Frenchman: "the foreigner will take our women and children!"; "Maybe he's a murderer"; "Send him back to his country." The old man replies: "he's my Frenchman!" The reply: "He's a thief; he's going to steal our chickens." Izidor thinks otherwise: "he's my luck, he came here to learn Romanes."

Izidor then receives a letter, written in Romanian, from his son. "I'm very happy to hear news of my brother, Radu. There are a lot of Gypsies in this jail. The director lets us play our music. The judge said I'll get out in six months. How are my daughter and my father and my brothers? [signed] Adriani." Gypsy woman cry as they listen.

While the letter is read, Sabina pushes Stéphane out of her way. He gazes at her three times, suggesting that he is becoming interested in her feisty ways.

The scenes are powerful and direct, without time for commentary. The old man cries in his house: "They locked up my Adrian. For us Rom, there is no justice."

Enter the Gypsy mafia in a shiny green Mercedes. The Gypsies kiss the mobster's hands, paying tribute to his gold. He needs musicians for his daughter's wedding. Izidor says they will play for six million lei (about $90, the equivalent of approximately one month's wage in Romania) and food. They haggle, but the mobster agrees, knowing that the village musicians are the best thing that he can get. The Frenchman is introduced, and the mobster promptly invites him to his daughter's wedding.

The old Gypsy then shows the mobster his nearly dead and beaten son, and tells of how they took Adrian for a thief. The mobster wants to help. He says that this boy should be taken to the hospital immediately, and that he will get Adrian out, he knows the prosecutor. Here the Gypsy mafia function exactly as their Sicilian counterparts: as the mediation between the poor and the government. Is this the intention of Gatlif? The stereotyping of the Gypsy mob corresponds to the Italian in ways that seem to be based in reality and in film. That is, it is as though Don Corleone (the Godfather) makes a special appearance in Gatlif's film.

The musicians pile string instruments into the Mercedes. Village girls will accompany as dancers. A Gypsy man says to Izidor: "I'm entrusting my daughters to you. Here's the virginity certificate. If she doesn't return a virgin, I'll cut your head off." Sabina screams at him: "Cut the crap. We're going to be late."

As in *The Godfather*, Gatlif draws the close connection between the mafia and their entertainment. This was a theme that began during the speakeasies of Al Capone in Chicago, where African-American jazz flourished. Since then the mafia has had its hand, in one way or another, in the entertainment industry, whether in New York, Las Vegas, or Hollywood.

Again the mis-understanding continues: Izidor proclaims that he is the Romanes teacher of Stéphane. While Stéphane, wholly absorbed in his own project, can only comprehend that the Mercedes have come for him, as if they were all wearing suits and ties in order to see a performance by Nora Luca. As they drive, the landscape of the area south of Bucharest becomes apparent: a flat landscape, with power lines, with a few trees, but mostly farmland. Factories loom as the industrial backdrop.

As they drive, a Gypsy woman who sits next to Stéphane sing songs. In the backseat of the lead car, Sabina's hair is being fixed. The camera draws in on her face through the rear window, as she stares, longingly, at Stéphane, causing the latter to smile at her. Their love for each other is now confirmed. The Gypsy woman in Stéphane's car notices this exchange, and says to him, "What are you after," while laughing.

The Gypsies from the village lead the wedding procession, with the girls in front dancing to singing, guitar, and fiddle. The camera cuts to above the procession in an artful moment. Stéphane carries a violin case, but he cannot sing. As they enter his house, the father symbolizes his resistance with an ax, while the crowd cheers. "If you come closer I'll kill you." The bridegroom, holding a bottle of brandy, answers with an offering to his would-be-father in law.

The bride sits on an elaborate Persian rug. Money surrounds her and is thrown at her, similar to the opening wedding scene of *The Godfather*. The music loses its village edge, as clarinet and accordion carry the tune, played by what looks like urban musicians. Sabina dances on the floor, making gestures calling attention to her womb. She bites the tie of a man dancing with her (an overtly sexual gesture). The Gypsy mobster has a tie with an American flag on it. They want Stéphane to work for them. Stéphane has no clue as to what is going on, as he led to a boy (Sami) who is a head mobster. Sami asks him in French, "Did you find your singer?" Then Izidor enters, and Stéphane has Sami explain to Izidor that he is looking for Nora Luca. The old Gypsy says that he knows a singer named Milan who knows hundreds of musicians.

At this point in the film, the dramatic tension has become ironic: Stéphane is searching for the perfect singer, the perfect moment in music, while he lives it. For the Gypsies, this is why he is a "Gadjo dilo": the Gadje (plural) refuse to appreciate the good fortune they enjoy everyday, and do not live in the here and now. The Gadje search for a happiness that remains elusive, while Gypsies are satisfied with the fleeting moments of everyday life.

The blaring Gypsy music is typical of Romanian weddings. Sabina walks by Stéphane who says to her, "you dance great." She speaks French, explaining that she used to dance in Belgium. Her facial expression says more than what she says. He mentions her husband, and then introduces himself. She says that she is Sabina and leaves. This exchange between the two is tender, and it is obvious at this point that they are in love with each other.

The familial theme (with Freudian overtones) that has been lurking in the background of the film so far becomes apparent when we learn that the tape of Nora Luca belonged to Stéphane's father. His attempt to find the singer who his father apparently heard on a trip to Romania is the attempt to gain the love and respect of his father.

Paun Milan is dead, and Izidor is heartbroken. They pour vodka on the grave, then Izidor dances while the accordionist/singer plays, to the snapping accompaniment of a Gypsy woman. The accordionist is none other than the contemporary Gypsy pop singer, hugely popular in Bucharest, who calls himself "Adrian Copilul Minune." Though he sings in a global pop style peculiar to Bucharest called "Manele," with Latino, Arabic-Turkish-Bulgarian, and Serbian rhythms, here he sings in a more traditional style.

The graveyard scene is one of the most moving in the entire film, and Izidor's response to the crying accordionist's lament expresses the tragedy of the film. At this point, we learn that Milan is Izidor's brother, and the pain is felt as familial loss.

While they go to visit Izidor's son in jail, Stéphane stays at Izidor's, attempting to return the goodwill of his hosts. He holds children, and then tries to get them out of his way as he sweeps a dirt floor in a house. The Gypsy women spy on him, calling him a faggot as he scrubs the floor. They then play a trick on him, bringing him inside a tent while Gypsy women — one of whom is Sabina — bathe themselves. He is chased out in due fashion. Again the theme of voyeurism is on the surface, crossed with the transgression of taboos.

Izidor returns and yells at Stéphane for acting crazy, and especially for cleaning up. But Stéphane has a surprise, a makeshift record player that allows Izidor to hear his dead father's music. Here we experience the generational flow of Gypsiness, as the sounds are immediately taken to heart by their Gypsy admirers.

Stéphane's immersion in Gypsy life is complete as he plays dice and bets with the Gypsies. A letter from Paris interrupts the game. Inside are one-thousand American dollars and a letter from his mother. He reads it, separated by a wall from Sabina. She sees the money, and leads him away to where she cooks. The Gypsies are surprised to learn that he only has a little brother. He eats next to Sabina, on the ground: here, he is completely assimilated to the Gypsy life, especially when we note that earlier he ate at a table set up especially for his convenience.

A car arrives, and we see why Stéphane sent for the money: he wanted to buy a car. They go for a ride through the countryside, and the car breaks down. While he curses at the carburetor, the Gypsies gather wildflowers in the forest. A perfect contrast: the Gypsies enjoy the beauties of nature, while the frustrated Frenchman swears and worries about his car.

With the car, comes the girl: Stéphane drives Sabina through the countryside in search of the singer. She is a little jealous, "what's with this singer?" Stéphane: she lives all over, pointing to his brain. She points to other body parts, as the car breaks down once again, this time the clutch.

They walk back to the village. Sabina's questioning continues, "There are other singers as strong as fire." Then Stéphane reveals his father's restlessness: his father was very sick, but he loved music and traveled to find it, bringing back recordings. Stéphane did not know his father very well, who died in Syria, with the nomads.

Stéphane continues his father's legacy by setting up a recording session with a Gypsy band in a bar. The music seethes with intensity — Adrian sings a Balkan-influenced song, "Tutti Frutti" — and Sabina attempts to seduce Stéphane with her dance. But he castigates her, telling her not to talk. His headphones separate him from the sonic moment and the Gypsy joy at their own music-making. Adrian leads the group. Stéphane does not have access to his own emotions; as he watches and grooves to the music, he tells Sabina again to be quiet. He does not understand that he has found Nora Luca in the person of Sabina.

He then becomes a full-blown ethnomusicologist, recording Gypsy singers much as Bartók would have:

It's a winter tale about Urza
Who in his anger killed his brother.
His anger passed and he realized he had ruined his life
For a fleeting moment
He ran away, hiding himself from the sky and the light.
Wherever he went he heard the echo:
'What did you do this winter?'
He met the beautiful virgin, Zambilla.
She fell in love with him.
Her father opposed their love and locked her up.
In despair the criminal let himself be caught.
Then Zambilla refused to eat.
To bring his daughter back to life
The father gave away his entire fortune
And got the Gypsy out of jail
They were free but poor ...

Sabina cries while listening to the song. Not understanding anything, Stéphane smiles at the pretty Gypsy song. What was the song about? Sabina tells him that it is a song about a man who kills his brother; but the analogy of forbidden love speaks exactly to the situation between Sabina and Stéphane.

Stéphane writes, again, a signification of his separation from the moment. Sabina tells him how Ceausescu stole from them. Izidor wants to go to Bucharest for female favors. He comes to the window so seriously, and we abruptly find ourselves in a nightclub in Bucharest. Adrian sings to clarinet and violin. Stéphane flirts with Sabina, and a picture is taken with Sabina, Stéphane, and Izidor. A woman belly dances to Gypsy music of the city, showing marked Arabic and Balkan influences, especially in the clarinet playing. Gypsies approach the stage, throwing money around. (The scene, in fact, is closely related to the Istanbul scene in *Latcho drom*.)

This shows a significant aspect of the Romanian-Gypsy psyché: the exhibiting of wealth through sharing it. Stéphane then approaches the stage, gives money and dances with the belly dancer. Izidor tries to get the foreign girls he flirts with to come back to his hotel room.

A man then dances, breaking plates in a ritual. Stéphane becomes obsessed with this, and does it while Sabina dances with him. The music reaches an ostinato, while the clarinet solos, a perfect synthesis of Turkish and Romanian styles. The dancing gets ecstatic.

Sabina then sings while Stéphane almost kisses her: it's Nora Luca, he exclaims, and he cries on the shoulder of Sabina. This is a transcendent moment of the film, as Stéphane is finally beginning to find himself.

Izidor begs Sabina for sex. "Just one time." Stéphane gets angry, and pulls Izidor from Sabina. In the next scene Stéphane and Sabina exert their passions, and she bites the pole. Non-source music is employed, the same kind of global pop that we heard at the beginning of the film. But they are interrupted, as Adrian returns from jail. The party ensues with drinking and singing, led by the Gypsy women. Adrian dances at his newfound freedom.

In the forest, by a river, we learn that Sabina was born there. They consummate their love by the river, and non-source music bursts in while they run naked through the forest. In the fast-moving scenes that follow, non-source music comes more to the forefront, in contrast to the earlier scenes with mostly source music.

Adrian then goes to a bar: "I'm buying drinks," while his mafia friends load the auto. Adrian: "I drink for those who sent me to jail." The barman replies that "I spit on your Mafioso Gypsy face." Adrian throws a glass, striking the man on the chin. The mobsters pull out knives. The three are chased to the breathing sounds of global pop: over this a musician sings "God, what did I do to you to be so black?"; Dmitru (the barman) is dead.

Adrian runs to the Gypsy quarter to hide. The music intensifies. Gypsies run as the mob of Romanians trash the Gypsy homes, burning it down. Chickens fly out from the fire. Gypsies run, screaming for their lives. The voice of the song merges with the voices and cry of the women screaming. Sabina returns crying, "my village!" Stéphane cries too, as he tries to pick her up.

Then we hear the real cry of Gypsy music, as she sees the charred body of Adrian. The scene cuts to the house where the unsuspecting Izidor and his band are playing for Romanians. The Gypsy woman dances on the table.

Stéphane and Sabina drive out to the wedding in a frantic hurry. Izidor is almost in a trance, playing the music of his hosts, when a crying Sabina comes from behind him. Izidor's pain is beyond anything yet in the movie, as he moans "Oh God, great Earth open up, and take me with my son."

We think Stéphane is alone with his tapes as he approaches the countryside. He digs a hole with a lug wrench, and then smashes his tapes with rocks. He buries the tapes in a hole by the stone marker we saw at the beginning, which is here a gravestone. He pours vodka on the grave, like the Gypsies. Adrian's voice is heard in his head while he dances on the grave. We know this as internal sound because of the way the sound is filtered.

In a stunning moment, the camera shows the inside of the car, through the window, we see a sleeping Sabina awaken, while Stéphane's dances in the reflection. She smiles as she watches him dance.

The latent main theme of voyeurism ends the film: that the Gypsies are watching us (the Europeans). This is the reversal of the typical spectacle of Gypsies in film, where we watch the Gypsies, or Gypsies provide an exotic or local color. Furthermore there is a perfect symmetry: the film ends exactly the way it began, with Stéphane whirling around, albeit now that he has become Gypsy, he dances as one. Sabina approvingly and lovingly look on.

BLACK CAT, WHITE CAT (1998)

> I transformed all the dirt going on in the world into a fairytale, and lifted everything at least one meter above the earth. The reality level of this story is very present, but the way it is done is opposite. I wanted to make an optimistic film. I couldn't live anymore with the luggage of history, the tragedy. If I couldn't make this movie, I would be hanging somewhere in a tree.
>
> Director Emir Kusturica

Black Cat, White Cat is a testimony to Balkan madness.

In the opening scene, as the two Gypsy protagonists stare out onto the water of the Danube, a river barge carries a gangster's truck (we know this through the presence of the machine gun). The music is a kind of silly music, played by a kind of flute; the next music we hear is source, as we see a violinist on the large Russian barge. The composed music imitates the sound of folk music. Thereafter follows Russian-style music as the Gypsies rush out to meet the ship for trade. A Jew's harp and clarinet are the main instruments, but the music again is supposed to evoke a style at once crazed and non-serious.

The next scene shows the mafia compound (these later turn out to be the good guys), where they try to make American whiskey. Matko (Birdie) goes to ask the Gypsy king, Grga Pitić, for a loan. While Birdie lies to his uncle that his father is dead, Birdie's theme enters, accompanied by a Jew's harp played by Birdie's boy, Zare. Birdie needs the loan for an investment scheme. The theme signifies that Birdie is lying, something he frequently does (it is used again when he tells his father that Grga is dead).

Germans enter the picture by ship, elegantly dancing on the top floor of the white yacht to a Viennese waltz. The Gypsies dream of being rich like their German and European counterparts.

Rap music plays as the Gypsy troublemaker and head gangster Dadan enters in his white limo, doing coke and gambling with another Gypsy and some Serbian prostitutes. "Pitbull" is the theme song for Dadan; the Serbian women answer that he is a "Terrier."

Black cat/white cat has a double meaning, referring to the two cats who show up from time to time, but also to the Gypsy boy (black) who is in love with a Serbian girl (white), Ida, who has been raised by an old and wise Gypsy woman.

Music possesses the power to heal. The boy brings a Gypsy band into the hospital to rescue his grandfather (the one who his father had said was dead). He dances out of the hospital accompanied to the joyous music. "What a life!" he proclaims as he floats down the river with a bottle and the band playing on. Later on, the Macedonian brass band is tied to a tree, while they perform to accompany the craziness of the water scene.

The magnificent wedding scene features Dadan dancing in a crazed fashion to the sounds of the pan-Balkan music. Dadan takes the microphone and sings:

> *I'll buy you a white carriage and half the world*
> *And three houses bigger than America*
> *Little girl*
> *You've won my heart*
> *If you were mine little girl*
> *You'd live like a queen*
> *A queen by day*
> *An empress by night*

His style of dance fuses disco elements into a Gypsy-Serbian wedding context. He asks the bride, his sister Ladybird, to dance. Because she was to marry against her will, she deftly escapes from the scene, which triggers the wildly comic finale of the film.

The music gives the overall impression of a comic farce, with a Balkan twist. Birdie's theme will accompany the waking of the supposed dead elder brothers, and the film ends happily, with money returning to the right hands, and with lovers united aboard the German cruise ship.

MONDO (1996)

The film opens like *Latcho drom*, with a narrative (though with a panoramic view of Nice):

> No one knew where Mondo came from,
> One day he showed up in our town perfectly unnoticed.
> We knew nothing of his family or home.
> Maybe he had none.

We then see Mondo walking the rich streets of the French resort. The perspective of the film is through the eyes of the young boy.

> He had surely come from far away
> The other side of the mountains
> We could tell he was not from here.

Mondo gets lost in the crowd, and the camera shows the people passing from Mondo's height. The first music we hear is weird, a dissonant Gypsy band — a fictional music. "Wait for me, wait for me," is what Mondo thinks.

The flute determines the musical action of the film. Sometimes the style is European, then Arabic, then Asian; indeed, tracing the configurations of the flute will lead to the essence of the film itself. Alain Weber was the musical consultant from the film. He weaves Macedonian-Gypsy brass music, Central African music, Rajasthani desert music, English choirs, Iranian and Arabic music into an elaborate and eloquent sounding fabric.

Mondo speaks French, and asks a man reading Flaubert by the sea to adopt him. The man replies that it is complicated to adopt a child.

Mondo barely escapes the wrath of the dogcatchers as he tries to sleep in a tree. (Later in the film, Mondo imagines himself as a dog as he looks on the people trying to help him after his collapse.) The cruelty of the persecution of animals is analogous to the indignity which Gypsies must suffer. We (the audience) are intended to identify with the dogs who are hunted, and resent those who try to catch them. Mondo runs into town, and stares through the windows of the shop. A solo flute plays an Irish-sounding tune. Mondo longs for sleep as he looks at the bed, then food as he sees the candy. We look at the boy from inside the candy factory, again, through the frame of the window.

Mondo wanders into an abandoned house (La Fontana Rosa). He focuses on things, such as bugs, flowers, cactus, fruits, with an intensity of someone living in the moment. The house has a Moorish flavor and energy. Then images of a water lily, and Mondo drinking a water drop. He eats a pomegranate. A breathy, wooden sound is heard as Mondo falls into a deep sleep. "how pleasant to sleep like that... when you sleep you're body has left the ground." The busts of writers speak to Mondo in his dreams — Balzac, Cervantes, Flaubert, Dickens. Frogs, a cat, and insects watch Mondo, who has gone far away.

The camera cuts to McDonald's and a modern French shopping area. Mondo goes into the store, following a family that he wishes he was part of. The material abundance of the West is apparent, as French children grab pies. Mondo eats some bread, still trailing the wealthy French family. He grabs some cookies. He hands an apple to the blonde girl, smiling; she smiles back, and then leaves him. A bald-headed man stares at him, eating popcorn. "You want some popcorn?" Mondo runs, and is chased.

The police arrest a refugee from Italy (though from beyond, from North Africa) as Mondo stares at them, hidden. Mondo is always only one step away from the same fate.

Mondo sits by the seaside. He pulls the boat ("Oxyton") toward him. An Arabic-sounding flute plays two phrases of a melody. Mondo invents his own song as he sleeps on the deck of the small boat. Arabic drums start up, and the sultriness of the flute's melody is answered by an Arabic reed pipe. The two instruments trade off while Mondo, in his dream, floats passed his fisherman friend. Mondo heads for the Red Sea in his dreams. Back on shore, Mondo sleeps in a cave by the ocean, shivering on the rocky shore. The flute re-enters to accompany the magically appearing oranges, a gift from God. On the oranges is Arabic writing. An Arabic-sounding song ("El Golla," by Moroccan flutist Abd El Hamid Hmaoui) led by the violins plays while Mondo gathers the oranges. A woman's voice is added over the song. Here we can experience the absolute continuum between Gypsy music and Arabic, real or fantasized.

Thi-Chin, the de facto Asian-adopted mother of the boy (for the state, the process is complicated), gets an Asian-sounding flute melody. This is the last time that we will hear the flute.

Mondo vanishes, disappears. The postman, fisherman, bakers, all, break down. The scene of the invisible cloud, the disaster hanging over the city is accompanied by church singing. Nice suffers from a collective guilt at their passivity in the face of Mondo.

Thi-Chin picks fruit from her garden. She holds a rock, "Toujours Beaucoup" (always a lot), written while Mondo was learning to read. The film's credit close with the earlier church singing.

CONCLUSION: THE NEW WORLD OF GYPSY FILM

The new world of Gypsy film is a unique development in mass spectacle. With its strong reliance on musical situations for the delivery of its message, it has strong ties with the nineteenth-century epic of Lisztean rhapsody. Musicality becomes the repository for the movement of the "emotionality" in these films.

What these films under the influence of Gypsiness exhibit that is lacking in contemporary film-making is the penetrating focus on acting in the here and now, the ineffable joy and tragedy of music-making that cannot be effaced by digital technology or the increasing busyness and business of post-millennial life:

C'est une musique qui crie la peur et la douleur d'un people qui a mal à son âme.

This is a music that cries out the fear and the pain of a people with an aching soul.

Diese Musik ist ein Aufschrei der Angst und des Schmerzes eines Volkes, dessen Seele leider.

Tony Gatlif, CD notes, *Gadjo dilo*

ACKNOWLEDGMENTS

A version of this chapter also appears in *European Meetings in Ethnomusicology* 10 (2003): 45–76.

Chapter Eleven

O lunga drom: The Digital Migration of Gypsy Music

Today the Roma and their history are a major topic of debate, discussion, and evaluation. NGOs working on behalf of Roma and governmental agencies negotiate the current situation and scope for future legal action. Roma groups are seeking minority rights, redress for past wrongs (including Nazi war crimes), and political representation in government. However, the commercial media, with a bow to political correctness here and there, for the most part continues to indulge in the stereotypes of "Gypsies." Perhaps nowhere is this better illustrated than in musical marketing, where Gypsy music as an exotic category is paradoxically allowed for by those activists who consider *any* use of the word "Gypsy" as pejorative and racially motivated.

In the space of this opposition between redress and marketing, an international Roma identity is and has been coalescing for some time. As we have seen, for centuries one of the great components of identity has been music, usually within a national landscape — Hungarian, Russian, Spanish, and so forth. Added to this, music as a proud emblem of achievement is increasingly playing a significant role in the creation of the modern, trans-national Roma community, as Gypsy bands from all over Europe learn of each others' existence, and of their shared roots in Indian music.[1]

Yet there are many who are concerned about the lack of music-making among Roma, citing the acceleration of cultural leveling under the global hegemony of mass-market capitalism increasingly dominated by American interest. The Roma organizer of New York's *Gypsy Festival* (1997), Frank Leo, worries about the decline of their music tradition, as Roma integrate into the American way of life; we can add that in Eastern Europe the threat is much the same. The following is from an article in *New York Newsday*, by Christine Popp:

> There were times, especially in Eastern Europe, when music in the Gypsy community broke out for celebration at the drop of a hat, remembered Frank Leo.

But that tradition, said Leo, whose grandfather emigrated from Russia around the turn of the century, has been in decline among those immigrants rooted in the culture here. 'Twenty years ago, everyone picked up a guitar or accordion; now they're too busy watching TV,' Leo said. 'They're breaking the Gypsy bond.'[2]

Leo's goals for the *Gypsy Festival* were to encourage Gypsy musicians to brush up on their musical skills, and also to present Gypsy art to New Yorkers.

Another strategy in identity-building is to focus on famous and successful personages within a culture's past, what we will name the "hall of fame" approach to the raising of national consciousness. Gypsy musicians commonly cited in this respect are János Bihari, Django Reinhardt, and Carlos Montaya. In his review of Kusturica's *Time of the Gypsies*, Hancock makes the following plea for the Romani hall of fame for educational purposes:

> Unless children also learn in school about the Romani contributions to the world, to the arts and to music, unless they learn that such well-known personalities as Yul Brynner, or Picasso, or Django Reinhardt, or Carmen Amaya, or Carlos Montoya, or Lafcadio Hearne, or Bob Hoskins, or Vita Sackville-West, or Mother Teresa or Charlie Chaplin are of Romani descent, they will continue to get an unrelievedly one-sided picture of a people only ever represented as immoral and dishonest. A balanced view, the non-Gypsy public's *kintala* [balance that preserves], will never exist for them.[3]

What is at stake is the balanced representation of the Romani people through artistic models, and that their contributions to world culture will be acknowledged as specifically *Romani*.

"JELEM, JELEM": THE ROMANI ANTHEM

Hancock's article appears on "The Patrin Web Journal: Romani Culture and History," one of the most informative Web sites devoted to Romani culture. The site includes an enormous amount of information and links to articles and books, including Hancock's *Pariah Syndrome*. Music is not so well represented, but there is a section on the Romani Anthem, "Gelem, Gelem" (also written as "Jelem, Jelem," "Djelem, Djelem"); it gets translated as "I went, I went"):

> *Gelem, gelem, lungone dromensa*
> *Maladilem bahktale Romensa*
> *A Romale katar tumen aven,*
> *E tsarensa bahktale dromensa?*
> *A Romale, A Chavale*
> *Vi man sas ek bari familiya,*
> *Murdadas la e kali legiya*

Aven mansa sa lumniake Roma,
Kai putaile e romane droma
Ake vriama, usti Rom akana,
Men khutasa misto kai kerasa
A Romale, A Chavale

I went, I went on long roads
I met happy Roma
O Roma where do you come from,
With tents on happy roads?
O Roma, O fellow Roma
I once had a great family,
The Black Legions murdered them
Come with me Roma from all the world
For the Romani roads have opened
Now is the time, rise up Roma now,
We will rise high if we act
O Roma, O fellow Roma

The idea of an anthem, in general, provides a profound instance for thinking the deep interconnections of music and nation building. The anthem functions as emblem of the nation-state, the equivalent of a musical flag. In the twentieth century, "supra" national anthems arose, as in the *Internationale* of the former Soviet Union, and some African anthems.[4] "Jelem, Jelem" fits into this category. What remains paradoxical about the existence of the Romani anthem, however, is that there is no aspiration for "Romestan," no nation-state to which it can attach. Further, there is not even the existence of a movement calling for a sovereign Roma state. Instead, the song cries for the freedom of the road (*droma*) in general, a universal road of the world.

On the Patrin site is a recording in Real Audio format that begins with an electric keyboard accompaniment, to a slow tempo. The quality of the recording is low, but made up for by an excellent performance. The basic chord progression, Em-Am-B7, is present, though the pitch is slightly higher than A=440. This imparts the quality of more tension in the vocal line. The singing intensifies as an obbligato violin enters. After the standard slow introduction, the tempo morphs into a disco beat, complete with a canned drum box and bass line, over which the accordion adds wild ornamentation. The singing style changes to the generic sound of European pop music; the arpeggiated and virtuosic figurations of the accordion intrusions outlining diminished sevenths, however, reminds us that we are still in Serbian or Bulgarian space.

"Jelem, Jelem" appears on many CDs produced since the 1990s, in various versions. A compilation CD, *The Gypsy Road: A Musical Migration from India to Spain*, features the Russian-Gypsy group "Loyko" playing it. The hybridity of their playing is a *tour-de-force* of contemporary Gypsy music. The slow, lamenting quality of the violin matches the traditional guitar accompaniment, played rubato, where the

Music Example 34 "Jelem, Jelem," guitar reduction.

guitarist the strums chords with the effect of a cymbalom. This kind of fast strumming as found in much Russian-Gypsy music is common to Europe, including flamenco guitar. The violin-guitar combo approximates the Russian analogue to the Romungro-Hungarian restaurant style. When the free rhythm section gives way to a regular 4/4 rhythm, the guitar plays in the standard pattern with upbeat accents (see Music Example 34). The tune's progression is in G minor, with a Phrygian E-flat chord resolving to D (Gm-Cm-D-E-flat-D-G etc.). The Phrygian half-step progression present gives Loyko's version of the song a Spanish, flamenco flavor. The violin's power is reserved for the modulation, which is done abruptly with an E major chord proclaimed on the guitar as V of Am. With the tune transposed up a whole step, the violin solo (after two verses) is a pure specimen of Gypsiness: sudden starts of fits, rising and falling arpeggios and scale passages. The tune ends with the violin's imitating the guitar, playing pizzicato, also slightly evocative of the balalaika of Russian folk ensembles. Whatever the timbral qualities may be, the aesthetic result of the pizzicato is pure nostalgia for a time long past, which Isabel Fonseca calls the essence of Gypsy song. Indeed, the following passage from Fonseca shows a poetic and etymological flourish in accord with the overall irony of the Gypsy anthem:

> Nostalgia is the essence of Gypsy song, and seems always to have been. But nostalgia for what? *Nostos* is the Greek word for "a return home"; but the Gypsies have no home, and perhaps, uniquely among peoples, they have no dream of a homeland. Utopia — *ou topos* — means "no place." Nostalgia for utopia: a return home to no place. *O lungo drom*. The long road.[5]

Romani activists would perhaps object to the romanticizing tone of the above passage, especially that most Roma groups are no longer nomadic wanderers and have a residence. And Roma leaders are politically seeking more rights and protections within the integrated lives of most Roma, not "the long road." But these kinds of criticism notwithstanding, Fonseca's passage does explain, in part, the cry of nostalgia present in modern, self-consciously stylized songs like "Jelem, Jelem," and other songs that fall under the tent of contemporary Gypsy music.

MARKETING GYPSY MUSIC AS A BIN OF NOSTALGIA

The nostalgia for the freedom of life on the road is the vortex for marketing contemporary Gypsy music CDs. This Internet post on a Flamenco message board explains the logic of this love of the road in the context of the struggle over "purity" in flamenco:

> Why do the flamenco Gypsies claim precedence in flamenco? Quite simply they had to survive. In the past they were persecuted as a minority, so had to struggle more for their own existence and recognition. The state wants to organize all our lives and document us, but Gypsies somehow did not fit into the system. *Them and us* [author's emphasis] almost created the mystery. But there is much more. *Their way of life is so appealing… just feel the freedom of wandering with minimal responsibilities! Live off the land and under the stars and sing your heart out in flamenco song….* [my emphasis] Or was it more down to earth, a cry in the dark about their hard life, their poverty and where to feed their child next? Such human struggle does allow the soul to throw up musical and poetic inspiration (compare the blues to the flamenco, both the music of an oppressed people). It also allows the Gypsy to suggest that he is more in touch with his ancestors on a spiritual level, thereby enabling a personal communication of his soul through the flamenco art form which in turn creates the concept of purity in flamenco. And so the story and justification goes on…[6]

This post encapsulates many of the associations used to sell Gypsy music. The message comes down to this: a persecuted, oppressed minority who express their pain directly in music and poetry.

Playing off the caché of this image, a flood of Gypsy music CDs has been produced for Western audiences. Most of these CDs find their way into the world-music section of large chain stores like Borders or Tower. Once there, however, it can often be difficult to determine which bin will contain Gypsy CDs. Because there are so many new CDs, including compilations, in the last ten years or so, "Gypsy music" seems to have been reinvented, precisely as Gypsiness. Even if this category exists autonomously, Gypsy music CDs can still spill over into other bins, including Eastern European, Russian, Spanish (Flamenco), Middle Eastern, and Indian ones.

While the bins can be explored for their commercial, sociological and ideological ramifications, their main relevancy for this book is that they can be used as a window into the question of Gypsy music — its essence, its history, its propriety — as we have posed it in chapter one. Significantly, the bins reveal the two layers involved in the reception and understanding of Gypsy music. Layer one has Gypsy music as part of the national heritage of the host country, while layer two has Gypsy music as an independent, autonomous category. Note that these layers are mixed and sometimes entangled in one another — in practice, their overlapping cannot be always or easily distinguished.

The oldest layer disperses Gypsy music into the Eastern European, Russian, and Spanish bins. This is Liszt's understanding: that Gypsy music marks a dynamic relationship between virtuosic, expressive, natural musicians and an active, encouraging, nationally united audience. In conveying their deepest joys and sorrows in their music, Gypsies enter a symbiotic relationship with the desires of the audience. After 1848, with the exodus of Hungarian and Gypsy musicians westward to Germany and France, the codes of popular "Hungarian" music were increasingly transferred to what was received as Bohemian music, in sensational fashion. Today, the popularity of Hungarian-Gypsy music has perhaps been overtaken by the flamenco world, at least in Western Europe and the United States. Because this type of bin has not been the subject of this book, we will not linger in it, but proceed to the divisions of the next.

THE THREE STREAMS OF THE AUTONOMOUS GYPSY MUSIC BIN

The autonomously conceived "Gypsy music" bin is much more complicated. It divides into three principle streams — folk music, music from below Turkey, and for lack of a better name, "Gypsy World Music." These labels are, again, for convenience, and do not denote an essence in-itself, but rather the coming quality of Gypsy music.

The first stream has roots that begin with the ethnographic demand for purity of folk materials as found in the writing of Bartók. Sárosi devotes a chapter to the ethnographical features of "Gypsy folk music." For the Hungarian researchers, the two main characteristics of Gypsy folk music are, first, that the Gypsies are non-urbanized villagers (again, non-urban being part of the definition of folk music), and second, that their music belongs only to Gypsy groups — that it not be shared by Hungarians, Yugoslavs, Serbians, or Romanians. It is assumed that this repertory is of non-European origins.[7] Since it is originally performed only for other Gypsies, the music of Gypsy folk musicians corresponds to "in-group" music; however, as it spreads on commercially available recordings, Gypsy folk music is quickly becoming "out-group" music. Now, it appears that at least since the fieldwork of the Csenki brothers, Imre and Sándor, begun in 1940, the idea has been accepted that Gypsy folk music divides into two broad types.[8] These are the slow songs, in Romani *meselaki dyili* (also called *loki d'ili*), and the faster dance songs, *khelimaske d'ili*. The slow songs have a flexible rhythm and more ornamentation. The dance songs are fast, and have "mouth bass-playing" using nonsense syllables ("bdi dabadaba," or Taraf's recent "Dumbala dumba"). In the "Music of the Earth" series, Kazuyuki Tanimoto's CD, *Hungary and Romania: Descendents of the Itinerant Gypsies, Melodies of Sorrow and Joy*, follows this division of Gypsy folk exactly, each track is even named accordingly. He even maintains, like Sárosi, that Gypsies possess no work, religious or nursery songs.[9]

The second stream of autonomous Gypsy music — music beyond the West — became visible with the first two vignettes of *Latcho drom*, the Rajasthani and Egyptian scenes. These recordings fill in the gap of the hypothetical "route" of the Gypsy nomads emanating from the Thar desert of northern India. As this route is increasingly accepted as historical fact, we can expect more music to emerge from "Gypsies" along its path.

Though it is tenuous at best to propose these peoples have anything to do with the contemporary Roma of Europe, it appears to be a viable and successful mode of marketing. Here we observe the merging of scientific hypothesis and business interest. Thus anything produced by these groups can be justified with an appeal to the latest Roma scholarship. For example, the Egyptian scene of *Latcho drom* was by the Nubian group "Les Musiciens Du Nil" who in 1997 released a CD titled "Charcoal Gypsies."[10] Their record company maintains that "'Charcoal Gypsies' continues to fuse the Saidi folk music tradition of the Upper Nile Valley with the force of Africa while sounding like just the sort of thing you'd hear during the wee hours of a quality rave."[11]

"Les Musiciens Du Nil" as a group predates *Latcho drom*; for something that is post-*Latcho*, we have the Rajasthani group "Musafir," formed in 1995. The name itself, which means "traveler" in Farsi, was inspired by the propelling and unifying concept of the Gypsy road. Since at least 1991 groups composed of virtuosos from Rajasthan have been touring Europe in festivals dedicated to the Gypsies, and in 1993 a CD appeared.[12] The two main castes (*jati*) who make up these groups are the *Manghaniyar* and *Langa*, both of whom are Muslim. Also in the "Music of the Earth" series, the CD recorded by Keiji Azami in 1980 is called *India: Traveling Artists of the Desert, the Vernacular Musical Culture of Rajasthan*, and features both Manghaniyar and Langa performers.[13] Released in Japan in 1992, we can surmise that the CD's release for Western audiences in 1997 has much to do with the perceived "Gypsiness" of these performers: the colorful and bright costumes of the female dancers, the nomadic lifestyle of caste musicians, the wildly ornamented and virtuosic vocal lines, and the use of bowed string instruments (the *kamache*) with strong percussion. Musafir, whose music appears on compilations like *The Gypsy Road*, was founded by Hameed Khan; their label is Blue Flame Records.[14] Their long-overdue second CD (their first was in 1995) was released in June 2002 and was titled *Barsaat*, which means "water". Their marketing is heavily predicated on Gypsies as spiritual bearers of music:

The musical form of interpretation is rooted in the music tradition of the 'Sepera' — *the Gypsies of Rajasthan*. The artists understand themselves as holy carriers of a spiritual tradition, that compared to the strict rules of the Muslim artists, allow women to be part of the music. A reason why on this particular production the core ensemble is supported by female vocalists, dancers and even fakirs.[15] [my emphasis]

Surprisingly for purists, the new CD eschews the sound of "authentic" folk tradition for something more contemporary. Their new producer, Music + Action (based in Egloffstein Germany), has latched on to the Roma connection, stating on their Web site:

Rajasthan, the province of India where this group comes from, is the ancient homeland of the Romany people. The music played by Musafir — Gypsies of Rajasthan — is thus a distant cousin of the musical styles of European Romanies.[16]

Perhaps because of this idea of the Roma's "distant cousin," the artistic director Hameed Khan decided to add a European bass line and drum synthesizer.[17] The result is a much heavier style for the group, and brings the music more in line with some Arabic and European pop trends of the last ten years.

The latest fusion by Musafir offers a bridge to the third stream of the autonomous Gypsy music bin — Gypsy World Music. Meant by this type are the numerous CDs produced with the burgeoning world-music audience in mind as intended listeners and buyers. This stream has the most amount of flexibility built into it, and invites the most controversy. For example, there is a recording by Csókolom, which means "May I Kiss Your Hand," with the title "Hungarian and Gypsy Fiddle Music and Songs."[18] The lead singer, fiddler and group leader is Anti von Klewitz, a Silesian from Zagreb; none of the other band members are Gypsy. Thus, when they perform the Hungarian-Gypsy song *"Amari Szi, Amari,"* does this count as Gypsy Music? Or is Gypsy music *as* Gypsy music only what is performed by Roma musicians? Or, can professional folk musicians participate in Gypsy music?

At the opposite spectrum to Csókolom is a group like Kalyi Jag. Not originally musicians, they started performing to raise awareness of Roma issues:

The Group was founded at the end of August 1978 of young Roma lawyers, educators, and working-class origin musicians coming from the territory of northeastern Hungary. There were several reasons for the foundation. On the one hand it became necessary to make widely known the real, authentic Roma culture, on the other to defeat by fostering our mother tongue the negative opinions, since through the language of music everybody is understandable and everybody can be loved. More positive communication can be transferred in music of Kalyi Jag gets to the knowledgeable human intelligence [sic]. At beginning the group had often played at workers' hostels, youth club, in camps and culture houses. Gypsy language songs, the most original, most authentic genre of gypsy folklore were of a great success. The group's name spread as a raging fire through the country. This was the first group in the country and in Europe who performed its own folklore on Roma mother language.[19]

The "raging fire" continues for Kalyi Jag, who perform arrangements of songs. The online Budapest Week has the following headline in May 2002: "Gypsy fire rages through Hungary: After success on Broadway, Kalyi Jag comes home."[20]

THE GYPSY-MUSIC BIN AS A COGNITIVE CONSTRUCT OF GYPSINESS

We will conclude with an exploration of the idea that the Gypsy music bin is a cognitive construct, an entrance and exit into a way of thinking about the world through a nomadic identity that is restless. The CD liner notes for Vera Bila & Kale's release *Rom-Pop,* perhaps summarize it best:

> It is said that one cannot sing the blues if one has never felt them. Similarly, one cannot perform Gypsy music if one has not led the nomadic life of a Gypsy. The music of Vera Bile and Kale clearly reflects the unique Gypsy experience.[21]

What is strange about this saying is that Vera Bile and her band members do not appear to have ever led a nomadic existence! In a role reversal like we have seen with Gatlif's *Gadjo dilo,* the Roma man disparages his *Gadje* female admirer, in the Romani song "I don't love her":

> *I don't love her but she follows me around*
> *She's a non-Roma, she loves a Rom, I don't love her*
> *She doesn't know the Rom, she is selfish*
> *She didn't talk with the Roma, she would be behind another*
> *I have a pretty Romani girl, she's black, she is poor, but she's ours.*[22]

The lyrics contain the fairly typical "us" versus "them" mindset; however, the political context for the song was tense. At the time, there were growing violent attacks against the Roma in the Czech Republic, culminating in the bizarre episode of an exodus of Gypsies who left for Canada. This was in response to a television "documentary" that aired, which was possibly an advertisement with racial motivations; on this show, the Gypsies learned that Canada would offer more opportunities and a better life. After more than one-thousand Roma left the country, the Canadian government responded with a visa requirement for Roma from the Czech Republic.[23]

Because of the marginalization of Roma, there are many ways of imagining this construct of Gypsiness. During the bitterness that ensued in the Czech Republic over the Gypsy-Canadian scandal, I had the opportunity to give a paper with Michael Beckerman at a conference in Prague.[24] Since we wanted the audience to enter into the topic quickly, we summarized six hypothesizes for what this Gypsy music bin might mean. The hypotheses do not compete with one another but can work together to explain what Gypsy Music is. Here I will state them in a condensed fashion, because the threads of each of these topics are woven throughout the book:

1) Gypsy music is authentic music expressing the spiritual orientation of the "real" Gypsies. Gypsies have their own unique experience of the world as a nomadic people, and their music bears this imprint. The singular Gypsy experience is based on genes, or lifestyle, or a combination.

2) Gypsy music is an expressive musical style, a language, that one can "speak." It must be capable of expansion via improvisation. Thus although Liszt and Brahms were not Gypsies, they were still able to speak the Gypsy musical dialect.

3) Gypsy music exists, but as a cognitive construction of the Gypsies and the Western mindset. As a self-perpetuating category, we hear Gypsy music *as* Gypsy because we really want there to be such a thing. For, Gypsy music connotes a mysterious brand of sensuality and connection with the Earth lacking in our Western everyday lives.

4) Gypsy music is a clever marketing ploy embraced by record producers and either "tolerated" or happily accepted by musicians. There is no real Gypsy Music; rather, the Gypsies play whatever people want to hear. Because they are brilliant showmen and entertainers, the Gypsies have convinced their audience and in turn themselves that Gypsy music is an authentic music.

5) From an ethnomusicological standpoint, Gypsy music acquires meaning as something culturally specific. What Turkish-Gypsy music might connote to a Western audience is quite different from what this music means in Istanbul. Thus the question of Gypsy music should be investigated according to the cultural reception and the context for its occurrence.

6) Gypsy music is part of a resurgence of sentiment for the unity of the Roma people throughout the world. That is, Gypsy music is a cultural expression of the political and nationalist urge toward group identity, functioning in a similar way as the constructs "Czech music," or "Russian music," did in the nineteenth century.

In the wake of these hypothesizes, I will now offer some further complications, as a way of problematizing our understanding of Gypsy music and group predication in general:

1) "Gypsy music," unlike other categories of world music, does not designate a specific geographic region; it is impossibly entangled in the musical property of various nations. Because of this, Gypsies can be imagined as "cross-fertilizers," as in Zakir Hussein's statement that Gypsies are like bees.

2) The vexing problems of any search for "origins" for Roma people; the linguistic evidence suggest Northern India yet beyond this, nothing is known scientifically or via documents. Furthermore, Gypsy groups throughout the world have lived apart for centuries. *It is thus the task of intellectuals to construct a unified national identity.* The Romani-rights movement has and is currently doing just that.

3) The reception of Gypsy music by the Romantics and especially Liszt comes down to expression, especially the deep notion of suffering. Our equation of "Gypsiness" captures this reception: I+V=E, where Emotion results from the combination of Improvisation (on-the-spot creation) plus Virtuosity (technique and the idea of innate musicality, whether or not this actually exists). Liszt's ideas seem up-to-date and contemporaneous to the current marketing of Gypsiness.

4) "Gypsiness" can be further defined as a set of ideas, both real and imagined, about Gypsies; its most common tropes are the road, journey, caravan, fire and the outdoors, sensuality, and nature. These symbols were most powerfully exploited in the events of film, especially *Latcho drom*. There is also the massive literary unfolding of these topics, with built-in negative stereotypes. Gypsiness stabilizes as a rhetorical strategy.

5) An ethnomusicological perspective might formulate issues in a wholly different way: Roma music in relation to a particular cultural context, understood via fieldwork; as insider vs. outsider music, or external vs. internal appropriation. The main problem with this kind of perspective, as I see it, is that ethnomusicological (and musicological, for that matter) discourse cannot control the wider signifier, "Gypsiness." Fieldwork tries to pin it down to this or that, but the predication remains unstable and uncontrollable. The category mutates before our eyes.

6) Composers engage with Gypsy music for a variety of reasons. For example, Rachmaninov's predilection for Gypsy subject matter at the beginning of his career, right as he was developing one of the greatest harmonic vocabularies in music history, vs. Bartók's critique of Gypsy music as popular Hungarian music. Despite Bartók's resistance, under pressure he becomes seduced by the codes of Gypsy music and it enters into his musical vocabulary in subtle ways. Janáček's Gypsy inspiration (*Diary of One Who Vanished; Makropulos Case*) is one of the greatest instances of a musical style that has nothing to do with Gypsies and yet everything.

7) The existence of a Romani flag (the wagon wheel) and anthem, both of which are markers of the nation-state, coincides with the resurgence of sentiment for the unity of Roma throughout the world. Paradoxically this occurs in an unprecedented fashion: with no claim for an independent country or territory ("Romestan").

8) The continued political persecution of Gypsies in Eastern Europe/world is a dismal reminder for the unsafe living conditions for Roma communities. The European concept of racism is a complicated matter, however, and there are other issues involved, including the economic oppression of most of the co-inhabitants in Eastern Europe, Russia, and the former Soviet Republics, areas where most of the world's Roma reside. We in the postindustrial capitalist countries cannot stand in simple judgment of what happens there.

CONCLUSION: ROMA REDRESS AND GYPSINESS IN MUSIC

As we have tried to argue, part of the problem of untangling the complications of redress concerns figuring out who the Roma are and where they came from. This problem of identity and origin cannot be solved by hard empirical scientific research alone — the documents that would establish the hypothetical route of Roma from Rajasthan to Europe never did exist, and the linguistic evidence linking the Roma to India can be open to a variety of interpretations. Thus if we assume that Roma identity is largely a cultural and social construction by both Roma and Gadje, then perhaps nowhere is this better documented than in musical discussions.

We can understand Roma redress as the intersection of practical or good-will projects and the politics of memory. "Memory" here refers not only to the narratives of historical representation, but also to the manifestation of this order through artistic means. The redress is under standing review by governmental task forces in various countries, including a multi-national one set up by the European Union commission in Strasbourg. There are also ongoing legal actions, some of which originate in the United States, which specify the Roma as victims of the war crimes of the Holocaust, and are seeking appropriate reparations. Today, there are two mutually conflicting avenues for addressing the Roma: 1) labeling Roma as constituents of the individual state; or 2) viewing the Roma as a cross-cultural unity, a transnational people spread across the world. Roma activists have been working for decades to solve problems at the local level, in the terms of the former avenue. The second alternative, Roma as a transnational people, still exists more in as a figure of the imagination, an unrealized project, and yet, most of the legal assumptions of the EU come out of it. Furthermore, this idea was prefigured in the nineteenth century's version of a pan-national Gypsy music.

In terms of generating actual stereotypes about the Roma, I have investigated what is revealed through music-making. Musicality partakes in spectacle, and beyond the sonic realm the act of music-making is intensely visible. Roma musicians offered a different, "Easternized" alternative to European performance practice. The positive trope of the exoticism became what I theorize as Gypsiness: the idea that improvisation combined with stunning virtuosity creates an emotionally charged atmosphere. We can cite as a reminder the descriptions of composers such as Barber or Shostakovich, or violinists like Menuhin, on the ecstatic atmosphere of Budapest or Bucharest restaurants and cafés when under the spell of Gypsiness. Yet the negative side of this is the nationalist view that although Gypsies possess their own performance practice, they do not play their own music, but steal the music of their European host country. Note that in musicology, the creator of the music is usually identified with the composer, not the performer. Thus the aporia: that Gypsy music names a style completely dependent on the folk repertoires of Europe, while the essence and force of Gypsiness remains sovereign from Western civilization.

Though the stereotypes reached a nadir during the nineteenth century, recently, as we have seen, they have undergone a fascinating renewal. The discursive unfolding of Gypsy music in film, CDs, and world music events presents a powerful and unified front for the affirmation of a new Roma identity. As we have shown, productions of Gypsy music crystallize around certain stable and nomadic signifiers: caravan, road, and route are the most prevalent. To take one example, and there are many,[25] for an event like *Gypsy Caravan,* produced by the prestigious and academically respected World Music Institute (New York), Roma intellectuals were used for and consulted on both the educational and promotional aspects of the show. Here are the most prominent ideas that were encountered: 1) all Gypsy music and music-making throughout the world are related — Gypsy music as transnational and multi-national; 2) some version of Gypsiness informs Gypsy music; 3) Gypsy music is natural, close to the earthly elements, and non-artificial; 4) Gypsy music is inherently painful, and contains the element of protest against their marginalization by a cruel world order. Yet despite the strategic embracing of a positive agenda which would unite multi-national Roma musicians, any other generalizations about Roma are characterized as completely false and untrustworthy.

Thus, some questions for us remain. In what theoretical space is it possible to write about the political issues facing the representation of Roma and their culture? Is "Gypsy music" a fictional unity, in fact? On the one hand, Roma intellectuals reject any attempt to attach general predicates to Roma. On the other hand, the same lobby does not hesitate to endorse a number of essentializing statements about the musical talents of Gypsies.

As a final consideration: what is at stake in the musical identity of Roma — the right of creative appropriation — is also at stake for the barriers facing the legal and bureaucratic establishment working on behalf of Roma. What complicates the temporality of the debt for the Roma is that they are an ethnically transnational and stateless people. A study of how music can exist trans-nationally, paradoxically appropriating while not appropriating, could turn out to be major contribution to strengthen efforts for redress by the Roma-Rights groups and legal organizations.

We conclude with a symbolic scene taken from Tony Gatlif's film *Gadjo dilo.* The ethnographer not only destroys his recordings of Romanian-Gypsy village musicians, but buries them in a gesture of mourning and reconciliation. Gatlif presents a dizzying collision of reality and fiction in this moment of the film, with what we think is the subtext for Gypsiness. In short, the idea that live Gypsy Music cannot be recorded, archived, and transferred digitally; the political analogue is that Roma rights and representation will continue to pose a complex challenge for world governments. It is here, poised between music and politics, that the figure of Gypsiness as both revealing and concealing might offer a constructive basis for the ongoing and coming aspirations of the Roma community.

Gypsy Music Discography

A. ARTISTS AND BANDS

Ando Drom. *Phari Mamo*. Notes by Christian Scholze. Network 26.981, 1997.

Barbaros Erköse Ensemble. *lingo lingo*. Notes by Sonia Tamar Seeman. Golden Horn Records, GHP 012-2, 2000.

Bílá, Vera & Kale. *Rom-Pop*. Notes. RCA Victor, 74321-27910-2, 1997.

Briaval, Coco. *Musique Manouche (Gypsy Music)*. Notes by Sandra Jayat. Auvidis, A 6219, 1996.

Budapest Gypsy Orchestra, The. *The Magic of The Budapest Gypsy Orchestra (A 100 Tagú Cigányzenekar Varázsa)*. Notes. HCD 10305, 1997.

Csókolom (May I Kiss Your Hand). *Hungarian & Gypsy: Fiddle Music & Songs*. Notes by Nora Guthrie. Arhoolie Records, CD 469, 1998.

Divana. *Music and Poets of Rajasthan*. Vol. 2. Notes by Alain Weber. Long Distance, ARC 331.

The Erkose Ensemble. *Tzigane: The Gypsy Music of Turkey*. Notes by Kudsi Erguner. CMP CD 3010, 1992.

Fanfare Ciocarlia. *Iag Bari: The Gypsy Horns from the mountains and beyond*. Notes by Grit Friedrich. Piranha, CD-PIR 1577, 2001.

Fodor, Sándor ("Netti"). *Kalotaszegi Népzene (Hungarian Folk Music from Transylvania)*. Notes by László Kelemen. Hungaroton Classic, HCD 181222, 1994.

Kalman Lendvay Orchestra. *Gipsy Music (Zigeunerweisen)*. Tuxedo Music. TUX CD 5001, 1990.

Kalyi Jag. *Cigányszerelem/Gipsy Love*. Audio and CD-Rom. Notes. Kalyi G+A Productions, CDK 001, 1998.

Kandirali, Mustafa & Ensemble. *Caz Roman*. Notes by Birger Gesthuisen. World Network, 54.037, 1992.

Kanizsa Csillagai. *The Boyash Gypsies of Hungary*. Notes by Helmut Pasquazzo. ARC Music, EUCD 1670, 2001.

Kolpakov Trio. *Rodava Tut*. Notes. Opre 95, n.d. [ca. 1998].

Kusgöz, Ahmet ve Arkadaslari. *Gypsies of Turkey*. Notes by Hüseyin Türkmenler, Diz Heller. ARC Music, EUCD 1635, 2001.

Lakatos, Sándor. "König der Zigeunergeigen." Capriccio, 2 CDs, 49 276 4 and 49 277 1, 1999.

Lakatos, Sándor Déki, and his Gypsy Band. *Dance the Csárdás! (Táncoljunk Csárdást!)*. Hungaroton, HCD 10218, 1994.

Loyko. *Gypsy Times for Nunja*. Notes by Christian Scholze. Network 37.993, 2001.

Lolov, Ibro & his Gypsy Orchestra. *Gypsy Music from Bulgaria.* Notes by Diz Heller. ARC
    music, EUCD 1476, 1998.
Musafir. "Niderli," "Banaa," and "Baalamji." USTAD REC. 0001, 1998 [promotional copy].
Nomad's Land. *Mouvances Tziganes.* Sunset-France, PS 65134, 1994.
Öcal, Burhan, and the Istanbul Oriental Ensemble. *Gypsy Rum.* Notes by Jean Trouillet.
    Network 57.944, 1995.
Papasov, Ivo and His Orchestra. *Balkanology.* Notes by Carol Silverman. HNCD 1363, 1991.
Pavlova, Zina. *Sing, Gypsy!* Monitor Records, MCD 71475, 1993.
Reinhardt, Django and Stéphane Grappelli. *Nuages.* Living Era: Original Mono Recordings
    from 1934-1941, vol. 2. Notes by Vic Bellerby. CD AJA 5138,1994.
Reinhardt, Schnuckenack. *Starportrait.* Intercord, INT 815.235, 1986.
ROM 2001 (Mongo Stojka). *Amari Luma.* SSR4023, 1995.
Santà, Andras et son orchestra. *Nuit tsigane–Gipsy Night.* Notes. ARB, AT 2729, 1994.
Sánta, Ferenc, Jr. *A Híres Prímás és Cigányzenekakra (The Famous Prímás and His Gypsy Band).*
    HCD 10245, 1995.
Senlendirici, Husnu & Laco Tayfa. *Ciftetelli.* Notes by Sonia Seeman. Traditional Crossroads CD
    6002, 2000.
Sesler, Selim and the Sounds of Thrace Ensemble. *The Road to Kesan: Turkish Rom and Regional
    Music of Thrace.* Notes by Sonia Seeman. Traditional Crossroads CD 6001, 2000.
Taraful din Baia. *Gypsies of Romania: Transylvania–Banat.* Notes. ARC Music, EUCD 1618,
    2000.
Taraf de Haïdouks. *Band of Gypsies.* Notes by Marc Hollander. Nonesuch/Crammed, 79641-2,
    2001.
_____. *Dumbula Dumba.* Texts by Marta Bergman. Cramworld, CRAW 21, 1998.
_____. *Honourable Brigands, Magic Horses and Evil Eye.* Musique des Tsiganes de Roumanie,
    vol. 2. Notes by Marta Bergman. Cramworld, CRAW 13, 1994.
_____. *Musique des Tziganes de Roumanie.* Notes by Marta Bergman. Cramworld CRAW
    2, 1991.
Tito Winterstein Quintet. *the best of.* Notes. Boulevard Records/Hammer Music. BLDCD
    528, 1995.
Tomasa, Jóse de la, María la Burra et al. *Cante Gitano (Gypsy Flamenco).* Notes by Phil Slight
    and Robin Broadbank. Nimbus Records, NI 5168, 1989.
Yuri Yunakov Ensemble. *New Colors in Bulgarian Wedding Music.* Notes by Carol Silverman.
    Traditional Crossroads 4283, 1997.

B. COMPILATIONS, COLLECTIONS, AND FIELD RECORDINGS

Bhattacharya, Deben. *Zingari: Route of the Gypsies.* The Living Tradition, no. 5. NE 9102-2,
    1997.
Dietrich, Wolf. *Gipsy music of Macedonia & neighboring countries.* Field notes by Dietrich.
    TSCD914, 1996.
Gadjo dilo: un film de Tony Gatlif. Warner, Princes Film 3984-23045-2, 1998.
Gypsies of Russia. Colors of the World Explorer Series. Allegro, ALL COTWE 116, 1999.
Gypsy Caravan. Liner notes by Michael Shapiro. Putumayo World Music. PUT 185-2, 2001.
Gypsy Dances. Featuring Kálmán Balogh, cymbolum; the group Méta; and András Farkas, Jr.
    & Ensemble. EasyDisc 12136-9017-2, 1999.

Gypsy Fire. Featuring Richard A. Hagopian and Omar Faruk Tekbilek. Traditional Crossroads, CD 4272, 1995.

Gypsy Music of Constantinople. Supervision of production: Petros Tabouris, with unsigned liner notes. Terra Musica, FM 1035, 1999.

The Gypsy Road: a musical migration from India to Spain. Notes by Dan Rosenberg and Angel Romero. ALU-103, 1999.

Gypsy Songs and Dances. Music by Vjaceslav Alexandrovic Grochovskij. Supraphon, 110449-2311, 1991.

Hongrie: folklore et musique gypsie. Atoll Music, 91114, 2000.

The Hungarian Gypsy Orchestra. Supervision of production: Petros Tabouris, with unsigned liner notes. Terra Musica, FM 1034, 1999.

Hungary and Romania: Descendents of the Itinerant Gypsies. Melodies of Sorrow and Joy. Field notes by Kazuyuki Tanimoto. Music of the Earth CDs, vol. 10. MCM 3010, 1997.

India: Traveling Artists of the Desert. The Vernacular Musical Culture of Rajastan. Field notes by Keiji Azami. Music of the Earth CDs, vol. 2. MCM 3002, 1997.

Latcho drom: un film de Tony Gatlif. "La musique des tsiganes du monde de l'inde a l'espagne." Caroline, Carol 1776-2, 1993.

Legends of Gypsy Flamenco. Notes. ARC Music, EUCD 1624, 2000.

The Magic of the Budapest Gypsy Orchestra. Notes. Hungaroton Classic, HCD 10305, 1997.

Music of the Gypsies: The Rough Guide. Notes by Catherine Steinmann. RGNET 1034 CD, 1999.

Road of the Gypsies (L'epopée Tzigane). Notes by Alain Weber. Two CDs. Network, 24.756, 1996.

La Route des Gitans. The Gypsy Road. Notes by Marie Costa. Auvidis Ethnic, B 6879, 1998.

Stelele Muzicii: Lautaresti. Vols. 1-11. Amma Service, Romania, 1999.

Sulukule: Rom Music of Istanbul. Notes by Sonia Seeman. Traditional Crossroads, CD 4289, 1998.

Taraf de Haïdouks. Notes by Marta Bergman. Nonesuch 79554-2, 1999. [Compiled from their first three CDs.]

Taraf: Romanian Gypsy Music. Notes by Speranta Radulescu. Music of the World, CDT-137, 1996.

Tzigane–Gypsy. Air Mail Music. Sunset France, SA 141038, 1999.

Tziganes: Paris/Berlin/Budapest/1910-1935. 2 CDs. Notes by Alain Antonietto. Frémeaux et Associés, FA 006, 1993.

Tziganes roumainie. Le plus grands artistes roumains de musique tzigane. Atoll Music, 91089, 2000.

Új Pátria Sorozat [New Patria Series]. Ed. and notes, László Kelemen and István Pávai. *Collected Village Music from Kalotaszeg.* Vol. 1. Fónó, FA-101-2, 1998. *Collected Village Music from the Transylvanian Plain.* Vol. 2. Fónó FA-102-2, 1998.

World of Gypsies. Vol. 1 and 2. ARC Music, EUCD 1613 and 1633, 2000 and 2001.

C. OTHER SOURCES

Bartók and Kodály. *Hungarian Folk Music.* Notes by Tully Potter. Pearl. GEMM CD 9266.

Bogár, István. Budapest Symphony Orchestra. Naxos 8.550110, 1988.

Cziffra, Georges. *Liszt: 10 Hungarian Rhapsodies.* Recorded in 1973. Great Recordings of the Century. EMI Classics, 7243 5 67555 2, 2001.

Fischer, Iván, cond. Budapest Festival Orchestra. *Brahms: Hungarian Dances.* Philips Classics, 289 462 589-2, 1999.

Jánosi Ensemble. *Rhapsody: Liszt & Bartók Sources.* Notes. Hungaroton Classics, HCD 18191, 1994.

Kronos Quartet. *Kronos Caravan.* Notes by Ken Hunt. Nonesuch Records, 79490-2, 2000.

Muzsikás. *The Bartók Album featuring Márta Sebestyén & Alexander Balanescu.* Notes by the band. Hannibal, HNCD 1439, 1999.

Notes

NOTES FOR CHAPTER ONE

1. In *The New Grove Dictionary of Music and Musicians*, 2nd ed., the article " 'Gypsy' [Roma-Sinti-Traveller]" (www.grovemusic.com, ed. Laura Macy) is written by an ethnomusicologist (Irén Kertész Wilkinson). Surprisingly, the article is silent on the use of Gypsy music by Western composers. Note a couple of things about the title: the marking off of Gypsy with quotation marks, and the bracketed politically correct terms for *some* itinerant groups who may or may not be Roma, in particular, German (Sinti) and British-Irish-Scottish (Traveller). Wilkinson's aim in the article is to underline "similar patterns in their musical practices and processes that reflect their shared values and ethos." Music as a unifying signifier; <http://www.grovemusic.com/shared/views/article.html?section=music.41427> (8 August, 2001).

2. The most prominent one was called "Csárdás" by the Brooklyn Philharmonic Orchestra, Robert Spano, Music Director, Michael Tilson Thomas, Artistic Director, February 20-21, 1998. The booklet contains articles by Jonathan Bellman, "The *Style Hongrois:* The Hungarian Gypsies and Their Imitators," and László Kelemen, trans. Peter Laki, "Hungarian Music, Gypsy Music, Folk Music."

3. The groundbreaking study is Benedict Anderson's 1983 and already classic *Imagined Communities: Reflections on the Origin and Spread of Nationalism*, rev. ed. (London and New York: Verso, 1991). Anderson defines the nation as "an imagined political community—and imagined as both inherently limited and sovereign. It is *imagined* [Anderson's emphasis] because the members of even the smallest nation will never know most of their fellow-members, meet them, or even hear of them, yet in the minds of each lives the *image* [my emphasis] of their communion" (6). The etymological links between "imagination" and "image" are significant; on the power of the imagination as a *reproductive synthesis*, see Immanuel Kant's *Critique of Pure Reason*, trans. Norman Kemp Smith (New York: St. Martin's Press, 1965 [1781 and 1787]), especially the "Transcendental Deduction" of the 1st ed., 129-133. With an ever-growing number of books and articles on the subject of nationalism (one need only to turn to newspaper headlines) Michael Hechter's recent book *Containing Nationalism* (Oxford: Oxford University Press, 2000) is a welcome navigation through the complexities of the topic.

4. "Nationalism/1. Definitions," www.grovemusic.com <http://www.grovemusic.com/shared/views/article.html?section=music.50846.1> (8 July 2001).

5. "Within a Budding Grove," review of *The New Grove Dictionary of Music and Musicians, Second Edition*," ed. Stanley Sadie, *New York Review of Books*, 21 June 2001: 29-32. Rosen feels that Taruskin does not "measure the complexity" of the questions of nationalism; Rosen also has reservations on Taruskin's treatment of "Spanish" and "Hungarian." To this latter, Rosen writes that "for Haydn, Schubert, and Brahms, the Hungarian idiom was a way of relieving the grandeur of the serious forms, and affirming a semi-Germanic identity through a Romantic identification with a home-grown peasant style that was an integral part of Austrian culture with no tinge of outside influence—that is, it was exotic without being foreign" (32). An entire article could be devoted to Rosen's thesis, itself a troubling pronouncement. Passages like this demonstrate the continued and massive bias in much present-day musicology toward "Germanic" — here mitigated by "semi" — and how even the notion of "Hungarian" is assimilated by this term. Further, Rosen rather naively posits a "peasant style" within Austrian culture — who are the Austrians in this context, and are they still German? Without any "tinge of outside influence": who is Rosen kidding here? Is he really proposing that we should understand Austrian works, within the incredibly ethnically diverse Hapsburg Empire, as an essential display of Austrianness? And as a corollary: why no mention of Gypsy within the Hungarian/Austrian context? Rosen's writing perfectly demonstrates an essentializing tendency within musicology.

6. See the standard American music-history textbook that continues to employ the now somewhat overburdened title, *A History of Western Music*, now in its sixth edition (New York and London: W. W. Norton & Company, 2001), by Donald Jay Grout and the recently deceased Claude V. Palisca (January 2001). Though much of Grout's prose has been effectively purged by Palisca and the new editorial "team," still, Palisca holds in the Preface that "the limits of Western music were generally agreed upon then [the 1950s, when Grout first planned the book], and hardly anyone doubted the value of studying its history. . . . In this edition I continue to respect the limits to aim for an *honest* and readable survey of the musical tradition *we* have known best" (my emphasis; xii-xiii). Who are "we" in this context? What is an "honest" reading? Nearly every sentence in the textbook could be torn apart and deconstructed to show a theoretical bias. Every fact is already an interpretation and a valuing of what is deemed important and significant by the writer. For example, take the "honest reading" of nationalism: "when Brahms arranged German folksongs and wrote folk-like melodies, he also identified himself with his own ethnic tradition. However, there is a difference in motivation and effect, because German music was dominant, while Bohemian composers were asserting their independence and distinctiveness" (646). Though perhaps there was a widespread cultural sense that "German music was dominant," still, why the need to continue to read music history this way? If a French composer felt some anxiety in relation to Germany, in that he "wanted to be recognized as the equals to those in the Austro-German orbit," is it still proper for us to interpret the French composer's music as a reaction to this anxiety? That he is "German," as it were, while he is writing music as music, "French" when he expresses his ethnicity? And what about the anxiety felt by German composers? Might we posit that they felt inadequate (whether they admitted it or not; it could be subconscious or even unconscious) in the face of the vibrant folk traditions, the performances of the Gypsies as one example among many?

7. See Jacques Derrida, *Margins of Philosophy*, trans. Alan Bass (Chicago: University of Chicago Press, 1982), especially xix: "The *propius* presupposed in all discourses on economy, sexuality, language, semiotics, rhetoric, etc., repercusses its absolute limit only in sonorous representation. Such, at least, is the most insistent hypothesis of this book. . . . The logic of the event is examined from the vantage of the structures of expropriation called *timbre (typanum), style,* and *signature.* Timbre, style, and signature are the same obliterating division of the proper. They make every event possible, necessary, and unfindable."

8. "*Ereignis*" is one of the keys to Heidegger's later philosophical writings. It is associated with law (*Gesetz*), gathering (*versammeln*), the saying of language (*Sage der Sprache*), and owning (*Eignen*). See *Unterwegs zur Sprache* (Stuttgart: Günther Neske, 1959), 258-60.

9. Carl Dahlhaus, *The Idea of Absolute Music*, trans. Roger Lustig (Chicago and London: University of Chicago Press, 1989), 9, writes that "the idea of absolute music—gradually and against resistance—became the aesthetic paradigm of *German musical culture* in the nineteenth century" (my emphasis).

10. Taruskin, "Nationalism/7. After 1848," www.grovemusic.com, (8 July 2001) quotes this remarkable passage from Franz Brendel's controversial 1859 and Hegelian influenced article proposing the term *Neudeutsche Schule*: "The birthplace cannot be considered decisive in matters of the spirit. The two artists [Berlioz and Liszt] would never have become what they are today had they not from the first drawn nourishment from the German spirit and grown strong with it. Therefore, too, Germany must of necessity be the homeland of their works." Setting aside the troubling aspect of Germanic assimilation in Brendel's pronouncement, we will only mention the use of the metaphors of eating and the growth of an organism as a way of discussing the dialectic of spirit.

11. Rhetorically this begs the question of who a Gypsy is. See Judith Okeley's discussion in *The Traveller-Gypsies* (Cambridge: Cambridge University Press, 1983) of the problem (really, danger) of racial and "one origin in space and time" theories (really, myths) concerning Gypsies. Okeley writes that the only thing that seems clear is that "there were plenty of indigenous recruits for nomadic groups who could have chosen to organize themselves to exploit economic opportunities on the road" (14).

12. This is also due to the tradition of ethnomusicological scholarship in these countries; many of these scholars feel that outsider work on music in their own country suffers from superficiality.

13. *The Critique of Judgment,* trans. Werner S. Pluhar (Indianapolis: Hackett Publishing Company, 1987). Kant's concern is to provide a universal and pure basis for a judgment of taste, where the beautiful can be determined independently of socio-economic or personal biases: "he must believe that he is justified in requiring a similar liking from everyone because he cannot discover, underlying this condition, any private conditions [my emphasis], on which only he might be dependent, so that he must regard it as based on what he can presuppose in everyone else as well . . . the judging person feels completely free as regards the liking he accords the object" (54).

14. See Karl Marx's "The German Ideology: Part I," reprinted in *The Marx-Engels Reader,* 2nd ed., ed. Robert Tucker (New York and London: W. W. Norton & Company, 1978). Marx writes that ". . . it [the revolutionary class] appears as the whole mass of society confronting the one ruling class. It can do this because, to start with, its

interest really is more connected with the *common interest* of all other non-ruling classes, because under the pressure of hitherto existing conditions its *interest* has not yet been able to develop as the *particular interest* of a particular class" (my emphases, 174). An open question: is there a common interest of musicologists, and is it a "particular interest of a particular (privileged) class?"

15. Carl Dahlhaus, *Nineteenth-Century Music*, trans. J. Bradford Robinson (Berkeley and Los Angeles: University of California Press, 1989), 35: "Viennese classicism is lauded for its universality, a universality that offsets the sense of disintegration, of divergent particularist trends, conveyed by nineteenth-century music."

16. Theodor W. Adorno, *Quasi una Fantasia: Essays on Modern Music*, trans. Rodney Livingstone (London and New York: Verso, 1994), in the original essay "Vienna" writes that "it is hard to imagine the Viennese climate of modern music without its naïve addiction to seemingly trivial everyday things" (211).

17. For this repertory see Géza Papp, "Die Quellen der 'Verbunkos-Musik: Ein bibliographischer Versuch," *Studia Musicologica Academiae Scientiarum Hungaricae* 24 (1982): 35-97.

18. Hechter, *Containing Nationalism*, in Chapter Seven ("The Demand for Sovereignty and the Emergence of Nationalism") qualifies the necessity of the demand for sovereignty with the need for "pre-existing social groups formed to provide their members with insurance, welfare, and other kinds of private goods" (125).

19. Carl Schmitt, *Political Theology: Four Chapters on the Concept of Sovereignty*, trans. George Schwab (Cambridge, MA: MIT Press, 1985); Schmitt defines sovereignty as the "power to decide on the exception." Commenting on Schmitt's philosophy of the exception, Derrida writes (*Politics of Friendship*, trans. George Collins (New York: Verso, 1997): "the exception is the rule — that, perhaps is what this thought of real possibility thinks. The exception is the rule of what takes place, the law of the event, the real possibility of its real possibility. The exception grounds the decision on the subject of the case or the eventuality (127)." An event (and as such all artistic phenomena), a singular and spontaneous happening, is on this reading grounded (*begründet*) in the exceptionality of the exception.

20. *Nineteenth-Century Music*, especially Chapter Five, "Trivial Music."

21. In a typically emotional posting on the e-mail discussion list "Romnet" Gregory Kwiek wrote: "Mr. Beckerman, I am an aware Rrom [note the double "r" spelling] and do not like to be reffured [*sic*] to as Gypsy in the first place. I find it incredibly offensive for a non-Gypsy group to call itself by that name. Only yesterday did I go to Patrin clicking on the Gypsy Lore Society's Education for Rroma in the U.S. How many gajze [without the dignity of a capital letter, as in Rroma] have gotten grants to go out and learn of the freaks." <Kz-1oner@webtv.net> "Re: Hot Air," 27 February 1998, <6500djm1@ucsbuxa.ucsb.edu> via <romnet-l@teleport.com>. The point, however, is well taken: that non-Gypsy scholars can benefit, professionally and monetarily, from studying the ethnic markers of a group like the Roma.

22. A substantiation of this, of which examples could be multiplied at length, again, occurred on Romnet. Ian Hancock posted a biting e-mail commenting on The Czech and Slovak Music Society Newsletter, Spring 1998 with the subject title "Any Roma around?," apparently reacting to the use of the word "Gypsy" to describe a paper I gave as part of the Martinu Festival in the Czech Republic, with five other graduate

students led by Michael Beckerman; <xulaj@umail.utexas.edu> (18 August 1999), <6500djm1@ucsbuxa.ucsb.edu> via <romnet-l@telelists.com>.

23. Trans. Edwin Evans (London: William Reeves, n.d.); this edition is the nine-teenth-century's English translation of *Des Bohémiens et de leur Musique en Hongrie*, new ed. (Leipzig: Breitkopf and Härtel, 1881), in German as *Die Zigeuner und Ihre Musik in Ungarn*. Note the deletion of "Hungary" in the title of the English edition.

24. *The Gypsy in Music*, 282.

25. *The Gypsy in Music*, 292-3, my emphasis.

26. Later published in his article, "Music: Pushing Gypsiness, Roma or otherwise," *New York Times* 1 April 2001.

27. Elliott Antokoletz, *The Music of Béla Bartók: A Study of Tonality and Progression in Twentieth-Century Music* (Berkeley, Los Angeles, and London: University of California Press, 1984). Though Antokoletz thinks that Bartók's music must be approached from above (trends in contemporary music) and below (Eastern European folk-music; 1), still, Antokoletz seems more interested in analyzing the "functions and interrela-tions of symmetrical cells" and their relationship to the "generation of interval cycles" (271). In short, he is more taken with Bartók's abstract compositional procedure, at least in the cited volume.

28. At this stage of our argument, this is a necessary though somewhat misleading statement. Bartók himself seems conflicted over Gypsy music, as we shall see in Chapter Nine; and of course, the appropriation of Gypsy music in Bartók's own music is relevant here. David E. Schneider takes this latter point up in his review of *Béla Bartók and Turn-of-the-Century Budapest*, by Judit Frigyesi, *JAMS* 53 (2000): 183-91.

29. 2nd ed. (Oxford UK & Cambridge U.S.: Blackwell, 1995). Fraser's book replaces Jean-Paul Clébert, *The Gypsies*, trans. Charles Duff (London: Vista Books, 1963). For another general introduction, see David Crowe, and John Kolsti, eds., *The Gypsies of Eastern Europe*, introduction by Ian Hancock (New York and London: M. E. Sharpe, Inc., 1991). On the borderline of fiction and non-fiction is Jan Yoors's poignant account of his adoption by Gypsies, in *The Gypsies* (New York: Simon and Schuster, 1967).

30. Fraser, *The Gypsies*, 12.

31. Fraser, *The Gypsies*, 10.

32. See Ian Hancock, "The Emergence of Romani as a Koïné outside of India," in *Scholarship and the Gypsy Struggle: Commitment in Romani Studies*, ed. Thomas Acton, 1-13 (Hertfordshire: University of Hertfordshire Press, 2000). Hancock is a leading linguist on the Romani language.

33. Carol Silverman, "Rom (Gypsy) Music," *Europe*, Timothy Rice, James Porter, and Chris Goetzen, eds., *The Garland Encyclopedia of World Music*, vol. 8 (New York and London: Garland Publishing, Inc., 2000).

34. On flamenco, see Claus Schreiner, *Flamenco: Gypsy Dance and Music from Andalusia*, trans. Mollie Comerford Peters (Portland, OR: Amadeus Press, 1996) and Bernard Leblon, *Gypsies and Flamenco: The Emergence of the Art of Flamenco in Andalusia*, trans. Sinéad ní Shuinéar, Gypsy Research Center (Hatfield, UK: University of Hertfordshire Press, 1995); for a good contemporary recording of *musique manouche* (the legacy of hot jazz), check out the group Coco Brival's CD *Musique Manouche (Gypsy Music)*, notes by Sandra Jayat (A 6219, 1996); for Balkan wedding music,

refer to the collection of field recordings by Wolf Dietrich, *gipsy music of Macedonia & neighboring countries* (TSCD914, 1996); on popular music, see Barbara Rose Lange's study of recent Gypsy-Hungarian rock music, "'What Was That Conquering Magic . . .': The Power of Discontinuity in Hungarian Gypsy *Nóta*," *Ethnomusicology* 41 (1997): 517-37.

35. (Northeastern University Press: Boston, 1993).
36. Bellman, *Style hongrois*, 213. The statement is indeed surprising, given the huge economic success of Brahms's early Gypsy works; see Taruskin, "Nationalism/11. colonialist nationalism," www.newgrove.com (8 July 2001).
37. "The Reflection of the Roma in European Art Music," *The World of Music* 38 (1996): 95-138, 134; note that Baumann's context of an ethnomusicological readership ensures that his use of the word "Roma" without Gypsy in parenthesis (as in Silverman cited above) will not be misunderstood.
38. *Gypsy Music [Cigányzene]*, trans. Fred Macnicol (Budapest: Corvina Press, 1978). See also his Folk Music: Hungarian National Idiom, trans. Maria Steiner (Budapest: Corvina Press, 1986), and his article "Hungarian Gypsy Music: Whose Heritage?," Folklor Digest 2 (1998), where he criticizes the view of Alan Antonietto and Patrick Williams that Hungarian music is Gypsy; again we note the dialectic of Liszt-Bartók in this more recent controversy: "Like Liszt almost a century and a half ago, they interpret literally the use of the term 'Gypsy music' to describe folk-based Hungarian popular music, and regard the popular Hungarian musical idiom of the nineteenth and twentieth centuries as the handiwork of Gypsies." This last article was posted on Romnet: Creative Intelligence Agency <poetburo@idirect.com> "Hungarian Gypsy Music, Part I," 23 January 1998, <6500djm1@ucsbuxa.ucsb.edu> via <romnet-l@teleport.com>(23 January1998). Sárosi's article is archived at <http://www.net.hu/Deutsch/hungq/no147/p133>.
39. *Gypsy Music*, 45, my emphasis.
40. The latest event is the Second Roma World Congress (Romano Lumako Kongresso), held in Lodz, Poland, 1-3 May, <http://www.romaworldcongress.org> (5 June 2002).

NOTES FOR CHAPTER TWO

1. The motif of music also appears in Gypsy folk tales. See the story "How the Gypsies Became Musicians," in Diane Tong, *Gypsy Folktales* (San Diego: Harcort Brace & Company, 1989), 102-03.
2. Aristotle, *On Poetry and Style*, trans. G. M. A. Grube (Indianapolis: Hackett Publishing Company, 1958), 4.
3. *Quasi una Fantasia: Essays on Modern Music*. Trans. Rodney Livingstone (New York: Verso, 1994), 1.
4. *Gypsies: A Multidisciplinary Annotated Bibliography* (New York: Garland Publishing, Inc., 1995), 289.
5. See Ian Hancock's reaction in *The Pariah Syndrome*, on the Web at <http://www.geocities.com/Paris/5121/antigypsyism> (15 May 2002).
6. "The Gypsies in Western Literature," (Ph.D. diss., University of Illinois at Urbana-Champaign, 1980), 4.
7. *The Style Hongrois in the Music of Western Europe* (Boston: Northeastern University Press, 1993, 91.

8. *Style Hongrois*, 76.

9. *Style Hongrois*, 69 (my emphasis).

10. See Gilbert Chase, "Origins of the Lyric Theater in Spain," *The Musical Quarterly* 25 (1939): 292-305, 298.

11. Angus Fraser, *The Gypsies*, 2nd ed. (Oxford UK & Cambridge U.S.: Blackwell, 1995), 99, notes the distinction between *Ciganas* [Portuguese] and *Gitanos* [Spanish]; he says that the former comes from the Greek word "*atsinganos*" the latter from the Spanish for "Egyptian." However, note that Cigan and Gitan sound similar enough. How can anyone claim to know where these words come from? Note that the word "Gitano" is seemingly contained in the word "*tsinganos*."

12. This brings up another topic which cannot be investigated in this context: Gypsies as actors and actors as Gypsies.

13. Bellman, *Style Hongrois*, 73.

14. For a plot summary, see Roland Hoermann, *Achim von Arnim* (Boston: Twayne Publishers, 1984), 92 ff.

15. Bellman, *Style Hongrois*, 74.

16. Miguel de Cervantes, "The Gypsy Maid," in *Six Exemplary Novels*, trans. Harriet de Onís (Great Neck, New York: Barron's Educational Series, Inc.) 1961, 91.

17. Cervantes, "The Gypsy Maid," 91.

18. Cervantes, "La Gitanilla," in *Novelas Ejemplares*, vol. 1 (Buenos Aires: Editorial Losada, S.A., 1938), 21.

19. The article by Jack Sage and Alvaro Zaldivar on Cervantes in the *New Groves*, 2nd ed., states that "there is less agreement about Roda's suggestion [in 1956] that the tunes named by Cervantes were those in vogue only in his day and were unrelated melodically to those found in cancioneros before 1550. www.grovemusic.com, ed. Laura Macy <http://www.grovemusic.com/shared/views/article.html?section=music.05312.1> (24 July 2001).

20. Adolfo Salazar, *La Música en Cervantes y otros ensayos* (Madrid: N.p., 1961), 163.

21. Bernard Leblon, *Gypsies and Flamenco: The Emergence of the Art of Flamenco in Andalusia*, trans. Sinéad ní Shuinéar, Gypsy Research Centre (Hatfield, UK: University of Hertfordshire Press, 1995), 68.

22. Cervantes, "La Gitanilla," 83.

23. Unfortunately, in the 1995 film *Moll Flanders*, the Gypsy reference disappears, as does much of Defoe's story.

24. Daniel Defoe, *Moll Flanders*, ed. Edward Kelly (New York: W. W. Norton & Company, Inc., 1973), 8.

25. For other functions, see Dougherty, "Gypsies in Western Literature," 89.

26. Henry Fielding, *Tom Jones*, ed. Sheridan Baker (New York: W. W. Norton & Company, Inc., 1973), 512.

27. Stanford University, "Pidgin and Creole Languages": "Between 1500 and 1900, there came into existence, on tropical islands and in isolated sections of tropical littorals, small, autocratic, rigidly stratified societies, mostly engaged in monoculture, which consisted of a ruling minority of some European nation and a large mass of (mainly non-European) laborers, drawn in most cases from many different language groups. Speakers of different languages at first evolved some form of auxiliary contact language, native to none of them, known as a Pidgin, and this language, suitably expanded, eventually became the native or Creole language of the community that

exists today." <http://www.sul.stanford.edu/depts/ssrg/pidgins/pidgin.html#Intro-duction> (15 May 2002).

28. Fielding, *Tom Jones*, 513.
29. Fielding, *Tom Jones*, 514.
30. Fielding, *Tom Jones*, 515.
31. Fielding, *Tom Jones*, 516.
32. Johann Wolfgang von Goethe, *Götz von Berlichingen*, trans. Charles E. Passage (New York: Frederick Ungar Publishing Co., 1965), p. x. For Goethe's own words on how the Gypsy scene "gratified" German company, see Dougherty, "Gypsies in Western Literature," 124.
33. For the German text, see "Götz von Berlichingen" in *Werke*, band IV (Hamburg: Christian Wegner Verlag, 1953), 165.
34. Goethe, "Götz von Berlichingen," trans. Charles E. Passage, 117.
35. Goethe, "Götz von Berlichingen," 166.
36. Goethe, "Götz von Berlichingen," 166.
37. Goethe, "Götz von Berlichingen," trans. Charles E. Passage, 119.
38. Sir Walter Scott, *Guy Mannering* (New York: R. F. Fenno & Company: Publishers, 1900), 19.
39. Dougherty, "Gypsies in Western Literature," 101.
40. Scott, *Guy Mannering*, 21.
41. Scott, *Guy Mannering*, 357.
42. Scott, *Guy Mannering*, 359.
43. Scott, *Guy Mannering*, 359-60.
44. "Randy" is the Scottish term for rough-mannered beggar, and also dissolute woman.
45. Victor Hugo, *Notre-Dame of Paris*, trans. John Sturrock (New York: Penquin Books, 1978), 86.
46. Hugo, *Notre-Dame of Paris*, 263.
47. Hugo, *Notre-Dame of Paris*, 226.
48. Hugo, *Notre-Dame of Paris*, 464.
49. Hugo, *Notre-Dame of Paris*, 482.
50. "Structure and Counter-Structure in Lorca's 'Romancero Gitano,'" *Modern Language Review* 77 (1982): 74-88, 86.
51. "Structure and Counter-Structure," 87.
52. Carl W. Cobb, *Lorca's* Romancero gitano*: A Ballad Translation and Critical Study* (Jackson: University of Mississippi Press, 1983), 5.
53. "Structure and Counter-Structure," 76.
54. Cobb, *Lorca's* Romancero gitano, 21.
55. Cobb, *Lorca's* Romancero gitano, 23.
56. D. H. Lawrence, *The Virgin and the Gipsy* (Cleveland and New York: The World Publishing Company, 1944), 36.
57. Lawrence, *The Virgin and the Gipsy*, 37.
58. Lawrence's own wife Frieda as the model for Cynthia.
59. Lawrence, *The Virgin and the Gipsy*, 43.
60. Lawrence, *The Virgin and the Gipsy*, 49.
61. Lawrence, *The Virgin and the Gipsy*, 49 (Lawrence's emphasis).
62. Lawrence, *The Virgin and the Gipsy*, 68.
63. Lawrence, *The Virgin and the Gipsy*, 69.

64. Lawrence, *The Virgin and the Gipsy*, 76.
65. Lawrence, *The Virgin and the Gipsy*, 94.
66. Lawrence, *The Virgin and the Gipsy*, 114.
67. Lawrence, *The Virgin and the Gipsy*, 127.
68. Liszt, *Gypsies in Music*, 218.
69. Though we have not treated the topic, Gypsies as represented in the plastic arts exemplify the same literary tropes.
70. *Gypsy Music*, trans. Fred Macnicol (Budapest: Corvina Press, 1978), 133.
71. See Carl Dahlhaus's *Esthetics of Music*, trans. William W. Austin (Cambridge: Cambridge University Press, 1982), 18, where he tries to narrow the focus of "expression," which has lost its specificity through overuse: "And the etymology of the word suggests that 'expression' means nothing else than 'testimony,' in the sense in which Wilhelm Heinse explained music as 'relieving one's feelings' and 'letting one's passions gush.' . . . Affections were represented, portrayed, but not 'dredged up from the soul,' not thrust forth from the agitated inner being." What Dahlhaus is getting at in this passage harmonizes well with the perceived interior qualities of Gypsy Music.
72. *Georges Bizet:* Carmen, Cambridge Opera Handbooks (Cambridge: Cambridge University Press, 1992).
73. *Carmen*, 3.
74. *Writing and Difference*, trans. Alan Bass (Chicago: University of Chicago Press, 1978), 197. What he means is that the author is absent and yet remains in control via writing.
75. *Carmen*, 128: "Again, there is ample evidence within the novella in support of such feminist readings. . . . A contemporary audience (influenced by the Women's movement, liberal sexual mores and sensitivity to issues involving spousal assaults) may be predisposed to side with Carmen against the irrational violence of José."
76. *Carmen*, 128.
77. *Gypsy Music*, 56: Regensburg, 1443, Konstanz, 1460, and Budapest, 1489; this last reference is to Queen Beatrix, who hired Gypsies to play on her island south of Budapest.

NOTES FOR CHAPTER THREE

1. *The Gypsy in Music* ["Des Bohémiens et de leur Musique en Hongrie," "Die Zigeuner und ihre Musik in Ungarn"], trans. Edwin Evans (London: William Reeves, o.p. 1859, n.d.), 319.
2. The idea of greater freedom is also stressed in the reformulation of tempo rubato by Chopin, Liszt, and others. For more on this see Richard Hudson's *Stolen Time: The History of Tempo Rubato* (Oxford: Clarendon Press, 1994).
3. *The Gypsy in Music*, 300: "The professional European musicians, and particularly the Jew, perceives in music nothing more than an industry; based on scientific calculations. For that reason it is they who are the most struck at first sight (or we should rather say, first hearing) by this musical anomaly [Gypsy music]."
4. *Beethoven*, 2nd rev. ed. (New York: Schirmer Books, 1998), 78.
5. See David Schulenberg, "Composition and Improvisation in the School of J.S. Bach," in *Bach Perspectives*, vol. 1, ed. Russell Stinson, 1-42 (Lincoln and London: University of Nebraska Press, 1995).

6. *Opus 200* (published 1836), trans. and ed. Alice L. Mitchell (New York & London: Longman, 1983).

7. *Harvard Dictionary of Music* (Cambridge, MA: Harvard University Press, 1946), 351.

8. *Thinking in Jazz: The Infinite Art of Improvisation* (Chicago and London: The University of Chicago Press, 1994), 4. Despite an ambitious program at the onset, Berliner's study seems to fall well short of saying anything new about the topic.

9. Susan McClary, *Carmen* (Cambridge: Cambridge University Press, 1992), 33-34: "Thus *Carmen* operates in part as an Orientalist work, but it also participates in another genre prevalent in nineteenth-century France: that of the racial *Other* who has infiltrated home turf." Also see: Jonathan Bellman, ed., *The Exotic in Western Music* (Boston: Northeastern University Press, 1998) and Georgina Born and David Hesmondhalgh, eds., *Western Music and Its Others: Difference, Representation, and Appropriation in Music* (Berkeley and Los Angeles: University of California Press, 2000).

10. *Nineteenth-Century Music*, trans. J. Bradford Robinson (Berkeley and Los Angeles: University of California Press,1989), 302.

11. Born and Hesmondhalgh, *Western Music and Its Others*, 16, her emphasis. Note that she means modernist in the restricted sense, we will extend it to denote, more broadly, the "modern project" (the Enlightenment).

12. Leon Plantinga, *Romantic Music: A History of Musical Style in Nineteenth-Century Music*, A Norton Introduction to Music History (New York: W. W. Norton & Company, 1984), 16.

13. Dahlhaus, *The Foundations of Music History*, trans. J. Bradford Robinson (Cambridge: Cambridge University Press, 1983).

14. Trans. Bernard Bosanquet (London: Penquin Books, 1993). After a nostalgic reference to the golden age of Greek art, where art "affords that satisfaction of spiritual wants," Hegel's dictum reads: "art is, and remains for us, on the side of its highest destiny, a thing of the past" (13).

15. Liszt, *The Gypsy in Music*, 30, writes of the "enthusiasm with which it [Gypsy music] has enjoyed in its own country of origin [for Liszt, Hungary] and the enthusiasm with which it has always been received in Vienna—that country of Haydn, Mozart, Gluck, Schubert and Beethoven. Haydn, as a genial old man, passed many hours in listening to it. Schubert knew it well, and even tried to translate some fragments of it for our use. That Beethoven gave it some attention is amply proved by pages of his work, several of his thoughts, and more than one of the voluptuous flights which occur in his later works." This latter claim is indeed tantalizing—Liszt hears in late Beethoven the influence of Gypsy Music.

16. "The Hungarian Gypsies and the Poetics of Exclusion," in *The Exotic in Western Music*, 74-103: "This is entertainment, which is ideally enjoyed in a rollicking, alcohol-lubricated atmosphere; it is not music to be politely and decorously 'appreciated.' Many musical decisions are made on the spur of the moment, depending on the musician's 'read' of the customer" (84). In this overly reductive passage, Gypsy music becomes like palm reading for heavy drinkers.

17. Liszt, *The Gypsy in Music*, 227.

18. Lewis Porter, "John Coltrane's *A Love Supreme*: Jazz Improvisation as Composition," *JAMS* 38 (1985): 593-621. In jazz studies, improvisation seems to be assimilated to the work of intellect (here, composition), to the conscious aim of the subject. Berliner

writes "In fact, when musicians speak of jazz as a way of life, they refer primarily to the unrelenting artistic demands of a jazz career and to a particular orientation to the world of musical imagination characteristic of jazz community members. They refer to the total immersion in the music's language that its rigors demand if players are to attain fluency as improvisers and enjoy continued artistic growth. Self-directed studies of jazz history, analyses of works by master improvisers, rigorous private practice routines, and interaction with other players in numerous bands continually sharpen abilities and replenish the artist's store of knowledge" (*Thinking in Jazz*, 486).

19. See Elmer Bernstein's score for *The Magnificent Seven* for examples of constructions of "Mexicanness" in music.

20. Nearly any recent issue of *JAMS* can be taken to show this. A recent volume (2001) has on article called "Re-placing Medieval Music" by Judith A Peraino. Her fears surface in the first sentence: ". . . explores reasons and methods [?!] for combining historical research in medieval music, here specifically music circa 1300, and critical theories associated with 'postmodernism.' " [No commentary is necessary—to place this word in scare quotes already states the absurdity!]

21. *The Postmodern Condition: A Report on Knowledge*, trans. Geoff Bennington and Brian Massumi, Theory and History of Literature, vol. 10 (Minneapolis: University of Minnesota Press, 1988), xxiv. The book can be read as a critique of authority—of "who decides what knowledge is, of who knows what need to be decided (9)?"

22. Schulenberg, "Composition and Improvisation," 5, sublates the distinction thus: "It should be evident that all improvisation is, to some degree, prepared ahead of time and is controlled by conscious planning. . . . But all written compositions, including those originating in improvisation, contain a certain moment of rationalization." Also, see John Rink, "Playing in time: rhythm, meter, and tempo in Brahms's *Fantasien Op. 116*," in *The Practice of Performance*, ed. Rink, 254-80 (Cambridge: Cambridge University Press, 1995): in terms of C. P. E. Bach's *Versuch*, "rhythmic liberties in the free fantasy were exercised in an ordered manner" (279).

23. "Interview [with Jean Martin], 16 August 1996," <http://www.shef.ac.uk/misc/rec/ps/efi> (19 January 2002).

24. On the "disjointure" (*Un-fug*) of the very presence of the present, see Jacques Derrida's comments on Heidegger's interpretation of the Anaximander fragment in *Specters of Marx: The State of the Debt, the Work of Mourning, and the New International*, trans. Peggy Kamuf (New York: Routledge, 1994), 25.

25. We can compare this to the process of the constitution for an originary presence: "An interval must separate the present from what it is not in order for the present to be itself, but this interval that constitutes it as present must, by the same token, divide the present in and of itself, thereby also dividing, along with the present, that is, in our metaphysical language, every being, and singularly every substance or subject," Derrida, *Margins of Philosophy*, trans. Alan Bass (Chicago: University of Chicago Press, 1972), 13.

26. Liszt disparagingly writes of the improviser who is a fake, continuing that "the people, whose judgment in the long run is both healthy and pure, will always prefer that an improviser who deals in charlatanism should reserve his lucubrations for others" (*The Gypsy in Music*, 319).

27. See Jacques Derrida, *The Gift of Death*, trans. David Wills (Chicago: University Press, 1995).

28. Immanuel Kant, *Critique of Pure Reason*, trans. Norman Kemp Smith (New York: St. Martin's Press, 1965). See the third antinomy, 409-17.

29. Franz Liszt, *The Gypsy in Music*, 297-98 (my emphasis).

30. See Alain Antonietto, "Histoire de la musique tsigane instrumentale d'Europe centrale," *Études tsiganes* 1/1 (1994): 104-33: "Caractérisée elle aussi, on l'a vu, par l'improvisation, l'effusion sonare, un employ systématique de la syncope et cette propension à transcender les matérieux les plus divers . . ."

31. The parallel activity in the Gypsy world would be fortune-telling.

32. Le Taraf de Haïdouks, *dosssier* [sic] de presse.

33. Antonietto, "Histoire de la musique tsigane," 106.

34. Liszt, *The Gypsy in Music*, 333.

35. See Hans-Georg Gadamer, *Truth and Method*, 2nd edition, trans. Joel Weinsheimer and Donald G. Marshall (New York: Crossroad, 1989), 301: "Consciousness of being affected by history [*wirkungsgeschichtliches Bewußtsein*] is primarily consciousness of the hermeneutical *situation*."

36. See the latest CD by Budapest's Muzsikás, *The Bartók Album* (Hannibal 1439, 1999).

37. *Road of the Gypsies* (Network LC 6759) is a two-CD set; Rough Guide's jacket to *Music of the Gypsies* (RGNET 1034 CD) has a quote from Rhythm Music Magazine, "these discs delve right into the heart of the region they explore."

38. For an analysis of how primal sexual desire can be marketed in music, see Richard Taruskin's discussion of *nega* in his article, " 'Entoiling the Falconet': Russian Musical Orientalism in Context," in Bellman, *The Exotic in Western Music*, 194-217.

39. The brain has evolved such that there are more regions of the brain that "construct" visual stimuli; is listening more primitive and undeveloped than seeing? Related: can *seeing* something called an improvisation help in the *hearing* of it?

40. Produced by the World Music Institute and David Eden Productions. I attended shows in Palo Alto (Stanford University) and Los Angeles, CA (University of California, Los Angeles), and both shows in New York City.

41. Exceptions would seem to be found in world music, especially North Indian classical music, with its focus on raga, meditation, oneness and unity; also Sufi music, or any music with strong ties to faith. New Age and Native musics might function as such in contemporary America.

42. "Pure desire" here describes the experience of something other than self-consciousness; see G. W. F. Hegel, *Phenomenology of Spirit*, trans. A. V. Miller (Oxford: Oxford University Press, 1977), 109.

43. Dahlhaus, *The Foundations of Music History*, 4.

44. *Kronos Caravan*, notes by Ken Hunt (Nonesuch Records 79490-2 2000).

45. *The Style Hongrois*, 12.

46. With perhaps the exception of Max Peter Baumann's article "The Reflection of the Roma in European Art Music," *The World of Music* 38 (1996): 95-138, itself somewhat based on an earlier article by Argenmüller.

47. *The Style Hongrois*, 103.

48. "Was heisst Improvisation," in *Improvisation und neue Musik*, ed. Reinhold Brinkmann (Mainz: Schott, 1979), 10.

49. "Rom (Gypsy) Music," in *Europe*, eds. Timothy Rice, James Porter, and Chris Goertzen, *The Garland Encyclopedia of World Music*, vol. 8 (New York: Garland Publishing, Inc., 2000).

50. "Rom (Gypsy) Music," 270.
51. "Rom (Gypsy) Music," 270.
52. "Rom (Gypsy) Music," 272.
53. "Rom (Gypsy) Music," 271. The exact sentence is "In contrast, some stylistic and performance elements, such as the propensity to improvise, are perhaps common to many European Rom music," and Silverman cites a 1987 article by Katalin Kovalcik. Though "perhaps" is obviously a convention, because so much hinges on it in this context, I would like to problematize it here: what is the exact nature of this academic convention? Politically, it is an escape route for the academic writer, displacing the truth of the statement. What arrives, in the "perhaps"? For a deconstructive view of "perhaps," see Jacques Derrida, *Politics of Friendship*, trans. George Collins (London and New York: Verso, 1997), Chapter Two is entitled "Loving in Friendship: Perhaps—the Noun and the Adverb."
54. I am following the standard definition of "music culture" as found in textbook *Worlds of Music*, ed. Jeff Todd Titon, 3rd ed. (New York: Schirmer Books, 1996): "Music, then, though a universal phenomenon (scientists even send out music in space capsules, hoping to communicate with intelligent beings in distant solar systems), gets its meaning from culture. Recall from the preface that by *culture* we mean the way of life of a people, learned and transmitted from one generation to the next" (1).
55. See Chapter Eleven for more ways of categorizing Gypsy Music.
56. Field notes Kazuyuki Tanimoto (Barre, Vermont: Multicultural Media, 1997).
57. "Thoughts on Improvisation: A Comparative Approach," *Musical Quarterly* 60 (1974): 1-29; 8.
58. "Thoughts on Improvisation," 11.
59. *Allegories of Reading: Figural Language in Rousseau, Nietzsche, Rilke, and Proust* (New Haven: Yale University Press, 1979), 281.
60. Ali Jihad Racy, "The Many Faces of Improvisation: The Arab Taqasim As a Musical Symbol," *Ethnomusicology* 44 (2000): 302-20, 304-07.
61. Racy, "The Many Faces of Improvisation," 308.
62. Racy, "The Many Faces of Improvisation," 315.
63. Racy, "The Many Faces of Improvisation," 314.
64. I have written about this in my program notes for the band, Arts & Lecture, University of California, 6 March 2001.
65. I wrote this section before going to Clejani. Still, I left this section unchanged, in order to record my initial impressions of this music before having done fieldwork. I had, however, seen the band in live performance and taken some lessons with Caliu.
66. Their tours have been hugely successful. In addition, they have recorded three CDs, and recently Nonesuch released a compilation drawn from these recordings. Their popularity was almost immediate, breaking the top ten of the European world-music charts with the release of their first CD, *Musique tsigane de Romanie, vol. 1*. Taraf was then featured in Tony Gatlif's 1993 film *Latcho drom* in an extended sequence set in their native Clejani.
67. In chronological order: *Musique des Tziganes de Roumanie*, notes by Marta Bergman (CRAW 2, 1991); *Honourable Brigands, Magic Horses and Evil Eye, Musique des Tsiganes de Roumanie*, vol. 2, notes by Marta Bergman (CRAW 13, 1994); and *Dumbula Dumba*, notes by Marta Bergman (CRAW 21, 1998).

68. Elijah Wald, "Romania's dancing outlaws," *Boston Globe*, 6 March 1998, D15-16, D16.
69. Taken from the liner notes to *Honourable Brigands, Magic Horses, and Evil Eye* (Cram World 13, 1994).
70. Hegel, *Phenomenology of Spirit*, 109.
71. "There is No 'One' Narcissism," <http://www.hydra.umn.edu/derrida/narc> (6 June 2002).
72. For the sake of argument; we could have also taken the orchestral concert.

NOTES FOR CHAPTER FOUR

1. Gilles Deleuze and Fèlix Guattari, *A Thousand Plateaus: Capitalism and Schizophrenia*, trans. Brian Massumi (Minneapolis and London: University of Minnesota Press, 1987), 381.
2. *Thousand Plateaus*, 381.
3. *Thousand Plateaus*, 381.
4. Program notes, *The Gypsy Caravan: A Celebration of Roma Music and Dance from India, Russia, Romania, Bulgaria, Hungary & Spain*, 9-10 April 1999, The World Music Institute, 2.
5. Hancock's speciality is Romani. More than any other person today he defines the Roma political agenda. Hancock represents the Roma on the Holocaust Committee Washington, D.C., an appointment he received from President Clinton. One of his current organizational associations is the Roma National Congress, which maintains http://www.romnews.com. Hancock states: "I believe that the Roma National Congress understands clearly that *technology* and communication are fundamental to the survival of our Romani people. With the creation of RomNews, and the constant, *daily* dissemination of information across the world, the RNC has achieved in a few years what the IRU has never been able to achieve since its creation. The RNC is based on Equal representation with no national leaders, no president or multiple vice-presidents. It recognizes the vital importance of education, and respects the maintenance of traditional Romanipe." "Statement regarding my position with the International Romani Union," (my emphases), www.romnews.com, <http://www.romnews.com/a/hancock> (29 July 2001).
6. For a similar view, but one which maintains that these proto-Rom groups were originally taken as slaves, forced to migrate against their will, see Roger Moreau, *The Rom: Walking in the Paths of the Gypsies*, rev. ed. (Toronto: Key Porter Books, 2002).
7. This reference to the "war machine" was written prior to 9/11. After 9/11 the definition of "war" in the Kantian sense—as the right of states—has been expanded to include groups outside of the state system.
8. For an in-depth analysis of the documentary evidence, see Angus Fraser, *The Gypsies*, 2nd ed., The Peoples of Europe (Oxford UK & Cambridge USA: Blackwell, 1995), Chapter Four, "The Great Trick."
9. I discuss this in a paper I delivered with Michael Beckerman in the Czech Republic, "Gypsiness in Music [4.1]," (presented at The Bohuslav Martinu Foundation's Festival, December 1997), 10-11. Recently this story (with footage) was featured on a program dedicated to Gypsies in Eastern Europe on ABC's television show "Nightline," 6 August 2001.

10. See Nicholas Van Hear, *New Diasporas: The Mass Exodus, Dispersal and Regrouping of Migrant Communities* (Seattle: University of Washington Press, 1998), 24. In Van Hear's four "migration orders," the Soviet Union and Eastern Europe constitute an order. My separation is arbitrary.

11. The remarkable Web site "650 Years of Roma Culture in Kosovo" documents the significance of Roma culture in Kosovo, <http://194.8.216.150:9080/inhalt.htm#Top> (29 July 2001); relevant is the link "Refugee Camp," where we read: "Since June 1999, 100,000 Roma were brutally forced to leave Kosovo by UCK (KLA) under the very eyes of NATO. They found shelter in camps in Serbia, Macedonia and Montenegro. The EU strategy of refugee containment near their 'home' works: only 10% found a hole into the 'stronghold of Europe,' taking high risks. Some were lucky, some used all their savings, some got help from relatives. Most refugees have to survive in the camps in the Balkans under inhuman and life-threatening conditions. Children and old people often do not have the strength to stay alive." Since the original Web site has disappeared, see "Gypsies of Kosovo" by Paul Polansky, <http://www.kosovo.com/gypsies> (12 January 2004).

12. *Thousand Plateaus*, 25.

13. *Thousand Plateaus*, 7.

14. *The Deleuze Reader*, ed. Constantin V. Boundas (New York: Columbia University Press, 1993), 31.

15. *Thousand Plateaus*, 23.

16. *Thousand Plateaus*, 12.

17. "On the Road to Gypsy Music," (paper read at the Regional Meeting of the Southern California Chapter of the Society for Ethnomusicology, University of California, Los Angeles, February 1998).

18. Thousand Plateaus, 349-50.

19. After discussing this point with Marin Marian Bălaşa, the ethnomusicologist from the Brailoiu Institute in Bucharest who first brought me to Clejani, I wonder if this is accurate. Marin acted as translator in my initial interviews with Caliu and other village musicians, and he maintained that they have no concept of what I was calling improvisation. Thus, though the musicians responded favorably that what they were doing was improvisation, there is the possibility that they were merely telling me what I wanted to hear—I was "leading" them, in a sense.

20. The Roma who came to America, most of whom settled almost immediately, intentionally kept a low-profile to avoid discrimination. Though there are some in-group Roma bands in America, music, a high-profile profession by definition, was not a viable career choice for American Roma.

21. See the Web site "The International Gypsy Jazz Archive," <http://www.nordi.no/music/hcr/archive> (29 July 2001). "The Django Reinhardt Swing Page" is at <http://www.hotclub.co.uk.index.html> (12 January 2004).

22. *Thousand Plateaus*, 19.

23. *Memoires for Paul de Man*, trans. Cecile Lindsay, Jonathan Culler, and Eduardo Cadava (New York: Columbia University Press, 1986), 15.

24. Sonia Tamar Seeman, "You're Roman! Musical Practice and the Creation of Social Categories among Roman (Gypsy) Communities of Western Turkey." Paper read at the Regional Meeting of the Southern California Chapter of the Society for Ethnomusicology, University of San Diego, February 2000. Seeman argued for a concept

of "glocality" as a locally grounded substitution for the semantics of globalization, in effect realizing the direction of influence from local to global. In my opinion, Seeman's situating of the origins of transnational categories as local productions misses the power of a transnational category: something becomes transnational precisely when it is *beyond* the local. And there is a representational problem at the heart of this reversal, namely, as soon as one chooses to represent a local identity-construct, as in her read paper, the local ceases to function as a local view; it is appropriated, as it were, by the international academic machine.

25. I witnessed this at both concerts in New York (April 1999).

NOTES FOR CHAPTER FIVE

1. On the 100th anniversary of the birth of Brahms in 1933, Bartók commissioned the musicologist Ervin Major to publish an article on the sources of the twenty-one *Hungarian Dances*. Major found that the Hungarian tunes quoted by Brahms are much younger than the ones used by Liszt in his *Hungarian Rhapsodies*. The tune of the Fifth Hungarian Dance is by Béler Kéler, and is a czárdása. An earlier version of this chapter is found in *European Meetings in Ethnomusicology* 8 (2001): 94–110.

2. Karl Geiringer, in *Brahms: His Life and Work*, 2nd rev. ed. (London: George Allen and Unwin Ltd., 1948), an influential biographer of the Bach family, Haydn, and Brahms, writes that Brahms invested Gypsy music with "an artistic form which raised it to a higher level. None of his predecessors and followers has approached his success in this direction" (218). Geiringer goes on to argue that the second volume of *Hungarian Dances* from 1880 are more "Brahmsian" than "Hungarian"; we might read here "serious" and "Gypsy," respectively.

3. One current trend is to read "hybridity" as the acceptance of difference. See Georgina Born and David Hesmondhalgh, eds., *Western Music and Its Others: Difference, Representation, and Appropriation in Music* (Berkeley: University of California Press, 2000).

4. Dahlhaus writes that the concept means that "even a very complex sonority becomes transparent with regard to its tonal relationships and can be understood *in its own right*," in *Schoenberg and the New Music*, trans. Derrick Puffett and Alfred Clayton (Cambridge: University Press, 1988), 123, my emphasis. In a way, the idea that something is understood "in its own right," on its own terms, in-itself, becomes a leading idea for musicological analysis itself.

5. See Adorno's pioneering essay "Vienna" for an introduction to this idea; the essay is in *Quasi una fantasia: Essays on Modern Music*, trans. Rodney Livingstone (London: Verso, 1992).

6. "A Fifteen Round Heavyweight Championship Between Antonin Dvořák and Mu-hammed Ali for the Crown of the Hapsburg Empire," Böhlav Verlag's *Schriften zur Volksmusik* (forthcoming, 2002).

7. We can compare three recordings of this piece (in the next section we will further develop this idea): 1) Iván Fischer conducting the Budapest Festival Orchestra, with Kálmán Balogh, cymbalom (Hungarton, 1985); 2) István Bogár conducting the Budapest Symphony Orchestra (Naxos, 1988); and 3) Lászlo Berki's *The Budapest Gypsy Orchestra* (Hungarton, 1997). These are three very different recordings of the same piece; the first two are attempts at "authentic" readings of the orchestral

arrangement, the third, Gypsy one a conscious articulation of the Romungro style (or, the assimilated Gypsy style, as heard in Budapest restaurants). The main difference between these recordings can be summarized in a word: exaggeration. The Gypsy version fits the Romantic stereotype: slower, schmalzier, and sexier. Also note that this rendition adds material to the A' section, two variations featuring deft clarinet work.

8. *Nineteenth-Century Music*, trans. J. Bradford Robinson (Berkeley: University of California Press, 1989), 151.

9. Naxos 8.550110 (1988).

10. Recorded in the Studio of Hungaroton, 1997 (HCD 10305).

11. According to Dr. Bălasa, the walls of the hall shook when he saw the group in Budapest.

12. "Budapest Gypsy Orchestra," <http://www.100violins.com/us/100/index> 17 March 2002.

13. "Some References," <http://www.100violins.com/us/100/index>.

14. Conversation, 21 March 2002.

15. Capriccio 49 276 4 (1999).

16. There is much confusion over the Lakatos family. Sándor Déki Lakatos continues to record, and is in many instances referred to without "Déki," thus leading many to think that the CDs are by his father. This confusion over identity, too, situates the performance situation of Gypsiness.

17. "A Vanishing Tradition: Gypsy Orchestras Are Getting Hard to Find" <http://www.geocities.com/Paris/5121/orchestras> (12 May 2002).

18. Released in 2000. The reference is to Lake Balaton, Central Europe's largest fresh water lake. Today a center for the wine and tourist industries, Balaton is also a rich cultural signifier for Hungarians. Its many palaces and spas offer a glimpse of Old Europe. Hubay's "Hullamzo Balaton" (op. 33, *Scenes of Czárdás* no. 5; translated as "[Choppy] Waves of the Balaton"), to which the CD refers, is a landscape painting of the waters of the lake.

19. *Táncoljunk Csárdást!* (HCD 10218, 1994).

20. Taking bowing technique to the next level is Roby Lakatos (b. 1965), the latest star of the dynasty, who records for Deutsche Gramophone. In his review of a Lakatos CD, Mike Gavin writes: "Roby Lakatos, youngest scion of the great Lakatos clan of Hungary, has stated his aim to bring Gypsy music into the twenty-first century by taking the musics that have plundered the Romany genius and giving them a Gypsy twist." "LIVE FROM BUDAPEST" <http://www.ronniescotts.co.uk/ronniescotts124> 13 May 2002. In this regard, see Roby's hot recording of "Hullamzo Balaton."

21. Recently the film music scholar William Rosar has brought the phenomenon of the "Gypsy" café style to my attention.

22. Philips 289 462 589-2 (1999); also recorded at the Italian Institute in Budapest.

23. Wayne Donnelly's anecdotal review of Fischer's Dvořák Eighth is emblematic: "Two years ago at Ravinia (the outdoor summer venue of the Chicago Symphony), I heard Fischer lead the most exciting Dvořák 8th I've ever heard. Riding home afterwards with an old friend who has played in the CSO for nearly thirty years, I listened with amusement as he complained. Fischer, it seems, wasn't content to just let them play a piece that they already knew perfectly, but insisted on their trying all sorts of new

phrasings. That might be OK, he said, during the winter when there was plenty of rehearsal time, but not when they had only one rehearsal for the performance. . . . When I [Mr. Donnelly] began listening to this CD, I immediately thought of that evening. Fischer wasn't interested in a routinely competent performance; he wanted something unique. And that's the same impression I get with these interpretations." <http://www.enjoythemusic.com/magazine/music/0202/dvorak> (14 May 2002.)

24. It is curious and not altogether clear why the credits say that József Lendvay Sr. plays "Gypsy violin," while his son (Jr.), mere violin.

25. As part of my research I have conducted informal interviews with audiences after this piece was played, and have received confirmation for this idea.

26. Soren Kierkegaard, *Either/Or*, part I, eds. and trans. Howard V. Hong and Edna H. Hong (Princeton: Princeton University Press, 1987).

27. See the essay "Différance," in *Margins of Philosophy*, trans. Alan Bass (Chicago: University Press, 1982), 10, where Derrida asserts that the neologism *différance*, perhaps one of the most enigmatic moments of deconstruction, as the condition for signification as deferral/differing though without the presence that these are dependent on, thus refers neither to the sign, to origins, or to the "authority of presence."

28. See Schoenberg's essay "Folkloristic Symphonies," in *Style and Idea*, ed. Leonard Stein, trans. Leo Black (Berkeley and Los Angeles: University of California Press, 1975), and Adorno, *Philosophie der neuen Musik* (Frankfurt am Main: Suhrkamp Verlag, 1978).

29. *Totality and Infinity: An Essay on Exteriority*, trans. Alphonso Lingis (Pittsburg: Duquesne University Press, 1969).

30. See his *Essays*, ed. Benjamin Suchoff (Lincoln: University of Nebraska Press, 1976), especially "Some Problems of Folk Music Research in Eastern Europe." There he speaks of nations and people as if they are found in nature. Thus "Old Romania" has the so-called "*hora lunga,*" long song, that is not found in any neighboring Eastern European country, but it occurs in the Ukraine, Persia, and Iraq. Bartók even hears it in an Arabic *maqam*. This kind of information is startling given Bartók's expertise in folk-song collecting, yet perhaps not so given that national essences during the first half of the twentieth century were thought to be something objectively real, that is, non-fictional. See Benedict Anderson, *Imagined Communities* (London: Verso, 1991), where nationalism is always imagined because "the members of even the smallest nation will never know most their fellow-members" (6).

31. Bartók, *Essays*, 32.

32. The CD *Rhapsody: Liszt and Bartók Sources* by the Jánosi Ensemble (Hungarton, 1994) tries to recreate the "Rákóczi March." The liner notes state that the "different variants of the "Rákóczi March" can be found everywhere in the countryside inhabited by Hungarians"; yet the Ensemble ends up playing versions allegedly by Turks and Romanians.

33. *The Coming Community*, trans. Michael Hardt (Minneapolis: University Press, 1993). It does not seem arbitrary that Agamben's discourse, a revival of the Scholastic term "quodlibet," occurs with a re-thinking of what "community" is in the society of the spectacle.

34. "Gypsiness in Music, Improvisation, and America: Toward a Deleuzian Philosophy of Music," paper read in San Diego at the Society for Ethnomusicology Regional Meeting, February 2000.

NOTES FOR CHAPTER SIX

1. Jonathan Bellman, *The Style Hongrois in the Music of Western Europe* (Boston: Northeastern University Press, 1993), 89, notes that for Peter Raabe "Liszt heard the voice of his own homelessness" in the Gypsies' music.

2. See John Rink, "Rhapsody," www.grove.com, ed. Laura Macy <http://www.grovemusic.com/shared/views/article.html?section=music.23313> (1 August 2001). The article proposes that Tomášek's opp. 40 and 41 (both 1810) were the first influential essays in the genre, which quickly became assimilated into the leisure of *Hausmusik*.

3. See, for example, the discussion in Bellman's *Style Hongrois*, 180-84.

4. Franz Liszt, *The Gypsy in Music*, trans. Edwin Evans (London: William Reeves, n.d.), 336.

5. "Music: Pushing Gypsiness, Roma or Otherwise," *New York Times*, April 1, 2001.

6. Quoted from Sárosi, *Gypsy Music* (Budapest: Corvina Press, 1978) 48; Sárosi zealously translates many of the Hungarian primary documents pertaining to the Liszt-Gypsy controversy.

7. *Gypsy Music*, 146. Brassai was a Kolozsvár professor who in 1860 wrote an essay called "Hungarian or Gypsy Music?"

8. *Liszt*, trans. John Victor (New York: Grossman Publishers, 1972), 115.

9. *The Gypsy in Music*, 387.

10. *The Style Hongrois*, 11.

11. Ironically Sárosi's book on Gypsy music is an attempt to show the Gypsy appropriation of Hungarian music: ". . . Their [Gypsies'] relationship to what they generally sing as their own—*flamenco* music is approximately the same as that of the Hungarian Gypsy musicians to their repertoire: it is not originally theirs"(35).

12. *The Style Hongrois*, 11.

13. *The Style Hongrois*, 6.

14. *The Style Hongrois*, 180.

15. *The Style Hongrois*, 199; in other contexts Bellman displays a tendency toward value judgment; he is particularly harsh when dealing with alleged Kleinmeister: "in contrast the legions of minor masters using the style hongrois were more likely simply to be exploiting a musical fad [. . .]"(133).

16. *The Style Hongrois*, 5.

17. Wilhelm von Humboldt, *Linguistic Variability and Intellectual Development*, trans. G. C. Buck and F. A. Raven (Coral Gables, Florida: University of Miami Press, 1971).

18. In this passage I am referring, obliquely, to Heidegger's discourse on nearness and the neighbor, and of its opposition to the parametrical interpretation of nearness through space and time. See his "Das Wesen der Sprache" in *Unterwegs zur Sprache*, 159-216 (Stuttgart: Verlag Günther Neske, 1959), 210 ff.

19. In the context of a discussion of Liszt, the reference to the masculine indefinite pronoun is intentional.

20. Alan Walker, *The Virtuoso Years, 1811-1847, Franz Liszt*, vol. 1 (New York: Alfred A. Knopf, 1983), 335.

21. Walker, *Virtuoso Years*, 433.

22. Walker, *Virtuoso Years*, 414.

23. Count Teleki also appears in Liszt's *Gypsy in Music*, 141, as the one who brought the Gypsy boy Josy to Liszt in Paris. An interesting aside related by Liszt: the French virtuoso Thalberg was present at this meeting.

24. Walker, *Virtuoso Years*, 435.

25. "The Interpretation of Liszt's Piano Music" in Alan Walker (ed.), *Franz Liszt: The Man and His Music* (New York: Taplinger Pub. Col, 1970); <http://www.mvdaily.com/articles/2000/02/pplords3> (19 May 2002).

26. Liszt's preference for uncivilized art prefigures Nietzsche's reevaluation of the concept of *Künstler*, where the artist's work is encompassed by a moral stance. In the *Genealogy of Morals*, trans. Walter Kaufmann (New York: Random House, 1969), he writes: "Let us, first of all, eliminate the artists: they do not stand nearly independently enough in the world and *against* the world for their changing valuations to deserve attention *in themselves!* They have at all times been valets of some morality, philosophy, or religion; quite apart from the fact that they have unfortunately often been all-too-pliable courtiers of their own followers and patrons, and cunning flatterers of ancient or newly arrived powers. They always need at the very least protection, a prop, an established authority: artists never stand apart; standing alone is contrary to their deepest instincts" (102).

27. Liszt, *The Gypsy in Music*, 299: "The civilized musician is at first so astounded by the strangeness of intervals employed in Bohemian [Gypsy] music that he can find no other way of settling the matter of his own mind than that of concluding the dissonances to be accidental . . ."

28. Liszt, *The Gypsy in Music*, 365-66.

29. Liszt, *The Gypsy in Music*, 368.

30. *The Future of an Illusion*, trans. James Strachey (New York: W. W. Norton & Company, 1961), 31.

31. Sárosi, *Gypsy Music*, 85.

32. Summarized in Walker, *The Virtuoso Years*, 323 ff.

33. I am referring to "passion" here as the suffering of pain.

34. In this paragraph I am relying on Heidegger's concept of the poetic in his *Unterwegs zur Sprache*.

35. Carl Dahlhaus, *Nineteenth-Century Music*, trans. J. Bradford Robinson (Berkeley and Los Angeles: University of California Press, 1989), 142.

36. Dahlhaus, *Nineteenth-Century Music*, 149.

37. Dahlhaus, *Nineteenth-Century Music*, 150 (my emphasis).

38. Sic., as shown by Philip Gossett, it is actually Sonnet 280; see Gossett's "Up from Beethoven," review of *Nineteenth-Century Music* by Carl Dahlhaus, *The New York Review of Books* (26 October 1989): 21-26.

39. Jacques Derrida, in a public lecture as part of a seminar on the death penalty, 19 April 2000, University of California at Irvine, discussed the function of the cutting/knotting of white bands in Jean Genet and the Gospels.

40. Liszt, *The Gypsy in Music*, 265.

41. Liszt, *The Gypsy in Music*, p. 265. See Hans-Georg Gadamer, *The Idea of the Good in Platonic-Aristotelian Philosophy*, trans. P. Christopher Smith (New Haven: Yale University Press, 1986), 10 ff. on the complexities of dialectical terminology—especially the term "*methexis*," or participation—in Plato.

42. Liszt, *The Gypsy in Music*, 334.

43. Susan Bernstein, *Virtuosity of the Nineteenth Century: Performing Music and Language in Heine, Liszt, and Baudelaire* (Stanford: Stanford University Press, 1998), 99 (my emphasis).
44. Bernstein, *Virtuosity of the Nineteenth Century,* 87.
45. Bernstein, *Virtuosity of the Nineteenth Century,* 91.
46. Bernstein, *Virtuosity of the Nineteenth Century,* 106.
47. Bernstein, *Virtuosity of the Nineteenth Century,* 100 (my emphasis).
48. Bernstein, *Virtuosity of the Nineteenth Century,* 100.
49. *The Romantic Generation* (Cambridge, MA: Harvard University Press, 1995), 491.
50. Rosen, *The Romantic Generation,* 492.
51. *Essays,* ed. Benjamin Suchoff (New York: St. Martin's Press, 1976), 323.
52. Walker, *The Virtuoso Years,* 442.
53. Piero Weiss and Richard Taruskin, eds., *Music in the Western World: A History in Documents* (New York: Schirmer Books, 1984), 359, commenting on Schumann's music criticism write that "it should be pointed out, for the benefit of those who are not acquainted with the characters' musical incarnations (as in Schumann's *Carnival,* op. 9) that the League of David's ultimate mission was to slay the Philistines." Ironically, it was Liszt who judged Schumann's music to be "Philistine."
54. From Liszt's essay "Berlioz und seine 'Harold-Symphonie' [1855]," in *Gesammelte Schriften,* ed. Lina Ramann, vol. 4, 1-102 (Leipzig: Breitkopf und Härtel, 1882), 69.
55. Liszt, *The Gypsy in Music,* 265.
56. Liszt, *The Gypsy in Music,* 266.
57. Jacques Derrida's *Spurs: Nietzsche's Styles,* trans. Barbara Harlow (Chicago: The University of Chicago Press, 1978), is devoted to this theme.
58. *Beyond Good and Evil: Prelude to a Philosophy of the Future,* trans. Walter Kaufmann (New York: Vintage Books, 1966), 169.
59. *Selected Letters,* trans. Adrian Williams (Oxford: Clarendon Press, 1998), 255-56 (my emphasis).
60. *Selected Letters,* 248.

NOTES FOR CHAPTER SEVEN

1. The analytical portions of this chapter were co-authored with Ildar Khannanov; note that an article based on this chapter was to appear in *The International Journal of Musicology 10* (Fall 2001) and is now forthcoming. Khannanov's penetrating insights into the essence of Russian-Gypsy music brilliantly combine his expertise in music theory, his primary field, with his ethnographic experience in the former Soviet Union, where he published folk songs of Tartarian nomadic tribes. Khannanov did his ethnomusicological studies under Ye. Drutz, who published *Folk Songs of Russian Gypsies (Narodnyie Pesni Russkilch Tsigan),* with A. Hessler (Moscow: Soviet Composer, 1988).
2. All translations are by Ildar Khannanov.
3. *Between Two Fires: Gypsy Performance and Romani Memory from Pushkin to Postsocialism* (Durham and London: Duke University Press, 2000), 35.
4. *The Writing of the Disaster,* trans. Ann Smock (Lincoln and London: University of Nebraska Press, 1995), 14-16.

5. This section is based on the book by S. N. Durylin, *Pushkin na tsene* (Moscow: Academia nauk SSSR, 1951), especially 29-33. Translations are by Ilja Gruen, who also kindly brought this topic and text to my attention.

6. *Sergei Rachmaninoff 1873-1943: Zwischen Moskau und New York, Eine künstler biographie* (Berlin: Beltz/Quadriga Verlag, 1991) 62.

7. *An Actor Prepares*, trans. Elizabeth Reynolds Hapgood (New York: Theatre Arts Books, 1948), 66.

8. Geoffrey Norris, *Rachmaninoff* (New York: Schirmer Books, 1993), 12. Norris also mentions in this context that Rachmaninov recalled that another member of Arensky's free composition class, Skryabin, also asked to take this exam; as Arensky did not like Skryabin, the latter was denied. Skryabin left the Conservatory and never returned.

9. *Pushkin na tsene*, 32, gives thirteen operas based on Pushkin's text, M. Ju. Wiegol'skii, V. N. Kashperov (1850), G. A. Lishin (1875, not finished), N. N. Mironov, M. M. Zubov (1894), Pavel Juon (1897), A. N. Shefer (1901), Lithuanian composer K. P. Galkauskas (1907), French composer A. Erlanger, Italian A. Torroto.

10. (Freeport, New York: Books for Libraries Press, 1934 [1970]), 79.

11. In Stasov's perception, oriental (*orientalnyi*) falls under the general category of the Eastern element (*vostochnyi element*), defined also as anything non-Slavic and non-European. Gypsy music, thus, is grouped with the *vostochnyi element*. However, one distinction that separates Gypsy music from this broad *vostochnyi element*—which in fact encompasses even China and Japan—is that Gypsy music is encountered inside of Russia. This has a few significant consequences, some of which are: 1) Russian composers were raised in an environment which contained Gypsy music (in the villages, Gypsy bands playing Russian folk music; in the cities, the choirs, and instrumental soloists and groups found in the restaurants and theaters); 2) it was an easy step to appropriate Gypsy musical language into a Russian paradigm. In a sense this language was already present in Russian folk music, which for composers was the source (*istochnik*) of artistic inspiration; 3) unlike Chinese or Arabic orientalism, Gypsy music allowed a composer quick access to the sphere of *vol'nost'*.

12. "Rakhmaninov's Student Opera," *The Musical Quarterly* 59 (1973): 441-48, 447; Norris also proposes Mascagni as a significant source for the opera, and notes that the opera was performed in Moscow in 1891 and that it would have been impossible that Rachmaninov did not hear it.

13. *Béla Bartók Essays*, ed. Benjamin Suchoff (Lincoln and London: University of Nebraska Press, 1976), 10.

14. We refer the reader to Martin Heidegger's text "The Origin of the Work of Art," in *Poetry, Language, Thought*, trans. Albert Hofstadter (New York: Harper & Row, Publishers, 1971), especially his discussion of "earth."

15. *Rachmaninoff and the Symphony* (Innsbruck-Vienna: Studien Verlag, 1999), 68.

16. See the discussion of *verbunkos* as a source of this work, in Richard Taruskin, *Stravinsky and the Russian Traditions: A Biography of the Works Through Mavra*, vol. 2 (Berkeley, Los Angeles: University of California Press, 1996), 1300-06.

NOTES FOR CHAPTER EIGHT

1. Nietzsche, *Twilight of the Idols/The Anti-Christ*, trans. R. J. Hollingdale (London: Penquin Books, 1968), 21: "There are more idols in the world than there realities: that is *my* 'evil eye' for this world, that is also my 'evil ear.' . . . For once to pose questions here with a *hammer* and perhaps to receive for answer that famous hollow sound which speaks of inflated bowels—what a delight for one who has ears behind his ears—for an old psychologist and pied piper like me, in presence of whom precisely that which would like to stay silent *has to become audible.*" The relevance of this passage to Romanology is the chain of signifiers starting with "evil eye" and running through "hammer" (the tool of the blacksmith), the ear, and the question of silence versus the audible.

2. This is the strategy proposed by Jaroslav Volek, "The 'Old' and 'New' Modality in Janáček's *The Diary of One Who Vanished* and 'Nursery Rhymes,'" in *Janáček and Czech Music: Proceedings of the International Conference* (Saint Louis, 1988), ed. Michael Beckerman and Glen Bauer, 57-81 (Stuyvesant, NY: Pendragon Press, 1995).

3. Kant, *Critique of Pure Reason*, trans. Norman Kemp Smith (New York: St. Martin's Press, 1965), 59: "I entitle *transcendental* all knowledge which is occupied not so much with objects as with the mode of our knowledge of objects in so far as this mode knowledge is to be possible *a priori*. A system of such concepts might be entitled transcendental philosophy."

4. Schoenberg and the New Music, trans. Derrick Puffett and Alfred Clayton (Cambridge: Cambridge University Press, 1987), 254; a characteristic statement is that ". . . for it could very well be that the hierarchy of sounds qualities which Schoenberg speaks, the priority of pitch and duration, is a fact which one has to take into account and not a mere assumption one can ignore" (my emphasis).

5. Janáček's earliest sketches for the work indicate that he originally conceived the role for soprano.

6. Recently it has been revealed that the original female inspiration, however, was in all likelihood Gabriela Horvatova, who vanished from Janáček's consciousness in relation to this work once he began to focus on Kamila.

7. Jaroslav Vogel, *Leos Janáček: A Biography*, rev. and ed. Karel Janovicky (New York: W. W. Norton & Company, 1981), 265.

8. In the discourse of the holy, national essence is transferred/bestowed on the peasantry. Note that for Hegel, in his *Philosophy of Right*, the agrarian class founds the state.

9. See Angus Fraser, *The Gypsies*, 2nd ed., The Peoples of Europe (Oxford UK & Cambridge USA: Blackwell, 1995); Gypsies had arrived in Moravia in the fifteenth century, and their presence would never have gone unnoticed (111). For more on the documentary evidence of the Gypsy arrival into European lands, refer to Reimar Gilsenbach, *Weltchronik der Ziguener. Teil I: Von den Anfängen bis 1599*, Studien zur Tsiganologie und Folkloristik, ed. Joachim S. Hohmann, vol. 10 (Frankfurt am Main: Peter Lang, 1995).

10. John Tyrrell, ed. and trans., *Intimate Letters: Leos Janáček to Kamila Stösslová* (London and Boston: Faber and Faber, 1993), 2 September 1918, 23. Beckerman, in "Kundera's Eternal Present and Janáček's Ancient Gypsy," in *Janáček's Studies*, ed. Paul Wingfield, 109-26 (Cambridge: Cambridge University Press, 1999), 122-123, quotes the relevant letters comparing Kamila to Zefka and *Makropulos Case's* Emilia Marty.

11. The proximity of the protagonist's name "Jan" and Janáček's own proper name is undeniable. Perhaps we could substitute the letter or signifier "J" to indicate these two layers: on the one hand, Janáček the composer, and on the other, the composer's desire to vanish into his "real" protagonist, Jan.

12. Volek, "Janáček's Diary," sets up the opposition of syntagma and paradigm (58) to describe this feature of artificial modality.

13. Volek, "Janáček's Diary," 72.

14. This is a very rich problem in dire need of further study that can only be touched on in this context. For an excellent overview of the problem, see Gheorghe Firca, *The Modal Bases of Diatonic Chromaticism*, trans. Carmen Paţac (Bucharest: Editura Musicala, 1984), 23; Firca's notes the paradox of calling Bartók's musical language *diatonic* chromaticism, and writes, in italics: "*This is the first structural chromaticism which was not generated by the alteration of the diatonic state to a certain extent, but by the very movement of the intrinsic elements of the diatonic system into a chromatic system, the movement both of the obvious elements and the latent ones.*" In other words, diatonic chromaticism delimits a structural and autonomous musical phenomenon. Might we venture to posit Janáček's modality as an autonomous structure?

15. *Spurs: Spur Nietzsche's Styles*, trans. Barbara Harlow (Chicago: The University of Chicago Press, 1979), 49.

16. Derrida, *Spurs*, 50.

17. Kant, *Critique of Pure Reason*, 189.

18. Jacques Derrida, *Glas*, Trans. John P. Leavey, Jr., and Richard Rand (Lincoln: University of Nebraska Press, 1986), 51.

19. We might, of course, critically question the whole notion that Jan's life with his Gypsy family in fact corresponds to the act of vanishing.

20. "Janáček's Ancient Gypsy," 121.

21. "Janáček's Ancient Gypsy," 119; Beckerman calls this the "Gypsy dance." The other kinds of music are the café waltz reminiscence and the idiot motive.

22. "Janáček's Ancient Gypsy," 125.

23. "Janáček's Ancient Gypsy," 120.

24. "Janáček's Ancient Gypsy," 126.

NOTES FOR CHAPTER NINE

1. Musicology, even in its postmodern guise as "New Musicology," remains strangely reticent to take seriously the implications of the deconstruction of the signifier and of broader narrative structures.

2. His best and most intensive fieldwork was carried out in Romania. See the monumental editions: *Rumanian Folk Music: Instrumental Melodies* (vol. I), *Vocal Melodies* (vol. II), *Texts* (vol III), ed. Benjamin Suchoff, forward Victor Bator, The Bartók Archives Studies in Musicology (The Hague: Martinus Nijhoff, 1967). Also see Bartók, with Zoltán Kodály, *Types of Folksongs 1*, trans. Imre Gombos, Collection of Hungarian Folk Music VI, Academia Scientiarum Hungarica (Budapest: Académiai Kiadó, 1973).

3. See the Hungarian CDs under the title *Új Pátria Sorozat* [*New Patria Series*], ed. László Kelemen and István Pávai, *Collected Village Music from Kalotaszeg*, vol. 1 (Fono: FA-101-2). Kelemen brought to the studios of Fonó Music Hall in Budapest Roma

"village" musicians from towns in what is now Romanian Transylvania for a series of recordings. His collaborator Pávai writes in the liner notes that "Ninety years ago, having visited villages in the Gyergyo basis (of Eastern Transylvania) Bartók, half jokingly, half angrily described in a letter, the hardships of collecting traditional folk music in the field; 'despite all efforts, what the collector of old Hungarian folksongs finds instead, are mostly art songs from the city or fashionable melodies. It seemed as if the traditional music was living its final hours, or maybe even its final moments.' Since then there have been countless references made to the 'final hour'. Has the 'final hour' really come?" (26). I wonder about the distinction between "old" and "fashionable": is it not possible to compose new melodies in the style of the old, thereby making the whole category of "old" impossible to delineate along scientific criteria? With oral music, the music might change every generation.

4. *Nineteenth-Century Music*, trans. J. Bradford Robinson (Berkeley and Los Angeles: University of California Press, 1989), 119.

5. Trans. Werner S. Pluhar (Indianapolis: Hackett Publishing Company, 1987), 174.

6. Béla Bartók, *Essays*, ed. Benjamin Suchoff (New York: St. Martin's Press, 1976), 6. Bartók's emphasis.

7. Page numbers in the following summary refer to Bartók's *Essays*.

8. Bartók, *Essays*, 321-22.

9. Bartók, *Essays*, 322.

10. Bartók, *Essays*, 322.

11. Bartók, *Essays*, 206.

12. Bartók, *Essays*, 207.

13. Judit Frigyesi, *Béla Bartók and Turn-of-the-Century Budapest* (Berkeley, Los Angeles, London: University of California Press, 1998); 248. On the one hand, Frigyesi is attuned to the Gypsy-verbunkos style evident in some of Bartók's music; on the other, she seems extremely sympathetic to Bartók's rejection of the sentimental-Romanticism of the nationalist Hungarian middle- and upper-classes, with which Gypsy music was aligned.

14. "Béla Bartók and the Concept of Nation and *Volk* in Modern Hungary," *The Musical Quarterly* 78 (1994): 255-87.

15. See Philippe Lacoue-Labarthe, *Musica Ficta (Figures of Wagner)*, trans. Felicia Mc-Carren (Stanford, CA: Stanford University Press, 1994). Lacoue-Labarthe says that "by most reckonings, nothing really has happened in more than two thousand years between music and philosophy, and that the history of their relations is, in a word, quite dull" (85). He goes on to say that the two cornerstones of the philosophy of music are Plato's rejection of the musician, and the enigmatic ontologico-political event of Nietzsche-Wagner.

16. Bartók, *Essays*, 501.

17. Bartók, *Essays*, 503.

18. Bartók, *Essays*, 506.

19. Bartók, *Essays*, 507.

20. Bartók, *Essays*, 173.

21. There is also the text on ethnomusicology by Bartók's brilliant and lesser-known Romanian counterpart, Constantin Brailoiu, *Problems of Ethnomusicology*, ed. and trans. A. L. Lloyd (Cambridge: Cambridge University Press, 1984); in a stunning passage, Brailoiu writes "Obviously, this point of departure is of paramount interest

to musicological research and explains the countless uncertainties of the researchers. Like 'musical folklore,' a recent term, its elders—the 'Volkslied,' 'chanson populaire,' 'folk song'—and its Italian younger brother 'etnofonia' all bear upon those people whose artistic practices are being studied. And the more elusive they become, *the vaguer the notion of folklore becomes, the wider the frame of the problem becomes*, the more sociology comes to bear upon criticism" (2, my emphasis). As an aside, Brailoiu's sociological prophecy has certainly turned out to be true for American ethnomusicology.

22. Bartók, *Essays*, 10 (my emphases).
23. "The Question Concerning Technology," trans. William Lovitt (New York: Harper & Row Publishers, 1977), 17: "Everywhere everything is ordered to stand by, to be immediately at hand, indeed to stand there just so that it may be on call for a further ordering. Whatever is ordered about in this way has its own standing. We call it the standing-reserve [*Bestand*]. The word expresses here something more, and something more essential, than mere 'stock.' The name 'standing-reserve' assumes the rank of an inclusive rubric. It designates nothing less than the way everything presences that is wrought upon by the challenging revealing." Take the CDs stored up in the new mega-stores, Borders, Tower, or Virgin—these CDs do not exist as autonomous products of technology, but stand there in the ordering of the orderable, ready to be called up to ensure the listening of the listenable.
24. See Frigyesi's "Béla Bartók and the Concept of Nation."
25. Bartók, *Essays*, 13.
26. *Béla Bartók: Studies in Ethnomusicology* (Lincoln: University of Nebraska Press, 1997).
27. *The Hungarian Folk Song*, ed. Benjamin Suchoff, trans. M. D. Calvocoressi, annotations Zoltán Kodály, Number 13 in the New York Bartók Archive Studies in Musicology (Albany: State University of New York Press, 1981).
28. Bartók, *Studies in Ethnomusicology*, p. 142; note the use of the word "scientific" as the focal point of Bartók's first sentence.
29. Bartók, *Studies in Ethnomusicology*, 143.
30. Bartók, *Studies in Ethnomusicology*, xiv-xv (my emphasis).
31. Bartók, *Studies in Ethnomusicology*, 144.
32. See Bálint Sárosi's article "János Bihari (1764-1827)," in Anita Awosusi, ed., *Die ungarische "Zigeunermusik,"* in Die Musik der Sinti und Roma, vol. 1, 66-79 (Heidelberg: Dokumentations- und Kulturzentrums Deutscher Sinti und Roma, 1996).
33. Zoltán Kodály, *Folk Music of Hungary*, trans. Ronald Tempest and Cynthia Jolly (New York: The Macmillan Company, 1960), 7.
34. Kodály, *Folk Music of Hungary*, 8.
35. Kodály, *Folk Music of Hungary*, 8.
36. Kodály, *Folk Music of Hungary*, 128; note that Frigyesi, "The Hungarian Revival Movement," in *Retuning Culture: Musical Changes in Central and Eastern Europe*, ed. Mark Slobin, 54-75 (Durham: Duke University Press, 1996), completely misses this point: "But they [Bartók and Kodály] spoke only about the artist whose aim was to create national music and did not think it necessary for the population at large to hear this music" (64).
37. *Gypsy Music*, 9.
38. "Hungarian Gypsy Music: Whose Heritage?," *Folklor Digest* 2 (1998) <http://www.net.hu/Deutsch/hungq/no147/p133> (8 July 2001).

39. His best one is "histoire de la musique tsigane instrumentale d'Europe centrale," *Etudes tsiganes* 1 (1994):104-33.
40. Sárosi, *Gypsy Music*, 23.
41. Fred H., post on Romnet, 23 January 1998.
42. Page numbers refer to Sárosi, *Gypsy Music*.
43. Sárosi, *Gypsy Music*, 143.
44. Sárosi, *Gypsy Music*, 145; Brassai was the author of "Hungarian or Gypsy Music."
45. Quoted in Sárosi, *Gypsy Music*, 146.
46. Sárosi, *Gypsy Music*, 149-50.
47. Sárosi, *Gypsy Music*, 253.
48. Sárosi, *Gypsy Music*, 253.
49. "The Hungarian Revival Movement."
50. Frigyesi, "The Hungarian Revival Movement," 65.
51. Frigyesi, "The Hungarian Revival Movement," 66-7.
52. Frigyesi, "The Hungarian Revival Movement," 68.
53. Frigyesi, "The Hungarian Revival Movement," 55.
54. Frigyesi, "The Hungarian Revival Movement," 73.
55. Frigyesi, "The Hungarian Revival Movement," 63.
56. Frigyesi, "The Hungarian Revival Movement," 66.
57. "Jocul barbatesc" and its arrangement by Bartók as violin duo number 32 are also found on Muzsikás, *The Bartók Album featuring Mártya Sebestyén and Alexander Balanescu* (HNCD 1439, 1999).

NOTES FOR CHAPTER TEN

1. See Giorgio Agamben's *The Coming Community*, Theory out of Bounds, vol. 1, trans. Michael Hardt (Minneapolis: University of Minneapolis Press, 1993). Agamben writes: "Today, in the era of the complete triumph of the spectacle, what can be reaped from the heritage of Debord? It is clear that the spectacle is language, the very communicativity or linguistic being of humans."
2. This is a reversal of the function of technology and the process Enframing *(Ge-stell)* in Heidegger. For a Heideggerian analysis of the phenomenon of homelessness with reference to Marx and Hegel, see Heidegger's "Letter on Humanism," in *Basic Writings*, trans. David Farrell Krell (New York: Harper & Row Publishers, 1977), 218 ff. For Heidegger, homelessness is the "symptom of the oblivion of Being," where Being remains unthought.
3. *The Coming Community*, 64.5.
4. Agamben, *The Coming Community*, 63.
5. *Film Music: A Neglected Art*, 2nd ed. (New York: W.W. Norton & Company, 1992), 216.
6. Quoted in Prendergast, *Film Music*, 217.
7. "Director's Notes," <http://www.czech-tv.cz/dokument/cernobila/english/director_note> (7 June 2002).
8. "Interview," <http://www.czech-tv.cz/dokument/cernobila/english/interview> (7 June 2002).
9. "*The Red Violin*: A Film by François Giraud," www.sonyclassical.com <http://sonyclassical.com/music/63010> (2 August 2001).

10. "Liner Notes," <http://sonyclassical.com/music/63010> (2 August 2001).
11. *Latcho drom: Un film de Tony Gatlif. Texte et photos de Denise Mercier* (Paris: K.G. Productions, 1993), 145.
12. Stephen Holden, "*Latcho drom* (Review)," in *The New York Times Film Reviews 1993-1994*, 318-319 (New York: Times Book & Garland Publishing, Inc., 1996).
13. Agamben, *The Coming Community*, 1: "The coming being is whatever being."
14. See Fredric Jameson, *The Political Unconscious: Narrative as a Socially Symbolic Act* (Ithaca: Cornell University Press, 1981), 79.
15. *Source Music in Motion Pictures* (Rutherford, NJ: Fairleigh Dickinson University, 1983), 15.
16. K. S. Kothari, *Indian Folk Musical Instruments* (New Delhi: Sangeet Natak Akademi, 1968), 77. The bowed string instrument in the sequence is the Kamaicha.
17. As producers will continue to claim "Gypsy" origins for groups from India, Egypt, et al., so we can expect scholars to continue to cast doubt on these claims.
18. Guenther Lewy, *The Nazi Persecution of the Gypsies* (Oxford: Oxford University Press, 2000), 223, unfortunately tries to hold that the "various deportations of the Gypsies to the East and their deadly consequences do not constitute acts of genocide," since these orders were "put into effect not out of an intent to destroy the Gypsies as such but in order to expel large numbers of this widely despised minority from Germany." For the opposing view, see Romani Rose, ed., *The Nazi genocide of the Sinti and Roma*, 2nd rev. ed. (Heidelberg: Documentary and Cultural Centre of German Sinti and Roma, 1995) and Wim Willems, *In Search of the True Gypsy: From Enlightenment to Final Solution*, trans. Don Bloch (London, Portland, OR: Frank Cass, 1997).
19. "Sinti & Roma," United States Holocaust Memorial Museum.
20. Carol Silverman, "Review of *Latcho drom*," *Ethnomusicology* 44 (2000): 362-64, notes that "the viewer is left to puzzle why these Slovak Roma are living in tree-houses," 363.
21. Similarly, we run up against the same problem in trying to define a *Gadjo* as a "non-Gypsy."
22. In the same vein, Silverman, "Review of *Latcho drom*," suggests that the film may be Gatlif's "tone poem to Romani music," 364.
23. Walter Benjamin, "Critique of Violence," in *Reflections: Essays, Aphorisms, Autobiographical Writings*, trans. Edmund Jephcott, 277-300 (New York: Schocken Books, 1978): "in this authority [the police] the separation of lawmaking and law-preserving violence is suspended," 286. When the French farmers act in the name of the police of the French state, the suspension discussed in Benjamin is realized.
24. Silverman, "Review of *Latcho*," 364, takes a different tact in her criticism of the film: "Despite Tony Gatlif's own Romani ancestry, the stance of Latcho drom fosters an outsider's gaze of 'looking into' an interior world, over high walls, into courtyards, onto a nomad's trail, etc. This serves to exoticize the subjects: Roma are a spectacle on display."
25. *Latcho drom: un film de Tony Gatlif* (Carol 1776-2, 1993).

NOTES FOR CHAPTER ELEVEN

1. See the CD *Road of the Gypsies* (Network, 1996), the song by one of the greatest nuevo flamenco singer, Camarón de la Isla (1950-92), "Nana del Caballo Grande," which employs a sitar.

2. Posted on "Romnet," <courbet@europemail.com> "New York Gypsy Festival," (20 November 1997), <6500djm1@ucsbuxa.ucsb.edu> via <romnet-l@teleport.com>.

3. "Dom Za Vesanje, O Vaxt a Rromengo: Time Of the Gypsies," Patrin, <http://www.geocities.com/Paris/5121/timeofthegypsies> (23 May 2002).

4. *The New Grove Dictionary of Music and Musicians*, 2nd edition, "National anthems," <http://www.grovemusic.com/shared/views/article.html?section=music.19602> (23 May 2002).

5. *Bury Me Standing: The Gypsies and Their Journey* (New York: Vintage Books), 5.

6. Simon Zolan, "It's in the blood . . . the Gypsies claim their precedence in flamenco," <http://www.flamencoshop.com/gypsy/itsintheblood> (25 May 2002).

7. Bálint Sárosi, *Gypsy Music*, trans. Fred Macnicol (Budapest: Corvina Press, 1978), 32. Sárosi, *Gypsy Music*, 32, says that the improvisational character of this music has roots that extend to Asia.

8. Sárosi, *Gypsy Music*, 24, notes their collection was published in 1955 under the title "Bazsorózsa" (Peony Rose).

9. Multicultural Media 1997 (MCM 3010).

10. Real World (CAR 2366). The Real World Web site "'The Musicians of the Nile': Charcoal Gypsies" notes that "frequently imitated and sometimes plagiarized, The Musicians of the Nile—lauded by the likes of Sun Ra and Keith Jarrett—have, for the last two decades, carried their majestic ancestral dream across the globe. The first 'Arab music' group to win universal acclaim, Les Musiciens Du Nil (their original name, the other being for promotional convenience) have been seducing audiences since being discovered in 1975 by Alain Weber, a man who has acted as their manager ever since" <http://www.caroline.com/realworld/nile> (27 May 2002).

11. *The Musicians of the Nile.*

12. *Divana: Musicians and Poets of Rajasthan*, second volume (Long Distance, 1996, ARC 331), notes by Alain Weber. Volume one came out in 1993.

13. Multicultural Media, 1997, MCM 3010.

14. *The Gypsy Road: a musical migration from India to Spain*, notes by Dan Rosenberg (Alula Records, 1999, ALU-1013); this was also the CD pushed by The World Music Institute at the *Gypsy Caravan* event.

15. "Blue Flame World Music: Barsaat, Musafir," <http://www.blueflame.com/index> (28 May 2002).

16. "Musafir: Gypsies of Rajasthan," <http://www.musik-aktion.de/MUSAFIR> (28 May 2002).

17. I am proposing that it was Mr. Khan or "Kawa" who came up with the idea for fusion, based on his work in fusion contexts in the 1990s. Refer to his biography on <http://www.musik-aktion.de/MUSAFIR>.

18. Arhoolie 469, 1998, notes by Nora Guthrie. Also see their Web site at <http://www.csokolom.com>.

19. "Kalyi Jag," <http://biomusic.mentha.hu/eng/zenekarok/kalyijag> (28 May 2002).

20. Edith Balazs, <http://www.budapestweek.com/performance6> (28 May 2002).

21. RCA Victor, 74321-27910-2, 1997 [recorded and released in the Czech Republic in 1995].

22. Translation from Romnet.

23. The episode is archived on the Patrin, "Roma Exodus from Czech Republic," dated 17 August 1997, <http://www.geocities.com/Paris/5121/czech1> (28 May 2002).

24. Unpublished manuscript, "Gypsiness in Music: version 4.1," 5 December 1997.
25. There will surely be many follow ups to *Gypsy Caravan* in the future; at the end of this writing a production advertised as *Gypsy Spirit: the Journey of the Roma* was announced, with Kalman Balogh as Music Director.

Bibliography

A. BOOKS AND ARTICLES

Acton, Thomas, ed. *Scholarship and the Gypsy Struggle: Commitment in Romani Studies.* A collection of papers and poems to celebrate Donald Kenrick's seventieth year. Hertfordshire: University of Hertfordshire Press, 2000.

Adorno, Theodor W. *Quasi una Fantasia: Essays on Modern Music.* Trans. Rodney Livingstone. London and New York: Verso, 1994.

_____. *Philosophie der neuen Musik.* Frankfurt am Main: Suhrkamp Verlag, 1978.

Agamben, Giorgio. *The Coming Community.* Trans. Michael Hardt. Theory Out of Bounds, vol. 1. Minneapolis: University of Minnesota Press, 1993.

Anderson, Benedict. *Imagined Communities: Reflections on the Origin and Spread of Nationalism.* Rev. ed. London and New York: Verso, 1991.

Angermüller, Rudolph. "Zigeuner und Zigeunerisches in der Oper des 19. Jahrhunderts." *Die "Couleur locale" in der Oper des 19. Jahrhunderts,* ed. Heinz Becker, 131-59. Studien zur Musikgeschichte des 19. Jahrhunderts, Volume 42. Regensburg: Gustav Bosse Verlag, 1976.

Antokoletz, Elliott. *The Music of Béla Bartók: A Study of Tonality and Progression in Twentieth-Century Music.* Berkeley, Los Angeles, and London: University of California Press, 1984.

Antonietto, Alain. "Des Bohémiens et de leur musique." *Études tsiganes* 32/2 (1986): 34-41.

_____. "Histoire de la musique tsigane instrumentale d'Europe centrale." *Études tsiganes* 1/1 (1994):104-33.

_____. "Musique instrumentale Tsigane d'Europe d'Europe centrale." *Études tsiganes* 32/4 (1986): 16-20.

_____. . "La musique tsigane mythe ou préjugés?..." *Études tsiganes* 32/1 (1986): 23-7.

Apel, Willi. "Improvisation." In *Harvard Dictionary of Music,* 351-52. Cambridge, MA: Harvard University Press, 1946.

Aristotle. *On Poetry and Style.* Trans. G. M. A. Grube. Indianapolis, IN: Hackett Publishing Company, 1958.

Atkin, Irene Kahn. *Source Music in Motion Pictures.* Rutherford, NJ: Fairleigh Dickinson University, 1983.

Awosusi, Anita, ed. *Die Musik der Sinti und Roma.* Vol. 1: *Die ungarische "Zigeunermusik."* Heidelberg: Dokumentations- und Kulturzentrums Deutscher Sinti und Roma.

Bartók, Béla. *Essays.* Ed. Benjamin Suchoff. New York: St. Martin's Press, 1976.

_____. *The Hungarian Folk Song*. Ed. Benjamin Suchoff, trans. M.D. Calvocoressi, annotations Zoltán Kodály. No. 13 in the New York Bartók Archive Studies in Musicology. Albany: State University of New York Press, 1981.

_____. *Rumanian Folk Music, Volume One: Instrumental Melodies*. Ed. Benjamin Suchoff, forward Victor Bator. No. 2 in the Bartók Archives Studies in Musicology. The Hague: Martinus Nijhoff, 1967.

_____. *Rumanian Folk Music, Volume Two: Vocal Melodies*. Ed. Benjamin Suchoff. No. 3 in the Bartók Archives Studies in Musicology. The Hague: Martinus Nijhoff, 1967.

_____. *Rumanian Folk Music, Volume Three: Texts*. Ed. Benjamin Suchoff. trans. E. C. Teodorescu. No. 4 in the Bartók Archives Studies in Musicology. The Hague: Martinus Nijhoff, 1967.

_____. *Studies in Ethnomusicology*. Ed. Benjamin Suchoff. Lincoln: University of Nebraska Press, 1997.

_____ and Zoltán Kodály. *Types of Folksongs 1*. Trans. Imre Gombos. Collection of Hungarian Folk Music VI, Academia Scientiarum Hungarica. Budapest: Académiai Kiadó, 1973.

Baumann, Max Peter. "The Reflection of the Roma in European Art Music." *The World of Music* 38 (1996): 95-138.

Beckerman, Michael. "A Fifteen Round Heavyweight Championship Between Antonin Dvořák and Muhammed Ali for the Crown of the Hapsburg Empire." Böhlav Verlag's *Schriften zur Volksmusik* (forthcoming, 2002).

_____. "Kundera's Eternal Present and Janáček's Ancient Gypsy." In *Janáček Studies*. Ed. Paul Wingfield, 109-26. Cambridge: Cambridge University Press, 1999.

_____. "Music: Pushing Gypsiness, Roma or Otherwise," *New York Times*. April 1, 2001.

Bellman, Jonathan. *The Style Hongrois in the Music of Western Europe*. Boston: Northeastern University Press, 1993.

_____. ed. *The Exotic in Western Music*. Boston: Northeastern Press, 1998.

Benjamin, Walter. "Critique of Violence." In *Reflections: Essays, Aphorisms, Autobiographical Writings*. Trans. Edmund Jephcott, 277-300. New York: Schocken Books, 1978.

Bernstein, Susan. *Virtuosity of the Nineteenth Century: Performing Music and Language in Heine, Liszt, and Baudelaire*. Stanford, CA: Stanford University Press, 1998.

Berliner, Paul F. *Thinking in Jazz: The Infinite Art of Improvisation*. Chicago and London: The University of Chicago Press, 1994.

Biesold, Maria. *Sergei Rachmaninoff 1873-1943: Zwischen Moskau und New York, Eine Künstlerbiographie*. Berlin: Beltz/Quadriga Verlag, 1991.

Blanchot, Maurice. *The Writing of the Disaster*. Trans. Ann Smock. Lincoln and London: University of Nebraska Press, 1995.

Born, Georgina and David Hesmondhalgh, eds. *Western Music and Its Others: Difference, Representation, and Appropriation in Music*. Berkeley and Los Angeles: University of California Press, 2000.

Borodin, Alexander. *Polovtsian Dances*. London: Ernst Eulenburg Ltd, 1988.

Boundas, Constantin V., ed. *The Deleuze Reader*. New York: Columbia University Press, 1993.

Brailoiu, Constantin. *Problems of Ethnomusicology*. Ed. and trans. A. L. Lloyd. Cambridge: Cambridge University Press, 1984.

Cannata, David. *Rachmaninoff and the Symphony*. Innsbruck-Vienna: Studien Verlag, 1999.

Cervantes, Miguel de. "La Gitanilla." In *Novelas Ejemplares*, vol. 1. Buenos Aires: Editorial Losada, S.A., 1938.

_____. "The Gipsey Maid." In *Six Exemplary Novels*. Trans. Harriet de Onís. Great Neck, New York: Barron's Educational Series, Inc., 1961.

Chase, Gilbert. "Origins of the Lyric Theater in Spain." *The Musical Quarterly* 25 (1939): 292-305.

Clébert, Jean-Paul. *The Gypsies*. Trans. Charles Duff. London: Vista Books, 1963.

Cobb, Carl W. *Lorca's* Romancero gitano: *A Ballad Translation and Critical Study*. Jackson: University of Mississippi Press, 1983.

Crosbie, John. "Structure and Counter-Structure in Lorca's 'Romancero Gitano.'" *Modern Language Review* 77 (1982): 74-88.

Crowe, David and John Kolsti, eds. *The Gypsies of Eastern Europe*. Introduction by Ian Hancock. New York and London: M. E. Sharpe, Inc., 1991.

"Csárdás." Brooklyn Philharmonic Orchestra, February 20-21, 1998. Jonathan Bellman, "The *Style Hongrois:* The Hungarian Gypsies and Their Imitators," and László Kelemen, trans. Peter Laki, "Hungarian Music, Gypsy Music, Folk Music."

Czerny, Carl. *Systematische Anleitung zum Fantasieren auf dem Pianoforte*. Trans. and ed. Alice L. Mitchell. New York & London: Longman, 1983.

Dahlhaus, Carl. *Esthetics of Music*. Trans. William W. Austin. Cambridge: Cambridge University Press, 1982.

_____. *The Foundations of Music History*. Trans. J. Bradford. Robinson. Cambridge: Cambridge University Press, 1983.

_____. *The Idea of Absolute Music*. Trans. Roger Lustig. Chicago and London: University of Chicago Press, 1989.

_____. *Nineteenth-Century Music*. Trans. J. Bradford. Robinson. Berkeley and Los Angeles: University of California Press, 1989.

_____. *Schoenberg and the New Music*. Trans. Derrick Puffett and Alfred Clayton. Cambridge: University Press, 1988.

_____. "Was heisst Improvisation." In *Improvisation und neue Musik*. Ed. Reinhold Brinkmann. Mainz: Schott, 1979.

Defoe, Daniel. *Moll Flanders*. Ed. Edward Kelly. New York: W. W. Norton & Company, Inc., 1973.

Deleuze, Gilles and Fèlix Guattari. *A Thousand Plateaus: Capitalism and Schizophrenia*. Trans. Brian Massumi. Minneapolis and London: University of Minnesota Press, 1987.

De Man, Paul. *Allegories of Reading: Figural Language in Rousseau, Nietzsche, Rilke, and Proust*. New Haven, CT, and London: Yale University Press, 1979.

Derrida, Jacques. *The Gift of Death*. Trans. David Wills. Chicago: University Press, 1995.

_____. *Glas*. Trans. John P. Leavey, Jr., and Richard Rand. Lincoln: University of Nebraska Press, 1986.

_____. *Memoires for Paul de Man*. Trans. Cecile Lindsay, Jonathan Culler, and Eduardo Cadava. New York: Columbia University Press, 1986.

_____. *Politics of Friendship*. Trans. George Collins. New York: Verso, 1997.

_____. *Specters of Marx: the State of the Debt, the Work of Mourning, and the New International*. Trans. Peggy Kamuf. New York: Routledge, 1994.

_____. *Spurs: Nietzsche's Styles*. Trans. Barbara Harlow. Chicago: The University of Chicago Press, 1978.

_____. *Margins of Philosophy*. Trans. Alan Bass. Chicago: University of Chicago Press, 1982.

_____. *Writing and Difference*. Trans. Alan Bass. Chicago: University of Chicago Press, 1978.

Dougherty, Frank Timothy. "The Gypsies in Western Literature." Ph.D. diss., University of Illinois at Urbana-Champaign, 1980.

Drutz, Ye. and A. Hessler, eds. *Folk Songs of Russian Gypsies (Narodnyie Pesni Russkilch Tsigan)* (Moscow: Soviet Composer, 1988).

Durylin, S. N. *Pushkin na tsene*. Moscow: Academia nauk SSSR, 1951.

Fielding, Henry. *Tom Jones*. Ed. Sheridan Baker. New York: W. W. Norton & Company, Inc., 1973.

Firca, Gheorghe. *The Modal Bases of Diatonic Chromaticism*. Trans. Carmen Paţac. Bucharest: Editura Muzicală, 1984.

Fonseca, Isabel. *Bury Me Standing: The Gypsies and Their Journey*. New York: Vintage Books, 1995.

Fraser, Angus. *The Gypsies*. 2nd ed. The Peoples of Europe. Oxford UK & Cambridge USA: Blackwell, 1995.

_____. "Authors' Gypsies." *Antiquarian Book Monthly* 22 (1993): 10-17.

Freud, Sigmund. *The Future of an Illusion*. Trans. James Strachey. New York: W. W. Norton & Company, 1961.

Frigyesi, Judit. *Béla Bartók and Turn-of-the-Century Budapest*. Berkeley, Los Angeles, London: University of California Press, 1998.

_____. "Béla Bartók and the Concept of Nation and *Volk* in Modern Hungary." *The Musical Quarterly* 78 (1994): 255-87.

_____. "The Hungarian Revival Movement." In *Retuning Culture: Musical Changes in Central and Eastern Europe*. Ed. Mark Slobin, 54-75. Durham, NC: Duke University Press, 1996.

Gadamer, Hans-Georg. *The Idea of the Good in Platonic-Aristotelian Philosophy*. Trans. P. Christopher Smith. New Haven, CT: Yale University Press, 1986.

_____. *Truth and Method*. 2nd ed. Trans. Joel Weinsheimer and Donald G. Marshall. New York: Crossroad, 1989.

Geiringer, Karl. *Brahms: His Life and Work*. 2nd rev. ed. London: George Allen and Unwin Ltd., 1948.

Gilsenbach, Reimar. *Weltchronik der Zigeuner. Teil I: Von den Anfängen bis 1599*. Studien zur Tsiganologie und Folkloristik, ed. Joachim S. Hohmann, vol. 10. Frankfurt am Main: Peter Lang, 1995.

Goethe, Johann Wolfgang von. *Götz von Berlichingen*. Trans. Charles E. Passage. New York: Frederick Ungar Publishing Co., 1965.

_____. "Götz von Berlichingen." In *Werke*, Band IV. Hamburg: Christian Wegner Verlag, 1953.

Gossett, Philip. "Up from Beethoven." Review of *Nineteenth-Century Music* by Carl Dahlhaus. *New York Review of Books* (26 October 1989): 21-26.

Grellman, H. M. G. *Dissertation on the Gipseys*. London: William Ballintine, 1800.

Grout, Donald Jay and Claude V. Palisca. *A History of Western Music*. 6th ed. New York and London: W. W. Norton & Company, 2001.

Hancock, Ian. "The Emergence of Romani as a Koïné outside of India." In *Scholarship and the Gypsy Struggle: Commitment in Romani Studies*. Ed. Thomas Acton, 1-13. Hertfordshire: University of Hertfordshire Press, 2000.

_____. "The Origins of the Romani People." *The Gypsy Caravan: A Celebration of Roma Music and Dance from India, Russia, Romania, Bulgaria, Hungary & Spain*, 9-10 April 1999, The World Music Institute.

_____. *The Pariah Syndrome.* Ann Arbor, MI: Karoma Publishers, Inc., 1987.

Hegel, G. W. F. *Aesthetics.* Trans. Bernard Bosanquet. London: Penquin Books, 1993.

_____. *The Phenomenology of Spirit.* Trans. A. V. Miller. Oxford: Oxford University Press, 1977.

Hechter, Michael. *Containing Nationalism.* Oxford: Oxford University Press, 2000.

Heidegger, Martin. "Letter on Humanism." In *Basic Writings.* Trans. David Farrell Krell. New York: Harper & Row Publishers, 1977.

_____. "The Origin of the Work of Art." In *Poetry, Language, Thought.* Trans. Albert Hofstadter. New York: Harper & Row, Publishers, 1971.

_____. *The Question Concerning Technology.* trans. William Lovitt. New York: Harper & Row Publishers, 1977.

_____. *Unterwegs zur Sprache.* Stuttgart: Günther Neske, 1959.

Humboldt, Wilhelm von. *Linguistic Variability and Intellectual Development.* Trans. G. C. Buck and F. A. Raven. Coral Gables, FL: University of Miami Press, 1971.

Hoermann, Roland. *Achim von Arnim.* Boston: Twayne Publishers, 1984.

Holden, Stephen. *Latcho drom* (Review). In *The New York Times Film Reviews 1993-1994*, 318-319. New York: Times Book & Garland Publishing, Inc., 1996.

Hudson, Richard. *Stolen Time: The History of Tempo Rubato.* Oxford: Clarendon Press, 1994.

Hugo, Victor. *Notre-Dame of Paris.* Trans. John Sturrock. New York: Penguin Books, 1978.

Husserl, Edmund. *The Crisis of European Sciences and Transcendental Phenomenology: An Introduction to Phenomenological Philosophy.* Trans. David Carr. Evanston: Northwestern University Press, 1970.

Jameson, Fredric. *The Political Unconscious: Narrative as a Socially Symbolic Act.* Ithaca, NY: Cornell University Press, 1981.

Janáček, Leos. *Zápisník Zmizelého (Tagesbuch eines Verschollenen).* Preface Bohumír Stedron, trans. Geraldine Thomsen. Prague: Státní Nakladatelství Krásné Literatury, Hudby a Umení, 1953.

Kant, Immanuel. *The Critique of Judgment.* Trans. Werner S. Pluhar. Indianapolis: Hackett Publishing Company, 1987.

_____. *Critique of Pure Reason.* Trans. Norman Kemp Smith. New York: St. Martin's Press, 1965.

Kenrick, Donald and Grattan Puxon. *The Destiny of Europe's Gypsies.* London, Fakenham, and Reading: Sussex University Press, 1972.

Kierkegaard, Soren. *Either/Or* (Part I). Ed. and trans. Howard V. Hong and Edna H. Hong. Princeton, NJ: Princeton University Press, 1987.

Kodály, Zoltán. *Folk Music of Hungary.* Trans. Ronald Tempest and Cynthia Jolly. New York: The Macmillan Company, 1960.

Kothari, K. S. *Indian Folk Musical Instruments.* New Delhi: Sangeet Natak Akademi, 1968.

Lajtha, László. *Instrumental Music from Western Hungary: From the Repertoire of an Urban Gypsy Band.* Ed. Bálint Sárosi, trans. Katalin Halácsy, transcriptions Béla Avasi and Éva Gábor. Studies in Central and Eastern European Music 3. Budapest: Akadémiai Kiadó, 1988.

Lacoue-Labarthe, Philippe. *Musica Ficta (Figures of Wagner).* Trans. Felicia McCarren Stanford: Stanford University Press, 1994.

Lange, Barbara Rose. "'What Was That Conquering Magic...': The Power of Discontinuity in Hungarian Gypsy *Nóta*." *Ethnomusicology* 41 (1997): 517-37.

Lawrence, D. H. *The Virgin and the Gipsy*. Cleveland and New York: The World Publishing Company, 1944.

Leblon, Bernard. *Gypsies and Flamenco: The Emergence of the Art of Flamenco in Andalusia*. Trans. Sinéad ní Shuinéar. Gypsy Research Centre. Hatfield, UK: University of Hertfordshire Press, 1995.

Lemon, Alaina. *Between Two Fires: Gypsy Performance and Romani Memory from Pushkin to Postsocialism*. Durham, NC: Duke University Press, 2000.

Le Taraf de Haïdouks. *Dossier* de presse. [Newspaper and magazine reviews.]

Levinas, Emmanuel. *Totality and Infinity: An Essay on Exteriority*. Trans. Alphonso Lingis. Pittsburg: Duquesne University Press, 1969.

Lewy, Guenther. *The Nazi Persecution of the Gypsies*. Oxford: Oxford University Press, 2000.

Liszt, Franz. "Berlioz und seine 'Harold-Symphonie' [1855]." In *Gesammelte Schriften*. Ed. Lina Ramann, vol. 4, 1-102. Leipzig: Breitkopf und Härtel, 1882.

_____. *Etudes for Solo Piano*. 3 vol. Kalmus Miniature Scores. New York: Belwin Mills Publishing Corp., 1978 (vol. 2).

_____. *The Gypsy in Music*. Trans. Edwin Evans. London: William Reeves, n.d. [o.p. 1859].

_____. *Hungarian Rhapsodies for Piano Two Hands*. 2 vol. Kalmus Miniature Scores. New York: Belwin Mills Publishing Corp., 1978 (vol. 1).

_____. *Selected Letters*, trans. Adrian Williams (Oxford: Clarendon Press, 1998).

Lyotard, François. *The Postmodern Condition: A Report on Knowledge*. Trans. Geoff Bennington and Brian Massumi. Theory and History of Literature, vol. 10. Minneapolis: University of Minnesota Press, 1988.

McClary, Susan. *Georges Bizet: Carmen*. Cambridge: Cambridge University Press, 1992.

McDowell, Bart. *Gypsies: Wanderers of the World*. Illustrations by Bruce Dale. Washington, DC: National Geographic Society, 1970.

Mercier, Denise. *Latcho drom: Un film de Tony Gatlif. Texte et photos de Denise Mercier*. Paris: K. G. Productions, 1993.

Moreau, Roger. *The Rom: Walking in the Paths of the Gypsies*. Rev. ed. Toronto: Key Porter Books, 2002.

Nettl, Bruno. "Thoughts on Improvisation: A Comparative Approach." *Musical Quarterly* 60 (1974): 1-29.

Nietzsche, Friedrich. *Beyond Good and Evil: Prelude to a Philosophy of the Future*. Trans. Walter Kaufmann. New York: Vintage Books, 1966.

_____. *Genealogy of Morals*. Trans. Walter Kaufmann. New York: Random House, 1969.

_____. *Twilight of the Idols/The Anti-Christ*. Trans. R. J. Hollingdale. London: Penguin Books, 1968.

Norris, Geoffrey. *Rachmaninoff*. New York: Schirmer Books, 1993.

_____. "Rakhmaninov's Student Opera," *The Musical Quarterly* 59 (1973): 441-48.

Okely, Judith. *The Traveller Gypsies*. Cambridge: Cambridge University Press, 1983.

Papp, Géza. "Die Quellen der 'Verbunkos-Musik: Ein bibliographischer Versuch." *Studia Musicologica Academiae Scientiarum Hungaricae* 24 (1982): 35-97.

Periano, Judith. "Re-Placing Medieval Music." *JAMS* 54 (2001): 209-64.

Plantinga, Leon. *Romantic Music: A History of Musical Style in Nineteenth-Century Music*. A Norton Introduction to Music History. New York: W. W. Norton & Company, 1984.

Porter, Lewis. "John Coltrane's *A Love Supreme*: Jazz Improvisation as Composition." *JAMS* 38 (1985): 593-621.

Prendergast, Roy. *Film Music: A Neglected Art*. 2nd ed. New York: W. W. Norton & Company, 1992.

Rachmaninov, Sergei. *Recollections told to Oskar von Riesemann*. Freeport, New York: Books for Libraries Press, 1934 [1970].

Racy, Ali Jihad. "The Many Faces of Improvisation: The Arab Taqasim As a Musical Symbol." *Ethnomusicology* 44 (2000): 302-20.

Rink, John, ed. *The Practice of Performance: Studies in Musical Performance*. Cambridge: Cambridge University Press, 1995.

Rose, Romani, ed. *The Nazi genocide of the Sinti and Roma*. 2nd rev. ed. Heidelberg: Documentary and Cultural Centre of German Sinti and Roma, 1995.

Rosen, Charles. *The Romantic Generation*. Cambridge, MA: Harvard University Press, 1995.

————. "Within a Budding Grove." Review of *The New Grove Dictionary of Music and Musicians, Second Edition*," ed. Stanley Sadie. *New York Review of Books* (21 June 2001): 29-32.

Rostand, Claude. *Liszt*. Trans. John Victor. New York: Grossman Publishers, 1972.

Salazar, Adolfo. *La Música en Cervantes y otros ensayos*. Madrid, 1961.

Sárosi, Bálint. *Folk Music: Hungarian Musical Idiom*. Trans. Maria Steiner. Budapest: Corvina, Franklin Printing House, 1986.

————. *Gypsy Music*. Trans. Fred Macnicol. Budapest: Corvina Press, 1978.

————. "Hungarian Gypsy Music: Whose Heritage?" *Folklor Digest* 2 (1998). [Reply to Alan Antonieto (1994) and Patrick Williams, "Les Tsiganes de Hongrie et leur musique"]

Schmitt, Carl. *Political Theology: Four Chapters on the Concept of Sovereignty*. Trans. George Schwab. Cambridge, MA: MIT Press, 1985.

Schneider, David E. Review of *Béla Bartók and Turn-of-the-Century Budapest*, by Judit Frigyesi. *JAMS* 53 (2000): 183-91.

Schoenberg, Arnold. "Folkloristic Symphonies." In *Style and Idea*. Ed. Leonard Stein, trans. Leo Black. Berkeley and Los Angeles: University of California Press, 1975.

Schreiner, Claus. *Flamenco: Gypsy Dance and Music from Andalusia*. Trans. Mollie Comerford Peters. Portland, OR: Amadeus Press, 1996.

Schulenberg, David. "Composition and Improvisation in the School of J. S. Bach." In *Bach Perspectives*. Vol. 1, ed. Russell Stinson, 1-42. Lincoln: University of Nebraska Press, 1995.

Scott, Sir Walter. *Guy Mannering*. New York: R. F. Fenno & Company: Publishers, 1900.

Silverman, Carol. "Rom (Gypsy) Music." *Europe*. Timothy Rice, James Porter, and Chris Goertzen, eds. *The Garland Encyclopedia of World Music*, vol. 8. New York and London: Garland Publishing, Inc., 2000.

————. Review of "Latcho Drom." *Ethnomusicology* 44 (2000): 362-64.

Solomon, Maynard. *Beethoven*, 2nd rev. ed. New York: Schirmer Books, 1998.

Stanislavski, Constantin. *An Actor Prepares*. Trans. Elizabeth Reynolds Hapgood. New York: Theatre Arts Books, 1948.

Taruskin, Richard "'Entoiling the Falconet': Russian Musical Orientalism in Context." In Jonathan Bellman, ed., *The Exotic in Western Music*, 194-217. Boston: Northeastern Press, 1998.

_____. *Stravinsky and the Russian Traditions: A Biography of the Works Through Mavra.* Vol. 2. Berkeley, Los Angeles: University of California Press, 1996.

Titon, Jeff Todd, ed. *Worlds of Music.* 3rd ed. New York: Schirmer Books, 1996.

Tong, Diane. *Gypsies: A Multidisciplinary Annotated Bibliography.* New York & London: Garland Publishing, Inc., 1995.

_____. *Gypsy Folktales.* San Diego, New York, London: Harcourt Brace Jovanovich Publishers, 1989.

Tucker, Robert ed. *The Marx-Engels Reader.* 2nd ed. New York and London: W. W. Norton & Company, 1978.

Tyrrell, John ed. and trans. *Intimate Letters: Leos Janáček to Kamila Stösslová.* London and Boston: Faber and Faber, 1993.

Van Hear, Nicholas. *New Diasporas: The Mass Exodus, Dispersal, and Regrouping of Migrant Communities.* Seattle: University of Washington Press, 1998.

Vicente, Gil. *Farsa de Ciganas.* In *Obras Completas,* vol 5. Ed. Marques Braga. Lisboa: Livraria sá da costa — Editora, 1953.

Vogel, Jaroslav. *Leos Janáček: A Biography.* Rev. and ed. Karel Janovicky. New York: W. W. Norton & Company, 1981.

Volek, Jaroslav. "The 'Old' and 'New' Modality in Janáček's *The Diary of One Who Vanished* and 'Nursery Rhymes'." In *Janáček and Czech Music: Proceedings of the International Conference (Saint Louis, 1988).* Eds. Michael Beckerman and Glen Bauer, 57-81. Stuyvesant, NY: Pendragon Press, 1995.

Von Arnim, Achim. *Isabella von Ägypten und andere Erzählungen.* Ed. Walther Migge. Zürich: Manesse Verlag, 1959.

Wald, Elijah. "Romania's dancing outlaws." *Boston Globe,* 6 March 1998, D15-16.

Walker, Alan. *The Virtuoso Years, 1811-1847, Franz Liszt.* Vol. 1. New York: Alfred A. Knopf, 1983.

Weiss, Piero and Richard Taruskin, eds. *Music in the Western World: A History in Documents.* New York: Schirmer Books, 1984.

Willems, Wim. *In Search of the True Gypsy: From Enlightenment to Final Solution.* Trans. Don Bloch. London, Portland, OR: Frank Cass, 1997.

Yoors, Jan. *The Gypsies.* New York: Simon and Schuster, 1967.

B. E-MAIL

Courbet, M. "New York Gypsy Festival," <courbet@europemail.com> "New York Gypsy Festival," (20 November 1997), <6500djm1@ucsbuxa.ucsb.edu> via <romnet-l@teleport.com>.

Creative Intelligence Agency,"Hungarian Gypsy Music, Part I," 23 January 1998, <poetburo@idirect.com> <6500djm1@ucsbuxa.ucsb.edu> via <romnet-l@teleport.com>.

Hancock, Ian. "Any Roma around," 18 August 1999,<xulaj@umail.utexas.edu> <6500djm1@ucsbuxa.ucsb.edu> via <romnet-l@telelists.com>.

Kwiek, Gregory. "Re: Hot Air," 27 February 1998, <Kz-1oner@webtv.net> <6500djm1@ucsbuxa.ucsb.edu> via <romnet-l@teleport.com>.

C. WEB SITES

Bailey, Derek. "Interview [with Jean Martin], 16 August 1996." <http://www.shef.ac.uk/misc/rec/ps/efi> (19 January 2002).

Balazs, Edith. "Gypsy fire rages through Hungary: After success on Broadway, Kalyi Jag comes home." <http://www.budapestweek.com/performance6> (28 May 2002).

"Barsaat, Musafir." Blue Flame World Music. <http://www.blueflame.com/index> (28 May 2002).

"Budapest Gypsy orchestra." <http://www.100violins.com/us/100/index> (17 March 2002).

Csókolom. <http://www.csokolom.com> (28 May 2002).

Derrida, Jacques. "There Is No 'One' Narcissism." <http://www.hydra.umn.edu/derrida/narc> (6 June 2002).

Donnelly, Wayne. "Review, Antonin Dvořák Symphony No. 8 in G major, Op. 88. Budapest Festival Orchestra, Ivan Fischer, cond." <http://www.enjoythemusic.com/magazine/music/0202/dvorak> (14 May 2002.)

Erdevicki-Charap, Mira. "Director's Notes." <http://www.czech-tv.cz/dokument/cernobila/english/director_note> (7 June 2002).

Gavin, Mike. "LIVE FROM BUDAPEST." <http://www.ronniescotts.co.uk/ronniescotts124> (13 May 2002).

Giraud, Francois. "Liner Notes [for *The Red Violin*]." <http://sonyclassical.com/music/63010> (2 August 2001).

Hancock, Ian. "Anti-Gypsyism." From *The Pariah Syndrome*. Patrin. <http://www.geocities.com/Paris/5121/antigypsyism> (15 May 2002).

————. "Dom Za Vesanje, O Vaxt a Rromengo: Time Of the Gypsies," Patrin. <http://www.geocities.com/Paris/5121/timeofthegypsies> (23 May 2002).

————. "Statement regarding my position with the International Romani Union," <http://www.romnews.com/a/hancock> (29 July 2001).

"The International Gypsy Jazz Archive." <http://www.nordi.no/music/hcr/archive> (29 July 2001).

"Kalyi Jag." <http://biomusic.mentha.hu/eng/zenekarok/kalyijag> (28 May 2002).

Kentner, Louis. "The Interpretation of Liszt's Piano Music." <http://www.mvdaily.com/articles/2000/02/pplords3> (19 May 2002). [Originally published in *Franz Liszt: The Man and His Music*. Ed. Alan Walker. New York: Taplinger Pub. Co, 1970.]

"Musafir: Gypsies of Rajasthan." Music + Action. <http://www.musik-aktion.de/MUSAFIR> (28 May 2002).

"'The Musicians of the Nile': Charcoal Gypsies." The Real World. <http://www.caroline.com/realworld/nile> (27 May 2002).

"National anthems. " www.grovemusic.com <http://www.grovemusic.com/shared/views/article.html?section=music.>19602> (23 May 2002).

"*The Red Violin:* A Film by Francois Giraud." www.sonyclassical.com. <http://sonyclassical.com/music/63010> (2 August 2001).

Rink, John. "Rhapsody." www.grovemusic.com, ed. Laura Macy.<http://www.grovemusic.com/shared/views/article.html?section=music.23313> (1 August 2001).

"Roma Exodus from Czech Republic." *Patrin*, dated 17 August 1997. <http://www.geocities.com/Paris/5121/czech1> (28 May 2002).

Sage, Jack and Alvaro Zaldivar. "Cervantes." www.grovemusic.com, ed. Laura Macy. <http:/
/www.grovemusic.com/shared/views/article.html?section=music.05312.1> (24 July
2001).

Sárosi, Bálint. "Hungarian Gypsy Music: Whose Heritage?," <http://www.net.hu/Deutsch/
hungq/no147/p133> (9 July 2001).

"Second Roma World Congress" (Romano Lumako Kongresso), Lodz, Poland, 1-3 May,
<http://www.romaworldcongress.org> (5 June 2002).

Stanford University, "Pidgin and Creole Languages" <http://www.sul.stanford.edu/depts/ssrg/
pidgins/pidgin.html#Introduction> (15 May 2002).

Taruskin, Richard. "Nationalism/1. Definitions," "Nationalism/7. After 1848." www.grove-
music.com, ed. Laura Macy. <http://www.grovemusic. com/shared/views/article.ht-
ml?section=music.50846.1> (8 July 2001).

Wilkinson, Irén Kertész. " 'Gypsy' [Roma-Sinti-Traveller']." www.grovemusic.com, ed. Laura
Macy <http://www.grovemusic.com/shared/views/article.html?section=music.41427>
(8 August 2001).

Zolan, Simon. "It's in the blood… the Gypsies claim their precedence in flamenco." <http:/
/www.flamencoshop.com/gypsy/itsintheblood> (25 May 2002).

Zygotian, Dork. "A Vanishing Tradition: Gypsy orchestras are getting hard to find." <http:/
/www.geocities.com/Paris/5121/orchestras> (12 May 2002).

"650 Years of Roma Culture in Kosovo" <http://194.8.216.150:9080/inhalt.htm#Top> (29
July 2001).

Index

Beethoven, Ludwig van, 6, 12, 43–44, 49, 54, 62,
73, 83–84, 94, 95, 96, 102–103,
126, 129, 143, 230n. 15
An die ferne Geliebte, 126
Hammerklavier Sonata, 96
Bell, Joshua, 174, 176
Bellman, Jonathan, 14, 20–21, 23, 46, 54–55, 61,
91–92, 154, 226n. 36, 239n. 1
Style Hongrois *in the Music of Western Europe,
The,* 14, 54–55
Benjamin, Walter, 127, 248n. 23
Berg, Alban, 6
Bergman, Marta, 233n. 67
Berki, László, 77–79, 236n. 7
Berliner, Paul F., 44, 230nn. 8, 18
Berlioz, Hector, 78, 84, 95, 97
Symphonie fantastique, 97
Bernstein, Elmer, 231n. 19
Magnificent Seven, The, 231n. 19
Bernstein, Susan, 99–100
Biesold, Maria, 115
Bihari, János, 70, 154, 158, 204, 246n. 32
Bile, Vera, 169–173, 211
I don't love her, 211
Birkenau, Poland, 184
Bizet, George, ix, 41, 46
Carmen, ix, 41
Blanchot, Maurice, 113
Blue Flame Records, 209
Bogár, István, 76–77, 236n. 7
Bohuslav Martinu Foundation's Festival, The,
234n. 9
Born, Georgina, 45, 230n. 11, 236n. 3
Borodin, Alexander, 72, 117–119
Polotvsian Dance, 117–119
Prince Igor, 117
Borrow, George, 40
Brahms, Johannes, 6, 14, 45–46, 54, 71, 73–78,
82, 84–86, 91, 103, 105, 127, 164,
212, 222nn. 5, 6, 226n. 36, 231n.
22
Hungarian Dance no. 5, 71, 73–84, 88, 105
Hungarian Dances, 54, 73, 82, 84–86, 164,
236nn. 1, 2
Brailoui, Constantin, 150, 246n. 1
Brassai, Sámuel, 91, 159, 239n. 7
Brendel, Franz, 223n. 10
Bruckner, Anton, 6
Brynner, Yul, 204
Budapest Festival Orchestra, 81, 236n. 7
Budapest Gypsy Orchestra, 77–79, 236n. 7,
237n. 12

Budapest Symphony Orchestra, 76–77, 236n. 7
Bulgaria, 52, 58, 193, 205
Burton, Richard, 174
Byron, Lord, 96–97, 113

C

Camerón de la Isla, 249n. 1
Canada, 211
Cannata, David, 121
Capone, Al, 192
Caravan, 215
Castiglione, Baldassare, 18
Courtier, The, 18
Ceausescu, Nicolae, 58, 183, 195
Cervantes, Miguel de (Saavedra), 20, 23–26,
34–36, 40, 42, 199
La Gitanilla, 23
Chaplin, Charlie, 204
Charap, David, 170
Charap, Mira Erdevicki, 170–173
Chaucer, Geoffrey, 18
Chicago, 192
Chicago Symphony, 237n. 23
Chopin, Friedrich, 4, 229n. 2
Chuvash, 156
Cine-poem, 185
Clébert, Jean-Paul, 225n. 29
Cleopatra, 174
Clinton, Bill, 234n. 5
Coco Brival, 225n. 34
Commercialism, *see* Marketing
Cooper, Gary, 166
Copland, Aaron, 168
Corelli, Arcangelo, 6
Corigliano, John, 168, 174, 176
Cremona, 174
Crosbie, John, 35–36
Crowe, Cameron, 174
Almost Famous, 174
Csárdás, *see* Czárdás
Csenki, Imre, 208
Csenki, Sandor, 208
Csókolom, 210
Cymbalom, 59, 71, 75, 78–80, 82, 87, 105–106,
173, 176, 183, 190, 206
Czárdás, 75, 79–80, 97, 141, 156, 162, 236n. 1
Czech music, 3–4, 72, 126–127, 131, 184, 212
Czechness, 73
Czechoslovakia, 138
Czech Republic, 65, 169–172, 211–212, 224n.
22